HALLIE
FLANAGAN

===

A Life in the
American Theatre

HALLIE FLANAGAN

A Life in the American Theatre

JOANNE BENTLEY

ALFRED A. KNOPF

NEW YORK

1988

THIS IS A BORZOI BOOK
PUBLISHED BY ALFRED A. KNOPF, INC.

Library of Congress Cataloging-in-Publication Data

Bentley, Joanne.
    Hallie Flanagan: a life in the American
theatre.
        Bibliography: p.
        Includes index.
        1. Flanagan, Hallie, 1890–1969.
2. Theatrical producers and directors—United
States—Biography. 3. Dramatists, American—
20th century—Biography. I. Title.
PN2287.F53B46 1988 792'.023'0924 [B] 87-46077
ISBN 0-394-57041-3

Manufactured in the United States of America
First Edition

FOR HELEN AND JACK
AND TO THE MEMORY OF
PHILIP AND FREDERIC

CONTENTS

ILLUSTRATIONS

(FOLLOWING PAGE 170)

Louisa Fischer and Frederic Ferguson, about 1883

Hallie Ferguson with her parents, about 1892

Kenneth, Hallie, and Gladys Ferguson, about 1903

Hallie Ferguson, age eighteen, starring in a high school production of *The Little Princess*

Murray Flanagan, about 1908
Courtesy of Betty Flanagan

Murray Flanagan, about 1915

Hallie Flanagan, about 1915

Hallie Flanagan with Jack and Frederic, about 1921

The Tomb Scene from *Romeo and Juliet,* 1925
Grinnell College Archives

Howard Wicks in 1925

Three versions of Chekhov's *The Marriage Proposal,* 1927
Performing Arts Research Center, New York Public Library at Lincoln Center

Dr. Horsley Gantt in Russia, 1930
By permission of the Alan Mason Chesney Medical Archives, The Johns Hopkins University

Frederic Flanagan in 1928

Philip Davis on Delos, about 1925

Scene from *The Hippolytus of Euripides,* 1931
Performing Arts Research Center, New York Public Library at Lincoln Center

Scene from *Sweeney Agonistes* in *Now I Know Love,* 1933
Performing Arts Research Center, New York Public Library at Lincoln Center

Joanne, Hallie, and Philip Davis in the garden at 12 Garfield Place, Poughkeepsie, about 1938

Hallie and Philip Davis in their car, about 1938

Hallie Flanagan Davis and Harry Hopkins in 1935
Grinnell College Archives

Scene from *One-Third of a Nation,* New York production, 1938
Performing Arts Research Center, New York Public Library at Lincoln Center

Hallie Flanagan Davis, 1935
Performing Arts Research Center, New York Public Library at Lincoln Center

Scene from Muriel Rukeyser's *Middle of the Air* at the University of Iowa, 1945
University of Iowa Archives

Hallie Flanagan Davis, about 1937
Library of Congress Federal Theatre Project Collection at George Mason University Library, Fairfax, Va.

Hallie and Helen Davis on the terrace of the Northampton house, 1943

Robert Schnitzer in 1943

Hallie Davis with her grandchildren, Frederic and Hallie Ann Flanagan, 1943

PROLOGUE: A MEMOIR

EVERY now and then, more often than not in New York, I meet someone who played a part in a Federal Theatre production. All actors grow animated describing the roles they've played, and the one I met recently was no exception. He'd had a part, he told me, in George Sklar's *Life and Death of an American*. "They had to close that show when Congress put Federal Theatre out of business." Interrupting himself as the room we were in grew crowded, he suddenly said, "Here comes my granddaughter. If I'm lucky, she's brought me a drink." A slim brunette wearing beads and slacks approached us, took his glass, gave him a fresh one, and kissed him. "Such a youngster," he sighed. "I had to tell her we had a depression. . . . You think she knows about Roosevelt? Just a name she read in a book. And the theatre he launched to give work to unemployed actors? Never heard of that either!" He laughed, she laughed. This old actor, I thought, is still acting. He's also getting tipsy. In a minute he'll give us a speech. And in a minute he did.

"Breadlines, Hoovervilles—today they're just footnotes in history. But they were real enough then, I can tell you. . . . Listen. If you grew up hungry, or if half the people you saw in the streets were hungry but a few were driving around in fancy cars, you didn't just watch, you joined. I joined Federal Theatre because it put on plays that made people mad. Happy-mad, mad-happy, those audiences reacted! Who wants a theatre that puts people to sleep? Ask her," he added, gesturing in my direction. "Her stepmother ran it. . . . Now *there* was a leader. We'd have followed Hallie Flanagan to the ends of the earth."

How often I've heard it. And not just from inebriated actors. Suddenly, as always on such occasions, I am back in the thirties watching scenes from the top of a staircase or the back of a theatre that are as clear to me now as they were fifty years ago. Hallie's on stage caught in a spotlight, or in a room full of people who circle her like planets. Is it her voice, low, clear, and vibrant; or her eyes which change with every inflection; or the colors she wears, as subtle as a warbler's; or the words she weaves into dazzling patterns that so captivate her listeners? At home she liked to quote Shakespeare, the Bible, and Whitman. She would do this with ease, intermingling their phrases with thoughts of her own. Hallie used language as others use saws, nails, and hammers—to build structures, the higher the better. Even so, did I know her? I am sure of two things. Hallie cared more on the whole about magic, *theatrical magic,* than she did about eating or sleeping. She also had a passion for order. She organized the Victorian house we lived in in downtown Poughkeepsie and the lives we led, my father's included, with the same thoroughness that she used to launch major theatrical productions.

My sisters and brothers and I had the same address as our parents during the years of our childhood, but we used entrances at opposite ends of the house. Hallie and Dad used the one at the front; the cook, the nurse, and we children went in at the back. The door and hall at the front led to the living room where our parents did their entertaining and to the stairs that went up to their bedrooms. The back entrance led to a kitchen, a playroom, and to the bedrooms we used. My stepbrother Frederic was ten years older; he went his own way. But my twin brother Jack and I, both six when Dad married Hallie, and our younger sister Helen, who was raised by grandparents before being brought to Poughkeepsie, were cared for by a Scottish nurse who ruled our lives by the clock. We got up at seven, went to school at eight, came home for lunch and in the afternoon to do our homework. Dinner with the nurse and cook was at five o'clock and we went to bed at seven-thirty so they could retire to their rooms and listen to the radio. Our parents we saw on special occasions and for an hour before bedtime, like children being reared in an English court. I used to lie in bed listening to the parties they gave in the evenings, wishing I were old enough to be invited or that I had been born into the family of my best friend, who was Irish Catholic and lived in a small house on the edge of town. The Dillons were poor, their entire house would have fitted into a corner of ours, but Alice ate with her parents and did her homework in the living room. Walking home after visiting her, I used to imagine myself telling Hallie the worst thing I could think of—that she was not my real mother. Hallie hated being thought of as a stepmother.

My earliest memory of Hallie (I was four at the time) is of walking beside her on a wooded path that circled a lake just beyond the Vassar College campus. Hallie was wearing a cape and hat and carrying a small wicker picnic basket. It must have been an early spring day. My father was walking beside her carrying a larger basket and an old blanket. Jack, eager to reach the rock overhanging the lake where we were to eat our lunch, was running along the path ahead of us. When we got to the rock, my father spread out his blanket and Hallie began unpacking the many small things she had put in her basket—thinly sliced sandwiches cut in circles and squares, cakes and candies in brightly colored tinfoil, elaborately wrapped gifts for my brother and me to which Hallie had attached pictures of flowers and stars. But I was resolved: I would not be enchanted. No one needed to tell me who was wooing whom and why. I had seen Dad kissing Hallie by the maple tree at the front gate. Shortly afterwards someone had asked me if I wouldn't like having a stepmother. That coming just after the kissing scene had given me my first premonition of disaster. What if this strange, unknown person came into our family? My own little kingdom, for so I thought of it then—myself in charge of Dad and Jack—would come to an end. With the conviction all young children have of possessing magic powers, I determined to ward her off by withholding my favor.

If Hallie was hurt when I stared past the treats she'd prepared and demanded one of my father's egg salad sandwiches, she did not show it. She went right on talking about the beauty of the lake and the buds that were beginning to open on the trees as if nothing unusual had happened. Perhaps, I've thought since, she realized that it would take time to win me. She made a second attempt a few months later.

This time it was summer and in Buffalo. My brother and sister and I had been sent there to live with our grandparents, and Dad had just come for a visit, bringing Hallie with him. There must have been talk of their marriage, for my grandparents had planned a party in their honor. On the appointed night we children were sent to bed, but I crept halfway down the stairs to see what was happening. I was sitting out of sight, I thought, when Hallie, dressed in a full-length red dinner gown, passed through the hallway, looked up the stairwell, and saw me. Without hesitating she climbed the stairs, sat down beside me, and took my hand. Could I keep a secret? She had noticed, she said, some small cakes in my grandparents' pantry. They were being saved for dessert, but she had made a plan. When no one was looking, she was going to tiptoe in there and tuck a few into her handkerchief. If I would go to bed, she would bring them up when the coast was clear. But no one must know of our secret. "Now run along, darling," she whispered. "I'll come up when I can." No one before had called me "darling." But it was not just what Hallie called me that gave me hope that evening. Since my mother's death, life in our home had grown gloomy. My father, lost in grief, had retreated into silence. Hallie's words made me feel that I had an ally and that I could choose how I wanted to live.

As I look back, I see that life in our family was not as easy for Hallie as I thought at the time. She returned from her marriage to my father and their honeymoon in Greece to become the stepmother of three small children who had been told that they had once had a clever, vivacious mother of their own. Less than a year later she was appointed to head Federal Theatre, which meant that she had to be away from home for weeks at a time. During the next four years she would return home for weekends, often bringing presents, but we were not always pleased. Once when she brought me a puppet I decided was less beautiful than the one she had given Helen, I glared at it and dropped it on the floor.

When she had time, Hallie included us in what she was doing. One afternoon when she'd been invited to Hyde Park to visit Eleanor Roosevelt, she took us with her, and Mrs. Roosevelt came out to greet us in a bathing suit. Another time, when Roosevelt was running for reelection against Alfred Landon, Hallie introduced us to Harry Hopkins. My brother's best friend, from a Republican family, had composed an anti-Roosevelt song, and we were all singing it boisterously as she and Hopkins entered the playroom. Hallie was embarrassed, though she tried not to show it. Later she told us that the New Deal was helping people who had been thrown out of work. It was not the first time Hallie made me feel that my rebellion was out of place. But she never rebuked me. The freedom she allowed herself she also extended to others.

There was never a time in my early life when I was not curious about Hallie. After Dad married her and we moved downtown, away from Vassar where Dad taught Greek, I got to know every inch of her study and bedroom. When they gave a party, I would stand at the top of the front hall stairs listening to the talk and peering down to see what everyone, especially Hallie, was wearing, as though in that way I might learn the secret of her power. I can see her now, standing by the front door greeting her guests in a long, flower-print dress that had a billowing skirt and sleeves gathered into puffs above her elbows. Hallie had once thought of becoming an actress. That ambition had gone, but she still saw gardens or rooms, wherever she happened to be, as settings where dramas might happen. I imagined her guests as characters in a play and since then have wondered if they saw themselves in the same way. Many actors and backstage workers have told me they forgot their own lives when Hallie directed. She drew them into a world of her own creation: that was her magic.

Hallie and Dad sometimes served wine or beer at their parties, but people never got drunk on liquor. They got drunk on ideas. "What would you think," Hallie might say, "of doing Chekhov in three manners?" or "What would you think of producing a play about energy?" The what-would-you-think approach caught people up. Loving invention, she generated a joy that became contagious. Everyone wanted to join. Discussion would follow, her music director would go to the piano, there'd be more discussion, then more notes at the piano. By midnight Hallie would have a musical score for her next production.

During the weeks when Hallie was away from home, I often went to her bedroom to gaze at her belongings. The walls of her room, so pale a shade of green they might have been painted by fairies, always held paintings. For a time a large watercolor of a daffodil painted by my sister hung above her bed. At other times this place was taken by a reproduction of Hallie's favorite painting, Franz Marc's *Blue Horses*. Near her bureau there was a photograph of her two young sons from a previous marriage walking hand in hand along a street in Iowa. Hallie had the largest bedroom in the house, and the only one that had windows looking out over the street and the side yard. There was an oriental rug on the floor, and between the corner windows a small chair and table where my father drank coffee in the mornings after bringing Hallie her breakfast on a tray. She would sit up in bed eating rolls and jam while he read her *The New York Times*. They had the sort of marriage, I decided later, that screenwriters sometimes portrayed in 1930s movies.

Hallie's clothes fascinated me. The dresses, skirts, and blouses in her closets had delicate scents that lingered long after she hung them up. She kept silk scarfs and chiffon nightgowns in her top bureau drawer which smelled of lavender or rose sachets. On her trips abroad she had bought many small boxes. Round ones made of onyx or wood sat on her bureau or lay on tables about the room. I especially remember two hand-painted boxes for stamps that she had bought in Russia—the insides painted dark red, the outsides depicting scenes of horses dashing through the snow, pulling people on sleds. Her most prized possession, however, was something no grown-up person who knew Hallie would have guessed she owned. In her top bureau drawer, inside a miniature, lavender-colored hat box, Hallie kept a white, six-inch-tall bear that she called Bimbo. Bimbo was German, a Steiff bear. His mouth was solemn, his tiny brown eyes had a tender expression. He was Hallie's toy, and no entreaty on the part of my sister or myself ever persuaded her to part with him. Where had she got him? We were dying to know, and Hallie, who enjoyed sitting up in bed in the evenings while we explored her belongings, also enjoyed our guesses, but we never learned a thing. Much later, my sister speculated that Hallie might have been walking along a street in some European city with a man who was in love with her, spied Bimbo in a window, and insisted she had to have him. Yes, I could imagine that happening: Hallie murmuring, "What a charming bear," her escort responding, the bear being bought on the spot.

Bimbo by this time is not the pure-white bear that he once was. The bright pink ribbon he wore around his neck when Hallie owned him has faded to a dull rose, and the lavender-colored hat box she kept him in has long since disappeared. But Bimbo's dark glass eyes are as bright as ever, and his expression just as solemn as it was fifty years ago. Today my sister and I alternate in owning him, reminding ourselves as we pass him back and forth of the pleasure Hallie took in keeping his origin a mystery.

Hallie loved Christmas and birthdays—any occasion she could

turn into a celebration. She spent hours every Christmas decorating the tree, setting the table, and wrapping presents. Each year there was a special new centerpiece, never anything Hallie bought; she could arrange holly, evergreen, and candles in dozens of ways. She made her own place cards; each person at the table got a rhyme or message that had been created just for him or her. She wrapped presents with care and each had to be unwrapped at an appointed time. Timing and sequence were as important in our living room as on Hallie's stages. If my sister and brother and I later joked about the roles we'd been given in Hallie's home productions, weren't we all willing accomplices, and didn't we enjoy her dramas as much as she did? The year my brother and I turned eleven, Hallie took us to New York to see the Federal Theatre production of *Pinocchio*. The entire cast sang "Happy Birthday" as the curtain fell, and there was a party afterwards with hot dogs and ice cream.

On another occasion Hallie and Dad drove us to Brooklyn to see the Federal Theatre Circus. When some tigers scared me, Hallie reached for my hand and led me down the street to a corner drugstore. I had ruined her fun and thought she might be angry, but Hallie turned the interruption into an adventure. We would have a special treat, she told me: hot chocolate with whipped cream. While we waited for this treat to arrive, she told me that fierce animals had once frightened her but she had got over it and I would too, that all I needed was a conquering spirit. When Hallie had a message to convey she looked straight at you; her dark eyes became thoughtful. The moment, the setting, and the quiet gravity of her voice have stayed with me. Drugstores today do not inspire intimate moments. Chrome, Formica, and long stands of merchandise have robbed them of any special quality; they seem as impersonal as supermarkets. But occasionally I come on one with small round tables and wrought iron chairs and I remember how Hallie's words touched me as we dipped and stirred our spoons in the whipped cream on top of our cocoa.

Hallie's home was her refuge, the place to which she returned to gather new strength for the coming battles, as Federal Theatre was never without its civil wars or its political opponents. She could not have done the job, she often told my father, without his help. This was true. When Hallie came home, Philip made sure she got the rest she needed; he guarded her privacy, listened when she needed advice, supported her when she felt discouraged, drove her where she needed to go. To some outside observers, it looked as though husband and wife had exchanged roles. Philip's relatives wondered if he had given up his own ambitions to further Hallie's, but he had chosen to play the supportive role and he never complained.

After Federal Theatre ended, my brother, sister, and I saw more of Hallie. During the week we still ate our meals in the kitchen, but on Sundays we had dinner with our parents. On Saturdays they took us on trips to New York or to see sites or villages in Dutchess County. In the evenings they read us stories, or Hallie invented wonderful ones of her own. In story-telling mood she could invent scenarios that made me want to live them, make up worlds I longed to inhabit, create myths I wanted to believe in. My brother and sister, who had meantime made strong attachments to other relatives, were not much impressed by Hallie's late attempts to be a mother, but I had been wanting a mother for a long time and I wholeheartedly welcomed the change.

Then very suddenly, in early 1940, Dad died of a cerebral hemorrhage. Hallie, who was not just devastated but guilt-stricken by this unexpected event, turned to me in her need. Though only eleven at the time, I became her confidante. In the evenings, when she was directing a play in her theatre at Vassar, she took me with her. When she was not rehearsing, she and I would settle into her study after dinner, Hallie to prepare for classes, I to do my homework, but sooner or later we would start to talk. Our conversations, which usually began with Hallie asking me what I was learning in school, would eventually turn to her girlhood in Iowa, a subject that never failed to fascinate me, for Hallie, with her great story-telling gifts, could make the years she had spent in Iowa at the turn of the century sound like a Garden of Eden.

Hallie's memories—of family celebrations, of evenings reading before the fire, of visits with cousins and trips up and down the Mississippi in summer, and of nut-gathering expeditions in autumn— gave her the strength she needed to go on living. She idealized her parents as she idealized their marriage. Her family, she came to feel, had had more fun than any she knew. All this became more and more important to her the older she got. Eventually she was to record these

memories in a sixty-page, handwritten autobiography she called
Notes on My Life.

Perhaps all of us create our adult lives before we live them. Being
inventive, we imagine a script filled with the joys and longings we
have experienced early in life and then launch it on the world and
hope for the best. Out of her experiences Hallie created a scenario in
which everything was possible—marriage, children, and total dedication to the art she had chosen. In one of her letters to my father
while she was running Federal Theatre, Hallie wrote that she wished
there were three of her: one to be his wife, one to look after their
home and children, and a third to do her job. In time she came to
believe, despite the deaths of a son and two husbands, that she had
achieved everything she wanted. In her autobiography she portrays
herself as a woman frequently torn between the demands of job and
home, almost always wondering whether or not she could earn
enough money to support her family after her husbands' deaths but
managing always to come out on top. It is a touching story, but like
most autobiographies it omits as much as it reveals.

When Hallie suggested to me one day that I might someday want
to write her biography (by this time I was in my thirties with a
husband and children of my own), I hesitated. She had already told
her story. Why repeat it? She said she was going to leave me her
diaries and other personal papers, and she did, but I put them in a
closet after her death and for many years tried to forget them. Later
I changed my mind. In her stories and plays Hallie had imposed
moral solutions, feeling perhaps that fiction ought to have them. But
her diaries made me realize that she was never sure she had made the
right choices. The challenge of discovering her began to grow and
eventually led to a determination to write this book.

When I told my sister, sometime late in the seventies, that I was
thinking of writing Hallie's biography, she had an immediate response: "We'll never know her!" We were sitting in her living room
in Snedens Landing fifteen miles north of New York City, eating
sandwiches and discussing the subject we had discussed dozens of
times before: Hallie. I was wondering, as I looked out over the
Hudson River, what Hallie would have said about the view. She
would have seen it as a setting for some imagined drama. She would
have invented characters and a plot. Although I knew what my sister

meant, I said I thought it *was* possible to know Hallie, but Helen's words remained a challenge. More often than I want to remember while writing this book, I wondered if she was right. The job of putting together the Hallie who was my stepmother with the Hallie who created three experimental theatres and a nationwide theatre project often seemed impossible. Someone outside the family could have done the job in half the time. But then, someone outside the family would not have had the memories I thought I had outgrown but which came back to trouble me when I started to put her story on paper.

There is more to say about Hallie, particularly about her role in the theatre; someday someone will say it. My purpose in writing her story has been personal. I wanted to discover her and to make her real for people who did not know her. Also, I think her life has meaning for the many women today who want to combine careers with child-rearing. Hallie did not find that easy, although she pretended otherwise.

PART

I

Midwest to East
1889–1934

1

Grinnell

HALLIE almost never talked about the earliest years of her life. "We traveled a lot," she said once. "For a time we lived in Omaha, after that in Chicago, St. Louis, and on an Iowa farm." She explained the moves by saying that her father, Fred, had been in business and that the company he worked for had failed. What she did not say, what I only discovered by looking into old telephone books, was that her father had been a traveling salesman who had lost one job after another during the depression of the 1890s.

While the Federal Theatre was preparing its last musical revue for a New York production, Hallie dropped in one day to watch a rehearsal. At the end of the first act of *Sing for Your Supper,* a boy comes running onstage with the news that his father has at last found work. People sing, they dance in the street, Papa is carried in on the shoulders of neighbors. No one cares what job he has found; he's employed at last, that's all that matters. Ned Lehac, who wrote the score for the first-act finale, "Papa's Got a Job," told me that Hallie wiped tears from her eyes when she heard that song. Robert Schnitzer, a friend, recalled that she wept after seeing Arthur Miller's *Death of a Salesman.* Neither Schnitzer nor Lehac had any idea what had moved her. There were a lot of things Hallie kept hidden. She was a very private person.

What Hallie did like remembering about her father was that he came from a spirited, adventurous family. The Fergusons came here from Scotland at the end of the eighteenth century, settled among other Scots in Barnet, Vermont, and took up farming. In the early nineteenth century Hallie's great-grandfather Alexander went west to help a neighbor establish a small Methodist community near Alton, Illinois. Many Fergusons, and many of their neighbors in Barnet and Monroe, moved to Godfrey during the Civil War. The early settlers built a school as soon as they had houses to shelter them. Ardent believers in education and in racial equality, several of these settlers went on to become preachers or teachers. Hallie's father grew up in a churchgoing community and in a home that put a high value on family life. He was one of nine children. His parents could not afford to send him to college; but he did get a secondary education and for a time taught physics and mathematics in the local high school. He made up his mind that his children would get the college education he had missed.

Sometime in the 1880s Fred Ferguson met the woman he wanted to marry. The salary he was earning was meager, not enough to raise a family, and he began looking about for a more promising position. Then he learned that Redfield in South Dakota had plans to build a college. The Dakotas were just then being settled. The few farmers who had moved there earlier were producing bumper crops. Homesteaders, entrepreneurs, and land speculators were flocking north to take part in building the towns that had begun to spring up along the railroad tracks, lured there no doubt by the posters the railroad companies put up in towns throughout the Midwest. "If you are a person of small means but lots of energy," one declared, "Dakota is the place for you."

After marrying Louisa Fischer, Fred went north, settled in Redfield, found a job selling harvesting machines, bought a plot in the land designated for Redfield College, and joined with those raising funds to erect a first building. The Dakota Boom, as it came to be called, was in full swing. The future looked promising.

South Dakota has an optimistic state motto, "Under God the people rule," but in fact it is the weather that rules in the state, and it was the weather that ended the Dakota Boom. When the growing season of 1888 brought drought and dry winds to the northern prairies, many homesteaders fled back to the states from which they had come. Others fled when the season of 1889 brought similar conditions. Soon no one wanted to buy harvesting machines and Fred was without work. Meantime Louisa had become pregnant.

Six weeks after Hallie's birth on August 27, 1889, Fred moved his family to Omaha, Nebraska, and began selling life insurance. For a short time thereafter it looked as though the Fergusons would prosper. Fred got a job with the Omaha Coal, Coke and Lime Company after the insurance company he worked for had failed. Because the country was in economic decline, many houses in the better sections of Omaha became available at reduced rents and Fred was able to move his family into a house in one of the better sections of town when Hallie was not quite two. But before she was four the country had entered a period of severe economic depression. Fewer people had money to buy coal, Fred's fortunes faltered, and eventually he had to move his family into a smaller house in a less prosperous quarter.

Fifteen years later, for a story she was writing in college, Hallie tried to recapture some of the fleeting, half-forgotten memories of the first six years of her life. Like many of Hallie's early stories, "The Truth" gives a highly idealized portrait of family life. The father of her story (a thinly disguised version of Fred Ferguson) puts on a brave front even when his prospects look least promising. The mother remains calm through every crisis. Virtuous, patient, and loyal, but unrealized as a character, she remains a shadowy background figure. Father and daughter both look up to her. Both feel they should emulate her virtues, particularly her respect for "the truth," but neither feels able to live by her high moral standards. Father and daughter have lively imaginations: when the world they hope for is not at hand, they invent it to fit their fancy.

In photographs taken at the time of her marriage, Louisa Fischer has a melancholy sort of beauty. There is a distant look to her eyes, as though she is dreaming of far-off places. "She was especially fond of flowers," Hallie recalled of her mother in later years, "and a superb housekeeper." As a girl Louisa had painted many pictures of flowers and landscape scenes, which hung on the walls of every house the Fergusons lived in.

Louisa was the daughter of German Catholic immigrants who

arrived in Alton, Illinois, at a time during the nineteenth century when the Mississippi River town showed promise of becoming an industrial center. Her father, Frederick Fischer, began work as a carpenter, prospered, put aside savings, and eventually accumulated enough money to buy a small grocery store. His wife, Amelia, ran their home in the well-ordered German manner, raising his six children to be courteous, proper, law-abiding citizens. Louisa and her three sisters attended Catholic school and learned sewing and cooking from their mother and drawing from a local artist. Drawing, and later painting, became Louisa's chief pleasure. On afternoons when she was not needed at home, she walked to the bluffs above the Mississippi to study and paint the river scene. In time, had the family continued to prosper, she might have gone to art school. But when Louisa was about thirteen, sometime in the 1860s, her father announced his decision to return to Germany to bring over other relatives. He left, promising to return, but was never heard from again. There was speculation in the family that Frederick might have drowned at sea. Some relatives thought he might have been robbed and murdered in transit. Inquiries were made, but nothing was discovered. Frederick's disappearance remains to this day a mystery.

After her father left home, Louisa's mother needed her to help run the store and look after the younger children. Later Louisa took up dressmaking to help make ends meet. As time went on she developed one overriding ambition—to serve the man she married with total devotion. Louisa's single-minded dedication to this goal, which was to last all her life, was unusual even in a day when devotion to home and husband was viewed as a woman's duty. Perhaps she saw some purpose in her father's disappearance. She may have come to the conclusion that he deserved something more than he had got from his wife. Whatever the case, after Louisa married Fred, she put his needs and comforts first. Her children were to recall that she treated him like a prince. "When my father returned home after traveling," Hallie's brother remembered, "my mother made us stay in our chairs until she had gone to the door to greet him and take his coat and hat. Only then were we allowed to run up and hug him."

Hallie's life during the years she lived in Omaha was divided between the weekdays when she was alone with her mother and the weekends when her father came home from his travels. The weekdays were quiet and uneventful. Louisa, as Hallie put it later, was extremely reserved. The weekends were just the opposite. When Fred returned, he took Hallie for walks, supplied her with picture books, and by talking about things that concerned him made her feel a part of the larger world outside her front door. When Hallie accompanied her father on train trips, she noticed that he would walk up and down the aisles, stopping to chat with everyone he met. If a baby began crying, or a young child became restless, Fred would seize a newspaper and transform it into hats, boats, valentines, whatever the occasion merited. In Hallie's eyes, he was master of every occasion; he could hold an audience spellbound.

Hallie was never in doubt about which part of the week she preferred. With her father, life seemed a drama that was rushing toward some wonderful climax. With her mother everything came to a standstill. To Hallie, Louisa was the beautiful princess who lived in a castle on a remote hilltop; one could never quite reach her. Hallie was filled with a longing she could neither define nor conquer and with a loneliness that was to haunt her off and on for the rest of her life. As she grew older she came to loathe cooking, cleaning, and household chores. Dailiness, she once remarked, was the hardest thing for her to bear, by which she meant days without change or diversion. She did not add that mothering small children also bored her, but this was just as true. Hallie enjoyed small children only on special occasions. She loved her children most after they had reached an age when she could guide their thoughts and take pride in their accomplishments.

A second daughter, Gladys, born to the Fergusons when Hallie was six, arrived during the worst year the Midwest had yet experienced. Stores closed, banks followed, and Fred soon found himself without customers. Meantime, Gladys began developing illnesses which no doctor could diagnose. Fred, insisting that the family misfortunes would soon pass, turned his thoughts to the future. What Hallie heard from him during this time was that the world was on the brink of the greatest century in history. America would lead the way, with new, unheard-of conveniences for everyone. Soon every home would have telephones, light bulbs, and bathtubs with running water. People would travel from town to town on fast, electric-powered trolleys. Apparently it never occurred to Fred that automobiles, then considered the playthings of the rich, might soon become more important than trolleys.

In his opinion about trolley cars Fred was influenced by his brother-in-law Paul Leffler, who had invented an idea for moving electric railway cars along a magnet-lined track. Leffler's Electro-Magnetic Railway Company was based in Chicago. The family, said Fred, would now move to La Grange, a suburb outside Chicago. He would sell stock for his brother-in-law's company and Leffler would pay him a small wage, plus stock in the company whenever he made a sale. This stock, he promised, would one day make the family's fortune. Fred was to go on repeating this promise until the company went out of business.

La Grange was famous for its fruit trees, and Fred, even before the family had resettled, began describing the pears and apples the family would grow. There was a tree outside Hallie's bedroom. She asked her father if it would one day have apples. "Of course!" said Fred. "They will grow there tomorrow." Next morning she awoke to find apples tied to all the branches. This was a story Hallie never tired of telling, perhaps because it came to represent her father's defiant response to affliction. In 1896 the Fergusons had never been poorer. They would never again face such an uncertain future, for despite Fred's boasts about his brother-in-law's railway company, the company's prospects were very uncertain: no track had been laid, no engines or cars had actually been built. Yet Fred continued to buoy his family's hopes, to insist that life should be enjoyed.

La Grange had a railway system that whisked commuters into Chicago in forty minutes, so Hallie, who often traveled with her father when he handed out leaflets to prospective buyers, got an early impression of the city she later described as "full of large, talkative men and the smell of cigar smoke." But the Leffler Company, though Fred managed to make the magnetic railway sound impressive to several small investors, never raised enough money to begin operations, and by the year's end Fred was once more out of work.

When Fred's business prospects floundered in Chicago, Louisa suggested moving to Alton to be near her family. During the next year Hallie's parents and sister lived with Louisa's mother and Hallie was farmed out to the family of her Aunt Amelia and Uncle Henry in nearby St. Louis. Hallie was now nine. To her St. Louis relatives she must have seemed an unusually mature and confident young lady. She had her mother's poise and her father's lively manner. From years of reading and being read to, she had a large vocabulary, which she did not hesitate to use. Having spent most of her childhood in the company of adults, she could appear socially at ease with her parents' contemporaries, but the appearance was at least partly deceptive. Away from her immediate family for the first time, Hallie felt terribly homesick. Later she was to say that homesickness was the worst feeling she experienced in childhood. Not wanting to disappoint her father, who had prepared her for this first separation by pointing out that it would be an adventure and an opportunity to do a lot of reading, she did read. To please her Uncle Henry, who tutored her in history, she studied the exploits of military heroes "by the hour." She also read novels and poetry, but her greatest discovery was learning that, like her father, she could overcome periods of unhappiness by looking beyond her immediate condition. Her Uncle Henry, whom Hallie later described as "huge, dark and mustachioed," intimidated her at first (he was so large he seemed awesome), but she discovered, after engaging him in conversation about Peter the Great, that he could be friendly, that he even seemed to like her. Being liked and admired had become essential to Hallie's feeling of well-being.

The Fergusons moved next to Sonora, Iowa, where Fred's parents owned a farm a few miles north of Grinnell. Sonora, with its clusters of farmhouses and broad rolling cornfields, looks today much as it must have in 1900. In midsummer under a clear sky the rise and fall of the fields, one shade of green growing into another, long, dirt, roller-coaster roads making troughs between them, makes one think of an untroubled sea. A bird plummets or calls, an occasional passing truck throws up clouds of dust, but nothing else stirs. Louisa was happy in Sonora. She had her husband to care for on weekdays as well as weekends, and nature at her doorstep. She went back to painting landscapes, and she redecorated the farmhouse with white woodwork and pale-colored walls, an act that apparently shocked the neighbors but delighted Hallie.

Fred worked his father's fields while waiting for the depression to end. He made a joke of farming, but his crops were bumpers. The two girls enjoyed watching their father harness his horses. Sometimes they made stick horses for themselves out of boughs they found in the orchard. Husking bees and square dances in the local Methodist church, reading aloud in the evenings, and the friendships she formed in the one-room country schoolhouse all contributed to Hallie's pleasure in living on a farm. Then, when Hallie was ten, her brother, Kenneth, was born and the family was complete. Toward the end of 1900 Fred found a job selling switchboards for a local phone company and moved his family into a modest-sized house in Grinnell. The family, he promised, would now stay put.

With the return of prosperity, Fred could have chosen to settle anywhere salesmen were needed. He chose Grinnell because many of his relatives had moved there. An aunt and uncle from his home town in New England had been early settlers. Grinnell had been founded by a group of men from the East who wanted to create a college and a Christian community. No one in Grinnell was expected to advance his livelihood at the expense of his neighbors; blacks as well as whites were to be welcomed; drinking was prohibited. As soon as Grinnell College was built, it became the town's pride. Fred looked on Grinnell as the Promised Land, the final settling place of his family after ten years of wandering, and Hallie came to see it the same way. In her later years, no matter how tired or discouraged she felt, the mere mention of Grinnell could restore her to cheerful thoughts. Serene was the word she most often used to describe her girlhood years in the small Iowa town. Life at the turn of the century, she liked remembering, was leisurely. There was time to dream, and think, and do what one chose. No one hurried. Horsecarts rumbled along country lanes, quickening their pace as they came into town. People took time to dress, for there was much to put on. Women wore petticoats, long skirts, and high-necked blouses. Children walked to school, men walked to work. At twilight, lamplighters lit the street lights, parents lit oil lamps inside their houses, and everyone helped with the chores. In the Ferguson house, children and parents gathered around the kitchen table after dinner to hear Father or Mother alternate in reading Dickens, Thackeray, or Scott. On weekends they put on plays in the living room for their parents' entertainment. In springtime there were picnics, in summer visits from cousins or trips to St. Louis, in autumn nut-gathering expeditions, and at Christmas a round of festivities. There were few family quarrels and no marital discord. Everyone went to church on Sunday; no one questioned the existence of God.

Fred and Louisa had lived through difficult times. When they finally settled, they directed their energies toward creating a harmonious family life. Hallie's two earliest memories of Grinnell make this clear. Fred had brought a horse to Grinnell from his father's farm and stabled it in a barn behind his family's house. He used the horse and a rented carryall to take the family on picnics and other outings. But after the neighbors complained that the horse's kicking kept them from sleeping, he felt obliged to return it. This was the first time Hallie saw her father depressed. "Be very nice to your father tonight," Louisa told the children. "I don't remember what we did to cheer him up," Hallie recalled, "but I do remember Father finally saying, Oh well, I can always ride Rob Roy." Rob Roy was the name of Hallie's favorite stick horse. Her other early memory of Grinnell was of the day her mother came to the rescue after mice ate up the May Day baskets she and her sister had made. Louisa "stopped her work, even turned off the oven, went to town, bought more tissue paper and worked all day making silver boats, pink hearts and blue roses, the most beautiful baskets we had ever seen." To help out, Hallie and Gladys concocted "soggy sandwiches, limp jello and fudge" for lunch, and Fred, when apprised of the situation, declared it was "the best lunch he ever ate."

Finally, the year Hallie turned fourteen, the Fergusons moved to the house they would occupy for the next twenty-two years. 1421 Broad Street, a white frame house in the best section of town, occupied a half-acre lot. With its ample lawns, large shade trees, and wide front porch, it had an air of prosperity. It was the home, one would have thought, of a well-to-do businessman, of a gentleman certainly. Fred must have got help from his parents to secure a mortgage. Some financial arrangement was apparently made, because Fred's parents sold their farm at this time and moved in with their son's family. Fred soon knew all his neighbors. When he walked down the street, impeccably attired in suit and top hat, often accompanied by his eldest daughter, he would lift his hat and ask after the health of everyone he met. His manner, some thought, was a little quaint, but Fred did not notice. He told people he was raising money for the college. He talked about his business investments, hinting that the stocks he owned in the Leffler Railway Company would one day make his family's fortune. He boasted about his children's accomplishments, particularly those of Hallie, who had started to write a novel. He never mentioned the fact that he was a traveling salesman. In his own view, he was a businessman with prospects.

Some of the information Fred gave his friends was correct— Hallie was writing a novel. She called it *Lady Glyde's Revenge,* and she read chapters of it aloud to her classmates at recess. This brief novel-writing effort came to an end a short time later when Grinnell built a theatre. Thereafter, Hallie's chief interest became playwriting.

Grinnell's Colonial Theatre was a typical nineteenth-century opera house with chandeliers, tiers of ornate boxes, two balconies, and an orchestra filled with red plush seats. The long row of footlights that lit the actors who arrived in town to give minstrel, vaudeville, and stock-company shows produced no subtle effects, but subtlety was not in vogue. Passionate love scenes, lingering death scenes, and heroic speeches were. People wanted the big emotions. These were the days of David Belasco's extravagant naturalism. Labor was cheap, and thirty technicians or more were often hired just to create an effect of snow falling, or of evening fading gradually into night, or, as in *Uncle Tom's Cabin,* of huge ice floes moving downstream. It was a time when trains carried carfuls of scenery from one town to another and stages became overloaded with scenic effects. Though Hallie would later scorn sentimental plays, elaborate sets, and melodramatic climaxes, these all thrilled her the first time she saw them.

A short time later Fred began organizing home talent shows in the family living room on weekends. He dragooned the younger generation, as Hallie's brother put it, into reciting poems or inventing skits. When Hallie took over, she at first suggested doing scenes from Dickens or Thackeray but then began bringing in scripts of her own—"mostly of the melodramatic, mortgage-overdue, villain-wants-debtor's-daughter variety," according to her friend Renna Norris. Once Hallie had discovered the pleasure of thrilling an audience with overblown emotional climaxes, there was no stopping her. "After she returned from a trip to the St. Louis Exposition," Norris recalled, "she kept us enthralled with descriptions of what she had seen." Hallie kept a diary on the trip, a dress rehearsal apparently for the performance she planned for her friends. As the train pulled out of the station she began: "This promises to be a very uneventful trip. The passengers are few: the usual bad little boy and his Ma; a young couple evidently having their first quarrel; several others, and then last and most interesting a pensive-looking black haired fellow, who I think is either an exiled Italian prince or at least a Russian spy. But Papa says he looks more like a barber or a book agent." Papa's down-to-earth comment on this occasion was not in keeping with his more usual inclination to make drama out of his everyday experiences.

During the days that followed, the Fergusons visited each building at the fair and Hallie continued to fill her diary with vivid descriptions of sights and reactions. Even the Machinery Building, the only one that failed to impress her, provided material for dramatic comment. "I held my nose all the time we were there because there was such an oily, greasy smell. If I had had four hands I would have stopped my ears too. Such a noise I never heard! Smash! Bang! Clash! all the time." The U.S. Government Building was the one Hallie felt she ought to like best—her father told her it was the finest building on the grounds. But in fact she was more impressed by the "fifty immense glass cases" of models wearing Parisian gowns in the Industry Building and by an exhibit of a model house—"a young couple's paradise." In a rhapsodic passage at the end of the diary, Hallie described the "million quadrillion tiny bulbs" which lighted the Exposition's palaces in the evenings. "Half way up Festival Hall the doors swing open and a torrent of water leaps madly down over the cascades between the rows of golden cupids. The rippling water dashes down, flashing in the opalescent light. The gondolas are filled and pull gayly out as the band plays Meet me in St. Louis, Louis, meet me at the fair . . ."

Her friends were not the only ones who noticed Hallie's growing theatrical bent. Her brother Kenneth observed that she liked to memorize passages from the Bible and quote them at opportune moments. "Her timing was perfect . . . I remember an evening. She was to put me to bed. Halfway up the stairs there was a landing where we stopped to look at the sunset. The sky that night was brilliant. Hallie watched, then she said, 'When I consider the Heavens, the work of Thy fingers, the moon and the stars which Thou hast ordained, what is man that Thou art mindful of him?' It was the right moment to say such a thing. I never forgot it."

As a girl Hallie's religious faith was as strong as her mother's. Fred went to church from time to time but Louisa, who had converted to the Protestant faith when she married Fred, never missed a Sunday service, and she took Hallie with her. At home she set an example of patience and solicitude that Hallie tried to emulate. When Gladys was diagnosed as having chorea, a nervous disorder that produced an involuntary twitching of the hands and feet, Hallie and Louisa took turns attending her. "They waited on her," Kenneth recalled, "and they got me involved too." A friend of the family who thought Gladys had probably suffered brain damage at birth remembered her as awkward, unhappy, and totally lacking in self-confidence, and one of Hallie's classmates concurred: "Life must have been a terrible burden for Gladys. Hallie was so graceful, but Gladys was clumsy, she was always saying the wrong thing."

Hallie modeled herself on her mother in other ways. She struck some of her friends as excessively proper. One evening when she was entertaining a group of girls, several boys dropped by, and a couple of them sneaked upstairs to pull apart the girls' bedclothes. Hallie did not take this as a joke. "She was scandalized," one guest remembered, "furious at the thought of bold males invading our private feminine quarters."

Also like Louisa, Hallie kept her deepest feelings hidden. When she fell in love for the first time she told no one, not even her closest friend. Later she recalled trying to find out where her idol lived. "Every time I passed his house, which on some pretext was every day, my heart would beat so that I could scarcely walk. I never spoke to this boy, nor he to me." This first love was a Polish boy who suffered from tuberculosis. He did not belong to the group of friends Hallie went with, he was an outsider. Her friends, she may have decided, would have thought her choice odd. But in fact it was typical of Hallie to be drawn to people who in one way or another stood apart from the crowd—typical too for her to fall in love with a person she did not know but could worship only from a distance. In the summer of 1907, when she went to Cedar Rapids to make up credits she had missed during the year she spent in St. Louis, she was terribly homesick. She overcame this feeling by falling in love with her German teacher, "a robust blonde by the name of Miss Plock." Miss Plock, Hallie said later, did not realize I existed. Each morning Hallie picked a bouquet of flowers and placed them anonymously on her teacher's desk. She got through the summer by idolizing a woman she never spoke to except in the formal setting of a classroom.

Hallie's childhood had taught her two very different sets of values. Her father had made her feel she was special and could accomplish anything she set her mind to. Her mother had made her feel that others' needs mattered most. She could not have known then how difficult it would be to resolve the double message her parents had given her. If they had quarreled or disagreed, she might have taken sides. But Louisa and Fred remained devoted to one another as long as they lived, causing Hallie to feel that marriage and family life were the goals she wanted also. Even later, after she had discovered the pleasures of exercising her talents, she tried to tell herself that everything she did was done for her family. Although it was Fred's encouragement that shaped her life, Louisa's ideals remained the ones that guided her thinking.

Murray Flanagan

ALLIE entered Grinnell College in the fall of 1907. Founded by
New England Congregationalists, it had as good a reputation
at the time Hallie went there as any university west of the Mississippi.
John Main, who became president shortly before Hallie matriculated,
set up an exchange system with Harvard professors. He inaugurated
lecture series which brought poets, religious leaders, and political
scientists to the college. He enlarged the faculty, established new
departments, increased the endowment, built a chapel, athletic field,
and swimming pool, and after Hallie's time several dormitories. His
innovations had one ultimate purpose—to build character. He
wanted his students, as he told them in weekly chapel talks, to grow
in wisdom so that when they moved out into the larger community
they would be equipped to change it. Many took his precepts to
heart. Harry Hopkins went on to become a top Roosevelt aide,
Chester Davis a director of the Federal Reserve Bank, Paul Appleby
an Assistant Secretary of Agriculture, Florence Kerr a top WPA
administrator. All responded to the social idealism that inspired
Grinnell's teachers as well as its president. None was more zealous
than Hallie herself. Invited to give the traditional last address before
the YMCA in 1911, she had no hesitation in telling her fellow
students that the love of truth should guide them: "A college woman

who goes out into the world having gained only knowledge, with no love for humanity, has failed."

She wondered later if she had been overly impressed by her teachers. She had worshipped them, she recalled, "in a sort of hierarchy: at the top President Main," with whom she studied Greek because he taught it; "next Miss Millard who taught philosophy and played Bach and had Sunday evenings to which her students were invited. As I remember it, the talk was very lofty and the food sparse, but we were awed by them anyway." She decided that President Main had tried to make Grinnell "into a Greek city-state, a self-contained realm of truth and beauty." She kept her admiration for Main's accomplishments as long as she lived, and it is not without interest that a quarter of a century later she married a professor of Greek at Vassar College.

This was the idealistic side of Hallie, the side she approved even later when she wondered whether Grinnell had overstressed public service. But she worried sometimes about another quality she saw in herself that conflicted with the virtues her teachers espoused. She enjoyed being popular, liked having admirers, went out of her way to make sure she kept them, then having achieved her aim felt an uncomfortable self-contempt. She was to explore this realization in the first short story she wrote in college.

Most of her classmates regarded Hallie as a leader. Renna Norris thought she assumed the role naturally. "She was impulsive, generous, venturesome, very loyal to her friends. She could hold her own in any argument." Some others thought Hallie worked too hard at collecting admirers, that she vamped people, young men in particular, and used feminine wiles to do it. One of her admirers was the young man who sat behind her in high school assemblies. His recollection was that "she liked to have very sharp pencils, I don't know why. When she needed them sharpened, I'd do that for her. I always carried a knife in my pocket." Hallie was later to say that one of the first things she learned about human relations was that "people like being needed." Part of her charm, apparently, was her willingness to reveal her emotional needs. Renna Norris recalled: "I felt flattered when she asked me to accompany her to the dentist to hold her hand." To some she gave the impression of being more than usually vulnerable. Rachel Harris wrote her after they had both become grown women, "You were so small and fragile, I thought you would always need someone to look after you."

Forty years later, Hallie's most vivid memory of the role she played in college centered on an event that took place in her freshman year. Hallie had been elected to the planning committee for the first freshman class party. The committee met in her house to decide which boys should accompany which girls. The decision was not to be left to choice.

> When we came to one boy's name, the chairman said importantly, "Now this is a problem. The dean of women called me in and told me that maybe he could either go by himself, or with a group. Because he's a negro, the only one in college." There was a silence, then a clatter—"how terrible, what shall we do?" I remember getting suddenly very angry and ashamed. I said it was all silly and that I would like to go to the party with him. (Of course this may have been just showing off or dramatizing it, but I think the main thing was a revulsion of feeling against injustice.) The committee was horrified, the boys said my parents would object. One boy said, "I would never go out with a girl who had gone out with a nigger." I said that no one could sit on our porch and call anyone that. The meeting broke up in a fight. . . . The affair came to little because the boy withdrew from college.

Hallie's father's comment when he heard this story was "By God, I wouldn't let anyone into college who couldn't recite the Bill of Rights."

Hallie took an active role in everything. She suggested staging the freshman party as an autumn picnic and with her friends collected leaves and branches to decorate the gymnasium. They created a bonfire by means of electrical devices, brought in swings and hammocks, and set up a fortune-teller's tent. The party, according to the college newspaper, was one of the best ever given.

At later periods during her four years at Grinnell, Hallie was president of the Literary Society and an editor of the college literary magazine and her class yearbook. She joined the Dramatic Club and acted in plays. In her senior year she was designated class poet and wrote a series of poems for the yearbook. "She had more ability than the rest of us," according to a friend who worked with her on the yearbook. The one thing Hallie did not do was enter into athletic events, although Harry Hopkins remembered that she "stood on the backs of students to cheer" and thus helped Grinnell to "win games over Chicago."

Hallie was later to insist that the "main thing that happened" to her while she was at Grinnell was Murray Flanagan. Murray came from a middle-class family in nearby Cedar Rapids. His father, whom Hallie rather meanly described as "a charming, completely lazy man who played the violin and had never, so far as I knew, had a job," had actually been manager of a wagon factory. When business in the factory slowed down, owing to improved methods of transportation, Murray's mother found work as a typesetter for the local Clinton newspaper, leaving the youngest of her six children, of whom Murray was one, to be reared by their zealous Presbyterian grandmother. According to Hallie, Murray had supported himself from the age of fourteen. In high school he not only won top marks but became an outstanding athlete. Hallie saw Murray as an ambitious young man determined to overcome the setbacks of his background. At the time she met him she was a senior in high school, he was a college sophomore and already something of a campus hero. While waiting on tables to earn his keep, Murray found time to join the football team, the Glee Club, the Dramatic Club, and the track team, where he distinguished himself as one of its fastest runners. "Although there were other brilliant and attractive people on campus," in Hallie's opinion, Murray was "the most versatile and promising." He was also good-looking. In the words of one of Hallie's classmates, he was "every young girl's romantic dream."

During his first two years at Grinnell, Murray lived in a room in town. Since there were no college dormitories at the time, this was the custom for out-of-town students. Hallie's grandparents died around this time, leaving their room empty. The Fergusons needed a tenant for financial reasons and Murray fitted the bill. He moved into the Fergusons' spare bedroom the same year Hallie entered Grinnell as a freshman.

Under one roof the two young people soon found they had much in common. Hallie's brother, Kenneth, recalled that they spent evening hours at the piano, "Murray playing and both of them singing 'I Love You Truly,' and songs like that. Murray also sang hilarious Irish ditties." As Hallie recalled it, "We had a gay time in what would today be called an extremely naive way. No drinking, no smoking, no sexual experimentation." During her freshman year, Murray one day took her for a walk, told her he was in love with her and wanted to marry her, but "was poor and had no right to get engaged till he got a job." They came to an understanding. Hallie would go out with other boys, preferably in a crowd, until Murray graduated, landed a job, and returned to Grinnell with an engagement ring.

But then, having made her conquest, Hallie discovered the pleasures of flirtation. She could not resist making further conquests and soon became aware that John Ryan, her speech professor, Grinnell's most popular bachelor, found her attractive. One day he wrote inviting her to visit him in his room. He had just discovered a story he thought would interest her. She had written one for his class which "dealt with love, the source of all artistic success. This story deals with jealousy, the cause of all artistic failure." He suggested she visit "any time Monday," adding that he was "idle" during the 10:15 hour. Prudence and the strong sense of propriety she had learned from her mother kept Hallie from accepting this invitation, but she did paste it into her scrapbook and, in midlife, on rereading it, remembered how jealous Murray had been every time she flirted with another man. Another instance of Murray's jealousy occurred after he had graduated and gone to work for the YMCA in Cedar Rapids. Before leaving he asked his best friend to "take care of" Hallie. Instead, the best friend fell in love with her. Hallie admitted that she had encouraged the flirtation. She thought it "unimportant," but when Murray learned about it he was furious.

Around the time Murray proposed, Hallie wrote a story that was later published in the college literary magazine. "Two's Company" contrasts two kinds of students. The hero, Fleming, is working hard to land a job and become a useful member of society. His roommate, Jack, wants to win the devotion of as many admirers as possible. Both men hope to win the love of a girl who lives in Philadelphia. Fleming (since the tale has a moral) wins out, while Jack ends by feeling a fool.

Fleming has the qualities Hallie idealized in her mother and in Murray: loyalty, unswerving commitment to others, and dedication to serving the community. Jack, on the other hand, has all the self-centered characteristics of a student who has not yet decided what he wants to do with his life. As he sits dreaming about the several girls he might invite to the school dance, he cannot decide what to do at the moment. He could take a cross-country tramp, he could be down at the river rowing. When he sees three of his friends strolling across the campus singing "For He's a Jolly Good Fellow," he wants to join them. All this time he is wondering: which girl shall he invite to the dance? He hits at last on an ingenious plan: he will ask several. Most, he reasons, will have to refuse, either from an inability to dance or because of a former commitment. By inviting all, he will win their devotion, and the girl he really wants will say yes. She, of course, turns out to be the one who has already agreed to marry Fleming. Hallie's portrait of Jack, the first in a long series of portraits she created of clever and charming but self-serving young people, shows her trying to resolve certain inner conflicts. Commitment to others wins out in this tale, as in others she wrote, but Jack, the clever, fun-loving hero, is the better-drawn character for obvious reasons: he was the one Hallie best understood.

As soon as he graduated, Murray began pressing for an early marriage. It was his wish to marry right after Hallie's graduation, but Hallie had decided she wanted to spend the next year teaching high school English. She got a job at nearby Sigourney High School, and was later to recall that "Murray's roses, telegrams, phone calls and appearances in a Ford Model T were the talk of the village." Hallie meantime was discovering how much she enjoyed teaching and the adoration of her students. When two of them rode to Grinnell on motorcycles the following summer to pay her a visit, however, Murray's jealousy erupted. "He was even jealous of me," Hallie's brother recalled. Kenneth, who was eleven at the time and proud of being a Boy Scout, said Murray got hold of his Scout manual one day, crossed out *Boy Scouts,* and wrote in "Boy Boobs of America." Whatever Hallie thought of this, she believed in Murray's talents and felt he was about to enter on a brilliant career.

What other members of her family thought of the Ferguson-

Flanagan match is not on record. But at least one member of Murray's family doubted that the marriage was a good idea for Murray. His younger brother, Lyle, thought Hallie was always "acting as though she were on a stage," and he blamed her for persuading Murray to give up his YMCA job and go into life insurance.

Hallie's persuasion was real enough. During the period of their engagement she introduced Murray to her uncle Will Fischer, who sold life insurance for the Northwestern Mutual Life Insurance Company in St. Louis, and Will offered Murray a job. Although he was enjoying his YMCA social service work, Murray agreed to switch to life insurance. No doubt he was coming to realize that once Hallie set her mind on some goal, there was no stopping her.

After Murray and Hallie had made plans to move to St. Louis, Murray took Kenneth into the Fergusons' back yard one day to show him some guns he owned. "I'm going to take good care of Hallie down there in St. Louis," he told Kenneth, "and I want to show you why you should never touch these guns." He fired them into the ground, Kenneth recalled, "and let me do the same. They had a tremendous kick and made a big hole in the ground and I was suitably impressed. But I was amazed that he thought St. Louis was dangerous."

Kenneth, who was a frequent visitor in the Flanagans' St. Louis apartment after their marriage—which took place on Christmas night 1912—soon noticed that Hallie's lack of interest in cooking and other household chores often put Murray in a temper. "He teased her when she burned the beans, and that happened quite often. When she left the house without her key, he called her the Keyless Kid." Murray took out some of his frustration on Kenneth. One Sunday morning Murray followed Kenneth out of the apartment house with his mouth full of water. Kenneth, who had dressed for church and was feeling that he looked quite smart, found himself splashed with water. "Naturally I retaliated," he said, "but then Hallie came out of the house and said she was ashamed of us both."

Before a year had passed, the young couple was having serious quarrels. On the occasion of their first wedding anniversary, Murray wrote Hallie a letter apologizing for his outbursts. Apparently their differences had reached a climax and Hallie had gone off to spend some days with a friend. Murray promised in his letter to change. He loved her as much as ever and had come to realize she was "better" than he was. None of this news reached the Ferguson household. Hallie, who felt it would have been disloyal to say anything negative about Murray, told her family only how successful he had become selling life insurance. This also was the way she presented her first husband in her autobiography. "He plunged into insurance with the zest and belief," she wrote, "which characterized all he did."

And then suddenly the Flanagans became lucky in a way that made up for Hallie's domestic failings. Will Fischer arranged to take his wife on a round-the-world trip, and he asked Hallie and Murray to take care of his house and two teen-age sons in his absence. During her second year of marriage Hallie acquired a taste for gracious living. She now had what she liked: an attractive house, servants to take charge of meals and chores, and two likable young men who enlivened the household but made few demands on her time. Later she remembered this year as "a great lark. Much of our life centered around Pilgrim Congregational Church where we both taught in the Sunday School." Once again Hallie had admiring students and a project that involved her. "She had us organize the class, elect officers and become interested in useful services," one student was later to recall.

At the end of that year Hallie became pregnant. The Fischers returned from their trip around the world and the Flanagans returned to an apartment. Their son, Jack, was born the following March, making Hallie feel for a time that life was "complete and marvelous." Murray bought a camera and the parents took turns taking snapshots. Jack's first bath, first steps, and first visits to grandparents were all recorded and pasted into an album. Murray was an attentive father and, when he was not too busy, helpful. But gradually, as the days stretched into weeks and months and Hallie found her life becoming a daily round of bathing, diapering, and feeding a young child, she became restless. She missed the stimulation of students and could not help comparing her life with her husband's. His work, she felt, was much more challenging than hers. And there was something else that troubled her. Hallie, who had begun by idealizing her husband, had come to feel that her own talents were as remarkable as his. At some point the thought entered her mind: why did it always have to be the woman who tended the family and advanced the man's career? Why not the other way around?

Hallie's marriage came at a time of upheaval. The historian Malcolm Cowley has written of "the bustle and hopefulness" that filled the years between 1911 and 1916. New ideas were being advanced in magazines, picture galleries, and experimental schools. Painters like John Marin were creating new art forms, Isadora Duncan was discarding the rigid dance patterns of the past, Amy Lowell was writing free verse, and a group of young actors and writers calling themselves the Provincetown Players was beginning to produce new kinds of plays. In her Fifth Avenue salon, Mabel Dodge was encouraging young people interested in the arts to "upset America" and bring an end to the Old Order. This ferment followed a pattern that had begun in Europe three decades earlier. When Henrik Ibsen's Nora walked out of her dollhouse and slammed the door on home and husband, the male-dominated world of the nineteenth century received a blow from which it never recovered.

Theodore Dreiser was one of the modern writers Hallie read and admired. In 1916 he wrote that the "ideal state of the human mind" was "not to cling too pathetically to a religion or a system of government, or a theory of morals or a method of living but to be ready to abandon at a moment's notice the apparent teachings of the ages, and to step out free and willing to accept new and radically different conditions." This was not the philosophy Hallie had learned from her religious mother, or her adventurous father, or even from her progressive-minded teachers at Grinnell, but it answered a need. She was to make Dreiser's ideas a central part of her thinking.

But not just yet. World War I had brought economic changes to the Midwest which had a more immediate effect on the Flanagans' way of living than the books Hallie read. By 1915, states west of the Mississippi were experiencing a boom, and Murray was offered a position as general agent for the Massachusetts Mutual Life Insurance Company located in Springfield, Mass. "It took us a year to decide to leave St. Louis," Hallie recalled. Murray accepted the position on condition that he could take his assistant, Mike Walters, with him. Mike had married Deborah Wiley, a close friend of Hallie's in high school, and the two couples had become inseparable. They decided to share a house in Omaha and, in Hallie's words, "to try the experiment of shared housekeeping." Since Hallie and Deborah were both pregnant, it was arranged that the two husbands would go to Omaha to find living quarters and set up the new office, and that the wives would follow in a few months' time.

Had Hallie been able to foresee the consequences of this arrangement, she might have acted otherwise. Setting up a new office and home, with no wife on hand to regulate his eating and sleeping habits, was a large undertaking for a man as dependent on his wife as Murray was. Kenneth thought Murray was so eager to do a good job that he neglected his health. He spent days organizing the office and nights going over the necessary papers; in the mornings, instead of eating a sensible breakfast, he would stop at the corner drugstore and order a pineapple sundae. Murray applied to the insurance business the same energy that had made him a star on the track team at college, and it eventually wore him down.

At first, no one realized anything was wrong. Hallie and Deborah joined their husbands in Omaha in October, and for three months the two couples enjoyed keeping house together. Then on Christmas Eve 1916, Murray came down with the flu. During the last two months of Hallie's second pregnancy he was terribly ill. It must have been a disastrous period for both of them. Everything, one imagines, which had brought them into conflict earlier—Hallie's frustration with domesticity, Murray's irritation at finding himself married to a woman who insisted on having a life of her own—must have surfaced. Jack had just turned two; Hallie's pregnancy exhausted her, and Murray's illness must have seemed the final impossible demand on her energies. From his point of view, Murray needed care, there was no such thing as too much. Two months after Hallie gave birth to a second son, Frederic, Murray's doctor decided that he should be moved to a sanitarium in Colorado Springs. Frederic was just three months old when Hallie had to pack Murray off to Colorado and return to Grinnell with her two children. She told herself that Murray would be back on his feet in a matter of weeks, or, at the most, months, but there were moments when she wondered. The insurance company agreed to pay Murray's medical bills, so Hallie did not have to worry about his expenses.

Despite her forebodings, Hallie was determined to stay cheerful. She wrote Deborah that the train trip back to Grinnell had been a "never-to-be-forgotten experience."

Everything went splendidly until ten o'clock when the porter came through and said we were nearing Grinnell, so I wakened both children, put on their coats, etc.—and from then on we had a scene of frightfulness. Jack wakened with one of those screaming spells—and Frederic got the colic, and we staged a duet. To cap the climax, the porter announced that we were one hour late, and they both howled all during that time. Jack had made a river and kept screaming at me not to spank him in such heart-rending tones that people looked out of their berths at me accusingly. Ken met us and we piled out in the rain into a taxi which broke down in front of the High School. Ken had to get out and hunt up another car (an open one). We got out and piled into that and drove howling away up Broad Street.

At home Hallie was distressed to discover that her old room was occupied by a boarder and that she and the children would have to sleep in the living room. The thousands of dollars' worth of Leffler Company stock that her father owned had become worthless, and Fred, now 63, was finding it more and more difficult to find work. As a result, the family had taken in boarders.

During the summer months Hallie looked after the children and wrote her husband almost every day. "His letters," she wrote Deborah, "are wonderfully brave and optimistic but he is dreadfully homesick." She was alternately encouraged and discouraged by the doctors' reports, which at first called Murray's case "effusion due to general weakened condition and heightened by a severe pneumonia and pleurisy," but later began to hint at a "tubercular condition." "The nurse says he is like a man who has been tired for years." By July she had given up any idea that he would be well in six months. She wrote Deborah, "At times I feel that my duty is so divided between Murray and the children that I am almost desperate . . . We just simply haven't the money to let me live in Colorado Springs with the children so that I could see him every few days . . . Murray and I both feel that we must face the separation just as millions of husbands and wives are facing a necessary separation today—and bring what fortitude we can to bear." Her great consolation during this difficult time was her two children. "Frederic," she wrote Deborah, "is the most adorable thing you ever saw. You and Mike would be crazy about him for he lies and chuckles and kicks and laughs out loud every time you speak to him." "I think he's going to be quite a person," she wrote in another letter, and "Jack is, as ever, angelic and devilish by turns."

Whatever difficulties Hallie had had with Murray during the earlier years of her marriage she now dismissed. Murray was her support and her support was vanishing. In a copy of *Les Misérables* that she was reading at the time, she underlined Hugo's description of a man who has just fallen overboard. The dying man reflects that he was once one of the crew, a living man, but that now he has nothing under his feet. "Around him are darkness, storm, solitude, wild tumult . . . within him horror and exhaustion." Whether Hallie was thinking of herself or of Murray, the passage hit home.

In December the sanitarium Murray had been staying in burned down and he was moved to another, where he was diagnosed as tubercular. Hallie recalled the next year and a half as a nightmare.

> Murray would have a hemorrhage and they would send for me. I'd rush out to Colorado. The children would get measles and I'd rush back to Grinnell. Finally the doctor in Colorado said Murray's only chance was to have me there all the time.

Hallie arranged to leave Frederic with Murray's parents and Jack with her own, but she was never reconciled to this arrangement. "I simply couldn't bear to think of them—used to wake up crying, felt terribly torn as to whether I had made the right choice."

During the daytime, when life took on a more cheerful aspect, Hallie found the routine at Glockner Sanitarium "in many ways a marvelous experience. Murray was like a magnet. From the first, he was a bed patient but every interesting person in Colorado Springs came to know him." She recalled conversations around his bed with a priest, a rabbi, an engineer who designed bridges, and a Japanese scholar. Murray "read omnivorously. Conversations with those who visited were both profound and gay."

Although Murray's current expenses were covered by insurance, Hallie still worried about the future. She had no domestic duties at

Glockner and at first had much free time. As she wrote later in her autobiography:

> During Murray's rest periods I rented a studio down town and advertised to get pupils in drama. I was so inexperienced that when they asked my fee I said $1 an hour, meaning *my* time. I had a class of 20, 3 days a week and when they each paid $1 I felt staggered—and gradually I was able to make all my own expenses. Murray never knew this. In fact no one did except one other girl at Glockner who was in the same situation. We rented the studio together and she taught, of all things, lace making, the only practical thing gleaned from a select girl's finishing school. It was all exactly like Helen Hokinson—and Ann and I used to vibrate between despair about our husbands and hysterical amusement over our "clients."

Hallie had written Deborah earlier of Murray's dark and depressed moods. He sometimes tried to subdue them with macabre humor, as when he suggested to Hallie that he should be sent up over Germany in an airplane so he could spit on the enemy. But gradually, as he came to realize he was dying, he counted more and more on his Bible. During one of Hallie's last visits, he read from Isaiah: "They shall mount up with wings like eagles, they shall run and not be weary." The passage must have made her think of the vigorous young man she had fallen in love with in college.

Much later Hallie wrote that Murray's death taught her the "first humility" she ever felt. "I began to see how childish I was, and I tried to grow up." She and Murray, she concluded, had been "as happy in their marriage as human beings *at that age* can be." She did not explain her reservation beyond saying that "love gets better as one grows able to grasp it." As usual, her fictional writing revealed more about her feelings than her public statements. In a later play she wrote—clearly about her marriage—Hallie's heroine comes to the realization that in relation to her husband she has been, as Shakespeare puts it, like "the base Indian" who threw a pearl away, "richer than all his tribe."

New Directions

Murray's death gave Hallie's life a new direction. After she returned to Grinnell, with a practical nurse to look after the children, she got a job teaching English at the high school. "I did not choose work," she said later, "I had to earn a living." That was true, but having to work also gave Hallie the opportunity to do what she wanted. She read avidly, particularly plays and poetry, and shared what she read with her pupils. One young man she taught that year recalled the dramatic hush that came over the classroom when Hallie read Synge's *Riders to the Sea*. "She was almost in tears when she finished, and so was the entire class. All she did when the class period was over was wave us out. And we all filed out the door. Nobody said a word."

Hallie and Kenneth, who had been close while they were growing up, became even closer after Murray's death. Kenneth, in his last year of college, was still living at home. "On Sundays," he remembered, "we often walked to the cemetery where Murray was buried. Hallie always took along some book of poetry that she wanted to read to me. She also knew a lot of poetry that she could quote by heart." She waited for the right moment. One late afternoon in autumn as they started to walk down the hill where Murray was buried, Hallie looked toward the distant town, stopped, and began to recite Edna St. Vincent Millay's "Afternoon on a Hill"—"the poem," said Kenneth, "that begins, 'I will be the gladdest thing under the sun! I will touch a hundred flowers and not pick one.' She got to those last lines, 'And when the lights begin to show up from the town, I will mark which must be mine, and then start down!' We did; we never looked back."

Hallie's own favorite story about the year she taught high school English had to do with a meeting she called at her home shortly after she discovered that pay had been deducted from the salaries of the teachers who were absent during the widespread flu epidemic of 1918–1919. Those who took on their work were also not paid, so the school system benefited. The teachers who met in Hallie's house agreed with her that something should be done, but before the meeting got started, someone went to the windows and pulled down the shades. The teachers feared losing their jobs. Their resolve to "do something" evaporated—fortunately for Hallie. Kenneth's recollection was that she had been cultivating the friendship of the superintendent of schools in the hope of landing a job teaching English at the college. Had the superintendent learned about her protest meeting, he would have been less inclined to help her.

However it came about, Hallie began teaching freshman English at Grinnell College in the fall of 1920, the year Grinnell introduced courses in playwriting and dramatic production in its curriculum. The man in charge of this program was William Bridge, a former minister and director of community theatre. Bridge formed a chapter of the Drama League of America, an organization that was sparking nationwide interest in amateur theatre. As local president of the League, Bridge met every Monday night with people in town who wanted to write plays or hear them discussed. Hallie attended regularly and began writing plays. Bridge thought she should try for an acting career, but Hallie insisted that playwriting interested her more. She had heard of George Pierce Baker, who was teaching playwriting to graduate students at Harvard, and decided she wanted to study with him. She had begun to hope she could earn a living in theatre.

Baker was an innovator and a key figure in the "new theatre" movement that got under way during the years preceding World War I. During extensive travels in Europe, where drama had long received

the respect accorded to painting, music, poetry, and novels, he saw
productions that provoked lively discussions of human problems.
Shaw, Ibsen, Maeterlinck, Hauptmann, and Synge, to name but a
few, were challenging people's thinking about the way they lived
their lives. American theatre, by contrast, was still dominated by
Puritan notions of what could and could not be shown in a
playhouse. American audiences demanded moral, inoffensive amusement—classics and light entertainment only. By the end of the
nineteenth century, theatre in America had become *show business,*
the profit motive predominant among those who controlled it. A
theatrical syndicate controlled the road companies; in New York
those in charge owned the theatres. The Shubert brothers owned
most of them, and newspaper critics praised their productions.

After Baker began teaching courses in the history and technique
of playwriting to graduate students at Harvard, two events occurred
that were to play a pivotal role in changing people's attitudes toward
theatre in the United States. On one of her American tours with
Dublin's Abbey Players, the Irish playwright Lady Augusta Gregory
gave this piece of advice to interested spectators: "Start your own
theatres. Train amateurs as we have done. Make your theatres in
your own image." That was in 1911. The following year Baker got
permission from Harvard to conduct a theatre workshop in connection with his English 47 course in playwriting. He went on to train
many who were to make theatre history, among them Eugene
O'Neill, S. N. Behrman, Sidney Howard, George Abbott, Philip
Barry, George Sklar, and Albert Maltz. O'Neill was later to say that
until Baker came along, most plays by Americans that were imaginative and original had been "almost automatically barred from our
theatre ... In the face of this blank wall, the bitterest need of the
young playwright was for intelligent encouragement." Baker offered
that encouragement. His larger aim was to make drama a force in
modern America just as it was in modern Europe.

Hallie, who had heard Baker lecture, also knew of the many
young people who had followed his lead. Alexander Drummond had
established a theatre department at Cornell, E. C. Mabie had started
one at the University of Iowa, Thomas Stevens one at the Carnegie
Institute of Technology in Pittsburgh, and Frederick M. Koch one at
the University of North Dakota. A group of amateurs in Province-

town, Massachusetts, had established themselves as the Province-town Players after meeting in one another's living rooms to perform plays for fun. The group, which included George Cram Cook and his wife, Susan Glaspell, Robert Edmond Jones, and John Reed, had such a good time with their first play that they had decided to move their enterprise into a shack on a wharf. Their first public perfor-mance—one-act plays by Reed and Glaspell—had proved successful and prompted them to seek subscribers, first in Provincetown and later for the small Playwrights' Theatre on MacDougal Street in New York City. By this time Eugene O'Neill had joined them.

William Bridge's innovations at Grinnell were part of this theatrical renaissance. By the spring of 1921 Bridge had started producing plays his students had written. He considered the lighting and sets at the Colonial Theatre old-fashioned and began experi-menting with more modern visual effects. Hallie became his assistant. By this time she was hard at work on her own first play and looking forward to its production at the Colonial. She called it *The Garden of Wishes*.

Hallie's first venture in playwriting is a one-act fantasy. Its central character, a forty-year-old woman who dreads growing older, goes to the Grantor of Wishes at the entrance to the Garden of Wishes to beg him to restore her youth. In the opening dialogue, the Grantor tells the heroine that although he can make her beautiful again, he cannot change her mind. This is all right, says the heroine; she is used to her mind, she even likes it. They talk, the heroine in a quite frivolous manner, and the Grantor tells her he considers her a badly spoiled person. "But you do like me, don't you?" the heroine inquires. The Grantor thinks this question is "beside the point," but ushers her into the Garden, where she regains her beauty and meets a young man who has just received the gift of words. When the young man sees the heroine gazing Narcissus-like at her reflection in a pool, he asks if she would mind posing while he writes a poem about her loveliness. At this the heroine bursts into "peals of delicate laughter," but then noticing that she has hurt his feelings resolves to be ladylike. In the course of their conversation the heroine, realizing that she has made a foolish wish, decides to leave the Garden and return to her husband. Previously she has told the Grantor of Wishes that her husband's mind is less subtle than her own and that she has become bored by her life with him because she understands him too well. In a final scene, the Grantor suggests that the heroine's husband is perhaps not as lacking in subtlety as she thinks. He too came to the Garden wanting something, though he turned back without revealing his wish. When the heroine expresses surprise and wishes she had been told this earlier, the Grantor says, "But you seemed to understand him so well." "We won't discuss that," the heroine jauntily remarks in her last line of the play, and off she goes to patch up her life as best she can.

There is much froth and frivolity in this play, but the mixture of contempt and compassion Hallie brings to the portrait of her heroine is anything but lighthearted. Her heroine's final realization that she has misunderstood her husband and wants to try again has poignancy. This was Hallie's first writing after Murray's death. As in college, when she wrote "Two's Company," she put many of her own qualities into the main character. She made her protagonist spirited and fun-loving, a person one may disapprove of but cannot wholly dislike. This time she added a judge to her story, a godlike figure who knows all and perhaps, but *only perhaps*, forgives all. Later, in a full-length play called *Free*, Hallie would turn this judge into a critical parental figure (a mother) and create a heroine who cannot decide whether to rebel against or agree with the judge's strict moral standards. Hallie was to spend her own life seesawing between the two positions. But first she was to face a second personal tragedy, one that happened without warning.

A week after the local newspaper announced that *The Garden of Wishes*, directed by Hallie, would soon open at the Colonial Theatre, Jack came down with spinal meningitis. There was no cure for meningitis in 1922, and the family doctor held out little hope for his recovery. Jack had always been frailer than his robust younger brother. While Frederic, in the years after Hallie returned from Colorado, went about the neighborhood making friends and exploring the terrain, Jack stayed indoors. Neighbors' children had been brought in to play with him but were told not to tire him. He turned to books. Though he was only seven, Hallie read him her own favorite poems. She even read him *The Garden of Wishes*, and Jack told her it was his favorite play. Jack had none of his younger brother's buoyant spirits, yet Frederic noticed, as others did, that

Jack was Hallie's favorite. He needed her more than Frederic seemed to. That was his advantage.

During the three weeks of Jack's illness, Hallie spent much of her time by his bedside. When he was not in pain, she encouraged him to talk. Sometimes she just held his hand. When he asked her one day what Heaven was like, she told him it was a place without pain— though this was the time, she later told Kenneth, when her faith in a heaven vanished. No God, she felt, would allow a child to suffer as Jack did. On one occasion a friend of the Fergusons heard his screams from the next block. Jack's death haunted Hallie for months. Thirty years later she wrote: "I remember his beautiful face and his small voice saying, 'A thing of beauty is a joy forever. Its loveliness increases. It will never pass into nothingness.'" Hallie had known Jack was remarkable. In time she came to feel he had been "too precocious" and that she had pushed him in that direction. Once more she blamed herself, feeling that she had put her own needs before others'. This time work did not help. During the spring of 1922 Hallie felt tired and lost. She burst into tears at the least provocation, and Frederic noticed. One day he blurted out, "I should have died instead of Jack." Hallie was stunned. Afterward she listened to her father, who told her that those who remained needed her. Life must go forward.

Hallie's determination to succeed was now fueled by her conviction that she had failed as a wife and mother. She had not followed her mother's selfless example, but selflessness was not something Hallie could easily embrace. Aware of her talents, she was eager to use them. And the world that was growing up around her was insisting that women had rights.

During the summer following Jack's death, Hallie went to Chicago to work under Irving Pichel and Alexander Dean, two men who had made names for themselves experimenting with new staging methods. That summer they were producing plays at the Chicago Three Arts Club. Chicago audiences, ever since 1912 when Maurice Browne, a young English poet, and his actress wife had converted the storage space of an office building into a community theatre, had become interested in modern plays and methods of stagecraft. Between 1912 and 1917 Browne and his wife produced works of Ibsen, Schnitzler, Shaw, Synge, and Euripides, among others. They made annual tours to nearby cities and publicized their production ideas in *The Drama, Theatre Arts,* and *Harper's Magazine.* Hallie was eager to follow their example.

When she returned to Grinnell later that summer, she put what she had learned into practice. William Bridge, who had started a summer theatre in the town park, gave Hallie her first directing job. Meantime she learned that a one-act play she had written had won first prize in the Iowa State Playwriting Contest and that it would be published in *The Drama* magazine and produced in the Des Moines Little Theatre.

Hallie's prize-winning play, *The Curtain,* was an adaptation of the second short story she had written in college. Story and play focus on a man who has been imprisoned for fraud and on his daughter, who believes him innocent. At a crucial moment, the father turns up at his daughter's apartment and asks her to hide him from the police. What he reveals amazes her. For years he has only pretended to make a living. All the time his income has steadily dwindled until finally, in desperation, he has resorted to fraud and become openly what he "had long been in secret, a liar." Thank heaven, he tells his daughter, she is like her mother, not like him. But an irony of the story turns on the final revelation that she *is* like her father: she too has lied, pretending to her family that things have been going well when in fact she has been having a hard time making ends meet. During the thirteen-year interval between story and play, Hallie's imaginative grasp of her two characters had deepened. She had come to know them in greater detail and learned how to make their confrontation dramatic. The moral of her play, which Samuel French published and which was widely produced in community theatres, remains the same: nothing good can come of telling lies. Yet Hallie, despite her moralizing, managed to create two likable liars.

It is not difficult to detect autobiographical elements in Hallie's creation. Hallie wrote her story about the same time as she became aware that her father's stock in the Leffler Railway Company was becoming worthless. There is no evidence that Fred became fraudulent in his financial dealings, even though the father of her story has many of Fred's characteristics. Rather, Hallie seems to have decided to make drama out of her realization that her beloved father's boasts were hollow: he was *not* going to make the family rich as he had always promised—he was barely able to meet the mortgage payments on the grand house he had purchased.

When Professor Bridge resigned the following January, Hallie inherited his courses in playwriting and dramatic production. She inherited, too, the small budget he had been given for producing plays and the large, barren room on the third floor of the administration building in which he had worked. "There was not a stick of scenery, no properties, no library, nothing," one of Hallie's first students recalled. "There was only a determined woman who wanted a theatre program at Grinnell." Hallie put her production students to work building model theatres; she taught her playwriting students how to dramatize short stories; she produced her students' plays. But she had larger ambitions.

The only shows that had previously attracted attention at Grinnell had been produced by the Dramatic Club under the supervision of John Ryan, the same speech professor who had written Hallie a flirtatious note when she was an undergraduate. Ryan's direction of plays, in Hallie's opinion, was old-fashioned and his choice of plays uninspired. "Ryan told you what to do," one student remembered. "Flanagan worked with you to develop an idea." Hallie was following the example set by Baker and other modern theatrical innovators. Sure that she was right and that her method would prevail, she went to President Main to suggest setting up a central dramatic council to coordinate all theatrical activities on campus. She got his support and was elected head of the council. Ryan then resigned from his position as adviser to the Dramatic Club, some said so as not to compete with her. But several of Ryan's students were outraged. As one of them put it: "The Dramatic Club was in no mood to have this unknown young lady take over the direction of its plays . . . I remember a meeting that [two of us] had with President Main and Mrs. Flanagan . . . Mrs. Flanagan was calm and dignified all through the meeting, and although I think she was hurt that the club's members did not want her she made no objection. This tempest in a teapot was over in a year," by which time most club members had become Hallie's students and admirers.

During the summer months, aided by students and local amateurs, Hallie ran Grinnell's summer theatre, a canvas-covered platform set up in the park with bleachers for four hundred spectators.

One of the people who worked backstage that summer was a shy young man named Gary Cooper, who had failed to get into Grinnell's Dramatic Club because its members decided he lacked acting ability. The club under Ryan's direction, several students later commented, had been snobbish and undemocratic. This was one of the things Hallie resolved to change. The summer season ended with Hallie playing the lead in Susan Glaspell's *Suppressed Desires*. The role called for a "passionate defense of home and husband," and Hallie, in the words of a local reporter, was "delightful."

This was a busy time for her. Baker had accepted her in his 47 Workshop at Harvard for the coming academic year. She was to leave for Cambridge (her first trip east) in September. Meantime, she enrolled Frederic, who was now six, in first grade and made all the necessary arrangements for his care. She realized she was going to miss him terribly—more, she thought, than he would miss her. Frederic was such an engaging, cheerful little boy that no one apparently realized that below his show of independence he was still the child who had poignantly declared, "I should have died instead of Jack."

Hallie was later to say that George Pierce Baker taught her everything she learned about theatre. She had heard him, during his nationwide tour of college campuses in 1921, tell audiences that drama could be a force in modern life as it had been in the time of the ancient Greeks. She was prepared to admire him, and she was not disappointed.

Tall, somewhat aristocratic in manner, sparing in his praise, and given neither to levity nor to sudden enthusiasms, Baker was in many ways Hallie's opposite. What the two shared was a passion for perfection. It was because of Hallie's eagerness to get every production detail right that she became Baker's right-hand woman the year she entered Harvard. At midterm she became his assistant. During classes she sat at his right hand and, according to a classmate, "he listened with great interest whenever she spoke or criticized our work." Discussions of student plays, designs, and scenery took place in a large rectangular room on the first floor of Massachusetts Hall. Rehearsals and productions took place on a small stage in Agassiz House. It was Hallie's job to attend rehearsals and keep Baker informed about sets, lighting, and costumes. She took her job seriously but kept a sense of humor about her duties. On a page of her Harvard scrapbook she drew a small stick figure holding a huge umbrella over a large drum and labeled the entry, "HF carrying drum through Harvard Square before taxi was signalled. The man said drum was very *preshus,* must not get wet."

It was also Hallie's job to carry student designs to a group of three experts and report their criticisms back to Baker. This was how she came to know Thomas Robinson, an architect and former playwriting student of Baker's who had stayed on after his degree as a consultant to the Workshop. Robinson was ten years older than Hallie—in the words of a friend, he was a "quiet, soft-spoken man with a pleasant smile and gentle manner"—and Hallie soon found they had much in common. Both had written plays, both had an interest in modern stage design. The work they shared brought them closer and resulted in a love affair. Hallie did not mention Robinson's name in *Notes on My Life,* no doubt because he was married. What she did say was that she had had an affair with an older, very gifted man who taught her a great deal about art and helped her regain a feeling of reality.

She made other friends that year, John Mason Brown, Donald Oenslager, and Philip Barber among them. The four often traveled to New York together to see plays and write the critiques which Baker required of his students. The plays Hallie saw in the 1923 season included Ibsen's *Ghosts,* with Eleanora Duse in the lead, the Martin Harvey production of *Oedipus Rex,* and the Moscow Art Theatre production of Gorky's *The Lower Depths.* "While watching the Russians," Hallie wrote for Baker, "I was in doubt as to how I felt about them. I was certain that the play was not the sort of thing I liked. I kept saying to myself, Suppose this is true? What excuse has it for being shown on the stage? . . . Yet I find that the play haunts my memory as few plays have done." She was particularly intrigued by the director's use of color to underline character. "Natasha's red stockings and shiny little shoes, in contrast to her soiled and bedraggled garments, are her last hold on romance. Natasha's faded pink dress is the one clean and hopeful thing in the entire play." Duse in *Ghosts* and Harvey in *Oedipus Rex* moved Hallie, but she took a strong stand against curtain calls. "I did not want Oedipus, after his blind and tragic exit, to reappear bowing and smiling . . . and I did not want to see Duse as a tired little old lady who ought to be put to bed. Why do they do it?"

She had no criticism after seeing Jane Cowl and Rollo Peters play *Romeo and Juliet,* though she afterward worried that she might have committed the "unforgiveable sin of rhapsodizing" over a production. After seeing it a second time, she concluded she had been right: it was the production "as a whole" that was impressive. "Here was no Belasco trick of a star's name to draw the crowd, and the other parts played by incompetents." All the actors were good. She studied the play and realized how much the director had contributed. His idea, to point up the urgency of youth, had carried the play. This idea would later animate Hallie's production of *Romeo and Juliet* at Grinnell.

When time permitted, Hallie began work on the full-length play Baker required of his students. When she visited his home, the huge wastebasket that stood by the tall stack of manuscripts on his library table reminded her that although many people wanted to become playwrights, only a few succeeded. Hallie wanted terribly to succeed. Baker advised his students to write on subjects they knew at first hand. Reading the works of contemporary playwrights, Hallie came upon Rachel Crothers's *He and She,* about a talented young woman who decides to compete with her husband in an art contest but discovers she must choose between her artistic ambitions and her role as a mother. Crothers's heroine gives up her career when she realizes the harm it will do her daughter. Here was a theme Hallie understood. She decided to borrow from Crothers's plot.

Hallie's heroine, Gloria, enters in act one strong in her newfound conviction that men and women ought to be equal partners in marriage. She tells her parents that she has decided to leave her husband and compete with him in an architectural contest. "I've gone on loving Peter for eight years," she tells her mother, "and gradually he has become more and more of a person and I've become less and less of a person until there's no Gloria left. There's just Peter Brandt's wife." She confesses that she has been unhappy in her marriage because she has felt jealous of her husband's work. "I have just as good a mind as Peter has. If I hadn't given up architecture I might have been building bridges" by this time. When Gloria's father expresses shock at his daughter's decision, she tells him, "From the time I was born you've told me that the only thing that counts is the self." At one climactic moment she asks her mother, "Don't you ever get tired of being a cushion for Father?" When her mother answers that she doesn't think independent achievement by women is impossible but that the "greatest achievement is not by a man nor a woman but by both, the woman through the man," Gloria blurts out, "but that's just the thing I resent! Why through the man? Why not the other way around?"

Her husband's arrival onstage brings the play to its big moment. "There was a time," Peter tells Gloria, "when we worked together, when I didn't have the feeling that you were disappointed in me." Peter says he has been "terribly lonely" in their marriage because he never felt she was with him and for him. "You don't quite believe in me. You're not sure that what I'm trying to do is worth your giving up anything you want to do." By the end of the play Gloria feels opposed by everyone she loves. "I feel as though I were being convicted of something," she says. Hallie gives Gloria no leg to stand on, so the ending comes as no surprise. Gloria returns to her husband, who has meantime been revealed as a wise and caring person, and tells him, "I want to come back and try it your way." Once again Hallie created characters who were like the people she knew. The parents of her play are idealized versions of her parents. Peter has Murray's best qualities. Hallie invented two boys who resembled her sons, and she put much of herself into Gloria. However, by having Gloria turn penitent at the end, she avoided the dramatic conflict she had posed in the play's earliest scenes. Crothers' heroine has a change of heart when she realizes her daughter is suffering. Hallie's heroine changes because she feels guilty.

Willa Cather wrote that "the world broke in two in 1922 or thereabouts." For Hallie it broke in two when Murray's death left her the double legacy of a troubled conscience and the freedom to pursue a career. Later she was to say that she never succeeded in becoming the playwright she might have become because her nature was not solitary. Baker told her she had the ability to write significant, full-length plays but that she would have to find time for intensive writing. She never found such time. The plays she wrote later were written quickly, almost always when her conscience troubled her. But Hallie was right in sensing that her nature was not solitary. Action, not writing, was to become her outlet.

Before Hallie left Cambridge in the spring of 1924, Baker told her she should spend a year seeing plays in Europe. She should visit England, Ireland, France, Germany, the Scandinavian countries, and Czechoslovakia; above all, she should see the work being done by Stanislavsky, Meyerhold, and others in Russia. If possible, she should talk with Gordon Craig, whose theatre designs had revolutionized European staging. Baker said he would give her letters of introduction. Hallie replied that she would not be able to make the trip without help from a foundation, so she began making inquiries, knowing she could count on Baker's endorsement. (Baker, in fact, gave her a high recommendation. He was to write the Guggenheim Foundation that she was "as distinguished a woman student as I have ever had in my 47 Workshop, and she holds her own well with the best of the men. She has distinct ability as a playwright . . . She showed herself so tactful and so effective as a liaison officer among the workers preparing each performance that I became sure she could safely be recommended to take charge of undergraduate dramatics in a college or university . . . She has prepared herself carefully for the work she wishes to do . . . I regard her as in all ways an exceptional person.")

Hallie was full of ideas when she got back to Grinnell. To impress a foundation, she would need to do a first-rate production— but what play would be right? She had been thinking of doing *Romeo and Juliet* ever since seeing the Jane Cowl–Rollo Peters production in New York. A course with Lyman Kittredge at Harvard had sharpened her appreciation of Shakespeare, and the theme of two young lovers thwarted by family antagonisms and finally by death had a special appeal. Would the play be too difficult for amateurs to perform? Would the Dramatic Club go along? For several months Hallie said nothing of her plans. She began by reorganizing the club. Under John Ryan's management, only actors had been allowed to become members. Those who worked backstage felt like second-class citizens. Hallie insisted that everyone who worked on a production was equally important. An improperly lighted actor could not give his best performance. In a sloppily constructed set, actors' talents were wasted. She got the club to agree to take in students interested in design and backstage work.

Among Hallie's students that year was one who listened more attentively than the others. Howard Wicks, from Des Moines, had been drifting, unable to decide what to do with his life. For a time he had tried chemical engineering, but this field did not use his abundant and diverse creative energies. Then he heard of Hallie's theatre course at Grinnell. After attending a class or two he became hooked. From then on theatre became Howard's "all-absorbing interest. My yen for skill in the technical field," he said later, "received Hallie's enthusiastic support, probably because she knew next to nothing about the technical side of theatre." Hallie did know the effect she wanted to produce, and this was enough for Howard. When the two got together they managed to find ways of scrounging materials that achieved the desired impression. "Hallie was an A-number-one wangler," Howard recalled. Either she persuaded someone, usually President Main, that she had to have money for a new curtain or spotlight or something else, or she found out how to get what she needed in other ways. He remembered a night when "Hallie got the idea that we needed the college truck. There was no one around to ask about it, but we happened to know that the keys were left in the car." Hallie, Howard, and an assistant went to the garage in the middle of the night, took the truck, got what they needed, and returned it. Unfortunately, someone realized that the truck had been missing during the night and reported the incident to the administration. Hallie was called in and dressed down, but there were no serious consequences. In Howard's recollection she had a way with the authorities.

When Howard heard Hallie say that "any form of creation is agony," he thought she was being melodramatic. Later, when he worked as technical director for the Theatre Guild, he decided she had been right. Howard wanted perfection just as much as Hallie did and was just as determined to get it. They both worked overtime to achieve the results they wanted.

Both were fascinated by lighting effects, but the classroom auditorium that served as a stage for student productions had nothing but a row of border lights. So Howard built "one of the most hazardous switchboards ever put in a theatre. I persuaded Hallie— she got the money someplace—that I needed a dimmer. There was a storeroom off the balcony of the classroom and Hallie got permission to cut a hole in the wall. At that time switchboards were made of slate. I scrounged around and found an old blackboard that could be cut and drilled. Then I mounted switches. I contrived it so that I could bring one light up on a dimmer and then close the switch and it would hold. Then I'd move the dimmer to another circuit so we could bring the lights up or have them any intensity we wanted." Howard could also sew. His mother had taught him when he was five to keep him out of mischief. There seemed nothing in fact that he could not do. Though he had never done blacksmith work, when Hallie needed wrought-iron candelabra, he borrowed a forge from somebody and learned how to use it.

With Howard in control of technical effects, Hallie felt confident by Christmas that she could create a *Romeo and Juliet* that would look and work right. She still needed actors. One student who learned of her plans recalled thinking that the Shakespeare production was bound to be a failure. "This was going too far. How could college students act convincingly in a Shakespearean tragedy?" Hallie had misgivings of her own. None of her students was quite right for Romeo. Grinnell's best actor, Bernard Craven, was not the romantic type so she asked him to play Mercutio instead. Hallie finally chose a nice-looking man for the male lead. He was not, in Craven's opinion, a very good actor, "but he was blond and the female lead was brunette and Hallie thought they looked well together." She had no difficulty in choosing a Juliet. Winifred Parker was Grinnell's most talented actress and in Hallie's opinion had "a lot of power, a lot of deep seated emotion." She would give herself to the role without reservation. Just before Christmas Hallie asked Winifred to give up another role so she could focus her energies on Juliet. Winifred agreed. Hallie was "an inspiring director," Winifred later recalled. "The rehearsals were long and hard but we were all very dedicated and she was patient with us. She never had us mimic her reading of a line, but explained what she wanted." The young woman in charge of the play's costumes also remembered Hallie's patience. "We were neighbors," she added, "so we always walked home from rehearsals together. She'd hold my hand and swing our arms to keep pace to the beat of some poetry she called Walking Poetry."

Hallie's conception of the play was above all youthful. She

decided to stress "hot blooded riot in the streets, with every man quick to give or avenge an insult; gay-hearted jesting on the way to the feast . . . Juliet a child until the moment where she first sees Romeo . . . Romeo running the whole gamut of youthful intensities." The pace would be swift, with quick scene changes. Some scenes would take place in front of the curtain, others on various levels on the full stage behind. Hallie decided to revert to the "bare boards of the Elizabethan stage," using only an occasional piece of furniture and relying on lights to create the mood. The love scenes were her major challenge, and she worked endlessly on these. Eventually she got her leads to work on them "without foolishness or embarrassment." Meantime, she got permission to do the production in the newly constructed high school, which had a stage and wings with adequate depth. Spotlights were ordered and costumes rented. Fencing lessons began, and an orchestra started work on a specially selected score. The play was produced on the nights of March 27 and 28, 1925, with the auditorium "luxuriously furnished" and with college girls, costumed as medieval pages, as ushers.

In the words of one spectator, "the curtain rose, the play began, and with each passing scene the audience became more thunderstruck." The fortunes of the star-crossed lovers, one professor recalled, "became the vital concern of the whole audience." The elaborate costumes added color to the drama. Few of those present had seen such spectacular lighting effects. "The sunrises and sunsets over the sea with the shining walls of the city in the distance" contrasted dramatically with the "cold sepulchral light in the priest's cell and in the Capulet tomb." Most striking of all was the final scene, which took place in the tomb. Howard Wicks had constructed a wrought-iron double gate at the rear and raised the entryway. On entering the actors had to descend into the tomb to arrive at Juliet's bier. Four medieval candelabra about 30 inches high, which Howard had created, held four white lighted tapers. The effect, just before the curtain fell, with Juliet lying on the bier in her white satin wedding attire, was, in everyone's memory, spellbinding.

Opinions differ as to what happened next. According to Winifred, the curtains closed, and "I got off the bier and walked to the wings in dead silence. Mrs. Flanagan and I stood looking at each other with eyes wide with amazement. Finally the applause burst, tremendous and prolonged." A student spectator recalled that when the final curtain fell, "the whole audience sat immobile. Not a hand moved to clap. There was just a death-like silence. For several moments no one moved from his seat. Then people stood up and began to move out into the aisles. Old friends were seen as we moved down the aisles, but not a word of greeting was spoken. No one wanted to break the spell."

Hallie's future had been decided. Frederick Keppel, President of the Carnegie Corporation, was in the audience as President Main's guest. After the show he went backstage and told Hallie that her production had moved him more than any Shakespeare he had seen. He asked her what she wanted to do next, and Hallie told him about her wish to travel in Europe to observe what was going on in European and Russian theatres. Keppel said he would recommend her to the Guggenheim Foundation, which was in the process of becoming established.

Meantime, through a friend who taught English at Vassar College, Hallie learned that the department was looking for someone to teach the course in playwriting and dramatic production, which Gertrude Buck had originated at the college in 1916. She told her friend she might be interested, and after a trip east for an interview she was offered the job at a salary of $3000. This was more than she was making at Grinnell, but it was Vassar's proximity to New York, even more than the money, that decided her.

New York in the twenties was where everyone interested in theatre, particularly anyone interested in experimentation, wanted to be. O'Neill's early plays, as well as plays by other new American dramatists, were being shown regularly at the Provincetown Playhouse. A second experimental group, the Washington Square Players, had by this time evolved into the Theatre Guild, which was producing plays by modern European authors. The stated ideal of the Guild was to shun commercial considerations and produce the best drama of the time. During the decade the Guild presented *Liliom* by Ferenc Molnár, two plays by George Bernard Shaw, Ernst Toller's *Man and the Masses,* and Elmer Rice's *The Adding Machine.* The successes of the Guild and the Provincetown Playhouse prompted a few commercial producers to venture money on promising new American dramatists. Some of the earliest plays of Sidney Howard, George S.

Kaufman, Marc Connelly, Philip Barry, Maxwell Anderson, George Kelly, Paul Green, and Robert Sherwood had their first productions in New York during the twenties.

Despite the pleasure she felt when she thought about the new life that awaited her, Hallie had some despairing moments as she prepared to leave Grinnell. How, she wondered, would she fit into an all-girls' college whose students were reputed to be wealthy and sophisticated? Away from home, she suspected, she was going to feel lonely.

From Pomona College in Claremont, California, where she taught a six-week course in theatre production that summer, Hallie wrote Winifred of the "great emptiness" she felt in her life. "Do you know which of your lines moved me most?" she asked, thinking back to *Romeo and Juliet*. "It was Alas that Heaven should practice stratagems upon so soft a subject as myself." (Later, Hallie was to write that the production was her "remembrance of Murray." Whatever troubles the young couple had had, she chose to remember only what was good in the marriage.) None of the students who studied with Hallie that summer had any inkling of what she felt. On the contrary, one student recalled that Hallie became "the darling of the campus." She produced *Arms and the Man* and, in her spare moments, befriended a young actor suffering from a terminal illness who had fallen in love with her. After Pomona, she returned to Grinnell to make final arrangements for the move to Poughkeepsie.

Grinnell was sorry to see her go. The "amount of work that her students were willing to do for her," Grinnell's English Department chairman wrote to Vassar's English Department chairman, had constantly amazed him. It was one of those hardworking students who paid Hallie her highest tribute. "Production at Grinnell," the student said, "returned to the more traditional style after Mrs. Flanagan left. We continued to do very credible jobs but we never again scaled the heights."

In Poughkeepsie Hallie and Frederic settled into a small apartment a block from the campus. Frederic, now eight, was enrolled as a day student at a nearby Quaker school. Hallie thought Poughkeepsie "quaint," and her first impression of Vassar was that its students were snobs. Nothing in her new surroundings resembled the Midwest world she had left. Poughkeepsie, two miles west of the college, is built on a series of hills that rise steeply up from the railroad tracks running along the Hudson River. From some of the hills there are magnificent views of the river, but the fashionable residences of well-to-do merchants which had been built to take advantage of these views had fallen into disrepair by the twenties. Poughkeepsie had had its day in the period of the river steamboats. It had come and gone; in Hallie's first opinion, it belonged to the past.

Vassar was in every way a more sophisticated college than Grinnell: its students were richer, its traditions more cosmopolitan. Founded in 1861 by a wealthy brewer, by the 1920s it had become a lively cultural center where liberal thinking, innovation, and feminist values were not just tolerated but encouraged. In 1925 three-quarters of the teaching staff were women. Hallie found herself surrounded by affluent students and brilliant scholars who took part in the life of the town and worked hard to eradicate economic inequality and social injustice. Not all of her colleagues were Socialists or activists, but most exposed their students to challenging points of view. Moreover, they had the backing of their president, Henry Noble MacCracken, and, according to one observer, the "sense of being a bit superior to the ordinary run of women." Many of these women were later to become close friends of Hallie's, but at the beginning of her stay at Vassar she missed "the simple, crude boys and girls of the Midwest." Even a year later, while traveling in Europe, she felt momentary despair at the thought of spending the rest of her life at the eastern college. "My God, I shall never be able to bear it. How can I go back? God help me to be able to do something more vivid in life than adding to the number of Vassar girls in the world."

Something else may have bothered her. Hallie was never as much at ease among scholars as she was among theatre people. When she went to Vassar for her first interview, the chairman of the English Department looked her over and passed on her only after deciding that she had a "nontheatric" personality. Vassar's scholars were proud of their high standards, and some of them looked on the applied arts, particularly the theatre, with raised eyebrows. These were the people, Hallie realized, that she would need to bring round if she was to build a campus theatre. She never thought of doing anything less. In fact, before leaving Grinnell, she urged Howard Wicks to go to Yale for further technical training, hinting that she might soon be able to hire a technical assistant. Her predecessor, Gertrude Buck, had staged student plays simply, but Hallie had no intention of following in her footsteps.

As soon as she saw the stage in Avery Hall that had been granted her for two nights a week, Hallie decided she had to have more space. She discovered that Avery had a basement, though the windows had been boarded up. Peering into this basement through cracks in the boards, Hallie discovered large rooms containing sinks that had been used for dye vats and stoves that had been used for glue pots during the World War I years when Vassar had had training courses for nurses. There were also stuffed animals, which might do, she suggested to a student, for Shaw's *Back to Methuselah*. After approaching the authorities and getting permission to use the basement rooms, Hallie and her students cleaned, painted, and furnished them. They became Vassar's greenroom, theatre classroom, storage space, and shops.

To celebrate their new acquisition that spring, Hallie, with her students' help, produced the fourteenth-century miracle play *Guibour*. "Disregarding the deficiencies of a small stage with no fly space, no wings and no light board, we built a station stage complete with cathedral, bailiff's court and Guibour's house. We even burned Guibour at the stake . . . Nobody much attended the production," Hallie wrote in *Dynamo*. But in the meantime she had been learning what could and could not be produced on a small, poorly equipped stage in an all-girls' college. One thing she learned, after producing two plays written by students, was that "whatever the Vassar tradition, you cannot have a theatre without men."

Her greatest pleasure that spring was learning that she had been awarded a Guggenheim Fellowship for the following year. Thirty-six other recipients, including four women, also won the $2500 stipend for 1926–1927, most of them, like Hallie, for study abroad. In applying for the fellowship, Hallie made the point that college productions ought to be directed by trained professionals. Whatever she learned abroad, she said, she would pass on to the noncommercial theatre. She needed President MacCracken's permission for the year's leave of absence, but this was not hard to get. MacCracken, an innovator and a strong believer in progressive education, was also a theatre enthusiast, and Hallie's ideas for an experimental theatre at Vassar had won him from the start. She had more difficulty deciding what to do about Frederic.

Like his mother and grandfather before him, Frederic had been developing into a charmer. A tousled redhead with a lively and inventive imagination, he had at the age of eight begun to exhibit the winning, outgoing personality which would successfully hide the turmoil he was to feel as an adult. In her play *Free,* Hallie had portrayed her heroine's younger son as a free spirit, a Peter Pan–like child who enjoyed nothing so much as engaging his grandfather in flights of fancy. Like Fred Ferguson, young Frederic preferred fairy tales to facts. It was his way, perhaps, of coping with the trauma of his brother's death and with the repeated separations he had endured from his mother. Well acquainted with his mother's emotional ups and downs, Frederic never gave Hallie the least indication of his own.

Frederic had enjoyed his first year at Oakland School and had made two good friends in the neighborhood, but he wanted to accompany his mother to Europe. Hallie's first idea was to enroll him in a Swiss boarding school where she would be able to visit him during his vacations. Her parents disapproved, pointing out that he might feel isolated, and they offered to move east to be near him. Meantime, Hallie had written to Henry Allen Moe, secretary of the Guggenheim Foundation, asking if it would be possible to increase her stipend to include a round-trip ticket for Frederic. She had just enough money from her husband's insurance, she explained, to pay for his schooling. When Moe turned down her request, she decided to board Frederic at Oakland and install her parents in her present apartment. Frederic had long since learned that his mother's career and freedom of action were more important to her than anything. He pretended to feel carefree and happy and in need of no one.

Just before her departure Hallie's former lover, Thomas Robinson, wrote to wish her bon voyage and said: "You drag adventure out of the sky, and paint and embroider and exploit it—so you will expect anywhere and anytime to find the world your oyster." He predicted that she was about to embark on a "voyage of adventure." He was right. Even before her boat left the pier on the last day of July

1926, Hallie was jotting in her diary what a "marvelous thrill" it was to find her cabin full of flowers, candy, baskets of fruit, letters, and wires, and then to go up on deck and see the crowds, "the flags waving in the breeze, and hear the orchestra playing *America*." Despite a brief notation later that afternoon that she missed Frederic and that her fellow passengers looked "very haughty," Hallie was soon finding excitement in her surroundings. She got an invitation to sit at the captain's table, which immeasurably buoyed her spirits. The captain, she decided, played his role impeccably. He could walk onto any stage "without changing a line." She wrote comments on other passengers as well: one looked the part of a man who "automatically gets to be the president of things"; another reminded her of David Belasco; and then there was a couple she considered "saintly"—they seemed to disapprove of cocktails being served at the captain's table. Hallie's diary notes read like those of a director preparing to launch a show about an ocean voyage.

The long, "utterly lazy" days on deck, watching the "receding quiet of the sky," gave Hallie a feeling of peace. She enjoyed the British custom of being served hot broth on deck at eleven and tea at four, followed by dinner, which was "most fun of all." She spent hours in conversation with several of her fellow passengers and felt cut off from the troubles of her past, ready to embrace new ways of seeing.

CHAPTER

4

European Adventure

HALLIE went to Europe to see new plays and new methods of staging. Playwrights like Shaw and Toller, who were exploring the complexities and social conditions of modern life, interested her particularly. She had no interest in sophisticated drawing-room comedies and was predisposed to dislike playwrights like Noël Coward, who addressed their plays almost exclusively to the upper classes. Her reaction to the 1926 theatre season in London, where Coward was the idol of the moment, might therefore have been predicted.

"Often I would have a bad moment of thinking I had gone into the same play by mistake. I saw this last night, I'd think as the leading lady lit her cigarette. . . . The English do drawing room comedy well. They live in drawing rooms, which we do not, and so they play in them naturally. But how tired, how deadly tired one gets of the drawing room." Telling herself she ought to be more tolerant, Hallie kept buying London theatre tickets. "I impoverished myself going to the theatre in London for seats are very high, almost as absurdly and wickedly high as in America. Usually I bought a cheap seat in the pit or gallery, but occasionally I decided this might not be fair to the play, so I would buy a stall seat and prance down to the fourth row. It was just as bad from there." After one Coward performance, the author appeared onstage with the leading lady to say "that the play was nothing, the play was very bad, but that the leading lady was so lovely the audience would not mind. I tried to imagine Ibsen coming before the curtain to say he knew the play was bad but the lady was lovely—I simply couldn't."

The "rites" that had to be performed in a London theatre gave Hallie cause for further comment. "You buy a program for sixpence . . . You rent from an attendant binoculars, the largest and heaviest seagoing opera glasses in the world; you arrange for tea or sweets or an ice to be served at that moment when your spirits are apt to be lowest. You break the seal and pore over the program. The seat meantime is growing harder and harder."

Hallie went on to Stratford-on-Avon hoping to get a different impression. She walked along the Avon remembering how Shakespeare's words had moved her so deeply the first time she read them that she could neither eat nor sleep. But the productions she saw there in 1926 left her cold. "Once there was belief in England, and amazement at the strangeness of life. Men crowded into an inn yard to marvel at ghosts and heroes." Since then men had ceased to wonder. "No bells ring in the lines of the dramatist, nor in the soul of the beholder." The unimaginative handling of the productions she saw in Stratford reminded Hallie of what she already believed— Shakespeare must be interpreted in new, dynamic ways if he was to reach modern audiences.

Hallie was later to recall the afternoon she spent with John Galsworthy as the high point of her stay in England. Galsworthy had written plays examining ethical and social problems, but his reputation had been made when *The Forsyte Saga* was published in 1922. The novel relates the history of a large family recently risen to wealth and success in the professional and business world. Critics have since decided that Galsworthy, lacking a profound understanding of human nature, had had a keen emotional attachment to the family in which he had been raised and a sentimental regard for the underdog. "He will be remembered," said one, "for his evocation of a vanished if somewhat unreal world and as the creator, in Soames Forsyte, of a dislikable character who yet compels sympathy." Hallie, who had a similar attachment to her family and a sympathy for the underdog, felt a kinship with this author who was more than twenty years her senior.

Every detail of his home in Hampstead caught her attention: "shadows falling sharply across clipped hedges; sunlight caught in the pattern of a bronze vase on the table; whir of motors passing rather far away . . . The house in its beautiful quietness of green turf and gardens is the wise and spacious place in which *The Forsyte Saga* might be written but not *The Silver Box*. The room, a perfection of soft tones and deep rugs and far vistas of green and gold, is of the mood of *The Man of Property,* but not of *Justice*. The John Galsworthy of the novels and the John Galsworthy of the plays are very different, and after seeing Mr. Galsworthy, I am more certain than ever that when he writes a play, he chooses a theme that has quickened his mind, but that when he writes a novel he does not choose a theme at all—the theme chooses him . . . John Galsworthy is so fundamentally a part of the mellow, seasoned novel of English life that it gets itself said through him."

Hallie left England feeling she had seen "no play, save one written by an Irishman, which might not have been conceived before the war." Shaw was, of course, the playwright she meant. "Long ago," she wrote in *Shifting Scenes,* the book about her European trip, "the English actor learned to enter a room—no mean achievement in art or life, to wear dinner clothes well, to convey or conceal emotion by underemphasis of tone and gesture. It is not his fault that the rest is silence."

Since Hallie was at heart a romantic, Ireland was bound to charm her. She must have known it would. When the Irish-American poet Norreys O'Conor spent a year teaching literature at Grinnell, he had talked with her about Ireland at length. Hallie had also seen the Abbey Players on their regular tours of America and like other theatre enthusiasts had been impressed by the direct appeal they made to modern audiences. As the boat she had boarded for Cork neared port, she went up on deck to see dawn coming up over the Irish Sea and the jaunting cars drawn up on the cobbled quay. Her first impression of Ireland was of "ruins of round towers where the monks once took refuge; an old grey stone castle half fallen across a stream where goats are nibbling grass; low whitewashed stone houses with little fields like pocket handkerchiefs; flocks of geese on the golden gorse . . . Like a song? but so is Ireland like a song, a wistful song that will come back to haunt one."

Norreys and his wife, Grace, met Hallie when her boat landed. The O'Conors owned a castle at Mallow near the Killarney lakes, and Hallie spent her first day rowing on these lakes, becoming more and more intoxicated by the beauty of her surroundings. "During the long, sun-filled afternoon an occasional Gaelic exclamation from our old boatman and the rhythmic splash of his oars are the only sounds on the Killarney lakes. Before the wistful loveliness of Ireland we are silent. For the mystery of color, jade and amber and amethyst, we find no words. Innisfallen is full of dreams."

She went on, after this interlude, to spend several days in Dublin, where on one memorable evening she met Yeats, Sean O'Casey, and Augustus John at the home of the poet, painter, and statesman AE and heard them criticize a recent Parisian art exhibit and denounce the cultural backwardness of America. Afterward Hallie reflected on how curious it was that "almost the only Irish characters in American literature were variations on the perennial Pat and Mike hauling bricks or tending bars," whereas the Irish people she met were "true aristocrats."

She was particularly eager to see the Abbey Players but decided after a couple of days watching rehearsals that their best days had passed and they were now living on their reputation. They still had, she wrote Professor Baker, a comradely spirit, but the productions she saw "lacked variety and power." The lighting was "conspicuously bad."

Hallie had meantime written to Yeats to ask for an interview. Mrs. Yeats replied, inviting her to tea. But conversation at stately Adam House, Hallie felt, never quite got off the ground. Yeats talked in a formal manner of the future of Irish drama, saying there had been no real drama since the Elizabethan period, which had been born of passion for romance. Future drama, he predicted, would be born of a passion for reality. Hallie—unusually for her—was equally formal, and "the afternoon somehow did not quite make it."

The high point of her stay in Ireland was the three days she spent visiting Lady Gregory in Galway. Lady Gregory, who with Yeats had been instrumental in starting the Abbey Theatre, was a grandmother by the time Hallie met her, and, although not as active as she had once been, was still full of vitality. Ireland's most renowned woman dramatist was living out her last years in the spacious surroundings of her late husband's family estate, Coole Park. As Hallie entered the gates of the great park, she felt as though she had arrived at a shrine. "We are in great avenues of trees, the seven woods of Coole stretching away to the left, orchards to the right, a long archway of holly and oak evergreen sweeping up the slope to the old gray house. Lambs are playing on the lawn, a flight of swans rises from the lake, and waiting by the portico, her black lace shawl blown about her welcoming face, stands Lady Gregory." For twenty years, poets, dramatists, and painters had gathered around Lady Gregory's fireplace to talk of Ireland and art and to read plays and poems in the making.

Lady Gregory had all the qualities and attainments Hallie valued most. She was an organizer, dramatist, innovator, and renowned hostess, and she carried all this off with a graciousness, warmth, and dignity that impressed everyone who knew her. During Hallie's visit she was full of reminiscences. Hallie listened spellbound while Lady Gregory described how the Abbey had come into being, how Synge and O'Casey had been nourished by it. In the evenings after their walks and talks before the fire, Hallie retired to her room to record what she could remember of the older woman's words. The idea of the Abbey, Lady Gregory told her, had been born in her summer house. "Yeats had written a play and Edward Martyn had written one, and I said, We'll have to organize a theatre to get them produced. The theatre was organized then and there, and the first rehearsal took place, as many early rehearsals did, here in the garden." John Millington Synge soon joined the group. Lady Gregory told Hallie,

I remember the evening when Synge read *Riders to the Sea*. It was a stormy night, with the lake beaten into spray, with rain lashed against the panes. Yeats was here and I think AE . . . Synge sat by the fire, bent over, frowning, and read as was his custom, without expression. The room grew instantly still. For the entire twenty minutes we scarcely breathed. When he finished we could not speak. He sat

bowed down in his chair, forgetting us. And we sat
forgetting everything except Ireland, and the sea, and the
sadness of human life.

Lady Gregory was equally eloquent about her first meeting with
Sean O'Casey.

> One night he dropped in at the Abbey Theatre, saw his first
> play and resolved to write one. The manuscript came in so
> carelessly scrawled on scraps of paper that it was difficult to
> read it, but I felt in it a flash of power. I had it typed in order
> to judge it more fairly, but in this form it was even more
> impossible. I took it back, told him that it showed a gift for
> making people talk as people do talk, and asked him to
> rewrite it. The revision took him a year. When we read it and
> saw that it wouldn't do, I think that I was as distressed as he
> was. Fortunately, being Irish, he added rage to distress, and
> swore he could get a play on in spite of us. The result was *The
> Shadow of a Gunman* which we at once produced.

Lady Gregory's granddaughters told Hallie that Shaw was their
favorite guest. He got lost one day in the woods, they said, didn't
come back for lunch or tea or dinner, and it was well past dark when
the search party found him. He pretended he hadn't got lost, but
after that he knew as they did that there were "presences in the
woods." Hallie too left Coole Park wanting to believe there were
presences in Ireland's woods. "The moss-covered rocks are beasts,
men and gods under enchantment," she told Lady Gregory's granddaughters. Ireland had cast its spell, even though no production
Hallie saw in the country nourished her ideas about theatre.

In Oslo, Hallie stayed at the Westminster Hotel—an unpleasant
place, she thought, "full of fishy odors and red-plush furniture," but
sacred because Ibsen had written his last four plays there. She visited
the room Ibsen had lived in and stood there thinking of the characters
in his plays who had moved her most. Then she returned to her room
to ponder the play of Ibsen's which meant most to her—*Little Eyolf,*
a drama seldom produced in America despite its modern theme.

Hallie must have been feeling homesick and lonely. At her

loneliest she was filled with regrets. Little Eyolf is a lame child whose father admits he has brought him up to be intellectually brilliant without paying attention to his true nature and whose mother admits she was never suited to be a mother. They talk and argue and blame one another at the very moment their son is drowning. After his death they are filled with remorse and decide to devote the rest of their lives to helping neglected children. It is not difficult to guess why Hallie found this play so painful.

In the nineteenth century Ibsen had led the fight in Europe against dramatic conservatism. His plays had startled a new generation of playgoers, but by 1926 Norway had returned to standard productions. Ibsen had been memorialized in a statue near Oslo's National Theatre and his plays were still performed, although in Hallie's opinion they were done as museum pieces to preserve the great man's memory, not to provoke new ways of thinking, and she was not enthusiastic about what she saw. But Norway's beauty moved her. In the country, along the fjords, in the villages, she found "settings for future dramas." It was mid-October, and wooden bridges were buried under snow. Hallie recorded seeing "wooden houses painted blue, orange and green—ugly little houses glorified with snow. The sun rises and the sky, which has been dim and vague and full of coming snow, takes on chromatic hues, casting a violet haze over the whiteness, turning the sheets of half frozen water into an incredible rose flame. A long line of horned oxen winds down the valley; women in full dark skirts and white kerchiefs are milking the goats; around the bend of a distant fjord comes a boat, the rowers black specks against the sunrise."

In Uppsala, Sweden, Hallie met Strindberg's widow, Harriet Bosse, and saw her perform in a theatre that was "Greek in conception, a lofty pillared temple." The actress was "unemphatic, cool, pondering rather than feeling her lines." The costumes were "of no place, no period, suggesting in their simplicity pilgrim robes." Bosse told Hallie that Americans must have a false impression of her late husband, that "Strindberg can be understood only if his plays are acted together, in a cycle, as we act him . . . All of his plays belong together, in the order written, like threads in a tapestry." But Hallie felt as she had in Oslo that the country's greatest dramatist was being enshrined rather than given new life.

She enjoyed what she saw of Sweden's other theatre better. Anders de Wahl was playing the lead in Pirandello's *Henry IV* and doing it, Hallie thought, with richness and a variety of emotional expression. After the performance he invited Hallie to his home to talk about acting. His house overlooking the Baltic, she noted, was "rich with evidences of travel in many lands: tapestries from Persia and Turkestan, cabinets of unset gems from Gibraltar and Egypt, editions of rare books in many languages, records of a quarter century on the Swedish stage." He told Hallie:

> When I am thinking out a part as I am now thinking out *The Emperor Jones,* I walk here on my balcony. You see how the spires and ships are reflected in the water? It is well for any artist to look often at reflections in the water and to remember that what he gives back is never the thing itself, never life, but the reflection of life.

Hallie never said how she came to know Erik Forsberg and his wife and daughter, but they became her hosts while she was in Stockholm. They took her on long drives to see the countryside, making innumerable stops for morning coffee, afternoon coffee, and "impressive Swedish dinners." Their friends also entertained her, so Hallie got to see a number of people's houses. Everything was "incredibly polished and shining," and the food people served was always "garlanded or garnished" or in ornate molds. One living room was done entirely in red. With her housewifely instinct Hallie noted exactly how food was laid out, how rooms were arranged, and what colors people used to furnish their houses.

If Hallie had had to choose two people who made her trip most worthwhile, Gordon Craig would have been one of them. An enthusiastic admirer of Craig's even before she left New York, Hallie did not know when she arrived in Copenhagen that Craig would be there. When he landed on Danish soil with scene and costume designs for a production of Ibsen's *The Pretenders,* he had not worked inside a theatre for almost fifteen years. The fiery, temperamental son of Ellen Terry and former lover of Isadora Duncan always encountered difficulties working with people. He insisted on having total control over every production he worked on. Co-workers, even those who found his ideas inspiring, grew impatient.

All his life Craig wanted a theatre of his own, such as Max Reinhardt had in Germany. England had not given him one, so he had settled in Europe and turned to writing. *The Art of the Theatre* (1905), which had established him as a reformer, was read by everyone interested in new scenic ideas. Craig advocated making scenery abstract and architectural. "I hate theatrical scenery," he was soon to tell Hallie. "It is not possible to put the human body against painted canvas and have either truth or art result. Three dimensions are needed, a background for the actor, simple but capable of infinite variety through light."

The American theatre critic Stark Young called Craig "a seed, an upheaval, a light and power in the art of the theatre . . . His influence is evident in the modern Russians, in Reinhardt . . . in Robert Edmond Jones . . . and in other American designers." Isadora Duncan wrote that "he was one of the few people I ever met who was in a state of exaltation from morning to night . . . An ordinary walk through the streets with him was like a promenade in Thebes or Ancient Egypt with a superior High Priest." Craig was about to become High Priest to Hallie as well.

At rehearsals, Hallie noted, Craig wore his "huge black coat flung back like a cape." He had "nervous hands" and a "sensitive, exalted face" like Ellen Terry's. The moment she saw him she felt he was a kindred spirit: poetic, dedicated, and dramatic in every fiber of his being. One of his critics said he was a dreamer and made the theatre seem a magical place, but to Hallie, brought up by a father who dreamed and conjured for his family's entertainment, this was no criticism. If theatre isn't magic, she would have said, what is it? Afterward she wrote: "I remember every detail of our meeting and our talks . . . the night in the Angleterre Hotel when I waited to meet him. It was after the theatre and crowds were coming in, filling the supper room and lounge. When the tall figure with the massive head and exquisite face with its long white waves of hair falling on the shoulders came in, everyone turned to look. Everyone always turns to look at Gordon Craig, and being an actor he loves it and plays up to it."

She had written him a letter that Craig apparently took to be a flirtatious invitation. Perhaps it was, though Hallie's flirtatious approaches were often made without serious intent. She was simply having fun. "What do you mean," Craig asked when he met her, "by

turning my world delightfully topsy turvy by beginning a letter To
Gordon Craig, Artist?" "But you are," said Hallie, "and to have you
suddenly materialize in Copenhagen turned me topsy turvy too. I
don't know what I wrote but I had to see you." "Come up and see
my drawings then," said Craig, "for they are the real me."

In the spacious room Craig occupied, there were maps on all the
walls: "a map of his beloved Italia, a map of Russia where he worked
with Stanislavsky." There were long tables with sketches and models
for *The Pretenders*. "We work here all day and all night," said Craig
happily. "We start at seven in the morning and we go on and on, and
we drink tea out of glasses. One of the glasses has a handle and we
give that to the one who is feeling the feeblest. And we are having a
magnificent time." When Hallie confessed that she did not understand *The Pretenders*, Craig was amused: "Neither could I for a long
time. I would read an act and then I would walk up and down and
say, My God what a terrible play. I cannot do a stage for that terrible
play. Then one night I read it all at once as all plays must be read and
I saw that it was a great play. I saw *The Pretenders* rising on steps.
I began to make steps and steps." He told Hallie:

> No stage design is worth its salt unless it helps the actor.
> That is what I have always said but people have always
> misunderstood me. I have always put the actors first but
> people think because I published designs in a book I
> thought the designs were more important than the acting.
> No. I published the designs because I hoped that stage
> people would like them and get me a theatre where they
> could be built for actors to play on. Actors did like them,
> but actors have no money. So my theatre is still unbuilt.

Hallie asked if he had wanted a theatre in England and he said,

> I have loved two things—the art of drama and England. All
> that I have said and done and written has been for one or
> the other of these two. Yet about both I have been
> misunderstood. People have said that I do not love England.
> I do love her. I love her too much to overpraise her. I love
> her too much not to see her faults. And people have said I

am too great an artist to be a man of the theatre. This insults me and insults the theatre. I am first and always a man of the theatre.

He began to talk about Italy. As Hallie put it, his conversation made sudden swoops. "When you go to Italy you will see gems of color, like the backgrounds of the old masters' paintings, and you will say, I always thought the colors were overdone." Craig laughed. "In Italy you will of course fall in love ..." He regarded Hallie speculatively. "You fall in love often, do you?" "Not in its most violent forms," said Hallie. This retort made Craig stern. "What do you mean?" he exclaimed. "There is but one form. And there is only one other thing beside it. That is work ... But I don't give a damn about love or work," he suddenly said, and, reaching for the sugar bowl, asked Hallie how many lumps of sugar she would take in her coffee. "On very special occasions I have three," said Hallie. "When I'm celebrating I even have four." "You shall have three," said Craig, "and I shall have six."

They went on talking, about Italian art ("about which I know nothing and he knows everything," Hallie confessed in her journal), and about woodcuts, acting, and the Danish actor Johannes Poulsen. "Poulsen is sweet," said Gordon Craig. "I could work with that man forever. Wait till you hear him shout and bellow around the stage! He is magnificent. I get completely worn out watching him die." They talked and talked, and every now and then Hallie would get up to go and Craig would say, "You have the most irritating complex about going home. When you go to call on strange gentlemen in their rooms in London, Dublin, Edinburgh, Oslo, and Stockholm, do you always keep jumping up and saying, It's so frightfully late, I really must be going?" "But it's after two," said Hallie. "I can't help it if it's a dozen," said Craig. "Time is only relative. Don't you know Einstein?" Hallie said no, she probably knew nothing. "I don't know what you do know," Craig replied. "I don't know why you're here. I don't know how you got here. I will not let strange young persons come to my rooms when I am creating Art. I do not really know who, why, or how you are. But there remains the gorgeous and astounding fact that you are—standing there with your little gold hat at a distracting angle saying, I really must be going home." "This time I am really going," said Hallie, "because I want to write down all you have said before I forget it."

"You are a very skeptical and critical young person," said Craig as he put Hallie into a taxicab, "and tomorrow we will have a very gorgeous celebration with six or seven lumps of sugar and you will then tell me the story of your life." "I will do nothing of the sort," said Hallie while the taxi driver waited impatiently. "We will discuss Art and Nature." "You are an anomaly and epitome of both," said Craig, "and that will be the last word I shall utter tonight."

Their flirtation continued the following afternoon when Craig phoned, asking where in the world she had got to. "You sound very small and far away." "I'm both," Hallie answered. "The latter can be remedied," said Craig. "I'm coming for you at once in a taxicab." He took her to the famous Copenhagen Oyster House, where there was a table waiting and an attentive interest on the part of the entire staff of waiters. Craig entered in his large black cape and soft black hat (set, Hallie noted, at a rakish angle) and regarded the small Danish flag that had been placed on their table with disapproval. "The lady is an American," he told the waiter. "We must have stars and stripes." This caused consternation and some excited conferences between waiters and management. Finally an American flag was produced, and Craig began the ritual of ordering dinner. Other dining room activities came to a stop as Craig consulted first one waiter and then another until at last he had the total attention of the entire staff. "The lady desires a Danish dish," Craig explained. "Why I do not know, but such is her peculiar request. Something Danish for the lady then, and let it be prepared in your best manner!" There were consultations, more discussions and flourishes on Craig's part, and a dish was finally decided on. Then Craig ordered whiskey and soda for himself. "But wait," he called out, as the waiter was about to leave. "Should I have it? I am having oysters, many of them, raw ones on shells. Should I at the same meal consume whiskey? Is there not some old tradition which forbids it?" Hallie meantime had noticed that the other diners had long since ceased to do anything but enjoy the play.

When the staff finally departed to the kitchen, Craig opened the Danish newspaper with as much ceremony as if he could actually read it. "What does the press say of us tonight?" he wondered.

"There must be something about one or the other of us since we are the only famous people in the state of Denmark." Hallie then produced her copy of one of his books, in which she had made margin notes and comments. "What funny little marks, what crazy little marks you make on my beautiful pages," said Craig. "And here I read, What does the man mean?—Oh you are an Enfant Terrible! But see, I will draw the answer on the table cloth," and he proceeded to do this. Over dinner they talked of his work and family. Hallie told him about Frederic, and Craig advised her, "Not too much school. He should travel, learn languages, read and look at paintings."

After dinner they wandered about the restaurant while Craig pointed with his cane at the pictures of ships. "Oh, this is nice!" he told the waiter. "Was it the gift of the painter or did the restaurant buy it? Oh you know, I like this place!" There was a large map marked Ostens Map, which Hallie interpreted to mean Oyster Map. "Of course," Craig exclaimed, "yes, of course it's an oyster map. Incredible, marvelous intuition of woman! I adore the oyster map and the restaurant and Copenhagen and you. Here we shall again rendezvous. I shall cable you from Italy to New York, Meet me at the Oyster Map, and here we shall foregather."

In writing down this dialogue afterward, Hallie recollected two special memories of Craig that she would always keep. "One was a day on which I slipped into the back of the theatre to watch Poulsen rehearsing the last act of *The Pretenders*. During the rehearsal Craig came onto the stage, strolling along with cape flung open and hat at its most fascinating angle. He sat down humbly at the edge of the box, but someone came and placed a chair for him and as he sat there in the wings, watching Poulsen act, he completely lost himself, and I read in his face the tribute one artist gives to another. The light fell in such a way that his great cloak faded away into the darkness of the auditorium, his hat gave a complete blackness of background to his white hair, while his beautiful face, the face of Ellen Terry, caught the high light, as did his nervous hand holding a white paper. A study in values, a Rembrandt study in black and white. I longed to be able to paint him.

"The other picture is of our talk on the walk home my last night. Again we had talked very late and we walked across the deserted square with Gordon Craig pointing out with his cane the lovely things in light, shadow, and architectural mass that will henceforth mean more to me because of him. I carried *Scene* which he had endorsed, With the best wishes of the kind author, and which he had gone over page by page, telling me how the woodcuts were done and what they meant. It was one of the high, white nights when life is incredibly beautiful."

"I want to live forever," Craig said.

Hallie thought of the enormous contribution he had made to the theatre. "You will," she answered.

But Craig was sad, and just for a moment Hallie glimpsed the disappointment hidden inside the artist who had entertained her with so much flair and bravado. "Life is going so fast," he replied quietly, "and I haven't yet done my work."

England, Ireland, and the Scandinavian countries had given Hallie much to think about. She had been delighted and charmed by the people she had met and the landscapes she had traveled through, yet nothing she had seen on stage had provided her with inspiration for the work she wanted to do. She had not expected it to. The Abbey Theatre's great moment in history had come and gone; as had the theatres which Strindberg and Ibsen had led in the nineteenth and early twentieth centuries. England was doing plays well, but not in a manner that could rouse Hallie's enthusiasm. The one place in Europe where theatre was still in a ferment, still experimenting and developing, was Russia. Theatre enthusiasts in search of new theatre went to Russia during the twenties and thirties, much as art enthusiasts in search of new art had gone to Paris in earlier decades. So Hallie left Berlin for Russia at the end of October with high expectations. She had read books and talked to people and had a good idea of what she would find.

After the Revolution, when hunger was rampant and most Russians were not only starving but cold and in rags, theatre became a national obsession. Peasants staged plays in sheds, factories formed drama groups, the Red Army and Fleet had more than twelve hundred theatres. In schools dramatizations became a part of the curriculum. Most if not all of this outpouring was mediocre, nearly all of it propaganda in favor of the new Soviet regime. But for Hallie the important point was that theatre had become a vital part of the lives of the Russian people; it voiced their concerns and encouraged their hopes for a better social system and might one day become a great new flowering of dramatic art. This at the time seemed quite possible. With Lenin dead just two years and Stalin not yet in absolute control of the new Soviet state, many people had similar expectations. Stanislavsky and Meyerhold, the great theatrical innovators who had begun their work under the czars, were still working in comparative freedom. The cloud of Stalinist suppression had not yet descended.

Too excited to sleep on the train bound for Moscow, Hallie remembered that certain people had warned her against going to Russia, saying she would see only what the government wanted her to see and people she met would be too frightened to speak openly. But how could a government, she wondered, that supported the Moscow Art Theatre, the Habima Players, the Chauve Souris, the Ballets Russes, and some of the greatest literature of modern times, be repressive? As soon as dawn came, she was at the window, ready to soak up everything in sight: "After the Polish frontier, an ever increasing austerity of landscape. Endless stretches of frozen ground, harsh, unyielding. Occasional fields in which peasants in broken boots and rough, dark garments bend over the stubble. Trees gaunt against a remote sky." Then Minsk: "Glimpses of the clustering wooden houses of the town. The platform full of Soviet soldiers in their olive uniforms." At the Borisov station: "A Russian beauty in full, black skirt; cerise blouse pulled tightly over abundant bosom; high heeled slippers; Spanish comb in her black hair." She was laughing and flirting while a "toothless old woman in the background" cried and mumbled. It all reads in Hallie's journal like the setting for a play, and that was exactly how Hallie saw it. The train moved on:

"Strange villages now, dirt villages. Enclosures with heaped-up dirt for walls, dirt yards, dirt huts with roofs of sod. Frowsy peasants peering from doorways. Millions of such peasants in Russia. Millions. Left for centuries to eat, sleep, live, love, work. Can any dream that they shall become free men? Some dare to dream it."

During her first days in Moscow Hallie was under a spell. The primitive condition of the city's streets ("cobbled and sodden with wet and slippery mud") made her feel she had entered a land where the important things mattered most. Moscow's rose, blue, and gold cathedrals stirred her with their strangeness. She saw the people thronging the streets as the creators of a "new heaven and a new earth." Soon she was wishing she could exchange her own values for those of the Soviets. Walking back to her hotel one day along the river, she began wondering how she could fit her "little life" into "this great life." Could she and Frederic share in it? Could they become part of the "vastness and the courage"?

Hallie's response to Russia in 1926 was wholly idealistic, based more on what she had read and hoped for than on practical realities. In part she knew this. Even while dreaming of shedding her bourgeois identity, Hallie could not help wondering how she would look in high Russian boots. Walking along the muddy streets of Moscow with her interpreter, she "murmured vaguely" that she "really ought to get galoshes. This was merely a passing remark, but the young man took it seriously. Certainly I must have galoshes. At once. With no delay. We entered a shop and galoshes were put upon my unwilling feet. I did not care for them. I am never fond of galoshes . . . I pled that I really craved, not galoshes, but the high Russian boots such as one sees on the stage, but at this the interpreter was horrified. The boots, he said, were much too expensive, I could not possibly afford them . . . I then suggested that the galoshes were too large. The interpreter said sternly that they could be bound on with string." And so they were.

At her hotel the doorkeeper was "a white-haired aristocrat" who greeted her each morning with a courtly bow, called a droshky, and tucked the robe about her in the grand manner. "One morning when I come downstairs, ask for my galoshes, and sit down to put them on, the old doorkeeper happens to be standing where he can see me. The two cloakroom attendants whose duty it is to sweep up each avalanche of snow from incoming galoshes stand stupidly watching me as usual. It has never occurred to me to be irritated by their stolidity; this is Soviet Russia—why should any person put on the galoshes of any other person? But the old man utters a furious ejaculation, strides into the cloakroom, seizes the two comrades, and with an avalanche of Russian terrifying to the ears, knocks their heads together, bangs them against the wall, flings them limp and stunned in a heap on the floor, spits upon them, advances to me as I sit petrified, kneels down, and in spite of my protests, proceeds, with a magnificent gesture, to put on my galoshes." Much as she believed in the "new freedom," Hallie's natural inclination was to enjoy the passing pleasures of the "old order."

Her stay in Moscow had lasted exactly one week when the Soviets celebrated the ninth anniversary of the October Revolution. In Red Square she found the "old Chinese Wall flaming with scarlet banners of the hammer and the scythe," the minarets of St. Basil's looking down "upon a vast crowd gathered from all Russia," and multitudes of Soviet forces. "Evergreen is upon the tomb of Lenin whose spirit walks abroad . . . As the hour of nine strikes, the bells in the tower of the Gate of Salvation chime out the Russian Revolutionary Funeral March. There is profound silence, tribute to the dead, a silence broken only when the band strikes up the Internationale." Then the parade starts: infantry regiments from the Ukraine, the Volga, the Caucasus, Siberia, Bessarabia, Georgia, and Armenia march. Next, the cavalry: "Turks from the five million Tartars on gray horses with sabers flashing as they charge down the hill to the river; giant Kalmyks from the Lower Volga on giant horses; Finns and Moravians from the Middle Volga; mountaineers under the blue and white pennons of the Caucasus dashing at breakneck speed down the cobbled streets." Next, processions of schoolchildren, then tanks and cannons, farm machines drawn by work horses, and finally the workers: "workers under banners, and workers under posters; workers drawn from the audience, which now dissolves, as spectators become actors and march along with their comrades; and when the formal procession ends, from intersecting squares still come the workers. Throughout the day, all Russia walks in the streets of her capital under her red flag." What she witnessed that day, Hallie decided, was what drama must have been like on the hillsides of ancient Greece: actors and audience become one through shared emotion, "great theatre because it is dedicated theatre," because it pays tribute "to a force outside itself with religious ecstasy."

In an interview with the director of the Revolutionary Theatre, Hallie learned that two kinds of theatres existed in Russia: Stanislavsky's Moscow Art Theatre and its offshoot studio theatres and the experimental and revolutionary theatres that had sprung up since the Revolution. Vsevolod Meyerhold, who had worked first under Stanislavsky, had become after 1917 the best-known producer of revolutionary drama, and it was his theatrical ideas that provided the leadership for the new theatres. Meyerhold was a fervent revolutionary, but as exacting as Stanislavsky in his artistic aims. He refused to do plays he considered mediocre and was fierce in his determination to shun the banal social-realist plays the Soviet bureaucracy wanted, a policy that was later to get him into trouble. But at the time Hallie went to Russia, he was still highly regarded.

Stanislavsky was sixty-three years old at the time Hallie went to his theatre to talk with him and to see a revival of Aleksei Konstantinovich Tolstoy's *Tsar Fyodor Ivanovich,* which had launched the Moscow Art Theatre twenty-eight years earlier. She observed, like every visiting director before her, the rightness of every detail. Each time an actor put on gloves or a hat, or walked on stage, the moment had been carefully designed to emphasize an aspect of character—vacillation, egotism, shyness or amorous expectation. "Watching the incomparable maturity of acting in Stanislavsky's theatre," Hallie wrote in her journal, "one has the feeling that centuries of training are behind each gesture, each inflection." No one, she thought, who saw *Tsar Fyodor* was going to be content for long with the acting in the lesser revolutionary theatres. But Hallie was also aware, as she sat in Stanislavsky's theatre, that she was witnessing the passing of an old order. She had seen the future, watching Russia's workers march in the anniversary parade, and the future was what she had come to Russia to see.

Stanislavsky told Hallie in an interview after the performance that he wanted to do a revolutionary play, though he would not do one simply because it was revolutionary. It would have to be exceptional, and he doubted that an exceptional revolutionary play would present itself in the near future: "We are too close to the Revolution to produce art reflecting it." He went on to say that he no longer understood what made young people enthusiastic. "Compare [the life of my generation] with the life of the present generation brought up on a regime of poverty and danger. We spent our youth in a Russia that was peaceful; we drank from the full cup of life. The present generation has grown up amidst war, hunger, world catastrophe, mutual misunderstanding, and hate. We knew much joy and did not share it with those near us to any great degree, and now we are paying for our egotism."

Stanislavsky concluded the interview by telling Hallie that even though he felt out of step with the temper of the new generation, he felt sympathy for young people and hoped to be able to help them with his knowledge and experience. He was the perfect gentleman, she thought. At the end of their talk, he took her to the theatre café and ordered her dinner. His courtesy and consideration touched her. Yet it was the more fiery and temperamental Meyerhold who was to make the more lasting impression.

Hallie had become fascinated by what she had heard of Meyerhold even before she entered his theatre. In 1918, for the first anniversary of the Russian Revolution, Meyerhold had created a sensation with his production of Vladimir Mayakovsky's *Mystery Bouffe*. Actors dressed as workers had leaped on stage from the audience and pulled down the curtains. Henceforth, Meyerhold proclaimed, there was to be no curtain separating actors from audience, there were to be no footlights, no proscenium arch. Steps and gangways to the audience would allow free access. Actors and audience were to be one.

The Death and Destruction of Europe was one of the first Meyerhold productions that Hallie saw. "Insolent rhythms," she noted, "mercilessly underscore the theme that the nations of the earth are dancing on a mine which is presently to explode capitalism and the bourgeoisie. America is on the list, and with a curious mingling of antagonism and amusement I watch a succession of scenes satirizing our national characteristics. In a Turkish bath several tired businessmen are being done over in order to prepare for putting across big deals on the morrow . . . Propensities to brag, to shoot up the town, to spoil their wives, to shake hands violently, are all caricatured as traits of overgrown, rather amusing, entirely immature children . . . [The play] continues with a scene in the French Cabinet, which pokes violent fun at political leaders, many of whom are greeted by shouts of derision from the audience." Hallie half expected to see spectators leap on the stage and take part in the action.

Invited to watch a rehearsal of *The Inspector General*, which Harold Clurman was to call the "single most brilliant production I have ever seen," Hallie studied Meyerhold as eagerly as she studied his stagecraft. His face she thought "magnetic and sinister," suggesting "more power and aggressiveness and animal magnetism than the artist's face usually possesses." Stanislavsky had been for Hallie the epitome of the invisible director. His conception prevailed because it was built on hours of preparation and years of working with his actors to perfect voice and gesture. Meyerhold's directing, Hallie noticed, was different. Many of his actors, lacking experience, appeared to be "mesmerized" by the force of their director's personality. "The man playing the Inspector is only a boy, very undeveloped. Meyerhold gives him the sense of the part, acts it for him, works on bits. Much is done by rhythm, for Meyerhold is essentially rhythmic. For instance, at one moment the Inspector leans to the group shaking his fist, then relaxes and allows them to place his cloak about him, then throws back the coat with a haughty gesture. Meyerhold tried to show the boy that it was a trick of rhythm in three: lean, relax, throw cloak. Again and again he did it." The actor worked until he got it. Meyerhold never seemed tired or irritated. His actors responded, they "took on some of his fire. When he left, the last act dragged."

When she saw Meyerhold's production of *Roar, China!* by Sergei Tretyakov, Hallie felt she had found what she came to Russia to see. The European trip had been teaching her to feel "pathetically grateful" for small pleasures in the theatre. To find a production where "conception, execution, acting and design were all a marvel of rightness" restored her faith. Meyerhold used "devices of reality"— real water, real boats—but treated them in anything but the usual realistic manner. "The stage has been stripped magnificently bare . . . [It is] a free high stage rising like a cathedral, lost in a fretted roof. No curtain, no footlights, no orchestra. Full use of lower boxes and side doors in audience for the actors. Use of aisle when it is needed. Wonderful use of lights with an infinite number of courses." The stage contained twenty usable levels. At the front, a wharf with steps leading to a river. At the rear, "little boats with sails went up and down or rocked back and forth but they never pretended to be real boats in real China." Behind the boats a great ship that looked real "only in the sense that it was made of wood and steel with real steps, girders and rigging."

The play depicted Chinese coolies being exploited by British imperialists and American capitalists. "The satire is at times overdone. But my God, what a production!" The coolies acted on the wharf at a different tempo and rhythm from that of the English and American passengers. "The coolies' acting was pitched to the sound of the Chinese reed instruments, Chinese guns, or lap-lap of the river. The acting on ship was pitched to the sound of American jazz, played by the ship's orchestra, to which the passengers tangoed." Each coolie was individualized. Each had different make-up; even their discolored blue blouses were distinct. "There is a magnificent scene of [English sailors] tossing bales of goods to the coolies who stagger off with them—much sweating, cursing, groaning. Some bales miss and go into the audience. The coolies are led by a little Chinaman in a silk kimono and straw hat who hits them with a fan and utters queer Chinese threats and chants. An American comes in, very good looking in sport clothes and Panama, notebook in hand ... He laughs at the coolies and flings them money. Some scramble for it but others fling it back in his face." Hallie was most moved by the acting of a character called Boy. "On the ship, two Englishwomen, both more or less sexually crazy, flirt and dance with the ship's officers— all played with an air of extreme artificiality, with the use of jazz enormously effective. They drink at little round tables. The American comes in and the American handshake and manner is satirized. They call for Boy. He appears, the marvellous tragi-clown—make-up of the clown in the Comedia, white suit, little frightened beautiful white face under tumbled black hair—comes down the steps, peers first at one, then at another; is sent for cigars, laughed at, sneered at, things thrown to him as to a dog. Off he goes, all in perfect jazz time, each pause, swerve, wistful glance so perfect that it tears you into little pieces."

Was Meyerhold "primarily artist or primarily revolutionist?" Hallie wondered what would happen if "the Soviet demanded a play of Meyerhold, revolutionist, of which Meyerhold, artist, could not approve." Would Meyerhold compromise his artistry to please the revolutionary government? Although she did not formulate her questions in exactly the same way that the Soviets would formulate theirs to Meyerhold twelve years later, her thoughts were to prove prophetic. When Stalin decided that socialist realism was the only art form the U.S.S.R. should tolerate, Meyerhold was labeled a formalist and advised to change his style. He reacted with proud defiance, affirming his right, and the right of all artists, to experiment. This was in 1936. Two years later his theatre was liquidated, and in 1939 he was arrested. He was shot in a Moscow prison in 1940. Stanislavsky, who died in 1938, was spared the news of this tragic conclusion to the great theatrical movement he had originated at the turn of the century.

Many theatre artists besides Meyerhold had begun their careers under Stanislavsky. Studios had evolved, and two interested Hallie in particular: the Second Moscow Art Theatre, known as MAT 2, and the Kamerny under Aleksandr Yakovlevich Tairov. Both were primarily interested in style: at the MAT 2 it was impressionism, at the Kamerny expressionism. An expressionist production of Yevgeni Ivanovich Zamyatin's *The Flea* was Hallie's favorite. "The background of the shallow stage is painted in audacious blurbs and blobs of color, blue sky with fat white clouds. And on the sky, the yellow moon and the wobbly yellow stars we once cut out of paper are stuck on, and you have the delicious feeling that you made them and pasted them there. The Emperor rides gloriously in a cardboard chariot with a coachman in the box. The officers prance in on stick horses which curvet and plunge and dance on their hind legs, and against the background of a glade spattered with forget-me-nots, the dolls dance to the music of the accordion man."

Hallie delighted in invention wherever and in whatever form she found it. She did not find it often in the revolutionary productions she saw after leaving Meyerhold's theatre. "Think of letting actors talk all they want to!" she complained in a letter to George Pierce Baker describing a "terrible" show she had seen in the Theatre of Improvisation. Yet the revolutionary theatres were what Russians wanted in 1926, and Hallie believed that the vogue would lead to something better. The time was not ripe for a flowering of the Soviet dramatic arts, she was to write in *Shifting Scenes*. Other, more important problems would have to be solved first.

Believing ardently that significant new art forms could and would eventually come out of the social ferment in Russia, Hallie was constantly on the lookout for their coming. When she went to see shows put on by a dramatic troupe calling itself the Blue Blouses, she became more hopeful than ever. Here was a new form indeed. The Blue Blouses had evolved from a form of educational entertainment that dramatized the news and came to be known as Living Newspapers. Living Newspapers had started very simply, when leading members of Soviet workers' clubs got up onstage to read newspaper articles to other club members. In a country where illiteracy was widespread, reading aloud had a practical, propagandistic purpose. It taught the illiterate what the government wanted people to know. The news was generally hopeful, always pointing to the glorious social and economic reforms the Soviets promised their citizens. Gradually these readings aloud had evolved into something more elaborate. Those presenting the material began developing roles, inventing conversations. Soon they were putting on masks, changing their clothes, and shouting slogans into megaphones. In time other elements were added—songs, dancing, acrobatics, declamations, pantomimes, and bits of film. Hallie found the Blue Blouses to be the best of the Living Newspaper groups. One of their stunts, a satire on bureaucracy, she thought particularly funny. A man looking for a job goes to an office for an interview with the girl in charge. While he is there, the phone rings. The girl begins a series of long-winded conversations, each one giving the man a chance for supporting action. Finally, in desperation, he kills her, but then, feeling alarmed, props up her body and puts the receiver in her hand. "Just as he slinks off, the phone rings and she immediately comes to life."

Russian friends had advised Hallie to travel third-class from Moscow to Leningrad if she wanted to know the people of the country. Hallie took this advice. She had three traveling companions: an overweight woman from the provinces, a Soviet officer who was writing a play against war, and a worker with a basketful of apples. The woman complained that her son, who was living in Moscow, had once been rich. His wife had worn fine clothes, and they had gone to dinners in the homes of their rich friends. Now, she said, he had to work; he lived in cramped quarters and his clothes were coarse like the clothes of their former servants. "The good days for Russia are over," she declared. Hallie looked at the Soviet officer, wondering if he would arrest the woman for voicing such complaints, but the officer looked amused. "Of course," Hallie wrote later, "I have no way of knowing whether he later shot her in the back."

After the woman and the worker had retired to the upper sleeping platforms, commenting to Hallie that sometimes these platforms fell down, and the officer had loaned her his army coat to use as a mattress, Hallie lay reflecting on the "curiousness of life." "Here am I, eating the apples of one comrade, sleeping upon the coat of another, and in momentary danger of being completely annihilated by the collapse of the third. Tovarish, indeed! I am at last becoming a part of Russia." But soon there was a jolt and the train stopped. It stood still so long it made Hallie think of a sentence in the Soviet guidebook: "If any train in the U.S.S.R. reaches its destination five days late, the money of the passengers will be partially refunded." "Gradually, one by one, the trainmen spill out. They walk back and forth, stamping on the snow, blowing on their fingers. They discuss the situation mournfully, gathering in groups, gesticulating toward the train. From the uncurtained window I can see that we are in the middle of a snowfield, and here, it appears, we are to stay . . . At first I am indignant. In any other country in the world something would be done. But since it is Russia, though the thermometer is bursting, they will sit down and talk it over. Gradually I sink into a sort of Russian-ness . . . After all, what is time? What matter whether we reach our destination tomorrow, or on some deferred tomorrow?"

By the time Hallie arrived in Leningrad, the Neva had frozen solid. Riding out one late afternoon by sleigh to see the river and the old city, beyond it the frozen plains and Gulf of Finland, she felt, though congealed with cold, that the trip was "magnificently worth freezing to see." But she was seeing Russia, she realized, as a privileged American tourist, and the contrast between her life and that of Russian artists distressed her. At the Leningrad School of Ballet she learned from a dancer how artists had lived during the years following the Revolution. "When we wished to fight we were told No. It is the artists who must be ready to save Russia from despair after war passes. So we worked to be ready. We worked for four years in rooms with no heat, often with two degrees of frost on the floor. We were cold and hungry. Shooting was in the street. We lived only for our work. The dance became our life." Two dancers, Semenov and Semenova, were rehearsing a show that was to open the following week. Semenova's stockings, Hallie noticed, were patched; her slippers were shabby. Working eight to twelve hours a day, she earned the equivalent of seventy-five dollars a month. Hallie thought of the comforts she had and felt ashamed.

An encounter with Nikolai Monachov, a leading Leningrad actor, gave Hallie a further glimpse of the difficult conditions under which Russian artists had been living. Monachov invited her to dinner in his apartment. "Today on the table you see red wine and white because we do honor to our guest," he said, "but in the hard days of the Revolution it was not so." Monachov had been a close friend of Richard Boleslavsky, the actor-director who came to America and taught acting in the twenties. He described their last meeting.

> The night I parted from Richard we sat at this table—no light but one burned down candle—no food for five days but the "cattle cakes," hard yellow cakes made for cattle. Often during those days a horse would drop dead in the street in Moscow and in an hour the bones would be picked bare. Richard sat at the table and put his head between his hands. "I shall go over," he said. Do you know how we went over in those days? We walked over the border and if we were caught we were shot. We could take no provisions, nothing. We might be shot, we might die of starvation, we might be torn by wolves in the lonely places. We went only when the point was reached where we could bear no more. Richard had reached the point but I had not.

When Monachov saw that Hallie was touched, he asked her to see Boleslavsky when she returned to America. "Tell him I forgive him." He showed her a black leather watch strap that Boleslavsky had made for him. "Tell him I wear it."

As in every country she visited, Hallie was well entertained. She went to the theatre almost every evening and was often invited to dine with people she met during the day. Because she was so courteously received, the few evenings she dined alone seemed desolating experiences. On one of them, sitting at a table in the hotel dining room, she felt so abandoned that when a man across the room lifted his wine glass to her, "invitation in his eye," she had a moment of feeling "Why not?" Hallie had traveled to Moscow with Velona Pilcher, who was London's reporter for *Theatre Arts Monthly*. The amusing and easygoing Velona had made a good traveling companion, but she returned to London before Hallie left for Leningrad. Hallie missed Velona most in the evenings. She was feeling especially lonely on the night she met Horsley Gantt, an American doctor who had gone to Russia after the Revolution as a member of the American Relief Mission.

Hallie was at the Artists' Club, a gathering place for musicians and actors, when she saw Gantt coming through the door. She remembered this moment afterward: he was "without exception the most striking looking man" she had ever seen. He reminded her of Abraham Lincoln. He was tall and slender; he had black wavy hair, "brilliant dark eyes, a strong nose and a cleft chin." She soon learned that Gantt had traveled to Russia soon after the Revolution to do what he could to relieve human suffering. He had stayed on to study with Pavlov and translate his books.

Gantt was quick to sense the impression he made on Hallie. He went straight to her table and spent the evening talking only to her. When he discovered that she planned to leave a day later, he insisted she stay on, and promised to take care of changing her ticket. Later, in her hotel room, Hallie wondered what their meeting would lead to. "Of course," she wrote in her journal, "I pretend [I am staying on] because of drama. But in reality I know it is to explore a new personality."

Gantt took her the next day to visit Pavlov's laboratory. Hallie, who had never before been much interested in science, found herself marveling at the orderliness, cleanliness, and meticulous attention to detail that she found in every room she visited. The rooms where the dogs lived were immaculate, as were the operating rooms and the postoperative areas set aside for the dogs' recovery. "The more I see of Dr. Gantt," Hallie wrote in her journal, "the more he becomes a complete puzzle." She was not sure what to make of his "clear, cold objectivity . . . Of course this is also the quality which makes him one of the most fascinating people I have met."

During the days that followed, Hallie and Lee, as she came to call him, often dined in his apartment. They talked endlessly about science, art, and Russia; they visited galleries and hired a droshky to ride miles across the Neva and out over the steppes; they attended late-night parties. Lee was different from any man Hallie had met. For one thing, he seemed uninterested in marrying. Though he was attracted to Hallie, he made it clear that his work came first. The more Hallie sensed his aloofness, the more she wanted to know everything about him. Her English interpreter told her Gantt was erratic. He worked like a demon for months and then disappeared; often he broke engagements. He was "ruthless," Hallie learned. "Any woman would think twice before marrying him."

On one of the evenings they spent together, she met the composer Aleksandr Glazunov, by then "a childish and helpless old man . . . A huge unwieldy mountain of flesh, slightly drunk, spilling wine on his shirt front, dropping cigar ash all over himself, listening unhearing to the music. Everyone good to him, wiping off the wine, brushing off the cigar ash. Various composers played, then Glazunov staggered to the piano, groped his way over the keys. Haltingly and like a child he began to play a few bars from Strauss's Blue Danube Waltz." Hallie felt she would never hear that waltz again without thinking of this "pathetic, tragic figure."

In mid-December, boarding a train for the trip back west, she felt sad at leaving a country and people she had come to love, but decided upon reflection that she was going just in time. "Why should I become lost over a scientist who must not fall in love?" In times of trouble Hallie gave herself stern words of advice, but this time it was not advice she could easily follow. The fascination of a man who would not allow anyone or anything to come between him and his work was irresistible. Besides, she had become accustomed to having things the other way, with men falling helplessly in love with her. Settling in her seat she tried to think affectionately of Grady Bates, the major who had often taken her to dinner and escorted her all over London. He was to meet her in Berlin, most certainly to propose marriage, but the farther she got from Russia the more certain she was that she loved Gantt.

Getting out of the country turned out to be an ordeal. At the Estonian border, frontier officials plowed through her luggage and confiscated three notebooks. When they saw her letters of credit totaling $300, they ordered her into the frontier station for questioning. While she was there her fellow passengers helped themselves to souvenirs and articles of clothing they found in her bags. Hallie was furious and began having second thoughts about the country she had just found so admirable. It was several weeks before she got all her papers back.

Bad news awaited her when she got to Berlin. Her father, she learned, was ill. She cabled her mother at once to ask if she should take the next boat home and, while waiting for an answer, tried to decide what to do about Grady Bates, whose intentions, she realized, were serious. Now he was coming to meet her in Berlin and there was going to be an end to a very nice friendship because Bates was the "marrying kind." When she said no to his marriage proposal, he would take himself off and find someone else.

Bates arrived the next day—Christmas Eve—with plans to take her to a party. Although Hallie did not feel up to it she agreed to go, then regretted it. The party was awful—"too much to eat, too much to drink, too many counts and barons and Americans." When one German she talked to about Russia made a sweeping condemnation of the Soviet regime, she felt ready to "kill him." Such was her mood. She was ready to go home. But the cable she received from her family the following day urged her to stay on. Her mother insisted that this was her father's wish, so Hallie abandoned herself to Bates's plans.

Bates and a friend had rented a car with the intention of showing Hallie Berlin and its environs. "There is an appalling amount of this city," Hallie wrote in her journal, "acres of shops, miles of placards, an infinity of motors, fur coats, enormous blue policemen, nurse-maids, students, and statues of emperors." She was displeased with the "endless procession of large, well-dressed people publicly con-suming food behind the plate glass of luxurious restaurants" and wondered if it was because she had just come from "bare Leningrad" that Berlin's excesses offended her.

Her impression of German theatres was similar. She found too much red plush, too much light from crystal chandeliers, too much scent on the women. "The theatre is being smothered . . . crushed under its own weight." She was disappointed to find so little of the experimental theatre that had been prominent in Germany in the earlier twenties. Innovation had given way to a "drama of entertainment." But there was one production that both fascinated and chilled her—Frank Wedekind's *Lulu,* the story of a woman who seduces a series of men and is finally killed by Jack the Ripper. "The play is acted upon levels which suggest the spiritual relationships of the characters. In the early scenes, when Lulu is at the height of her beauty, she is played above the men who crouch about her, hating each other, desiring her. In the later scenes she is no longer consistently above her lovers in power, but now up, now down; therefore Erich Engel designs a staircase upon which and around which the scenes of enslavement and revulsion, passion and murder are enacted." Watching early seduction scenes, Hallie felt she had never seen anything so sexually frank on any stage: one of Lulu's lovers pulls out a gun and rams it between her breasts, and Lulu puts her arms around him and kisses him, holding the kiss until he drops the revolver with a groan. Hallie's first thought was that this was "terrific theatre." She got so caught up that she could "scarcely look" when Lulu entered with Jack the Ripper. She later concluded that the play, however brilliant, was a "descent into nausea and despair"— not a theme that could inspire her.

She had ambivalent feelings too about the productions directed by the great Austrian director Max Reinhardt. Having just come from Russia, Hallie was acutely aware of the contrast between Meyerhold's political commitment and Reinhardt's total lack of it. "Max Reinhardt, unlike Meyerhold, is not consumed by any single idea. Each play he produces is a new empire, with a new set of machines to be evoked for the conquest." She concluded that Reinhardt was a "master of machines" in danger of being enslaved by them. He was saved by his Austrian "lightness and volatile brilliance" but was, on balance, overefficient, "with no room for the occasional divine accidents of art."

Hallie made a point of jotting down her observations when she returned to her hotel after seeing a show. The next morning she would go over what she had written to refine and elaborate. She had already decided to write a book and was eager to finish it before returning to Vassar. When she had discussed the book with Craig in Copenhagen, he had suggested the title *A Passionate Playgoer.* He thought it should be impressionistic sketches of people, places, and theatres, and Hallie took his advice. But she was finding it difficult to set aside the long hours she needed to get the job done. The constant series of distractions, including time spent with Grady Bates, kept her from feeling lonely but also interfered with her work. Without much hope that Henry Allen Moe would extend her Guggenheim grant, Hallie nevertheless wrote asking if this was possible. "I have no time to do more than take copious notes," she lamented. She added that she had written several chapters that Craig liked, but this was an exaggeration. Perhaps Hallie had read Craig some of her notes on English, Irish, and Scandinavian productions, but nothing in her journal indicates she had finished "several chapters" by the time she got to Denmark. While she was in Berlin she read a preliminary draft of her Russian chapter to Junius Wood, a former student who had become Moscow correspondent for the Chicago *Daily News*. This was a dispiriting experience. Wood did not share Hallie's enthusiasm for Russia.

There was something else that kept her from concentrating. Hallie continued to wonder what was going on at home. Her mother's cable had given her little information, and she could only guess at the state of affairs in Poughkeepsie. She thought constantly of her father. And she missed Frederic. It was "strange" being away from her family at Christmas. Without Bates, life would have been "unbearable." Bates proposed marriage, as Hallie knew he would. Although she felt grateful for his kindness, she told him they had too little in common. A few days after Christmas she saw him off on his train. "My happiness, he calls me," she noted, "but it isn't to be." A few hours later she congratulated herself on having said the right thing.

Hallie was now alone in Berlin. For the first time since leaving New York she was without suitors, admirers, or friends. Germany's capital city had failed to charm her, she had little liking for the Germans she had met, and there was nothing in the productions she was seeing to engage her full attention. She visited museums, took walks, and tried to work, but could not throw off the feeling of being among strangers in a strange land. By New Year's Day 1927 she had become "so horribly lonely and depressed, I feel I can't live. I want to go home. Would it be cowardly?" Then, on January 3, Hallie learned from a letter that her father had died four weeks earlier. "Oh God," she lamented, "—and I never knew." Her mother had not wanted to tell her because it had been her father's last wish that she finish her trip. He had died, she now realized, while she had been falling in love with Lee Gantt in Leningrad.

It had been her parents and brother, but particularly her father, who had helped Hallie most after Jack's and Murray's deaths. Life must go on, Fred Ferguson had counseled, because those who survived needed her. And her work was important. Hallie now tried to give herself this same advice. She had plans to go on to Dresden, Prague, Vienna, Italy, and France before sailing for home. Interviews and plays awaited her. She decided it would be cowardly to give up. She would not be cowardly, would not disappoint her father's last wish for her.

She was enchanted by Dresden, "with its lace-like bridges over the Elbe, its castle, its baroque yet miniature elegance." Walking through the city at twilight, she felt as though transported into a fairy tale, and the exquisite toys she saw in every shop window enhanced this impression. But Dresden's theatres, like those in Berlin, were a disappointment. "The German stage today is reactionary," drama critic Wolfgang Schumann told her. "For a brief time we had in Germany a fierce, new drama to meet new needs." The postwar expressionist artists protested against war, the government, and moral standards, but eventually, when they found that the world remained unchanged, they gave up their protests and audiences went back to demanding what they had always demanded, entertainment. Apparently Schumann had not heard that Bertolt Brecht planned to produce *The Threepenny Opera* in Berlin the next year. Schumann took Hallie home to meet his wife, Eva, who translated books from English into German, and the three quickly became friends. Their house, Hallie noted, was full of books, and they enjoyed good conversation. She felt at home. The Schumanns made Hallie their guest for several days, showing her the city, introducing her to people, and doing much to dispel her sadness and misery. Hallie never forgot their kindness. During the early years of the Second World War she sent them packages of food and clothing. After Dresden was bombed, she tried for months to discover what had happened to the couple who had shown her so much consideration at a time when she needed it most; but she never did.

Heartened by her Dresden visit, Hallie arrived in Prague in high spirits. "Prague must be seen, felt, heard and smelled," she wrote. "Of all the cities in Europe it is perhaps the gayest, the most

captivating and the most odoriferous." Hallie had read something
about Prague's history, but she had not anticipated its "unlimited
capacity to surprise." Walking through history, she found its winding
streets, archways, corridors, and low vaulted passageways, its sudden
glimpses into courtyards built hundreds of years earlier, its walks
along the river, and its steep steps ascending to the castle overlooking
the city an endless fascination. All appeared as a "succession of stage
settings" for the "succession of actors" who had lived there. The
people in the streets were "vivid, eager, frankly curious, child-like,
quick to laughter, tears or blows." She paused to watch a passing
scene: "thronging the streets a laughing, talking crowd, strolling,
flirting, sometimes fighting. A group meets another group. Recognition. Laughter. Everyone kisses everyone else. Passers-by stop and
gaze in unabashed and friendly interest. Two men meet, one gets out
a book, reads aloud, gesticulates with his cane. The other shakes his
head. They argue while the crowd eddies around them. A pretty girl
comes out of a shop, drops a package, toys roll in all directions.
People stop, rush after the toys, return them to her with laughter . . .
The crowd strolls on, exhilarated by the incident." The Czechs liked
being entertained, they liked entertaining. In this, Hallie thought,
they were like the drama-loving Russians. They were a people after
her own heart.

There is a contradiction here, for Hallie often used the word
"entertainment" scornfully. When a theatre production offered her
nothing but entertainment, she could be scathing in her criticism. But
in fact it was only certain kinds of entertainment that bored her.
What she considered banal, for example, were English ladies and
gentlemen smoking and conversing in drawing-room comedies, or
bourgeois American boys and girls meeting, breaking off, and then
making up. She abhorred this sort of play, because she could not
identify with any of the characters or with the authors' limited points
of view. On the other hand, she was completely open to being
captivated by an imaginative children's show or by a simply plotted
peasant drama which carried no message and which dramatized
nothing more complex than villagers enjoying the daily round of
their existence. She saw both in Prague.

The peasant plays reminded her of medieval miracle plays. They
were primitive in emotion and simple in plot, she recorded, but they

made a direct appeal to spectators wanting an "intensification of their own experiences and a strong statement of their own beliefs." Prague's Kingdom of Marionettes, one of Europe's most renowned puppet theatres, entranced her even more. The Kingdom of Marionettes had been started by a group of businessmen and nontheatrical professionals who wanted to have a good time. In this it resembled the Provincetown Players, who at the beginning had also had no higher ambition. The Prague group got together to make puppets, then began putting on occasional shows. Soon their productions became so popular that the city offered them the use of a hall Sunday afternoons. "We are really doctors, lawyers, and merchants," the group's scene designer told Hallie, "but on Sunday we become children. We do it for fun—the children's fun and ours." After seeing one of their shows, Hallie reflected that she had once objected to puppets because they lacked facial expression. She changed her mind. The unending cheerful expression of the puppet hero of *On Earth, in Hell, and in Heaven* was the smile of "supreme urbanity of soul." Kasparek was "the personification of aplomb, the apotheosis of a good sport." He met Death, a tall gentleman carrying a scythe, with abandon. He went through Hell and Heaven with equal equanimity. Being unfit for both places, he ended as a cherub. Hallie wrote an article about the show for *Theatre Arts Monthly* that was published a few months later.

Then there were Czech plays dealing with social problems. Hallie had hoped to see Karel Čapek's *R.U.R.*, a protest against modern mechanization, but it was not on. Čapek was Czechoslovakia's best-known playwright, and Hallie wanted to talk with him. A meeting was arranged, but it proved a disaster.

To begin with, Čapek had no idea why he was supposed to talk with the lady who had arrived from America. His face, Hallie recalled, held one message throughout their interview: "Why in the name of God do you molest me?" Hallie made the first error: she mistook Čapek for his secretary when he walked into the room where they had planned to meet. (He was small, she wrote in her journal, and looked totally uninteresting.) "Will you give this card to Mr. Čapek?" she inquired. "I think he is expecting me." "I am Mr. Čapek," the playwright replied. "Oh, of course!" said Hallie.

Each effort she made to rectify her initial blunder added to

Čapek's discomfort. Here, in part, is Hallie's report of their conversation.

ME: Everyone tells me I am to be guided by your advice in Prague.

HE: Oh—no—

ME: I'm so disappointed not to see your new play.

HE: It isn't on.

ME: Or I hoped I might see *R.U.R.*

HE: I don't like that piece.

ME: (flabbergasted) You don't? Really?

HE: Do you?

ME: (all on fire, he has actually asked me something; now we are getting on) I like it all except the epilogue. I've always thought the epilogue must be a bad translation.

HE: Can't say.

ME: (after giving him messages from people I've met in England and from one person I didn't meet) I hope you're coming to New York so that you can write *Letters from America*. (Why am I talking like a Cook's tour?)

HE: I feared I might have to go to America. The danger is past.

ME: Oh, I see.

HE: Quite.

ME: (trying for an exit line) I wondered if you'd suggest anything I ought to see in the theatres in Prague? Something distinctly Czech?

HE: I never go to the theatre.

ME: Oh.

HE: Sorry to be so rushed tonight. You'll come in again?

ME: Oh yes—yes (more and more fervently as I fall down the stairs) Oh yes—yes—thank you!

Hallie labeled this incident How Not to Make an Impression.

The Czechoslovakian government subsidized several theatres. Professors at the University of Prague helped manage them, and townspeople took a lively interest. Here was a country, Hallie reflected, where theatre was a vital part of community life. When curtains fell, there was "no air of finality," for spectators, swept up by their enthusiasm, went off to coffee houses to talk about the plays they had seen and to reenact bits of them for interested bystanders. Hallie left Prague feeling a little wistful, wondering at the contrast between what she had just experienced and what New York City had to offer.

She went on to Vienna, but here the homesickness Hallie had felt earlier returned in full force. There were several reasons for this. Vienna in 1927 seemed the ending of an era. Hallie sensed the bitterness people were feeling in the aftermath of World War I. Travelers from the States, she was told, "still say of Vienna, How charming! How gay! When they walk along Lord's Lane they do not remember the old days when Vienna was the capital of the Empire, nor the terrible days of the war. They see magnificent buildings, and do not guess that many of them are only shells. They hear people laugh, they see them buy flowers. They do not know that a Viennese must always laugh, must always buy a flower even when he is sad. They see only surfaces, not the emptiness within."

Hallie found the same emptiness in Vienna's playhouses. Whatever was new and experimental was apt to perish before it could attract an audience sufficient to support it, while the established national theatres, "with their heritage of aristocratic tradition, elocutionary acting and operatic methods of production, suffer from fatty degeneration." Max Reinhardt's productions expressed the bitterness of the day. His production of Somerset Maugham's *Our Betters,* Hallie thought, was brilliantly done, but she had no sympathy for what the play expressed. "Here is banality, brilliantly expressed through rhythm and patterned movement: each character enters to his own musical motif; and all of the trite formalities— *Thank you* and *How are you?*—are sung and danced to equally trite musical arrangements . . . the performance is flawless expressionism, never representing life, but presenting the essence of the play through artificial, highly stylized action." While the director in Hallie applauded Reinhardt's talent, her American optimism recoiled from the onslaught of so much cynicism. The public, she was told, wanted "fine clothes, feasting and luxury," and, in the theatre, a dramatization of society life rather than anything that provoked thought. Hallie was probably not conscious of how much her own liking for fine clothes and luxury fueled her objections. She, too, for different reasons, had been trying to master cynicism, bitterness, and despair. She had no wish to see her feelings mirrored onstage.

Hallie had been looking forward to hearing from her family. Surely there would be letters waiting for her when she reached Austria's capital city. But there was nothing. No letters, no cables, not even a postcard with the cheerful kind of message Frederic sometimes sent, "Dear Mother, I love you." Hallie became obsessed with the thought that Frederic might have forgotten her. "I can't sleep, can't eat, can't write," she wrote in her journal in mid-February. "Today at the hotel, next table to mine, a mother came in and sat down with a boy Frederic's age. I had to get up and leave. Of course I know he doesn't miss me this way. He's used by this time to doing without me, but that's the terrible part." When she wrote these words, Hallie had become so absorbed in her own misery she forgot that Frederic, alone in a Quaker boarding school and having just lost the only father he had known, was probably feeling even more miserable than she was. "He's the one really important thing I have," she lamented. Since Murray's and Jack's deaths, Frederic had become her "salvation." The idea that she might lose him was terrifying.

It was at this point in her life that Hallie made her one and only trip to a psychiatrist. She must have been desperate indeed. It was not a part of Hallie's make-up to seek outside help—one solved one's problems, she believed, not by looking into cause, motive, or early hurts in life, but by action. Hallie never revealed what the psychiatrist in Vienna told her, though it is reasonable to guess that he reminded her of what her son and mother must be feeling. A few days later, on Jack's birthday, Hallie remembered that "he would have been twelve today." She tormented herself by thinking how different life would have been if Jack and Murray had lived. By this time there would have been a third child, a daughter; they would have lived in a "beautiful house"; they would have found "peace and security." Even while warning herself, "I can't do this," she returned to the same thoughts the next day. "The loneliest thing in the world would be to travel this way if one were not doing a definite job . . . Only work helps."

Italy put Hallie in a different state of mind. In the Goldoni Theatre in Venice, where she heard operetta "gloriously sung" but "indifferently acted," she puzzled over the fact that "none of the gorgeous color of Italy or of Italian painting" had found its way to the modern Italian stage. But she felt at home. She was once more in a country "where life in its intimate phases was lived in public," where the streets themselves were stages, where people ate, drank, bargained with customers, punished their children, washed their clothes, fought, and made love in the open. She was amused by the theatre audiences—the gallants in boxes who paid "ardent tribute" to the actresses, "sending up huge baskets of roses, carnations and lilies" between the acts, and was more disposed than usual to be tolerant of the flaws she found in productions. "Sets totter whenever a door bangs, the footlights glare, the prompter chants the play line by line . . . there is never any sense of a director having mastered the play, no pattern in acting, no grouping," but there was always "rhythm, the music of marvelous voices," and the "apparent spontaneity of Italian acting." Italy's theatre carried "no message, no group striving, no setting." It did not reflect the time, place, or social order. "It is the miracle which occurs when a person on the stage, through some incredible alchemy, lights a torch in the imagination of the beholder."

Caught up in this mood while traveling from Venice to Florence, Hallie enjoyed the attentions of a handsome young officer in her railway compartment who kept glancing in her direction. "How unpleasant it must be to get old and have no one to flirt with," she wrote in her journal to keep herself from looking at him. She was wedged between a thin lady wrapped in layers of coats and a fat gentleman who was reading the *Neue Freie Presse*. She continued taking notes. "Other passengers get on, and the young officer manoeuvers so that he and the fat man change seats, and now it is becoming very exciting because he is talking to me in Italian, and God only knows what he is saying. I pretend to be absorbed in my writing and only murmur Si, Si." But not for long. "We go out and

stand on the platform and have a cigarette, and in spite of the fact
that he now knows I do not understand a word, he speaks very fast
and wildly—alternately kissing my hand and the end of my scarf . . .
We go back and I pretend to go to sleep which doesn't make things
better. We reach Bologna and here it seems he has to leave. This
becomes very tragic but he finally gets out and stands on the
platform, sword in hand and hat off as my train pulls out . . . The
thin lady has been looking on very disapprovingly. She thinks I am a
Bad Woman but I am fond of the young officer and I adore being
made love to in Italian."

The productions Hallie saw in Florence gave her the feeling she
was being subjected to an endurance test. "All the front boxes are full
of fat men who examine the actresses avidly through opera glasses."
Most of the actors were showy, loud, and totally without talent.
"Perhaps because life in Italy is so charming and gay, and the climate
so favorable to life out of doors, there is less need for theatre. It really
is so incredibly bad that there must be some explanation."

In Rome, Luigi Pirandello told Hallie that the dramatic arts in Italy
had not developed. "Our government," he said, "has never recognized
drama as an art." The playwright had just returned to Italy after
touring Germany with *Six Characters in Search of an Author*. They
met in the reception room of Pirandello's apartment, high above a
Roman street. Hallie told him she was hearing the distant street sounds
as if they were in one of his plays. "Relentlessly flowing," said Pirandello, "a great river relentlessly flowing—and we think we need to
make little paper boats of plays to sail on its surface." Hallie was later
to describe Pirandello as "quiet, simple, direct, like a child." He was
in middle age, "tall and slender, with a beautiful head, dark hair,
mustache and beard, intense, alive eyes, mobile hands." Thinking that
she might want to do one of his plays, Hallie asked how he wanted
them staged in America. "In a fine balance," the playwright replied,
"between the seen world and that other world which many of us know
exists only a hairsbreadth from the actual. Perhaps this balance can be
shown by muted tones of the voice in contrast to full tones; or by
wavering gesture in contrast to sharp lines of every day; or by light,
which seems to be to best express subtle things in the theatre." Hallie
was to remember Pirandello's advice when she produced the American
premiere of *Each in His Own Way*.

Italy brought out a side of Hallie with which she was often in conflict. She did not like viewing herself as pleasure-seeking or acquisitive, yet she knew that that part of her existed. Her admiration for Russia derived in part from her view of Russians as a people committed to idealistic goals. When Hallie met idealists she felt humble; a part of her wanted to be like them. But she was not altogether like them, and in moments of intense self-scrutiny she knew it.

While visiting the palazzo of a former Italian nobleman in Milan, Hallie became acutely aware of how much she loved beautiful rooms, fine clothes, and luxurious living. Poldi Pezzoli's palace, she noted, was "vibrant with the presence of a rich and vigorous personality." Walking through the rooms he had furnished with exquisite rugs, vases, paintings, and china, she immediately felt how much she had in common with the fun-loving egotist she imagined him to have been. "I can see Pezzoli," she mused, "welcoming his guests with an expansive gesture. He must have been a splendid looking person, a bit vain, opulent in tastes and desires." He had been proud, she decided, but had had a "childlike simplicity." She was sure he had "loved living, people, wine, food, soft fabrics and sunlight. Probably he spoiled his women and showered them with gifts and was quite unscrupulous in leaving them when he was tired of them." That Pezzoli's love of luxury made him vain and unscrupulous was a leap of pure imagination on Hallie's part. A leap that carried with it all of her puritan American upbringing.

Hallie's eagerness to discard this aspect of her background, as well as her inability to do so, is nowhere more apparent than in the notes she wrote about productions she saw in Paris. Probably, she admitted, it is "impossible for any American to look at a steady succession of French plays with the detached intellectual acumen of the French." Most of the French plays Hallie saw were primarily concerned with sex. "Don't you tire of the interminable theme?" she finally asked a Parisian playwright.

"That is your American morality objecting," the playwright, Stève Passeur, commented. "You are building up a defense mechanism because you are really shocked." He went on to discuss a play they had both seen where a man and his mistress converse in bed. "It is amusing, this extreme sensitiveness of Americans to the sight of a bed."

"On the other hand," said Hallie, "it seems to me naive that a bed should be considered perpetually thrilling."

"Everyone knows that people talk in bed," Passeur replied, "that some of the most interesting conversations in the world are held in bed, and why hasn't a dramatist a right to use them?"

"Evidently he has," rejoined Hallie. "Evidently in France a dramatist can do anything."

Oh no, Passeur insisted, a French playwright should not be sentimental. Sentimentality, because it was false, was the real immorality. He had the impression that Americans considered any play dealing with "free love" immoral.

But Hallie, who considered herself liberated, was not willing to concede this point. Love, she insisted, was not free when encumbered by possessiveness, jealousy, and economic pressure, as in the French dramas she had just seen. She went on to support the Russian concept of love: what a man and woman could achieve together was more important than "any amorous relationship between one man and one woman."

What could they achieve together, Passeur wanted to know— "Revolution?"

This conversation was brought to a conclusion by the third person present, a drama critic. Neither Hallie nor Passeur, Leon Smyser thought, was going to convert the other. Hallie left it at that. Parisian theatre, she had already decided, no matter how brilliant or well done, was not for her. She missed meeting the master of French experiment, Jacques Copeau. He had left the Vieux-Colombier and moved to a village in Burgundy two years earlier. She missed meeting Copeau's two most distinguished disciples, Charles Dullin and Louis Jouvet, and one of the boldest of all French innovators, Gaston Baty. Workshops Baty had founded for dramatists and actors had closed down a year or two earlier. Hallie had arrived in Paris at the wrong time. She was glad to get to the Riviera.

She began her stay by visiting her friends the O'Conors, who had rented a villa in Menton, a mecca for expatriate artists and intellectuals. Living within sight of the Mediterranean, having time to write, not having to worry about money, and meeting people she liked was a heady experience, and Hallie savored every minute of it, even while feeling she ought to go home. She became friendly with Pauline Schubart, a vivacious, attractive American who had graduated from Smith about the time Hallie had graduated from Grinnell. Pauline had two sons, aged eight and twelve. Her husband, Henry, a self-made man who had been earning $8000 a year and up in textiles since he was twenty, was taking a year off to try (as he put it later) to save his marriage. Hallie did not know this: she thought the Schubarts had an ideal marriage and she supported Pauline's wish to do more with her life than bring up two children. Pauline wanted to write. "She had no real talent for it," her son Mark recalled years later, "but she was ambitious and she was influenced by the people around her."

The Schubarts invited Hallie to spend a weekend in their villa at Cap d'Antibes. Hallie found their life intoxicating. Every morning after rising she went out onto a terrace that had a broad view of the Mediterranean. She luxuriated in the rich tapestry of colors—greens from emerald to jade to ultramarine, blues like spring forget-me-nots, wistful grays. She felt that the Schubarts must be entirely happy. Certainly she was. They went down to the sea to bathe, drove to Cannes and Vence, took a cruise to the island of St. Honoré, dined out, and in the evening sat on rocks overlooking the sea. They talked endlessly about marriage, children, the arts, Russia, and the pleasures of living on the Riviera. Hallie wrote in her journal, "Pauline has lovely clothes and exotic things from Babinis for her rooms. Her husband and her two boys adore her." On the day they visited Cannes, she suddenly exclaimed, "Oh I can't help loving luxury!"

"You're so damned contradictory," Pauline observed, "with your love of luxury, your rapture over beauty, your quivering toward scents, sounds and fabrics—and your mental acceptance of Russia."

Hallie also liked Henry. "One of his manifold perfections," she noted, "is that he gets up early, makes breakfast and brings up a tray of coffee, rolls, jam, and oranges." Hallie and her hosts met for the first meal of the day in the master bedroom, Hallie in a negligee, Pauline wearing orange pajamas. While Henry shaved, Pauline confided to Hallie that at moments like these she "almost" felt her marriage was not a failure. Hallie, who both wanted and feared married life, thought Pauline was simply being amusing. From where she sat, Pauline had everything: a good-natured husband who waited on her, endearing, intelligent children, the freedom to write if she chose (for there were governesses to help look after the children), and an abundance of money to make everything possible. "She believes in equality of the sexes," Hallie observed, as if this conferred all benefits and settled the matter.

In subsequent years Pauline had a difficult time, though Hallie did not keep up with the Schubarts long enough to find this out. Unable to persuade her husband to stay in France with the children while she returned to New York to explore her talents, Pauline walked out on Henry periodically but was shattered when he left her for another woman. "She wanted to be liberated and married at the same time," her younger son, Mark, observed years after he had become dean of the Juilliard School. "It wasn't something that my father had any way of understanding."

The Riviera was a relaxed conclusion to Hallie's Guggenheim trip. Hallie had crossed the ocean to explore whatever was daring, original, and of high quality in the theatres of Europe. She had met and talked with several prominent theatre artists, seen some exciting productions, and sharpened her sense of what was good and what was outmoded. If American directors had much to learn from Europe's theatres, they also, Hallie felt, had their own destiny to pursue. She had every intention of becoming part of that destiny.

5

Experimental Theatre at Vassar

HALLIE returned to America to find that her mother was not well. Louisa had had eye trouble for some time and was now going blind. After her husband's death she had moved to Detroit to stay with relatives, and Frederic, after his school let out, had joined her there. Louisa, Hallie discovered, had become more reserved than ever. That summer she began having attacks resembling those of an epileptic, which no doctor could diagnose. She did not want to return to Iowa. Grinnell, she told Hallie, had meant "Fred and only Fred. I couldn't stand to be there without him." Her sister and brother-in-law made her welcome at Melville House, a big house they had bought in the Ford factory region of Detroit where they taught courses in adult education to immigrant factory workers. From this summer on, the place became a second home to Hallie. She made frequent trips to visit her mother and in time came to regard Melville House as her "antidote to Vassar."

She spent the summer becoming acquainted with the workers in her aunt's house, taking Frederic on trips to the Ford plant, and getting her book in shape to submit to a publisher. When she finished her Copenhagen chapter, she sent it off to Craig and was distraught when he replied that her words about him were sentimental and untrue. Hallie wrote back that she was broken to pieces. Craig countered, "Cheer up, dear good child. I think you can't be so nice in pieces. How can you put a nice hat on pieces?"

> I write in a queer way and you, like one or two others who love me, try and write in the same way and it leads to a poor result. You are a great dear but you must stop it. For your own sake you must not go on writing like this. I'll tell you what to do. Take as a model some very *plain clear* writer— Schopenhauer or Emerson—and try to write like him. Practice that and you will find you are writing twice as clearly within a month or less ... As for being hurt, don't mind that. It won't do you a scrap of harm, and you *know* I'm no ogre.

Hallie told him he was being merciless and wrote Velona that perhaps she should not even look for a publisher. Velona told her not to mind too much what Craig thought and to go ahead and publish "no matter how bad [the book] is. There are many who, unlike Gordon Craig and me, will profit from reading you." Others to whom Hallie sent chapters found them interesting, but no one gave her the praise she had hoped for. She did more revisions and was relieved when Craig found her Copenhagen chapter much better.

At the end of the summer she began making preparations for her second year at Vassar. Fred was to continue at Oakwood School in Poughkeepsie, though no longer as a boarder. Her class in Dramatic Production would be large. Thirty-five girls had signed up for it, and she was to have Howard Wicks as her technical assistant. Wicks was to come up from Yale, where he was getting a master's degree, every Friday and Saturday, which meant she could do an ambitious program of plays.

If any of the thirty-five girls who gathered in the Avery Hall greenroom for their first class with Hallie in the fall of 1927 thought that the course was going to be easy, they soon learned otherwise. Hallie entered the greenroom carrying Craig's *On the Art of the Theatre* and Stanislavsky's *My Life in Art*. She placed these books and a red alarm clock on a small round table in the room's center. Student chairs were arranged in a semicircle facing her. Several

students had heard that Hallie was an inspiring teacher, and some
had decided they were not going to be impressed. But when Hallie
began to speak, the room became instantly still. "She could command
an audience just by the tone of her voice," was one recollection.
Hallie discussed her idea of theatre. It could bring people together,
change their ideas, and enlarge their way of looking at the world. The
Greeks had known the power of theatre, so had the English of
Shakespeare's day, but America was only now getting to know it.
Although Broadway was still doing old-fashioned scripts in old-
fashioned ways, American audiences were beginning to demand
something more. A new theatre had emerged in Europe and was
emerging in Russia. Hallie talked about Craig, Stanislavsky, and
Meyerhold and sent her students off to the library to read about
expressionism, impressionism, and constructivism. Within weeks she
had fired most of them with an enthusiasm approaching her own.
During the discussions that followed, an idea emerged: why not do
Chekhov's *The Marriage Proposal* three times in one evening, each
time in a different manner?

The Marriage Proposal has three characters—a landowner,
Chubukov, his daughter, Natalya, and their vacillating neighbor,
Lomov, who fears marriage but has decided the time has come to
propose to Natalya. All the action takes place in a half-hour. Lomov
calls on Chubukov and asks for Natalya's hand in marriage. Natalya
is called for, Chubukov leaves, and Lomov, as soon as he sees
Natalya, becomes violently agitated. Instead of proposing he gets
into an argument with her over who owns a meadow bordering their
properties. Before long they are shouting at one another. Lomov
leaves. When Natalya hears from her father that Lomov was about to
propose, she has hysterics and demands that he be brought back. The
two young lovers then get into a second violent argument, this time
over whose dog is superior, his or her father's. Lomov passes out and
is taken for dead. When he comes to, Chubukov joins the hands of
the two lovers and tells Lomov, "You'd better get married as soon as
possible." With a third quarrel just beginning and Chubukov becoming hysterical, the play ends. It is farce in the best Chekhov manner.

Hallie's plan was to begin by staging the play realistically, as
Chekhov had intended. A simple set—a room with the minarets of St.
Basil's glimpsed through recessed windows, richly colored Russian

hangings on the walls, a few pieces of ornately carved furniture, a brightly polished samovar on the table, and a handsome oriental rug on the floor—would suffice to suggest the real room of a well-to-do landowner. She could borrow these furnishings from townspeople. Sunlight would stream through the windows, steam would issue from the samovar, and there would be Russian beards on her actors' faces. Hallie did not like using girls in the men's parts but felt she had not yet earned the right to challenge a deeply embedded Vassar tradition. First she would need to be accepted; later there would be time to make changes.

After a brief intermission the audience would return to find that the stage had become an abstraction. A large painted hanging at the back would show violent clashes of color in a geometric design that would serve to suggest the underlying tensions in the play. A few simply designed stools and tables would accentuate the geometric patterns of the hanging. The actors would be masked and would speak in rhythmic monotones, the tempo of each adjusted to fit individual character. Costumes would also suggest the essence of character. Lomov, in a sickly green and yellow, would move in jerks, and for each step forward he would take two back. In contrast, Natalya would wear orange, and her movements would be forward and sharp like her character. Everything would be done expressionistically to reveal the essence of the play, "the eternal, deadly struggle between man and his implacable enemy, woman."

The style that appealed to Hallie most would be saved for last. Here Meyerhold's constructivist ideas would come alive on the small Vassar stage. When the audience returned after a second intermission, it would find no curtain or hangings of any sort, just a bare stage extending by steps into the audience and up the aisles, "a stage undecorated, unset save for those elements of reality—seesaws, swings, ladders—on which the rhythms of the play (could be) best expressed." The stage would have become a space for the actors who "would cease to be characters, as in realism, or abstractions, as in expressionism." This time they would be acrobats in "dark work suits and skull caps, undifferentiated save for Natalya's scarlet handkerchief." And they would act their parts under direct stage lighting and against the exposed walls of the stage.

Hallie later described an early scene: "The father leaps down the steps, and looking out into the lighted audience cries, Whom do I see?—Ivan Vassilevitch—and up the aisle to meet him comes the reluctant lover. He might be any one of us and thus takes us with him." She decided that playground equipment would be ideal for the two lovers, who were, after all, funny, argumentative, competitive children. So Natalya swung furiously as she insisted that the meadows belonged to her family. She slid down the slide and ran into the audience to escape Lomov's verbal attacks. The two lovers used the up-and-down motion of the seesaw to emphasize their alternating one-upmanship. Hallie had seen Meyerhold use a swing and a seesaw effectively in staging a play by Ostrovsky. This was undoubtedly her source.

To learn the skills that would be needed to carry out this production, Hallie's students met with Howard Wicks on Fridays and Saturdays. As one student put it, "Many of us didn't even know how to boil water, because we'd been brought up in houses with cooks where the upstairs maid took over on the cook's day off." Hallie too knew next to nothing about backstage matters. She might stay after a rehearsal to watch girls climb ladders to install lights, but she never climbed these ladders herself. Once, watching a perilous installation, she remarked, "I really don't think you should be up there," but the girls knew better. Hallie wanted her actors' faces lit, she wanted specific lighting effects, and it was their job to make this possible.

One of the first things Howard Wicks did was find the city dump. The two hundred and fifty dollars allocated for a production, he thought, was just about enough to buy a little grease paint, a few rolls of cloth, and some lumber. As at Grinnell, ingenuity would be the order of the day. Lighting was his first concern, but what confronted him in Avery Hall was abysmal. Instead of spotlights above the stage and beam lights aimed at the stage from above the auditorium, he found ceiling lights hidden by frosted glass panels— "appropriate for an art gallery or a museum perhaps, but a curse for a theatre." The switchboard for the stage consisted of a panel of heavy-duty tumbler switches which could be heard going *klonk klonk* whenever a circuit was turned on or off. There were no dimmers. Hallie told Howard she wanted beam lights installed above the auditorium to provide lighting for the apron area. This meant getting the permission of Professor Washburn, who had been giving psychology lectures in the auditorium for twenty years. So Wicks was sent off to get the necessary approval.

Patiently but without much tact, Howard explained to Professor Washburn that beam lights focused on her face during lectures would serve to keep her students' attention. "Young man," said Professor Washburn, "I have been lecturing here for twenty years and I have never needed any spotlight to keep the attention of my students." Hallie managed to patch up this misunderstanding and the beam lights were installed. But to operate them a student had to climb a ladder through a hole in the ceiling, walk a plank laid down between two crossties, and manipulate the lights from a crouched position. Accidents were bound to happen. At one rehearsal a girl manning a beam light put her foot through a glass panel, sending bits of glass all over the first five rows of empty seats. No one was hurt, but Hallie used the incident to petition the college for money for a catwalk.

The Marriage Proposal, performed in November 1927, was an instant success. *Theatre Arts Monthly* and *Theatre Magazine* reviewed the production favorably, the latter in a long article describing the constructivist version of the play.

> It is hard to say just why this constructivistic method resulted in an extraordinarily human and sympathetic performance. Probably it is because of the genuine intimacy established between the audience and the actors, who not only leave the stage frequently to mingle with the audience but address many of their speeches directly to the spectators. A bond of personal friendliness is created, one strong enough to outweigh the onlookers' sense of strangeness at the unfamiliar setting and to make the burlesqued action seem natural; as, for instance, when the overjoyed father hearing that his daughter is asked for in marriage, breaks into the Flea Hop, explaining confidentially to the audience, "I don't know why I'm behaving so idiotically." The machines also become reconcilable with normal human behavior and their use points much of the action. When Natalya and Lomov begin their first conversation they use the swings, going back and forth in unison as they chat

amicably, but as the impending discord looms, Natalya breaks the even rhythm, sending her swing ahead of Lomov's. Another of their arguments takes place on the seesaw, punctuated by violent bangs, until Natalya jumps up, leaving Lomov lying exhausted across the board.

The Provincetown Players had employed expressionist techniques in producing plays by Eugene O'Neill in the early 1920s, but no one before Hallie had used Meyerhold's constructivist techniques in an American production. This was one reason *The Marriage Proposal* in three manners created a stir that spread far beyond the Vassar campus. The *New York Times Magazine* of May 13, 1928, commented that "Chekhov's play done in three manners has made an impression on the great world of the theatre." *Woman's Journal* reported that Hallie had "won the respect of a profession ever derisive of the academic theatre." Anticipating the production's success, Hallie had invited writers, critics, and other New York professionals to see the show. They would continue to see whatever she directed in the years that followed.

Interest continued. A Smith College professor staged a scene from *Twelfth Night* in five manners, and other colleges followed suit. The *Encyclopaedia Britannica* and *The Golden Book* printed photographs, and George Pierce Baker invited Hallie to bring the show to Yale. But there was an anticlimax to all this fanfare. "Our success and fame," a student recalled, "had reached Broadway and several big shots came up from New York to see a special production that we gave just for them. That time the show was a devastating flop from beginning to end." Hallie had rehearsed her actors and crew so that the production went like clockwork. Everyone worked with the precision of professionals, but no one, after all, *was* professional. Students later felt they had become "too self-assured and smug": cues were missed, the timing was off, technical details were mishandled.

Hallie was beside herself. She got us all down into the Green Room afterwards and gave us the most disparaging and dramatic HELL. Of course, we felt as badly about it as she did. But she had more at stake. She was dressed in a beautiful long dress and she paced back and forth berating us until we were all nearly reduced to tears.

A few weeks later Hallie's students put on a skit that proved effective propaganda for the catwalk she wanted. Administrators were invited to attend *The Mystery of the Campus Murders,* which begins with the disappearance of several students from a college campus. A detective is hired and soon discovers that the missing girls have all been taking Dramatic Production. He goes to a rehearsal where he hears the technical director telling the director that all the lights are on and the director demanding more. "What do you think this scene is, Orpheus in the Underworld?" At this the technical director pales. Someone, he mutters, must go up to the beams. "So what!" says the director. A victim is chosen. Her companions gather round her, chanting their farewells. She is anointed with oil, trussed up in ropes, and yanked out of sight. Suddenly there is a crash of glass, all the lights go out, and a body hits the stage. The technical director says to the director, "I did warn you. I did say there was an element of danger." The director remains calm. "Please see," she replies, "that the stage is swept in time for tonight's rehearsal." Hallie's students, it seems, regarded their tiny director as a hard-boiled taskmaster.

Hallie's playwriting class was smaller than her class in production. Few students at Vassar wanted to write plays, and even fewer, Hallie thought, had the talent for it. But she had one student among those she taught her second year at Vassar who did. This was Molly Day Thacher, who later married Elia Kazan. Molly also had political interests and a knowledge of the agitprop plays that had been done in Germany during the early twenties and were still being done in Russia. She wrote a propaganda play against war and capitalism for Hallie's class and Hallie produced it. Although *Blocks* was not the first agitprop play to be done in America (some had occasionally been produced in New York by the Workers Drama League), it was the first to be produced on an American college campus.

The plot of *Blocks,* like the plot of all agitprop plays, is simple. Tan Man and Green Man, the two men who represent power, compete for a pile of blocks that occupy center stage and symbolize the world's possessions. Each man owns a worker and each worker is instructed to fight for the blocks. After they kill one another, they are celebrated as heroes who died for God, country, and honor. Tan Man and Green Man, in striped pants, cutaway jackets, and top hats, alternate in chanting, "Gave themselves gladly, the youth of the nation. Bright with their plumes on them, just as they died. Wash all the blood off them. Don't let the wounds show. Glory and pride." It was strong meat for an elite girls' college, and it caused a stir. It also cemented Hallie's reputation as a campus innovator.

But it was not Hallie's innovations alone that caused the controversy that grew up around her in succeeding months. Many faculty members at Vassar shared the socialist point of view expressed by *Blocks;* they came and applauded. But something bothered them. As Hallie's reputation grew and an increasing number of students asked to take her courses, some members of the faculty, particularly those in the English department, began complaining about the time her students spent on productions. Their grades were slipping in other courses: This was one thing they said. Another was that Hallie was not a scholar. *Where,* one professor wanted to know, had she got her training? And what were her students learning? Maybe to handle lights and put on make-up, but was that in line with Vassar's time-honored tradition of scholarship? Irritation was also growing among students: while most wore skirts, sweaters, and pearls in 1927, Hallie's D.P. students went about in shirts and blue jeans, their fingers streaked with paint, their hair smelling of sawdust and turpentine. A few flaunted this dress. They were "Hallie's girls," an elite group. Hallie had become the center of a cult.

Hallie allowed, even encouraged her students to call her by her first name. Her classes were informal, her manner colorful (she once threw a shoe at a janitor who insisted on cleaning the auditorium while she was rehearsing a play). She wore hats and a red cape she had brought back from Russia. Some said her auburn hair was really a wig. She was a bit more than the academic community had bargained for.

Hallie's reaction to the less personal of these criticisms was immediate and practical. She decreed that no girl with less than a B average could take D.P. She reassured faculty members that she would not usurp time that should be spent writing papers for other courses. But she could do nothing about students who "took every pipe course [they] could, so that *nothing* would interfere with D.P." and who "even refused Yale proms if they would interfere with what we were doing in the theatre."

Chief among Hallie's critics was C. Mildred Thompson, the dean of the college, defender of academia, and as strong-minded as Hallie herself. Thompson commanded great respect and some fear among Vassar's scholars. She had no doubt that she had been appointed to defend Vassar's high standards against all potential rebels, and she made the course in Dramatic Production her number-one target. One of her jobs was to reassure mothers that their daughters were getting proper food and rest. D.P. students asked for late-night passes so that they could work in the theatre till midnight; this was bad enough. But what annoyed her most was having to give academic credit for work that was fun rather than scholarly. At one time relations between Hallie and Dean Thompson became so strained that when teachers went to the faculty lounge for a cup of tea, they had to decide whether to join "Hallie's people" on one side of the room or "the dean's" on the other.

The controversy concerned different views of education. Most faculty members believed that Vassar had an obligation to train its girls in scholarship. Even if they did not become scholars they would learn to think clearly about a variety of subjects. Hallie had no quarrel with learning to think. But the dean wanted her to justify the teaching of theatre by approaching the subject academically, giving scenes from plays as illustrations of different periods in dramatic history—and this Hallie was not prepared to do. She was an artist; she believed that the only way to learn theatre was to create high-quality productions. Still, the criticisms hurt. After making tactful efforts to placate the opposition, Hallie thought out her position in detail. The following spring she gave a speech in which she said, "If a student's ideas gush forth in a four thousand word topic on the character of Caliban, we regard it as a legitimate part of the educational process. If, however, his ideas are made visible through the acting of the role of Caliban, or through the designing of a background against which Caliban may appropriately move, we are not sure the process is educational." Surely she had Dean Thompson in mind when she added, "We say [to our students] in effect: sidetrack any vital art interest you may have for four years while you fill your mind with standardized information. If after half a decade you still have any desire or any aptitude left, go on to a school of painting, or acting, or music. Following this system we

have, of course, killed the artistic ability in many students." Hallie
thought that theatre, as part of a liberal-arts education, had specific
values to teach: "In the production of a play the student does not
express himself. He expresses Sophocles or Shakespeare or perhaps
one of his contemporaries. It is this very release from the concentric
circle in which the student dwells that constitutes one of the greatest
values of creative drama. The student must expand emotionally to
understand persons of another age, another environment, another
point of view . . . He must learn to work as one of a group in which
he is important only as he relates himself perfectly to every other
member of that group." Even without hearing this speech, Dean
Thompson must have sensed (correctly) that Hallie would soon be
asking for more money, more staff, and a bigger and better theatre
plant to bolster her belief in the educational value of theatre.
Fortunately, the dean had no authority over Hallie. President Mac-
Cracken told Hallie not to worry. The male president made a point
of staying outside the conflicts that often raged among the brilliant
female members of his faculty.

"Hallie's pioneer period at Vassar," recalled a student, "was of
relatively short duration, but so dense and tense that I picture her
sleeping in a full suit of armor, with sword and dagger by her side,
ready to slay the next dragon." Her students enjoyed the controversy
immensely as it gave them the opportunity to rush to their teacher's
defense. "Those who opposed Hallie," said one, "were green with
envy. The dean wasn't nearly so popular as Hallie, and she never got
a Guggenheim."

Hallie also had some staunch supporters among members of the
faculty, several of whom became close friends. Genieve Lamson, a
geography professor who spent vacations with brothers and sisters
on a farm in rural Vermont and whose most animated conversation
was about horses and cows and silos, was one of them. Genieve was
completely different from Hallie, but she had qualities Hallie admired: she was practical, loyal, and down-to-earth. Jo Gleason, a
humorous, easygoing professor of psychology, became another good
friend, as did Agnes Rindge, Vassar's sophisticated art historian.
Hallie was as eclectic in her choice of friends as she was in her choice
of plays. She made friends with her colleagues in Kendrick House,
the new faculty residence with apartments for twenty-five women

teachers that opened soon after she returned from Europe. Hallie was one of the first to move in, and she now had a charming apartment with a bedroom for Frederic, and a living room with fireplace, as well as meals in the Kendrick Hall dining room.

Communal living freed Hallie from domestic chores and many maternal responsibilities. Kendrick employed a houseboy and four maids who tidied the apartments daily and cleaned them once a week. When she wanted to get away for a weekend, friends offered to keep an eye on Frederic. She had never imagined, she told a colleague, that a group of women could run their lives so well, "without carping or petty jealousies." The Kendrick way of life, which was to be hers for the next six years, made her feel that Vassar was home.

Freddie, as he was called by these ladies, quickly became a great favorite. He was the only child in the residence and a great charmer with his curly red hair and engaging high spirits. Hallie felt he had inherited Murray's Gaelic charm and her father's zest for life. Phelps Riley, Fred's best friend at the time, later remembered him as the instigator of good-natured pranks and escapades. "I sort of envied him," he said. "He did what he wanted; he didn't seem to have any restricting inhibitions." Apparently, everyone, including his mother, regarded Fred as a carefree, happy boy who would sail through life on his charm. No one, not even Fred himself, seems to have recognized how rootless he felt. Hallie counted on his high spirits to lift her when she was tired, and Fred played the role that was expected of him. By this time he had become accustomed to fitting in.

Hallie's two closest friends were her cousin Frances Youtz and Frances's husband, Philip. The Youtzes lived in an apartment in Washington Heights in New York City and Hallie was always welcome. Whenever she could get time off from work, she went to visit them and see plays and museums. During the days the Youtzes took long walks, and Philip, who had studied architecture, pointed out the latest architectural marvels. Hallie, who labeled these walks the "daily constitutional," often joked that her legs did not comply with her brain, but she was glad of the exercise and of the Youtzes' concern about health, as she often neglected her own. In the evenings after the theatre, the three friends returned to the apartment to discuss the show. Their talks, sometimes heated, always animated, gave Hallie a chance to sharpen her critical powers. Hallie found she could relax with the Youtzes almost more than with anyone else—they liked to laugh as much as she did. Writing them later in her life of the "trilogy of pleasures" they had shared, "love, laughter and work—what better?," she recognized how much this friendship had helped her feel at home in the East.

Hallie had other reasons for visiting New York City. She was renewing friendships she had made at Harvard and meeting new theatre people at the office of *Theatre Arts Monthly*. Hallie had sent the magazine's editor, Edith Isaacs, two articles from Europe, and both had been published. Mrs. Isaacs belonged to a small but influential group of American theatre workers and intellectuals who were striving for quality productions, not just in New York but across the country. Her magazine, which was serving the cause of experimental theatre, was read by every forward-looking theatre person of the time. Although Harold Clurman later described the twenties as "the coming of age of the American theatre," most Broadway openings continued to pander to audience cravings for mere entertainment.

Hallie thought this was inevitable. The New York professional theatre *could not* be consistently daring. Backers had to be repaid; speculators hoped for high returns on their investments. Experiment could only exist where money was not the goal. That was why she felt so strongly about experimenting in a college theatre. At the end of the 1927–1928 college year she got permission to rename the Theatre Workshop the Vassar Experimental Theatre. "It should not expect to please everyone at every production. The plays we put on are never ends in themselves." They are searches "for a more swift, simple and expressive means of communication."

In the fall of 1928 Howard Wicks became the full-time technical director of the Vassar Experimental Theatre. Feeling that a "young instructor should conduct his classes with dignity," he was surprised one cold rainy afternoon when his students arrived at the greenroom, stopped at the door to remove their wet shoes and stockings, and arranged them in "neat rows extending from the doorway. Barefoot and wrapped in fur coats, they came to their chairs waiting for me to begin as if nothing unusual had happened. I couldn't believe it. Said I to myself, This is crazy, but just take it in your stride, Wicks.

Beginning my lecture as if everything were normal, I was interrupted a bit later by a few polite snickers from the back of the group where several girls were trying to get their bare feet into the pockets of fur coats being worn by those sitting just ahead of them." Feeling that his "dignity had just flown out the window," Howard decided that from then on his approach would be "more or less informal." His students were enchanted with this young man from a small Midwestern town whose mother had taught him to sew. They had never met anyone like him! Besides, he could do anything: hang lights, construct sets, cook, make masks and wigs, and design costumes. Many of the girls were eager to learn these skills for themselves. Howard wore dungarees and a blue shirt when working in the shop, and soon his students began arriving in similar outfits. In no time they were inviting him to dinner in their dormitories and he was inviting them to dinner in his downtown apartment: he got himself on the dean's approved list. "Their pleasant compliments spurred me on. I made greater and greater efforts to have something special to feed them. Sea foods fascinated me because I had not known them in Iowa, and one evening I decided to start dinner with a shrimp cocktail. I carefully peeled the shrimp, arranged them in small glass bowls with lettuce and topped them with an appropriate sauce. The girls were a bit hesitant about enjoying this special treat and one of them asked casually how long I had taken to cook them. 'Aah!' I said. 'Cooking them had not occurred to me.'"

Soon afterward Hallie, who often got the urge to play Cupid, decided that one of Howard's pupils would make him the perfect wife. Howard, who had no intention of marrying anyone, thought Hallie must be joking or out of her mind. But she was serious— though in this instance seriously mistaken. The girl, who later became Lyndon Johnson's ambassador to Denmark, thought the idea so preposterous she wondered how Hallie could have had it. Sometimes Hallie understood characters in plays better than she understood the characters of her friends and students.

Later in his life Howard Wicks recalled that his students constantly questioned him about Hallie. She was as much an enigma to them as she had been to Gordon Craig when he had called her an anomaly. Had she been named after Halley's comet, was one question

Wicks was asked. And why did she always wear a hat? Most important: did she wear a wig? Howard did not think so, but he was wrong. Hallie had bought an auburn wig—no doubt to enhance an image of youthfulness when her hair became prematurely thin—at the same time she had changed her birth date from 1889 to 1890, just before she moved east in 1925. It is of interest that she chose a wig that was the color of her mother's hair. Until this time Hallie's hair had been black like her father's.

Hallie and Howard had little in common outside the theatre. In off hours she went her way and he went his. But at the theatre they set their sights on the same goal. "Sure we sometimes got on one another's nerves," Howard said. "That's inevitable when two people are working together so intensely. Neither one of us was going to settle for anything less than perfection." He had no difficulty accepting his secondary role. "For each show I was guided by the background Hallie envisioned. She had proven herself right so many times that the longer we worked together the easier it was to take her ideas." In the fall of 1928 Howard got an opportunity to construct the kind of set he most enjoyed doing. He was far from enthusiastic about Hallie's expressionist and constructivist ideas. Realism suited him better, and realism was to be used for the play Hallie co-authored with one of her playwriting students.

At first, Hallie did not take much notice of the thin, shy girl who signed up for her playwriting course in September. Janet Hartmann was a loner, the sort of student, one of her classmates remembered, who "disappears into the woodwork when the library closes." But when Hallie asked her students to bring in dialogues, those Janet submitted were the most dramatic. Janet had invented two characters—an inhibited girl who is painfully aware of her inability to cope with the world and everyone in it and a mother who feels she is justified in shielding her daughter from their less-cultivated neighbors. Hallie encouraged Janet to write a full-length play. At what point she decided to go further and become Janet's collaborator is not known, but the three-act drama that resulted, and that became the hit of the 1928–1929 Vassar season, was unquestionably masterminded by Hallie. It contains structural complexities beyond the ability of a beginner, motifs and a theme that had preoccupied Hallie in an earlier play, and at least one character that no one but Hallie could have invented.

The Sky Will Be Lit Up is a love story. Tina Dane, a pathetically shy young woman who lives with her mother in a somber mansion at the top of a high hill, falls in love for the first time with the reporter who arrives at the mansion a few days before it is to be sold. Mother and daughter, on the verge of poverty, are about to move into a smaller house. Tina, who has shied away from conversations with ordinary people because of her mother's snobbish attitudes, discovers the pleasure of talking with Henry Nolen, a man almost as shy as she is. Late in the play she makes the painful discovery that Nolen is married, but she also becomes able to challenge her mother's views and to rejoice at leaving the mansion. The theme of discarding the past was probably Hallie's, for the idea intrigued her most of her life. And there is one character in the play whom Hallie unquestionably invented. This is Fips, the twelve-year-old son of a neighbor. Fips has Frederic's charm and high spirits and an additional quality that few people knew Frederic had. For a young boy, Fips is unusually compassionate and perceptive. He goes out of his way to cheer people up. Frederic played this role when the show was produced.

Hallie decided she also had to have a male actor for the role of Henry Nolen. She had rebelled for some time at Vassar's tradition of putting women into men's parts, and she finally won her point. But no one she knew of could convey the necessary impression of awkwardness and shyness. And then one afternoon at an elegant cocktail party in nearby Millbrook, she spotted a man across the room who looked as though he did not belong there. She asked about him and discovered that in fact he did belong, he had inherited the Mather furniture fortune. The dramatic contrast between Mather's origins and his evident discomfort interested her and she crossed over to him, introduced herself, and asked him if he had ever acted in a play. Philip Mather said he never had but that he would be willing to try. On the following day he turned up onstage at Avery Hall.

Hallie had given the role of Tina to Kay Ewing, a talented actress in her production class. She handed Kay and Philip scripts, a teapot, and cups and asked them to pour and drink imaginary tea while they read. Kay later recalled how hard she tried to keep the pot from shaking as she poured. As she handed Philip a cup, it rattled in its saucer. Philip was equally awkward. "I'm sorry," he called out to Hallie, who was seated in the auditorium. "I'm afraid I'm wasting your time." But Hallie, who had just seen exactly what she wanted, called back, "You have the part."

Kay was "breathlessly naive" at rehearsals, according to Christine Ramsey, who played the role of her mother. "Philip Mather was modest and shy, downtrodden even. Pretty soon you could just feel this thing coming together between them. Hallie had a way of drawing out what you didn't dream you had within you. It was as though she had a magic touch that opened you up. And she made everything come from you, never from imitating her." After a good rehearsal everyone "felt high. After a poor one they felt dejected but more inspired than ever to live up to Hallie's expectations next time."

Howard Wicks was delighted at the opportunity to create a real room in a real house. Hallie wanted a staircase and an entrance to an upstairs room. At the local junkyard Howard found a solid walnut rail, balusters, and a newel post and designed a flight of stairs to fit them. His students studied pictures of Victorian decor, and one of them created stencils for the carpet and wallpaper. "The illusion of a decaying, grand old house was beautifully conveyed," according to the campus reviewer, who noted such details as "the unfaded areas on the walls where a highboy and clock had been, the antimacassar and chair covers, and the magnificent height of the windows."

Hallie often made decisions spontaneously. At a dress rehearsal, while Howard and his crew were setting up floods and spots to light an exterior scene through a Victorian window, they heard Hallie call out from the house, "Leave it! Don't change a thing!" She was "ecstatic over a perfect illusion of the out-of-doors that had unintentionally been created."

There was applause for the set when the curtains drew apart on opening night and applause for the acting and the play when they closed. "Exquisite in detail, beautifully and wholly formed," raved the campus reviewer. One student thought the production did more to win the hostile faculty to Hallie's side than anything else. And everyone agreed that there was an "overwhelming advantage" in having men play the male roles.

Janet Hartmann's brother, who was only seven when the play

was produced, recalled that there was much talk about it in the family. "One of the stories was that Hallie Flanagan asked Katharine Cornell to read the play and that Cornell was impressed and told my sister to rewrite it for a New York audience. I cannot verify the accuracy of the story." Neither can anyone else. Janet, her brother added, "had a tragic life. Hallie Flanagan arranged a fellowship for her at London University. She met her husband-to-be in England, but she never wrote another serious piece. She had a brain-injured daughter, and later many serious mental problems." Unlike many of Hallie's students, Janet did not keep in touch with her teacher after her marriage, so Hallie never knew the sad events of her later life.

Hallie sent a copy of the script and an invitation to visit the college to Gordon Craig. "It might be possible for me to get to America and Vassar College," Craig replied, but he felt uncertain. He suggested she come to Italy instead.

> Do you see any future in regard to your work in Vassar? For my part, I think that it is around the artists that groups should gather, rather than at institutions . . . You have now gone through your training and reached a point in your life when you will have to consider—what next?—and I think you are able to undertake more difficult work. It is not only aristocratic mothers who keep a girl away from life as you write in your play, but idea-less institutions may be keeping Hallie away from Art and all it could offer.

It would be fascinating to know Hallie's response. Craig continued,

> I have been planning for some time to build some small houses in a group among trees, and a theatre of my own kind in amongst them—there to train a company of performers. I see the need of recommencing *The Mask,* re-establishing my school, and although no longer thirty years of age, rousing up.

He hinted that Hallie had marvelous "faculties of management" and with a "clever assistant" would be the right person to help him achieve his goal. Two years earlier Hallie had sat at Craig's feet. She had felt like a disciple, but she no longer saw herself in a secondary role. At Vassar she was discovering that she had an audience, devoted students, increasingly respectful colleagues, and the kind of atmosphere where she could work unhindered. She wrote Craig that going to Italy was out of the question at the present time. But she *was* thinking about traveling.

"If I could have a year's extension of my fellowship," she wrote Moe at the Guggenheim, "it would be wonderful. Do you think there is any chance?" She told him her first trip abroad had made her "want more and more" and suggested two possibilities: "a study of dramatic forms in Yugoslavia, Turkey and India, with particular reference to folklore as it relates to drama" or "a study of dramatic forms in the Orient and Egypt, with particular reference to traditional methods, the use of masks, the use of rhythmic acting."

Two months later Hallie had to retract this request. Her mother's ill health made it necessary for her to spend the summer in Detroit. Furthermore, Louisa had been unable to keep up the mortgage payments on the Grinnell house, and Hallie feared it would be lost through default, as indeed it was a few weeks later. Although she now felt happily settled in the East, the loss was a blow. Hallie often spoke of houses that had been home as though they were parts of her body. The large, comfortable house on Broad Street had been her first, the place where she had spent some of her happiest years. Coming after a series of makeshifts, it had special significance. She had been married there. It had housed her and her children after Murray's death. It was where Jack had died and where she had lived while starting her career. Hallie thought of it as the place she could always return to. Her determination, fierce at times, to discard the past and move on into the future was as strong as it was because of opposite pulls in her nature. It took Hallie most of the summer to recover from feeling that a part of her had disappeared forever.

Hallie's book about her European trip was published in 1928 and universally well received. Hiram Motherwell, writing for the *New York Times,* called *Shifting Scenes* a "brief and gay reminiscence of her experiences." The London *Times* described it as a "very lively book of impresssions . . . gay, informal, penetrating, a little gossipy at times but abounding in good sense." Newspapers and magazines were unanimous in finding Hallie's style light and charming. The Poughkeepsie *Sunday Courier* noted that the book was "youthful," and this, in retrospect, seems a good adjective to have used. Hallie's occasional excessive enthusiasm, her near worshipful attitudes toward Craig, Meyerhold, and Stanislavsky, among others, and her spirited impatience with everything that was not new in the theatres she visited shows that *Shifting Scenes* was a first book. With its sometimes lyrical passages and flights of fancy, it reflects the kind of writing Hallie had done in the past, not the leaner, more incisive style she was beginning to develop. As a student put it, the book was a "Hallie Valentine," somewhat in the style of the amusing letters she often wrote to her friends.

Hallie's students who graduated in 1929 were the last to enter a world they could think of as safe and secure. Hallie's production of *Blocks* had reminded them that conflicts between management and labor were reaching crisis dimensions. But, in general, America's theatres had shown more interest, in the twenties, in Freud's insights than in those of Marx. This was to change in the next decade as theatres began challenging audience complacency by revealing the underside of American economic life.

A Campus Romance

HALLIE first met Philip Davis, Vassar's only male professor of Greek, in the fall of 1925, the year they both joined the Vassar faculty. Philip was a bachelor fresh out of Princeton and, in the words of one of his students, "pale, melancholy, handsome and very romantic looking." Hallie soon learned that girls without the slightest interest in Greek were taking his courses just so they could get to know him. In the spring they invited him on picnics. President MacCracken, rumor had it, advised Philip to marry to keep his students from falling in love with him, but in fact Philip was engaged. In the fall of 1927 he brought his wife to live in a house just off campus. Ten months later she gave birth to twins. But she died a year and a half later when a third child was born.

Several months afterward, in early 1930, MacCracken called Hallie to his office to ask her to put Philip in a play "to get him out of his blackness." Philip, said MacCracken, was drinking heavily and missing classes. Hallie, who had seen Philip crossing campus "looking lost to everyone and everything," remembered her own lost feeling after Murray's death and was glad to be helpful. She had just started casting Ernst Toller's *Masse Mensch* (*Man and the Masses*), a poetic drama about poverty and revolution that had been produced first in Berlin in 1921 and later by the Theatre Guild, and she gave

Philip the role of Man. "His face," she was to recall later, "like something on a Greek coin, and his voice, used to haunt me in the scene in which he faces the whirling planets and says, Life, life . . ."

Masse Mensch introduced the Vassar community in early 1930 to the work of a playwright who was also a political activist. Toller wrote the play in a German prison while serving time for having joined a workers' rebellion. The rebellion, which taught him that violence did not breed better conditions for the masses of workers, also taught him despair. He put his vision into poetry and his drama into expressionist form. Hallie envisioned a stage with a raised circular platform connected to the floor by steps on one side and a ramp on the other. Behind the platform stood a large central pillar. Players stepped into spots of light to recite their lines. Choruses of workers appeared out of the shadow to chant:

> We who are huddled forever
> In canyons of steel, cramped under cliffs of houses,
> We who are delivered up
> To the mockery of the machine,
> We whose features are lost in a night of tears . . .
> Out of the depths of factories, we cry to you:
> When shall we, living, know the love of life?
> When shall we, working, feel the joy of labor?
> When shall deliverance come?

The campus reviewer thought the show "by far the most significant piece of work the theatre has done . . . During the cumulative beat of the scenes we surrendered ourselves to the emotional sweep of the play." Hallie sent Toller pictures of the production, and he wrote back that he was "moved to think of students so young and so fortunate, in so young and fortunate a land, turning their thoughts to the problems of justice, speaking out for the miserable masses of men."

For her second major production of the 1929–30 season Hallie chose Pirandello's *Each in His Own Way*, which had not been produced in America. The Italian playwright, best known for his ideas about the relativity of truth, had a profound sympathy for women, and in *Each in His Own Way* he portrayed the most tormented and guilt-stricken of all his female characters. A beautiful actress, Delia Morello, has a reputation for seducing and destroying men. We learn during the opening scenes that two men have committed suicide on her account and that the night before she was to be married to the second of them, she ran off with another man. In Pirandellian style, this event is afterward discussed by a number of gossips, each of whom has a different interpretation of Morello's motives. When Morello appears, having been persuaded by one of these interpreters that she acted as she did because her fiancé idealized her from his own need while refusing to understand her true self, we at first believe her. She had spent a night, she admits, with the "other man" because she was desperate, unable to see any other means of escape from a marriage which would have destroyed them both. She is comfortable with this version of the truth until that other man arrives and both he and Morello realize that they have been passionately attracted to one another all along. It is not difficult to understand the appeal of this morally complex play to Hallie, who ever since her husband's death had been exploring such themes in plays and stories, sometimes with remorse, sometimes with self-justification.

The emotional center of *Each in His Own Way* is Delia's self-torment. A modern, conscience-stricken woman, she is constantly trying to discover who she is, what she believes, and if there is anything genuine about her. Does she have a true self? In her most poignant speech, she says,

> I struggle and struggle, suffering all the while—I don't know—as though—as though I were not quite myself, as though I were constantly groping around to find myself . . . to understand the woman that I really am, to ask her what she really wants, why she is suffering so, and what I ought to do to tame her, pacify her, give her a little peace.

And later,

> Truth? What is truth? . . . Nothing is true! I should like to see with my eyes, or hear with my ears, or feel with my fingers, one thing . . . just one thing . . . that is true . . . really true . . . in me!

Delia feels free only when she ceases to care about her lover. At the end of the play, as self-doubting as ever, she has a moment of peace, a moment of feeling nothing, before she is caught up once more in the maelstrom of her conflicting passions. Spectators in the audience (as well as characters in Pirandello's play, for what the playwright gives us is a play within a play) get caught up in this melodrama. One of them, recognizing her own story in Morello's, rushes backstage at an intermission and slaps the actress. In this and other "real-life" interludes, which Pirandello wrote as separate scenes, the story of certain spectators parallels the story taking place on stage. In Hallie's acting version of the script, she had her audience characters rush up onstage from the auditorium at certain intervals to break up the onstage action. She did not expect that this would produce a third drama, a "real-life" Vassar incident, but this is what happened. For Hallie and her stage manager, Pirandello's play became a play within a play within a play.

One of the men she found to play a spectator role was an Italian scholar at Vassar. At one point in the play he was to dash onstage from the auditorium, pick up Delia, and carry her offstage. But on opening night he was not in his dressing room and could not be found. Much perturbed, Hallie alerted his understudy, then anxiously stationed herself at the rear of the theatre. Halfway through the show, she heard a commotion in the lobby. Her stage manager beckoned. "Our scholar," he whispered, "is outside and has gone crazy." Hallie went out to the lobby, where she found her delinquent actor in a black hat and long, dilapidated raincoat thumping himself on the chest and telling the stage manager he could not go on. "Are you crazy?" asked Hallie. "The performance has started and it's almost time for your cue." But the scholar kept pointing to his raincoat. "I have nothing on under it," he told her. "Nothing!" And he dashed out the door and accosted a latecomer. "Give me my clothes!" he demanded. "My clothes!" "Sir," said the latecomer, "I do not know who you are and I certainly know nothing about your clothes." And she sailed into the lobby with an air of outraged dignity. By this time Hallie was furious. She told the scholar that his presumed nudity was a matter of indifference, that his cue had already been given, and that his understudy was taking his part. At the word "understudy," the scholar cast off his raincoat, burst through the door to the auditorium, and tore down the aisle. He was fully dressed in impeccable evening attire. The audience was none the wiser. His subsequent exit from academic circles, Hallie later recalled, was "almost as abrupt as his exit from the theatre. There were those who felt that his nerves had been shattered by over-arduous rehearsal." But Hallie, reflecting on Pirandello, chose to believe that he was "merely exercising the right of any Pirandello character to break the fetters chaining him to 'this masquerade called reality' . . . the right, the necessity even, of engaging in actions as passionately incxplicable as life itself."

Most of Hallie's productions made enormous technical demands on those who worked backstage. When wigs were needed for the Pirandello production, one student recalled, "it required unraveling hemp rope, dyeing it and knotting strands into the mesh of dish cloths." When Hallie wanted a train sound for a play one of her students had written, Howard created a mechanism for cranking roller skates over loose cleats and housed it in a closet directly opposite the stage stairs. Communication was by bucket-brigade hand signals from the stage, down the stairs, and around corners. "It was about as gut-busting," according to one of those involved, "as the boiler room on a submarine chaser during World War II." "Hallie was a task-master," another student agreed, "but you felt pleased that you had been honored to do the job, so you gave your best. If she felt you were doing a good job, she never failed to tell you. If she was disappointed, she showed that too. I think her honesty with her students was a great part of her magic." All of Hallie's students spoke of her magic: her ability to fire others with her own vision and dedication. Howard thought Hallie was "exhausted much of the time, just under a constant strain. She would never admit it to anyone, and the minute she was with people there was some kind of spark that came up so they didn't realize how exhausted she really was."

In a professional theatre company Hallie would have had the help of set and costume designers, a lighting expert, and a professional stage manager, but she would not have had the freedom of the small Vassar theatre. Here she was able to learn from her mistakes and develop into a skilled director. Though she sometimes complained of overwork, she was grateful to MacCracken, who supported her against all opposition and provided a financial security that might not have been available in another setting.

Even so, she often felt restless. She was not an academic; she needed the stimulation of talking with people involved in nonacademic endeavors—one reason her aunt and uncle's house in a working-class Detroit neighborhood became her "antidote to Vassar." Above all, she wanted to travel. In the spring of 1930 she got the idea of taking a group of students to Russia. By organizing the trip and acting as guide, she would take care of her own expenses. When Philip Davis heard of this plan, he asked if he might write to her in her absence. Since acting in Toller's play, he had begun attending late-night rehearsals, then walking Hallie back to Kendrick. Hallie said yes. Philip's loneliness touched her.

Several of the seven students Hallie took to Russia in the summer of 1930 had studied with her and heard her talk of the innovations taking place in Russian theatres, and all were excited at the prospect of seeing the new socialist experiment in action. Russia, many people thought, was going to usher in at last a just social order. The western democracies had failed to solve the problems brought on by industrialism. As Malcolm Cowley put it later, there was the hope that people in the future would "go marching with comrades, shoulder to shoulder, out of injustice into the golden mountains."

On reaching Leningrad, Hallie wrote in her journal, "Oh, I was right. Russia is what I thought it was, only infinitely more. It is a country of free men, it is a land of workers. They exist to help others." When several Russians in a theatre gallery spat on the little Vassar group the next evening, Hallie felt ashamed of being an American. "We are the reason for the revolution. We and our kind may cause the next one." The thing that intrigued Hallie, as it had the first time she visited Russia, was that the country seemed to be composed of selfless individuals. Her students, influenced by their teacher, were soon writing home that it was thrilling to visit a country with such idealistic aims, though one of them later admitted that rooming with Hallie could be exhausting as well as stimulating, since "she talked about Russia even while she brushed her teeth and took her bath."

In Moscow the group was disappointed to discover that Meyerhold and Stanislavsky were out of the country. In Stanislavsky's absence the Moscow Art Theatre was presenting a crude social satire against capitalism. The Russian theatre, Hallie discovered, had changed. In 1926 propagandistic theatres had existed side by side with brilliantly innovative ones. Now theatres everywhere were explaining the aims and achievements of the Revolution. One production, *Oil,* "took four hours and every known stage device including an orchestra, cinema, radio, an expressionistic setting of oil wells, oil drills and oil tanks, to explain the value of oil for Russia's economic future. The result was a confusing yet exciting theatrical omnibus," Hallie wrote in an article for *Theatre Guild Magazine.* "The dictatorship of the proletariat has destroyed style and with it the artist who refuses to serve the collective." She explained this by acknowledging that hungry people have other concerns. She still believed that Russian theatre, though often crude, had "blood in its veins" because it was helping to build a new and better social order.

After Moscow, Hallie went on alone to Constantinople. "Here people are sleek," she noted while sitting in an outdoor café. They are "soft and overfed" or "ragged, ill looking and vilely dirty." She was not sure why this made her so angry—perhaps because it placed her among the soft and overfed. The day before, on a shopping spree, she had bought presents for Frederic and a necklace, ring, and earrings for herself. "I refuse to write what they cost," she commented. "They are exquisite, I adore them, they would have cost three times as much in America . . . and all this is merely rationalizing my extravagance . . . Oh God, what an inconsistent, vain, idle and passionate fool I am. And how I love my earrings. They are the color of light coming through plane trees."

She thought of Murray while she was sitting in the café and of how much fun they would have had seeing the city together. "Perhaps one reason marriage survives," she reflected, "is that it is a good deal of fun. Being in love never is fun—it's thrilling, exciting, agonizing, and blissful, but it's never fun. But having won through all the tumult of the blood, I suppose a man and a woman must have a lot of fun just being together." She wrote Frederic that she was very homesick for him and very disappointed he had not written. She had decided to return home earlier than planned and wanted to know if he was glad.

For Frederic, now approaching adolescence, his mother's moments of missing him and needing him were difficult. In his early years, when he had needed her, she had often been unavailable. After he became a grown man Fred confessed to a friend how desperately lonely he had felt when Hallie went to Europe in 1926 and parked him at Oakwood School. Her letters from abroad telling him how much she missed him and what a good time she was having must have been a torment. He reacted apparently by not writing his mother when she was away. Hallie, who did not understand her son's feelings, continued to look on him as gay and charming, very much like her father. She did sometimes worry that he was growing up without her own commitment to idealistic goals. "I wish I could know for certain," she confided in her journal, "that Frederic won't get fat in body or mind."

When she returned to Poughkeepsie, Hallie wrote a story about a group of luxury-loving, pleasure-seeking young people who get together for a party in Greenwich Village. All except one spend the evening drinking, engaging in silly flirtations, and talking about things one can buy abroad. The exception, a young man who has just spent three years in a monastery, quotes lines from the Bible as the party gets louder and sillier. "The moon shall be turned to blood," he prophesies. Like the Christ figure hanging on the wall (an art object someone has bought in Italy), he gazes at his companions with "eyes full of agonized comprehension." When the guests are at their drunkest, someone falls down the stairs and the Christ figure crashes to the floor, symbolizing no doubt the end of the hedonist twenties. If Hallie was once more trying to put the part of her she condemned behind her, she soon found an opportunity to exercise the faculty she most approved in herself, her social conscience.

In the fall of 1930 few people anticipated the prolonged Depression that was to follow the stock market crash of 1929. Hallie herself did not, but she was aware that unemployment was growing. And she learned when she got home that a severe summer drought had ruined many farmers in a broad area stretching from Virginia to Arkansas. She began wondering how the Vassar theatre might help focus attention on the plight of those in distress. Then, in March 1931, a former student phoned Hallie from upstate New York to ask if she had read Whittaker Chambers's story about the drought in the

March issue of *New Masses*. Hallie read it and told the former student, Margaret Ellen Clifford, "Let's dramatize it." They did, and got Chambers's permission to produce it. Two months later *Can You Hear Their Voices?* opened at Vassar.

Hallie and Margaret Ellen's dramatization departed considerably from Chambers's story. They invented new characters, introduced information about unemployment and the decrease in farm production, and changed the story's message. Chambers had presented a problem with a communist solution. Hallie and Margaret Ellen gave no solution. Instead they ended their play with a question, Can you hear what the farmers are saying, and what will you do about it? In the original story, farming families in Arkansas grow increasingly desperate and turn finally to the one man in town, a communist, who has a plan of action. Hallie and Margaret Ellen interspersed scenes of farming families with scenes of a wealthy congressman's family in Washington. In an early Washington scene the congressman and his daughter discuss the drought over breakfast. The daughter wants to know why somebody doesn't do something about it, to which the congressman replies, "What should you suggest doing, my dear? The bishops have prayed for rain, I believe." The congressman has a greater interest in his daughter's coming-out party. When she pokes fun at the party, he says he is worried about the education she is getting. He did not send her to college "to acquire biased, radical ideas about collective farming." In subsequent scenes, a farmer's wife smothers her baby so she won't have to see it die of starvation while the congressman gives a party for his daughter costing more than two hundred and fifty thousand dollars. After the communist hero has told his sons, "Remember that every man ought to have the right to work and eat . . . See if you can't help make a better kind of world for kids to live in," a lowered projection screen tells the audience: "These boys are symbols of thousands of our people who are turning somewhere for leaders. Will it be to the educated minority? CAN YOU HEAR THEIR VOICES?"

The play, later considered the "earliest noteworthy variant of agitprop theatre to be written by authors outside the Communist Party," won immediate critical acclaim. The *New York Times* called it "smashing propaganda," and *New Masses* lauded it as "the best play of revolutionary interest produced in this country." Hallie noted that "some conservatives found the play radical and some radicals found it conservative," but none of this worried her at the time. It had achieved its purpose, which was to rouse public interest in the plight of farmers. It was produced in theatres across the country: the Hedgerow Theatre near Philadelphia, the Cleveland Playhouse, the Beaux Arts Theatre in Los Angeles. College theatres followed suit. When it was published, there were requests for copies from theatres in Greece, China, Hungary, Finland, Denmark, France, Russia, Spain, and Australia. The Shanghai People's Theatre wrote Hallie that *"Can You Hear Their Voices?* was produced last night before the working class people of Shanghai as a part of our protest against Japanese imperialism."

Meanwhile, the letters Philip had started sending to Hallie when she went abroad continued, even though they met frequently. The letters were not about love, she remembered later. They were "about philosophy, music, art, life, and love," parts of them written in Greek, some of them illustrated. But love letters or not, they conveyed serious intentions. Hallie must have realized that Philip was falling in love with her. She was fond of him and liked his company. Grady Bates, she may have remembered, had taken himself off after she rejected his marriage proposal. She did not want the same thing to happen with Philip. Yet she did not want to consider marriage at this time. The idea of marrying again, while it was never far from her mind, frightened her. Ever since Murray's death, when she had begun to explore what she considered her wifely failings in stories and plays, Hallie had had misgivings about what she could bring to a marriage. Her job made enormous demands on her time, and often exhausted her. She looked for admirers to bolster her energies, but admirers could be forgotten when she got back to work. Husbands could not. And Hallie was still infatuated with Lee Gantt.

After he returned to America from Russia, Lee had taken a job at Johns Hopkins University. He had visited Hallie in Poughkeepsie but only to tell her that he was engaged to be married. After he and his wife were settled in their new home in Baltimore, he invited Hallie to visit. "Maps of the Moon," a story Hallie wrote after this visit, gives an indication of how she was feeling.

She gives her heroine, Thane, many of her own characteristics. Thane arrives for a visit at the home of a man she has formerly loved.

Lee and his wife, Paula, greet her warmly. Lee shows her around, then takes her to the roof of the house, where he has installed a telescope and drawing board to draw maps of the moon. Thane realizes that he still attracts her. "How perfect," she reflects. "Other men would be content to fling bridges across the rivers of a continent—Lee must pierce the interstellar spaces." Her response to the man she once loved is still worshipful. Afterward, drinking tea in the couple's living room, Thane is suddenly struck by the thought that she will never be an intimate part of his life. "For how many years now," she wonders, "has this gone on? For how many more must it continue?" Since first meeting Lee ten years ago, since the first long look across a crowded room, she has felt totally under his spell. There had never been a word from Lee. No sign that he cared, nothing. "Yet thereafter, she who scorned sentimentality, became a laughable example of it." Thane recalls how she has run from love and proposals of marriage, how she has thought only of Lee when other men made love to her. Finally she begins to torture herself by imagining what Paula must be thinking of her: "Thane has plenty of men. Why does she want Lee? She doesn't want marriage, she doesn't want children." She wants only to draw him into her net of admirers. "She wants to disturb him, and she does." By the end of the afternoon Thane has convinced herself that Paula wants her to "go away and never come back."

Around this time Hallie began another story about a rich American woman who goes to Russia with the expectation that everything she wants will fall in her lap. Isabel feels humiliated and rejected when she meets a man more interested in his work than in pursuing a flirtation. Hallie did not finish this story. There was no place to go with it. Isabel has no redeeming features.

Philip's letters to Hallie, all of them lacking in self-importance, must have made Hallie realize she was playing with fire. It was not something she really wanted to do. Philip's feelings for her were genuine, and Hallie knew it. She wanted to do the right thing and apparently felt that the right thing was once more to involve Philip in a play. For some time she had been thinking of producing Euripides' *Hippolytus*. A few months after falling in love with Lee Gantt in Russia, she had seen Ludovisi's relief of Aphrodite in Rome. Here was the "real thing," she reflected: the willful, vengeful goddess who

destroyed Hippolytus because he disdained love. During the following year she continued to ponder the "terrifying" character of
Aphrodite. Envisioning a stage for the struggle between Hippolytus
and Aphrodite, she began to imagine one dominated by the "vast,
brooding" statue of the goddess, at the same time wondering,
"Could we build such a statue? Her voice should seem to fill the
theatre."

In December 1930 she asked Philip to read the play to her in
Greek. The language, she decided—"strange, splendid, and bar-
baric"—suited it. Although her students did not know Greek, they
could learn it. Most of those in the audience would not know Greek
either, but plays, she reflected, "would be better if we didn't
understand them so well." The important thing was that those who
watched would have a "powerful, emotional sense of what the play
meant."

Philip agreed to train Hallie's actors in ancient Greek and to play
the role of Hippolytus. By June 1931 Hallie was writing the
chairman of the Greek department that "archaic simplicity" would
be "the keynote of the production." On either side of the proscenium
arch there would be "vast sculptural figures, caryatids, one of
Artemis and one of Aphrodite." From these brooding, ominous
figures would come the voices of the goddesses. "Against their
unmoved calm, mortals shatter themselves in vain." Masks would be
used to reveal the essence of character. A listening chorus would
follow every development of the play with an intensity she hoped
would be duplicated in the audience.

To Gertrude Brown of the music department, who had agreed to
write a musical score, Hallie wrote: "There are two warring motifs—
the *Aphrodite,* dark, passionate, intoxicating but sinister (lots of
strings), and the *Hippolytus-Artemis,* sharp, clear and piercing
(brass, trumpets, lots of body to this music)." Passion against reason,
female against male: this was to be the prominent motif. During the
summer and into the fall Hallie continued making plans. To get
details right, she pored over plates in Richter's *Sculpture of the
Greeks.* To understand Greek dance, she studied Emmanuel's
Antique Greek Dance. In September, with her new technical director
and his wife, Lester and Philena Lang (Howard Wicks had left to
become technical director for the Theatre Guild), Hallie began

supervising choreography, mask making, and set construction. She explained to the Langs that she wanted huge statues to emphasize the superior power of the supernatural over the human. The first spotlight, on Aphrodite and her uplifted hand, just as she appears in the Ludovisi relief, was to remind the audience that "love is the most terrible gift of the gods." This theme was to be underscored by the Aphrodite chorus of women, who would move in such a way as to suggest that they were drawn to the goddess against their will.

After much thought Hallie decided to give the leading role of Phaedra to Elizabeth Tappan, a Latin professor who later became an Episcopalian nun. She gave the role of Theseus to President Mac-Cracken. She had been thinking about both roles for two years. "Phaedra is strong," she noted in her journal, "but subtle. She is entirely subjective, full of dreams and reveries. She leads a secret life in her imagination, and like all introverts she imagines herself at the core of every situation. She is never too lost in grief to remember how she looks. The nurse sees through her perfectly, but Theseus, her husband, does not know her at all." In casting Philip as Hippolytus ("a hunter, cold, with bare muscular cleanness and the unconscious arrogance of the pure"), she was casting against type. Philip was none of these things, and in retrospect Hallie was to say that giving Philip the role of the man "conquered by Aphrodite" was "not a very intelligent thing to do on the part of a woman who had no desire to fall in love." At the time, however, her concern was to involve him in something beyond his personal tragedy.

The three principals were to wear masks. Each had to lie on a table while a layer of cold cream, then a layer of plaster of Paris, was placed on their faces. In Philena Lang's recollection, "It took about fifteen minutes for the plaster to harden. The men took it very well, but Elizabeth Tappan almost fainted and we had to remove the plaster quickly. After she recovered she said she would try again, and the second time there were no problems." Meantime Lester and his crew were building the statues. "The basic forms were made with small meshed chicken wire that was shaped and supported over light wooden frames. The forms were then covered with papier-mâché. When dry, a light-colored coat of paint made them look like very solid statues, but raising them into place was a major undertaking, with much shouting and some cursing as ropes pulled them up and assistants anchored them in place." The costume crew made black wigs and sixth-century B.C. tunics for the women in the Aphrodite chorus; they made blue-gray cloaks for the chorus of hunters, representatives of Artemis. Theseus got a black tunic and silver helmet, Hippolytus a white tunic. Phaedra wore black accentuated by a red wig. No detail went unresearched. Costumes, masks, wigs, music, set, and movement were all based on sixth-century B.C. sources.

As rehearsals got under way, excitement grew. "It was a tremendously emotional experience for everyone involved," one student remembered. A reporter from the New York *Herald Tribune,* after watching a rehearsal, reported that the production was to be the "première presentation in modern times of this famed classic in the tongue in which it was first heard" more than two thousand years earlier. A reporter from the Associated Press photographed President MacCracken holding the mask he would wear as Theseus, and the picture appeared in numerous newspapers.

Mary McCarthy, who had studied playwriting with Hallie, recalled a famous first-night incident. Halfway through the show President MacCracken forgot his lines and substituted a Greek version of "To be or not to be," a speech he had apparently learned as an undergraduate. But the chairman of the Greek department, who was deaf, was sitting in the front row with an ear trumpet. She was greatly concerned, Miss McCarthy recollected; fortunately, others failed to notice.

Hallie had become accustomed to success. But nothing she did before or after at Vassar won as much praise as her *Hippolytus* in Greek. The reviewer for the *Herald Tribune* thought the acting "splendid" and the choruses "superb . . . in groupings borrowed from painting and sculpture of craftsmen long forgotten, they mirrored the tragedy-laden verses of the protagonist." The Pough-keepsie *Sunday Courier* called the production a "gigantic *tour de force* . . . the experience bowled you over." Mary McCarthy thought the show "absolutely marvelous, the most remarkable performance of a Greek play I've ever seen, then or since. It gave one a new conception."

The British classical scholar Gilbert Murray wrote Hallie after seeing photographs that the two gigantic statues gave the play "exactly the background that it needs and which Granville-Barker and I were never able to attain. We could not get the statues and we never had a stage which had room for them." The two Englishmen would have been surprised to learn that the statues cost twenty-five dollars apiece and that they had been put on a stage that was barely twenty-two by sixteen feet. When you want to do something badly enough, Hallie thought, you find a way.

Love affairs between faculty members are probably unusual on any college campus; one more often hears of affairs between professors and their students. Certainly they were unusual, if not nonexistent, during the thirties at Vassar, where most of the men who taught were married and most of the women had chosen to dedicate their lives to teaching rather than to marriage and family. So when Hallie and Philip began spending a good deal of time together during the rehearsals of *Hippolytus,* their students noticed. "Here was this man," one remembered later, "so attractive and looking like he needed to be saved by someone, and this woman who seemed to be saving him." "We all sensed," said another, "that they had a tremendous rapport. When Philip arrived a little high at the dress rehearsal, Hallie didn't mind at all. With anyone else she would have been furious."

Although Hallie and Philip were discreet about their sexual involvement, which probably began during rehearsals, speculation continued. Whenever their romance began, it meant more at first to Philip than it did to Hallie, who wrote later that she had had several love affairs after Murray's death but that none of them took precedence over her work or her life with Frederic. Her affection for Philip, far from making her conclude that they should spend the rest of their lives together, made her wary. She vetoed the idea of marriage as soon as Philip mentioned it. He should look, she thought, for someone younger, someone who had the time and energy to care for his children. Philip did not listen, or if he did, refused to believe what he heard. That Hallie needed him every bit as much as he needed her was clearer to him than to her.

When she thought about Philip, Hallie focused on their differences. Philip was eleven years younger. He had been reared in comfortable circumstances. He came from a well-to-do Princeton family. His father had taught at the Princeton Theological Seminary and written a dictionary of the Bible. The Davises (there were six children, of whom Philip came fifth) spent winters in their large, comfortable Mercer Street house, their summers in an equally large house on Lake George, where all six children had learned to swim, row, hike long distances, and paddle a canoe. Until his wife's death, life had been easy for Philip—or so it seemed to Hallie. He had sailed through Princeton and through graduate work at the American School of Classical Studies in Athens, then married a wealthy Buffalo girl whose parents showered the couple with expensive gifts. Hallie disapproved when Philip drank to alleviate his occasional black moods, and once when he turned up drunk at her apartment, she sent him away. Still, they had interests in common—music, poetry, literature, and a passion for working against injustice. One of Philip's sisters was later to recall that Philip was always concerned for people in need. His eldest sister remembered him as the "black sheep" of the family. "He did what was expected, as I did, but neither of us quite belonged to the genteel Princeton world in which we were raised."

Philip recognized long before Hallie did that their common interests mattered more than their differences.

Having spent the summer and fall of 1931 engrossed in the history and artistry of the ancient Greeks, Hallie was ready by early 1932 to tackle something more recent. Moreover, she felt committed to do what she could to bring the growing economic crisis before the public. The Depression was worsening, its effects on working-class people becoming more and more apparent. By 1932 the unemployed numbered more than thirteen million. Thousands of people were wandering about the country in a fruitless quest for work. Thousands of others had set up Hoovervilles, encampments of squatters who created makeshift homes out of junked cars, old barrels—whatever they could find to protect themselves from the cold and the rain. In the mining towns of Kentucky and West Virginia, evicted families put up tents. Children went barefoot. Hunger stalked cities and towns across the country. Relief funds from private and government sources were everywhere inadequate. Hallie's first effort to bring this state of affairs before the public had presented the plight of farmers and asked its privileged audience, "What do you intend to do about it?" *Can You Hear Their Voices?* had avoided Chambers's communist message, but the two plays she was to produce in late 1932 did not.

Miners on Strike and *We Demand,* both propaganda playlets rather than full-fledged dramas, had been written by members of the New York City Workers Laboratory Theatre, one of the many workers' theatres that had sprung up in response to the Depression. Hallie became aware of this movement after she began receiving copies of the journal the members put out. *Workers Theatre* magazine encouraged its readers to form similar groups across the nation. It also published short plays written by members of the Workers Laboratory Theatre. The two plays Hallie produced at Vassar had been published in this journal. Both derived from the agitprop form, neither had any great artistic merit, but Hallie felt they had the simplicity of vision she believed was needed at the time. Like many artists of the period, Hallie had no doubt where she stood on the age-old controversy whether art should or should not be used as a weapon. She liked to quote Walt Whitman, who was reputed to have said that "the trouble is that writers are too literary . . . There has grown up the doctrine, art for art's sake . . . Instead of regarding literature as only a weapon, an instrument, in the service of something larger than itself, it looks upon itself as an end . . . To me that's all a horrible blasphemy."

Hallie told her students about the workers' theatre movement, and some went with her to the New York Lyceum to see the first national competition of workers' theatres in the spring of 1932. Fourteen theatres—from Chicago, Philadelphia, Newark, and New York—performed, most of them in English, but a few in German, Hungarian, or Ukrainian. Excited by what they saw, several students urged Hallie to produce two workers' plays at Vassar. Hallie did, without foreseeing the uproar that would follow.

On opening night, students who hoped to collect money for the National Committee to Aid Starving Miners attached a form to the program asking for contributions. This became part of the problem: several members of the audience felt it was in bad taste for a theatre to solicit funds. Others were shocked at the communist message the plays expounded. Many writers for the Workers Laboratory Theatre made no secret of their communist sympathies. One of the plays their journal published gives its communist hero the last word: "Yes, I agitate for the defense of the Soviet Union, the only country in the world where there are no more exploiters, the only country in the world where the workers are free, the only country in the world where the worker rules." This message was implicit in both plays that Hallie produced at Vassar.

During the days that followed, a group of parents and trustees called on President MacCracken in protest. The president replied that his teachers had the right to present controversial material. Several faculty members rallied to Hallie's support. Helen Lockwood wrote in the *Vassar Miscellany News,* "Whether we like it or not, the rising of the masses is the incoming tide of our time. As we have failed to order our industrial machinery fast enough, their left wing has become increasingly active." While Lockwood considered the workers' plays unsatisfactory from an artistic standpoint, she concluded that the educated classes would be wise "to take immediate steps to understand their full meaning."

In June, Hallie attended a conference of workers' cultural societies sponsored by the John Reed Club of New York. Nineteen theatre groups sent delegates, and one group performed. In an article she wrote for *Theatre Arts Monthly,* Hallie noted that a red banner with the words "Workers of the World Unite" was on the wall behind the speakers' platform and that many messages from theatres in the U.S.S.R. suggested that these workers' theatres should be modeled on those of the Soviets. "But as the meeting progressed, a number of speakers emphasized the fact that the problems of America are not the problems of the U.S.S.R., and consequently that, although workers here must study the proletarian theatres of other countries, they must work out their own ideas and their own style." The skit that was performed Hallie thought childish. She wondered how workers unused to the simplest stage techniques would learn the skills necessary to create good theatre. "The treatment of economic and industrial themes, aside from some burlesque of the upper classes, is deadly serious, perhaps because people who are hungry are not apt to be humorous about the situation."

The editors of *Workers Theatre* magazine, who had hoped to win Hallie's total support, discovered instead that although she lauded the vitality of workers' theatre groups, she remained objective about their present achievements. Ironically, it was to be her article in *Theatre Arts Monthly* that the House Un-American Activities Committee would find greatest fault with when it called her to testify in 1938. The committee's objection was that since Hallie failed to criticize the communist views of the workers' plays, she must have supported their wish to overthrow the United States government. In fact Hallie never saw herself as part of a proletarian movement. She was a rebel within America's middle class, a position she indicated at the conclusion of her article, when she wrote that if workers' theatres ever succeeded in their herculean task—the reorganization of our social order—she and others like her would become an "involuntary audience."

Although most of Hallie's close friends believed as she did— that the greatest threat in the early 1930s came from those in America who showed indifference to the poverty and suffering around them—she did have a few friends who saw an equally disturbing danger coming from Soviet Russia. During the summer of 1931, while planning *Hippolytus,* she began seeing a lot of two people who were to become close and lifelong friends, despite their political differences. Nikander and Katharine Strelsky, a "white" Russian and his American wife, were living year round in an unheated summer cottage near Wappingers Falls, New York. Nik, as everyone called him, had grown up in the Ukraine, a son of landed proprietors. He had fled from Kiev as the Reds were storming the city, been captured, escaped, and joined the White Army. Later he had lived for a time in Constantinople, where he earned a living by managing a ballet theatre for the armies of the occupation. An American admiral helped him get to America, but his health was bad, and he spent his earliest months here in a sanitarium recovering from tuberculosis. It was there, in Saranac, that he met Katharine, also a tuberculosis patient. Just before Hallie got to know them, Nik had found a job teaching Russian to some Vassar students and teachers. Later he got a job on the faculty. Hallie and Nik spent many hours discussing Russia, and though their views differed they became good friends.

Philip also liked the Strelskys. By this time he had become an important part of Hallie's social life. During the summer of 1932 Hallie worked with Philip on some mimes he was translating from

Theocritus. The more they worked together, the more she depended on his clear, honest judgments. Philip, who was not at all "theatric," could look at situations with a clear, unprejudiced eye. He was becoming a ballast for Hallie's heady enthusiasms, and though it scared her a little to perceive how much she needed such a ballast, she was coming to realize that Philip's feeling for her mattered. When he again proposed marriage and Hallie raised objections, he told her he had considered the matter of their ages and come to the conclusion that although she was certainly too young for him, her youth might be nice for his children. Hallie laughed. She liked Philip's humor and what she had begun to think of as his "dear, quiet strength."

7

Indecision

IN the summer of 1932 Philip persuaded Hallie to visit his in-laws in Buffalo, where Philip's father-in-law, Ausburn Dwelle, owned a glass factory and a large comfortable house. If Philip was becoming attached to a new woman, he and Mrs. Dwelle wanted to meet her. Hallie agreed to the visit with some foreboding. Her anxieties increased when she noticed the many photographs of Philip's wife that hung on the walls. In one, Philip and Helen were standing in wedding attire in the Dwelles' rose garden. A ray of sunlight enveloping Helen's hair made her look angelic. "I have never been the least reconciled" to Helen's death, Hallie wrote to Mrs. Dwelle after the visit. "The only saving element is that at the height of her youth, beauty and love, she became immortal, remaining for all of you eternally young and fair." In her flowery way Hallie must have been trying to show respect for the Dwelles' loss. She may also have realized that whoever married Philip would have to compete with the Dwelles for his children's affections. Philip's children spent their vacations in the Dwelles' house.

As usual when she was in turmoil Hallie wrote a story. "Pearls Found in a Bottle," which was published three years later, is about a working-class girl who is courted by a wealthy gentleman. Proud, aloof, and unhappy, Olga is determined to keep her independence.

But her suitor, Rand Perry, is as determined to win her as she is to resist. "You think your money means a lot to me, don't you?" she asks him. "Well, it doesn't. I mean to get out of this town someday for good. But I don't need you to take me out."

> In the end, of course, he was too much for her . . . Near the close of the summer she got so thin and desperate-looking that he felt sometimes that he was killing her. But he could not give up. Sometimes when he came up the steps in the evening she would turn and look at him in a haunted way, like an animal.

Philip, like the fictional Rand Perry, was extremely persistent. He had answers, many of them humorous, for all Hallie's objections. When she asked him why an affair would not suffice, he said he had designs on her cooking. "It was well-known," Hallie remarked later, "that I cannot cook even an egg." Domestic chores, Philip assured her, would be taken care of: he had a cook, and the Dwelles were paying someone to look after the children.

One thing in Philip's favor was Frederic, who liked Philip from the moment he met him. Hallie felt Fred needed a father and that Philip would be a good influence. Fred was now a boarding student at Pawling School in Poughkeepsie. Hallie had sent him there, she told an editor at *Redbook* magazine who wanted her to write an article about sending children to private schools, "not because I feel the quality of education there is superior, and not because I believe in special privileges for the leisure class, to which incidentally I do not belong, but to counteract the too great feminine influence of a mother and a woman's college combined."

Fred made several attempts to persuade his mother that he was not where he wanted to be. He often phoned her from Pawling pretending to be the headmaster. "This is Dr. Gamish," he would say, "and I am sorry to have to tell you that Fred has been expelled for smoking." Hallie would hear this, Phelps Riley remembered, and for a moment be dreadfully upset. She did not get the underlying message, however, no doubt because she also knew that Fred was popular, active in sports, and getting decent grades.

In the fall of 1932, Hallie and Philip began working together on a sequence of mimes they decided to call *Now I Know Love*. Mimes have been described as brief dramatic episodes. The mimes Philip had translated from Theocritus had been written as popular entertainments for the marketplace or dinner table. A student in Hallie's playwriting class, Mary Crapo, wrote a modern mime, and Hallie decided that T. S. Eliot's dramatic fragment, *Sweeney Agonistes,* could also be included in this category. She wrote him asking for permission to produce it. Hallie had an unerring instinct for what was seminal in the theatre, and she recognized before anyone the dramatic potential of Eliot's small gem. (As a writer for the *New York Times* would put it later, "without *Sweeney Agonistes,* the works of Samuel Beckett, Harold Pinter and Sam Shepard are unimaginable ... By imitating jazz chants and vaudeville ditties, Eliot created an entirely new dramatic idiom.") Eliot replied from Eliot House at Harvard, where he was lecturing on poetry:

> I have no objection to your doing *Sweeney,* what there is of him, though I cannot imagine what anybody can do without me there to direct it. The action should be stylised as in the Noh drama—see Ezra Pound's book and Yeats' preface and notes too [*At*] *The Hawk's Well.* Characters ought to wear masks; the ones wearing old masks ought to give the impression of being young persons (as actors) and vice versa. Diction should not have too much expression. I had intended the whole play to be accompanied by light drum taps to accentuate the beats (esp. the chorus, which ought to have a noise like a street drill). The characters should be in a shabby flat, seated at a refectory table, facing the audience; Sweeney in the middle with a chafing dish scrambling eggs. (See "you see this egg.") (See also F. M. Cornford: *Origins of Attic Comedy,* which is important to read before you do the play.) I am talking about the *second* fragment of course; the other one is not much good. The second should end as follows: there should be 18 knocks like the angelus, and then
>
> *Enter an old gentleman. He is in full evening dress with a carnation, but otherwise resembles closely Father Christ-*

mas. In one hand he carries an empty champagne bottle, in the other an alarum clock.

THE OLD GENTLEMAN: Good evening. My name is Time. The time by the exchange clock is now nine forty-five (or whatever it is). I come from the vacant lot in front of the Grand Union Depot, where there is the heroic equestrian statue of General Diego Cierra of Paraguay. Nobody knows why General Cierra is there. Nobody knows why I am there. Nobody knows anything. I wait for the lost trains that bring in the last souls after midnight. The time by the exchange clock is now 9:46.

SWEENEY: Have you nothing else to say?

OLD GENTLEMAN: Have you nothing to ask me?

SWEENEY: Yes.

OLD GENTLEMAN: Good.

SWEENEY: When will the barnfowl fly before morning?
           When will the owl be operated on for cataracts?
           When will the eagle get out of his barrel-roll?

OLD GENTLEMAN:
           When the camel is too tired to walk farther
           Then shall the pigeon-pie blossom in the desert
           At the wedding-breakfast of life and death.

SWEENEY: Thank you.

OLD GENTLEMAN: Good night.
(As Old Gentleman leaves, the alarum clock in his hand goes off.)

I will let you know if I can possibly come on May 6th.

Hallie had her own ideas about how to portray Sweeney, the disillusioned gentleman who wonders how it would be to live on a cannibal isle where

> Two live as one
> One live as two
> Two live as three
> Under the bam
> Under the boo
> Under the bamboo tree.

She had no intention of displaying her character in a mask scrambling eggs at a refectory table inside a shabby flat, but instead saw him dressed in the sort of attire a civil servant in India might have worn, his back resting against a huge pillar, his legs shod in riding boots, his eyes staring out into space as he says,

> I knew a man once did a girl in
> Any man might do a girl in
> Any man has to, needs to, wants to
> Once in a lifetime, do a girl in.

"If you saw the play," Hallie wrote to Eliot, "done against a realistic background, I have a feeling that you would be disappointed, because after all, isn't the realistic background as obsolete as arbitrary rhyme in poetry?" Still, she worried about what Eliot would think when he saw her production. After having given her such explicit instructions, would he feel that his work had been betrayed?

On the morning of May 6, Philip drove to Cambridge to pick up Eliot. On the way back they stopped at several bars. Hallie was frantic by the time they arrived. "Oh, I thought you'd miss it!" she exclaimed. "I wish I had," Eliot murmured, but he took his seat. The audience was moved by the pastoral poetry of Theocritus, grew restless watching Dorothy Parker's *Telephone*, which Hallie had dramatized, but was riveted by *Sweeney*. Eliot thought Hallie's *Sweeney* "entirely different from" his own conception, but liked it "very, very much," in fact was "inclined to think Mrs. Flanagan's way of presentation better" than his own might have been. "*Sweeney* is still a fragment to me; I can only see it as part of a longer play, but Mrs. Flanagan successfully produced it as a complete dramatic unit."

Philip shared honors with Eliot that evening, the *Herald Tribune*'s reviewer giving as much space to his translations as to *Sweeney*: "Mr. Davis rendered the hexameters of Theocritus in vigorous and beautiful prose.... Mr. Davis's lines moved the audience deeply." After the performance, cast, crew, and friends met at Philip's house to celebrate. Hallie recalled that the "philosophical discussion engendered by the play continued most of the night in a flow of Eliot prose and verse." It was helped along by a keg of beer that Philip had stored in the basement. While guests gathered, he handed glasses around, disappearing now and then to fill a large pitcher. "Where is this beer?" Eliot wanted to know. He was told it was in the basement. "Then let's go there," he said, and all disappeared down the stairs to continue their talk by the beer keg.

The next day Eliot discussed poetry from the stage of Avery Hall. Hallie described the occasion in *Dynamo,* the book she wrote about Vassar:

> Roaming about the setting of his own play he talked about poetry with impersonal lucidity.
>
> "My poetry is simple and straightforward," he declared; and when the audience laughed he looked pained. "It is dubious whether the purpose of poetry is to communicate anyway. Poetry ought simply to record the fusion of a number of experiences." Later when asked about *Sweeney Among the Nightingales,* he said, "I'm not sure it means anything at all." And he went on to develop the point that a poem may be like a still life, the meaning of which we do not formulate—"We merely estimate the way the painter has used planes and angles."
>
> To student questions from the crowded house he was painstakingly exact, though sometimes cryptic.
>
> "Was the production what you expected?"
>
> "The moment expected may be unforeseen when it arrives." (This line he later used in *Murder in the Cathedral.*)
>
> And to the student who asked why he did not write Sweeney differently, he said thoughtfully, "To be a different poem a poem would either have to be written by the same poet at a different time, or by a different poet at the same time."
>
> One questioner, referring to the lines,

> Every man has to, needs to, wants to
> Once in a lifetime do a girl in,

asked hopefully, "Mr. Eliot, did you ever do a girl in?" Mr. Eliot looked apologetic and said, "I am not the type."

Most people who watched *Now I Know Love* experienced *Sweeney* as the high point of the evening. But there was one exception. A few days after the last performance Hallie heard from an editor of *Workers Theatre* that her production was only "half worthwhile" because Eliot gave off "the pessimism of capitalist imperialist civilization in crisis in its final stage of decay." The writer went on to tell her she was squandering her time, energy, and craftsmanship on unworthy material. "We expect it generally in the bourgeois theatre but not in the Vassar Experimental Theatre." Unknown to Bernard Reines, Hallie had become increasingly critical of the workers' theatre movement. When a young playwright sent her his propagandistic play asking for comments, she told him she thought that all propaganda plays, including her own, were "too simplified to be very good dramatically. All workers' plays I have seen suffer from this fault."

By September 1933 *Workers Theatre* had changed its name to *New Theatre* in an effort to attract a wider audience. It was the period of the Popular Front, and the magazine's editors now wanted articles from liberals as well as radicals. The new board asked Hallie to become a contributing editor and she accepted. Other contributing editors included Lee Strasberg, Sidney Howard, Erwin Piscator, Virgil Geddes, and Anita Block. Molly Thacher, Hallie's former student, now married to Elia Kazan, was on the magazine's editorial board and kept Hallie informed as to how the magazine was doing. She told Hallie she hoped it would become the most important theatre magazine in America—but *New Theatre* lasted only until 1937.

During the summer Hallie polished her recent short stories and sent them off to a New York agent for his comments. She was also working with Philip on a book they hoped to publish, *Acting Versions of Ancient Mimes*. Philip was to leave for Athens in August. He and Hallie had each been granted sabbatical leaves for the coming

academic year. Philip planned to live at the American School of
Classical Studies, making frequent trips to the island of Delos, where
he had begun collecting information for a book on building inscriptions. Hallie was to meet him there in the spring. It was Philip's idea
that they marry in Athens, but Hallie would not commit herself. She
had not been feeling well, whether from overwork or uncertainty
about her future or a combination of both. "I can't seem to do my
work here or anything else," she wrote a friend in the spring. "My
technical director, Lester Lang, and I work all the time," she wrote
someone else, "—a state which I do not regard as ethical or
satisfactory." It was not just exhaustion that bothered her. Hallie
was forty-four and at a midpoint in her career. She was a success at
Vassar, but she was not sure she wanted to stay there. Gordon
Craig's suggestion that she should be thinking of new opportunities
had hit the mark. She would have welcomed a new challenge,
something nonacademic. But what? Often she dreamed of having
more time to write, but she needed to keep on making a living. And
nothing she had written had made much money.

Hallie could not have been encouraged by the letter she received
from her New York agent. In August she heard from August
Lenniger that although he was "on the whole favorably impressed"
by her stories, he felt they were "too intellectual, not popular
magazine material." He supposed she had "not paid much attention
to market requirements" and was "probably one of those writers
who have to write what they feel regardless of standards." He
thought he could sell her stories if she made them slightly more
commercial. He suggested she become a regular reader of *McCall's,
Redbook, Good Housekeeping,* and *The Ladies' Home Journal.*
Around this same time Hallie heard from *The New Yorker* that the
mime she and Philip had sent them was not right for the magazine
and from Oxford University Press that there was not much of a
market for *Acting Versions of Ancient Mimes.*

September 1933, one of Hallie's students later recalled, was a
heady time at Vassar. The campus was "full of ferment," and so was
the town. Roosevelt had been President only six months, but already
people were hopeful that his progressive measures would solve the
problems that Hoover's administration had not. In the middle of the

month, cities across the nation celebrated people's hopes in a series of parades. "Such an amount of baby-petting and flag-waving as is going on in these parts," Hallie wrote a former student, "you have never seen. It makes me feel that we should do a revue called *The Blue Eagle* or *One Year of a Century of Progress*." Revue songs could be called "Beer Coming Back," "Dollar Going Down," and "Prices Going Up." It would "give everyone a chance to act, sing and dance." Hallie headlined her letter "Summer Headquarters of Roosevelt, Recovery, the New Deal, the Blue Eagle and me."

One of the students in Hallie's playwriting class that fall showed a particular talent for dialogue, Hallie thought. She was Mary St. John, a bright, articulate girl from a wealthy background. "Muriel Rukeyser, Elizabeth Bishop, and Eleanor Clark were all classmates of mine," Mary recalled. They were "friends and editors of the *Miscellany News* which I chaired. They were heady company, as was Mary McCarthy, who was a year ahead of us and at the time took a dim view of our political bent. We were certainly left of center"— influenced, she thought, by the "radicals" on the faculty, including Hallie. "But—I suddenly just realized this—Hallie's impact was artistic rather than political. We built sets inspired by Russian constructivism, we wrote in the style of the Living Newspaper, but it was the theatre that really counted."

Hallie encouraged Mary to write a play, and Mary wrote *American Plan,* an episodic piece in which twenty-five scenes contrasted the lives of workers with those of their bosses. Forty years later Mary considered the play "terribly dated. We were simplistically oriented against wealth." Theatre as Hallie taught it, she reflected, "was an instrument for education. Hallie was wonderful in a college setting. Her contribution was broader than theatre." Mary also remembered Hallie as "temperamental in the way theatre people are. She could blow up at you and then build you up. She responded emotionally to things."

The set for *American Plan,* another of Hallie's and Lester's modern constructions, focused on a staircase and upper platform and provided several acting areas where the lives of rich and poor were contrasted. In one scene, the corporation president's daughter is married on the upper platform, accompanied by the music of Mendelssohn's Wedding March, while an endless succession of the unemployed file past below. Throughout the production Hallie used music, as Brecht and Piscator had done, to stimulate a feeling of irony. Reactions to the production showed more concern with the play's political implications than with its artistic merit. The *Miscellany News* reviewer seemed pleased that *American Plan* provided "no theoretical solution." The audience was presented with problems, she thought, but propaganda was avoided. The managing editor of *Scholastic Magazine* thought it a good play to produce because it conveyed "the social-economic problems of the present crisis in a way that young people can understand." A year later, however, when the play was produced by the Little Theatre in Birmingham, Alabama, an industrialist in the audience found its premise communistic. "If the Little Theatre people had known as much as I know about the undercover operations of communistic elements in the Birmingham district," he declared, "they would never have dared to produce such a play." It was the beginning of a period when radicals and progressives of every shape and color came to be lumped together. Hallie and Mary St. John had wanted to point up inequities in the current social situation. But this, more and more, would be considered a dangerous thing to do.

Hallie next turned her attention to a Soviet drama that had played to packed houses in Russia but not yet been produced in the United States. She considered Alexander Afinogenov's *Fear* "one of the three great Russian plays since the Revolution.... It was originally banned as being counter-revolutionary, but later accepted as part of Russia's plan of self-criticism." "No American play," she told President MacCracken, "criticizes American government as drastically as *Fear* lashes the Soviets." Hallie's Russian friend Nikander Strelsky and two students of Russian made a translation of the play which Hallie turned into her own acting version.

While she was working on the script and before she had started rehearsals, she received a letter from May Sarton, then twenty-one and at the time more interested in acting and directing than in writing. Sarton had acted with Margaret Ellen Clifford at a summer theatre in Gloucester, Massachusetts, and had then been an apprentice under Eva Le Gallienne with the hope of making herself a place in the theatre. When she first wrote to Hallie about *Fear*, it was to say:

It has been brought home to me that there is no place for
the young actor to grow up in—one year of observation in
a working theatre like the Civic Repertory; the playing of,
shall we say, five walk-ons; and several parts in student
productions—is an excellent introduction, little more. In
looking back to Europe I became aware that the creative
theatres such as Copeau's had nearly always started from a
small group of amateurs who were willing to take a long
time about growing . . .

With this in mind Sarton and other apprentices were planning to
present a series of rehearsal performances of modern European plays
which the New School for Social Research had agreed to sponsor.
Would Hallie be interested in seeing her group perform at Vassar?
One of their productions would be *Fear*, in a different translation,
but it would not open until Hallie's had closed. Hallie replied that
she was very much interested and attended Sarton's group reading of
Henri Lenormand's *The Secret Life* in November. After meeting with
Hallie, Sarton wrote:

I hasten to tell you how delighted I am to have at last "seen
the leopard" and found him such a charming creature. I had
conceived you as a very large positive and rather abrupt
lady with black hair—and I still cannot quite fit the two
images together: before H.F. and after H.F. so to speak.

Hallie subsequently wrote to Sarton about some of the difficulties
she was having with Afinogenov's play. "Our translation has to be
worked over at every rehearsal. The entrances and exits are driving me
crazy! There is scarcely one which is either motivated or reasonable . . .
Don't you find the line-up of forces very confusing?" She had still not
completed the casting, which called for many more men than women,
and was finding the play "far beyond our acting abilities: I have no
good person for Borodin and am spending my vacation trying to pump
a little life into the terrible men of the cast! I feel rather guilty to be
attempting this play—it should be produced by a really expert
company!"
Hallie had met Afinogenov in 1926 in Moscow during a rehearsal
of one of his earlier plays. She had heard him speak and been struck

by his concern for the way the Revolution was affecting character. The play *Fear,* as its title suggests, has to do with the state of mind of Soviet Russians within a scientific institution fourteen years after the Revolution. Borodin, its central character, based to some extent on Ivan Pavlov, is a former aristocrat who believes that scholars rather than politicians should run the country. His counterpart, Yelena, a young Soviet scientist, considers Borodin's views foolish and outdated. In the earliest scenes the author contrasts Borodin's passion for science with several other characters' greed for power. Later in the play, no doubt forced to this conclusion by Soviet censors, he has Borodin admit his mistakes and agree to work for the Soviets. The strength of *Fear,* however, is in its character delineation. Proletarians, former aristocrats, almost everyone in this play, loses dignity at one time or another as he or she struggles to survive in the climate of fear the Soviets have established.

Lester Lang's set emphasized the difference between the old and new orders. Borodin's room, though shabby, "is still a rich room, with rugs, hangings, ikons, books, a samovar," while Yelena's "contains a large uncurtained window out of which one sees the smoke stacks of factories. Everything in it is plain and bare and machine-made: a desk with stool, a wooden bench, a poster glorifying industrialization." In Hallie's words "Fear stalks through the scenes, yet this fear is combated by the fearlessness of those who believe in a new order." The contrast, whether or not Hallie was aware of it, reflected conflicts she had been struggling with: her own love of "old world" trappings versus her belief that a new order, whatever it might bring to her personally, was what she should be fighting for.

The production aroused much interest among theatre professionals. The reviewer for the *Herald Tribune,* interpreting the play as a plea "for a square deal for the survivors of the Czaristic aristocracy," thought "there was nothing lacking in this production. Broadway would find it hard to do better." The *New York Times* reviewer expressed surprise that Broadway had not recognized the play's merits before Hallie had. RKO studios, Warner Brothers, and the Theatre Guild all wrote asking to see copies.

While rehearsing *Fear,* Hallie had been making plans for her forthcoming sabbatical. Hoping for a renewal of her Guggenheim

Fellowship, she wrote to Henry Allen Moe, "The life of a producer is rather like the life of a camel. He must come to an oasis now and then in order to drink before continuing his long tramp through the desert." When Moe turned down her request, she looked elsewhere for funds for the European trip. In November a letter arrived from Leonard Elmhirst asking whether she would be interested in becoming director of theatre at Dartington Hall, an experimental arts center in Devon, England. He offered to pay her fare to look Dartington over. Hallie replied that she could come in February.

Dartington, she learned, was situated on a high 800-acre tract of land that had once belonged to Richard II. Several stone buildings, which in medieval fashion surrounded a large, open courtyard and looked out over a vast sweep of fields and downs, had become under the Elmhirsts' direction a refuge for artists and intellectuals. Dorothy and Leonard Elmhirst had wanted to create an ideal community: they had built a progressive school as well as an arts center, rooms for weaving and pottery making, and farm buildings in which Leonard carried out experiments in farming and husbandry. His wife was the former Dorothy Payne Whitney who, with her first husband, Willard Straight, had founded *The New Republic*. Dorothy's wish to give her children, Michael and Beatrice Straight, a modern education had resulted in the founding of Dartington School. It was patterned along the lines of A. S. Neill's Summerhill, where children learned to read only after they expressed a wish to do so. Dartington, like Summerhill, was progressive with a capital *P*. Hallie, who by this time had become identified with the progressive movement in education, was a natural choice to lead Dartington's theatre program. She was flattered to be asked, but wanted to see the school before coming to any decision.

Meantime she had been working to expand the Vassar Experimental Theatre by soliciting funds from the parents of her wealthy students. One parent donated five thousand dollars, and Hallie, without consulting the president, used part of this money to finance architectural plans for a new theatre building. This naturally got her into trouble with the comptroller and president, who reminded her that building plans remained a function of the college. After they patched up this difficulty Hallie went on to remind MacCracken: "Mr. Lang and I have both had serious physical breakdowns this year and have been told by our doctors that we cannot continue to do between us the work usually done by four or five people. Our hope is that the theatre after seven years has proven itself of sufficient value to the college to make its requests possible." She asked for three things: a switchboard, a new curtain track, and a full-time secretary to handle sales of plays and an "extremely heavy correspondence." The music and art departments, she pointed out, had larger staffs. The president replied that a new switchboard would be constructed and that he hoped to be able to give her the money for a secretary. After consulting with the board of trustees, he offered Hallie a somewhat larger budget, which included money for an office assistant.

Hallie spent a Sunday visiting Frederic at Pawling before she boarded a boat for England. "It was a good visit," she noted in her diary. "We went to the Pawling diner for luncheon and made plans for his coming to Europe in July. In the afternoon we walked over to the chapel which we had all to ourselves and he played the organ." The next day her friends in the English department gave her a luncheon, and in the evening Kendrick House gave her a farewell dinner. At her last class in Dramatic Production, a group of students marched in singing and presented her with a huge cake with the words "Experimental Theatre, 1925–1934" on it. The next morning several of them went to the railroad station to see her off.

"The last two years have been my best years at Vassar," Hallie wrote to one student a week later, "largely because of you and the small group waiting in the cold at the station. I left you with such a pang of realization that I wouldn't be there to see you graduate." Affectionate friendships with students had meant much to Hallie during her unmarried years. Her students had been her extended family, her children as well as her co-workers. Realizing that this might soon change, she spent a couple of days missing them terribly. She was a "badly spoiled person," she wrote in her journal after finding her cabin filled with baskets of fruit, flowers, books, fountain pens, a traveling clock, and piles of letters, most of them from admirers. In an effort to restore the lost connection with those she had left behind, she began a series of "Dear Theatre" letters. "Not only is there a winter garden on this boat with rather dejected palms and pink sofas," she wrote, but there hangs in the salon a complete assembly of photographs of London society. The Duchess of Northumberland is there looking at a picture book, and Sybil Thorndike looking down her nose; Ruth St. Denis holding baby, Princess Bibesco. Dame Clara Butt is there, swathed in furs; Rebecca West looking surprised in a jewelled headdress, and Gladys Cooper lying down uncomfortably with a shawl wrapped around her. There are a great many poses of Lady Lavery, sometimes with a Nubian slave, sometimes a crystal ball . . . My favorite is H.H. Princess Antoine Bibesco with a monkey . . . It makes me feel we should revolutionize the greenroom—go in more heavily for the personal touch . . .

Here the dramatic quality of the ship ends: there are only 24 cabin passengers, which, together with the extravagant nature of your floral tributes has landed me at the Captain's table. He is a very nice man in spite of the fact that he has written a book called *Ship Ahoy!* which I gather we are all supposed to buy. He appears seldom, due to the ice and general frigidity, which leaves at our table a nice old gentleman from Toronto who hates New York, a man and his wife, both quite jewelled, who Travel a Great Deal, another mysterious man, very melancholy, who eats fish and says nothing. All are so British that I feel deformed holding my knife and fork the way we do.

In time the man she at first described as mysterious and melancholy grew expansive. Hallie found the stories he told about Cambridge "delightful." He turned out to be a professor of zoology, the director of a museum, and the author of many books. The couple she had described as traveling a great deal talked about India so vividly they made Hallie "long to go there." She was beginning to enjoy her companions, even though they *were* British, when a "frontal attack of British humor" on the evening of the ship's concert did her in and she noted, as she had on an earlier trip, that she did not understand the English at all and sometimes thought them "of all races the most foreign . . . Their jokes were simply unspeakable and . . . everyone got drunk."

However, it was not just, or even mainly, her fellow passengers who made Hallie feel "rotten," as she put it in a letter to a friend. She had embarked on a trip that was to end by meeting Philip in Athens, and she was still undecided whether she wanted to marry him. Could she manage a family of six and also do her work? She had once told a Vassar friend that she wished she had a daughter. Philip had two, but how would they feel about having her as a stepmother? One day, observing a family with children ranging in age from six to sixteen, she had the "nice feeling that everything is possible," but the next day she was just as certain that marrying Philip was the last thing she should do. Before embarking, she told herself sternly that she must "get to work and either stop loving Phil or marry him." Gordon Craig had invited her to visit him in Genoa, and she thought that talking things over with him might help. She wrote him a long letter saying she planned to go to Italy in a month's time and would he please cable her in London if it was not convenient for him to meet her.

On February 21, Norreys O'Conor met her boat and took her to his house in Kensington, where she spent a pleasant evening before going on to Devon. At Dartington Hall, Leonard Elmhirst and his stepdaughter Beatrice Straight gave her tea and settled her in a comfortable room overlooking a small church and graveyard dating from the fourteenth century. Hallie was charmed by the "apparent contradiction of Dartington: a fourteenth-century castle and modern houses by Lescaze." The medieval buildings surrounding a large courtyard were starkly beautiful in their setting on a high hill overlooking miles of downs. Leonard Elmhirst had planned a tour of the estate for the following day. He showed Hallie everything he thought might induce her to come to Dartington. She learned that she would be working with Kurt Jooss, whose ballet *The Green Table* she admired. She saw a rehearsal of a dance-drama that was being jointly produced by students, faculty, and workers from nearby orchards and farms. She met with students who were making pottery under the direction of the famous potter Bernard Leach. She saw buildings where wine was being made, others where cattle were being bred, still others where woodworking and weaving were going on. All the crafts, Hallie told herself, were being revived "not as romantic gestures of some vague back-to-the-soil dream, but as practical ventures." Others would later describe Dartington as impractical and utopian. But Hallie was having a wonderful and restful few days, and for a brief time she thought seriously about taking the job. She told Elmhirst she was on her way to Greece, probably to marry Philip Davis. He assured her that Dartington could also hire Philip. She left him with the impression that she was interested.

Back in London she spent ten days seeing plays, meeting old friends, talking with Dartington Hall trustees, going to art galleries, and doing research at the British Museum for a production of *Antony and Cleopatra* she wanted to stage. Grace and Norreys O'Conor gave a dinner in her honor at which she met "lots of interesting people—Sir Philip and Lady Gibbs and Hugh Fisher the etcher, and Lord Dunsany (very strange) and A.E., now living in London, very much a voice from the past." The high point of the London visit was a luncheon with T. S. Eliot and a tea he gave for her the following day. "We have had the most crazy and amusing times," she wrote to Esther Porter, a former student and presently her office assistant at Vassar, "and we talk entirely in Sweeney-ese. Eliot thinks Sweeney the best play he ever saw, and of course this makes me think him very discerning."

From Paris she wrote to her students that

> say what we will about the modern theatre building, there
> is nothing in the world so like a theatre, so much a theatre
> as the Comédie Française; so red and gold, so crystal
> gleaming, so floridly aristocratic ... There is something
> about the bell ringing before the curtain—the long sustained
> ringing as the lights dim—that raises expectancy and the
> pulse beat.

"These letters get fearfully grimy," she added, "because I carry them around and write at odd moments—just now in a sidewalk café with an organ grinder playing and a man sweeping the street with an orange broom."

She kept thinking of Craig, hoping he could advise her about Philip. But when she arrived in Genoa, expecting him to meet her, he was not at the railroad station. Next day a letter from Mrs. Craig informed her that the Craigs had awaited her arrival for two weeks and then left the city. "Oh how ghastly!" Hallie noted in her journal. "They never received my letter."

Craig's next communication must have made Hallie realize that he was having an even more difficult time than she was. Her worries about marriage must have seemed small beside his feeling of having been abandoned by an uncaring world.

> I had thought to speak to you of an idea which I have in my head—but now you'll be going north and will not have any serious intention of altering all your plans—changing the whole course of your life—and generally joining an artist who both wants and needs some assistance—but who will be damned if he'll try and persuade anyone to render him any. Besides, I expect my road is a bit too hard travelling for anyone else. I've never provided myself with a big cash box, so as to make it easier—and no one seems ready to give me the funds for a theatre—or a school—or a centre—or even for "The Mask" which showed what it could do without funds. But then no one was ever ready to provide any artist with funds for his schemes.

He went on to say that he wanted to know whether she thought he could establish a center "by getting, say, 100 pupils and making a school with them and perhaps HF to look after them." Dartington Hall, he told her, struck him "as a trifle idiotic—pompous and purposeless . . . An idealist bent on reforming all things and with too much money to know how to do it is of little worth."

If Hallie did not quite arrive at Craig's view of Dartington, she had nevertheless been having second thoughts about the job. Ten days before hearing from Craig she wrote the Elmhirsts that she was feeling doubtful about accepting their offer. She had heard from the chairman of Vassar's English department, who was reluctant to extend her leave of absence, and from students who said they would not return to Vassar if Hallie was working abroad. She wondered if the Elmhirsts would like to hire her to run a summer course in 1935. "Mr. Lang and I could plan a wonderful course, and we might wish to do it for several consecutive summers."

There is no indication that Hallie ever considered Craig's suggestion that she run a center for him. She may have thought the idea financially impractical, and by this time she was even more unwilling to be second in command than she had been at the time of his earlier proposal. They continued, however, to exchange letters and in April Hallie heard:

> It's a good thing that your future husband is (interested in the theatre) for I suppose you have no idea of giving up that work—unless you took up Greek archaeology—why not?—or is it rude to suggest that? Well, it's not an entirely stupid suggestion . . . I don't know how it is in America but in England women more often like to help their husbands and share in his work than they like to ask their husbands to go in for the particular hobby or work which they happen to have been at . . . Thank God anyhow that you are not an artist for your days would be even more upside down than they are now. As it is you are in great demand all around—a husband demanding you—a great college ditto—a baronial hall ditto—a son and all your pupils—Why, you should be as happy as ten cinema stars.

With its statement that she was "not an artist" and its hint that she ought to be thinking of helping her future husband rather than expecting him to help her, the letter must have evoked a strong response. Perhaps Craig, because he was unhappy himself, was trying to upset Hallie. If so he succeeded. "It is of course difficult for me to comprehend," he wrote at the end of one of his letters, "why anyone should globe trot—going to five or six places instead of one. I am so convinced of the importance of concentrating and not dissipating in a work of this kind." This time Hallie exploded, and Craig in his next letter wrote:

> I note a rather sad or cross tone in your letter . . . I hope you've not been worried or ill. I suppose sometimes, when in love, troubles do come along and upset—but so do they anyhow—so no use worrying, is it? But I'm none the less sorry if you're grieved about anything. Oh by the way I'm awfully sorry to have thought for a moment that you are a globe trotter—so forgive me; . . . NO YOU ARE NOT a globe trotter and never were. You were, when I knew you,

a particularly charming puss-in-boots—and there it is—and
I am awfully sorry if you feel out of sorts but I'm sure you
will soon be yourself again.

She was not. From Naples she wrote to Esther Porter that her life was
a "stormy sea, very much at variance with the calm bay of Naples."
She might get married, she might go to Greece or Egypt, she might
even go home. In another letter she described herself as "hungrily"
reading the news that arrived from the Vassar theatre. Meanwhile
she and Philip were exchanging letters and telegrams, Hallie from
Naples, Philip from Athens. Hallie worked on a scenario for a play
she had thought up on the train from Genoa, then walked about the
city, spent a day by the sea, walked some more and during her
ramblings met tourists who provided her with "one of the most
exciting days" she had had in a long time. She described this in a
letter to her students.

> It really started Friday—that is to say, as I was leaving the
> hotel Friday morning an elderly American lady said to me,
> "I beg your pardon, but my husband and I are consumed
> with curiosity as to whether you are English or American."
> (This was doubtless the effect of my old tweed suit.) She
> then went on to say that they hadn't seen an American for
> weeks, that they were just finishing a trip around the world,
> and that they thought Naples horrid—"Just a line of hotels
> and men trying to sell you coral beads." I told her I never
> stayed in the vicinity of the hotel and asked whether she and
> her husband would care to come with me. So we started off
> on a wild day. We went to the flower market, and the fish
> market, we walked along the Esplanade and took tram 20
> and went to Villanova and looked down on the world, we
> had Turkish coffee and *mozzarella in carozza*, which
> according to my Italian means *cheese in a carriage* at a
> coffee shop, and we ended by going to a wild Dopolavora
> show. . . .
>
> Well, to get on to Palm Sunday, Mr. and Mrs. E. of
> Seattle were so thrilled by our day that Mr. E.—who, it
> develops, is a manufacturer of that silver stuff they put on
> radiators—well—someone has to. Only imagine enough

radiator polish to send people on trips around the world! Mr. E. decided, probably with what was left of the polish, to charter an airplane and take us to Rome for Palm Sunday. So we left in great state in a very small, shaky plane, with a grand Italian officer with cockfeathers hanging out of his aviator helmet in the most futuristic manner. Can you imagine rising over the Bay of Naples and soaring over terraced gardens, and then over Rome? Over the Tiber, over the Colosseum, over the white grandeur of Rome? We got very excited and Mr. E., who had had quite a few sips of white wine to fortify him for the experience, went so far as to say that Italy from the air was almost as satisfying as Hollywood.

Did I say that this was on the morning of Palm Sunday? There were endless processionals of monks carrying palms, and endless parades of the army and the navy, and more bands than I have ever heard, even at the N.R.A. Because by one of those curious strokes of fortune, we were seeing Rome not only on Palm Sunday, but on the occasion of the Plebiscite—every citizen had to vote for the officers suggested by Mussolini.

Hallie would soon have more to say about Mussolini.

The flow of letters between Hallie and Philip continued, their future plans still uncertain, until finally Hallie asked Philip to meet her in Naples. In her journal she wrote:

> It is best. I long to go to Athens and marry him—but I am not well enough and he must see just how I am and decide whether it is not too great a risk. At least—spring in Sicily— a week together—is something.

Years later a friend of Philip's would remark, "There was never any question who wore the pants in that marriage. Philip did. He was very protective of Hallie." And Hallie seems to have been well aware that this was true. At least in her diary she acknowledges that he must make the important emotional decision.

She had three days to wait for his arrival—it was the beginning of the Easter weekend—and she decided to spend the time visiting friends who had rented a house on the island of Capri. Here she witnessed, and thought "more impressive than anything I've seen in the theatre since I came," a torchlit procession of villagers winding their way through the town to the church on the night of Good Friday: first came schoolgirls wearing white dresses and black veils, next young men carrying swords veiled in black, then the old men of the village "bearing life-sized, horribly emaciated images of Christ." While more young girls holding dead lambs that dripped blood over their white dresses walked to the chanting of hymns in the light held by torches, the old women of the village, all of them dressed in black, wept in a way that reminded Hallie of Irish keening. "But Phil would not like Capri," she noted in her journal. "It is too fixed up—arty—gigolos with sandals and painted toe nails. I didn't like it except the beauty."

Back in Naples, Hallie unpacked, repacked, and waited for Philip. When he arrived, at eight in the evening on Easter Monday, they walked to a high point overlooking the city, ate spaghetti, drank white wine, and decided to go to Taormina. "We are in a trance," she wrote. For the moment at least Hallie was without fear. Whatever Philip decided, whatever he felt, must be right. "Phil says all I need is rest for a week, and then Greece and marriage."

At Taormina they booked a room with a balcony overlooking the sea and went off to visit the ancient Greek theatre. Philip walked around, taking notes and measurements. Hallie seated herself on the hillside, and looking out over Mount Etna, the Mediterranean, broken columns framing the sea, and a "riot of flowers," she described in her notebook the scene before her:

> wild geranium, scarlet poppies, white and yellow daisies, clover, pink asphodel, wild narcissus, bleeding hearts and great hedges of cactus and bowers of wisteria . . . The plain of Naxos stretches away to the sea—green lizards dart in among the rocks—a church bell rings in the town very far away. Aside from that no life, no sound. There is a certain silence about a place which is full of the sense of the past which is unlike the silence of nature alone . . . This vast theatre open to sun and wind, commanding views of unparalleled splendor, needs superpeople to fill it . . . It makes all modern theatres seem petty.

Two days later they went to Syracuse, which Philip described as
the "home of bigger and better tyrannies." He talked a good deal
about Fascist Italy and ancient dictatorships, drawing parallels
between them. In the evening they watched ships come into the
harbor and after dinner took a walk to the central square to see
Syracuse Cathedral and the Greek temple inside it. "We go to the
cathedral every afternoon to see the light fall across the Greek
columns," she noted. But even while Hallie was soaking up history
and being entranced by Sicily's beauty, she began to wonder if there
was something escapist about Philip's preoccupation with the past.
She wondered why archeologists made such an effort to understand
what had happened thousands of years ago when there was so much
to learn about what was happening in the present. When Philip told
her that one must know the past in order to understand the present,
she told herself he was right, but then wondered if he was. She felt
this way particularly on the day Phil took her to the outskirts of
Syracuse to visit its ancient fortifications. "Philip is climbing perilously about making measurements, I suppose, and re-living the
history he knows so well," she noted in her journal. She decided there
was something "formidable and sinister about this landscape":

> the tumbled gray rocks, like gravestones of the millions
> who died here—Athenians greedy for conquest, wanting a
> corner on Sicilian wheat and wine; Syracusans, and the
> mercenaries they hired, dying defending a city for Diony-
> sius; Carthaginians perishing of fever in the swamps.
> Thucydides tells all these stories and it is evident that I must
> read Thucydides ... To me there is futility rather than
> grandeur—all the youth wasted, all the strength lost, all the
> love kept waiting ... all a part now of yesterday's ten
> thousand years.

Ordinary activities—a puppet show and a good dinner in the
evening—restored her spirits. Hallie enjoyed the noisy audience at
the puppet show, with many spectators standing in the aisle, some
leaning on the stage, almost all shouting. "Phil suggests many ancient
audiences behaved this way—that the long declamations and bom-
bastic speeches were necessary to shout down the audience." Back in
their hotel room they discussed the future, and Hallie in a burst of

confident optimism decided that "Philip is always right and I am always wrong and I hope this is no exception." She would go through with the marriage, she would become a stepmother to his children, but first she wanted to see something of Africa. They decided that Philip would work at Syracuse and Agrigentum while Hallie went to Africa, and that they would then sail for Athens. Philip called her African trip her "flight into Egypt."

Next morning, watching him from the railing of the boat taking her to Tripoli, Hallie reflected on his qualities—"quietness, dear laughter, delicacy, strength, dark power"—and wished she could be "Aphrodite for him always." But she found herself once more questioning the marriage. As she watched Sicily and Philip receding she felt "more alone than ever in my life. Defenseless." To remedy matters, she began conversing with her fellow passengers. By evening she was drinking wine with them. Next morning she rushed on deck to take in her first sight of the African coast.

> palm trees rising from the sea against a sky of hard, fierce blue. Africa seems at first sight painted on the sea. There is no background, only a long low line of palms and white roofs punctuated here and there by mosques and minarets and by tall watch towers circled with black and white mosaics ... [It looks] theatric and unreal—exactly like a backdrop for a musical show.

In Tripoli she walked on the white marble esplanade along the sea, took special notice of the "abnormally brilliant" flowers and their "almost overpowering fragrance," mused on the "danger" that lay behind the African façade, and reminded herself that it was "absurd" to think that "anyone can know anything about Africa by coming and staying on the façade." "Officers in full uniform," she observed, were "everywhere." Hallie had made the trip to Africa to witness a dance and drama festival—tribes from various parts of the continent were doing native songs and dances "to preach the glories of Fascism"—and she found herself making comparisons between Russian and Italian propaganda:

> It is amazing to me to see how many of Lenin's plans for developing a state Mussolini has taken over. Many of his

speeches, which are posted *everywhere,* are almost literal leninism: his organization of the Balilla is like that of the Octybrati; the Dopolavoro is like the Komsomol—both with the important difference that the Italian stresses nationalism and the Russian internationalism.

The Dopolavoro, which was Mussolini's organization for the physical, artistic, and cultural life of the workers, existed, Hallie conjectured, to make Fascism acceptable. She and Philip had seen some of the government-sponsored artistic projects in Italy and Sicily and had discussed their political significance. Her interest in the Italian-sponsored African projects was also, apparently, more histor-ical than artistic, for once in Africa she took few notes on the dances and dramas she had supposedly gone there to see, reserving her enthusiasm for the Roman ruins being excavated at Leptis Magna and for the prehistoric temples on Malta and Gozo. "How it would amuse you," she wrote to her students, "to know that I am now whirling through the Libyan desert

> not via camel or donkey, but in a superb Isotta Fraschini car belonging to the Italian government . . . all because it is *Britannia* after all that rules the waves. Sir Ronald and Lady Storrs—His Excellency being late Governor of Cyprus and of Jerusalem are here—and Mussolini seems to have given them the keys to Africa—and they have adopted me—we are seeing everything and going everywhere—

Hallie did like traveling with people of means! She liked "whirling" through the desert because it made her feel like a special and privileged being. She liked living in style, liked having others attend to the mundane details that accompany the pleasures of traveling. So when the Storrs invited her to accompany them on an airplane trip to Malta and Gozo, she was delighted. But visiting the islands' temples and hearing myths about Ulysses and Calypso made her long for Philip, and, by the time she was on her way back to Syracuse a day later, she concluded that it had been "a long, long week" and she was eager to hear about Agrigentum and "daring to be happy."

Even after her return, Hallie continued to waver. At moments everything seemed possible; other times her doubts were so great she felt physically ill. One night she saw "pictures of people on the ceiling—sinister and strange." Two days before the date set for the wedding, Hallie was still noting in her journal that she was undecided and that Philip's tenderness and her love for him were "combined against" her reason. By this time they were staying in a hotel room in Athens. On the day before they were to be married, she was visited by the wife of one of Philip's colleagues, a down-to-earth woman and a scholar, who was later to say she thought everything Hallie told her—about being too old and not strong enough to take on the responsibility of a family—was ridiculous. Sensing Mrs. Sterling Dow's disapproval, Hallie told herself that she would always be an outsider with Phil's friends. She decided to leave for Naples the next morning. Once more it was Philip who reassured her. On April 27, after a morning Hallie characterized in her diary as "indescribably awful," she and Philip were married in St. Paul's English Church, with two of Philip's colleagues being "dragged off the tennis courts to act as witnesses."

Philip had spent much of his sabbatical studying building inscriptions on Delos, the small, uninhabited island in the Aegean that the ancient Greeks had worshiped as the birthplace of Artemis and Apollo. According to legend, Delos had drifted through the Aegean until moored by Zeus. There, atop Mount Cynthus, the steep crag in the island's center, Leto had given birth to his twins. Each May on the plains below, the ancient Greeks had celebrated the event with processions, dramas, and holy offerings brought over from the mainland. Philip knew the island well. He had done research for his doctoral thesis on Delos and was now doing further research for a book he planned to write. He persuaded Hallie that Delos would make an ideal setting for their honeymoon, although it contained only a multitude of ruins and a single, small house and museum for the use of the archeologists who dug there. Living conditions would be primitive—there was no plumbing or electricity—but they could bathe in the sea and they would be waited on by Jan and Janni, a father and son who had dug for Philip and had agreed to act as cook and housekeeper. During the morning Philip would continue his archeological studies while Hallie worked on articles and a play that she had begun on the subject of archeologists.

Hallie's first impression of the island was of a "blaze of white marble whipped by the blue Aegean . . . No trees . . . Scarlet poppies and purple ever-lastings thrust up from the ruins of temples, bazaar, and streets . . . A red mountain in the middle." Time, she was later to write, "is lost on Delos." The ancient Athenians had decreed that no one could be born or die there. Twenty-five years after her marriage, Hallie would remember how she had spent the two weeks of her honeymoon.

We rose at dawn and ran down to swim in the sea while the sun colored it with sheets of saffron and rose. We breakfasted on the stone terrace, Jan and Janni bringing us black bread, goat's milk and sometimes, with excited shouts, a plover's egg. After breakfast all three men would disappear into the museum adjoining the house where Phil was reading stones. And from then until noon the island was mine. I came to know every inch of its past and present, and every morning, under the bronze torso of Apollo, or between the paws of one of the little sphinxes, I would find a note from Phil—usually a few Greek words which sent me searching through the Greek lexicon. At noon we had another swim and breakfast all over again—and then we took a siesta lying on steamer chairs on the terrace, Phil reading Aeschylus until we fell asleep which was usually very soon. Then the museum again for Phil and Janni, while I watched old Jan slap our clothes clean on the hot rocks, or hunted for herbs by the sea for our salad. At four we explored the island and Phil would say, "I read a stone today that says that in 400 B.C. Nikias built a bridge from Samos to Delos, to bring over some dancing girls . . ." When the dark came down swiftly like a curtain, we would race back to the house where Jan and Janni had lit our lamps and heated water for our baths. One curious accident enhanced the whole picture—We had brought digging clothes to wear by day and thought we had brought the other suitcase full of just a change of tweeds. Instead we'd brought the one with our evening clothes, so every night on Delos we dined like the English in African wilds, in evening clothes. This had a profound effect on Jan and Janni—and the latter took the sailboat one day and reappeared with gold earrings and a red sash in which he served us fish or octopus, fresh herbs, red wine. After dinner was cleared away, they would come in and bow goodnight and we would see their little torches glaring down by the sea where they slept. They always locked us in before they left and we kept up the fiction that we should not breathe the night air—but they probably knew that after sufficient red wine we would dance on the flat roof or ride the marble lions in the moonlight.

These memories leave out many details, some of which Hallie no doubt preferred to forget. In the mornings she worked on her production plans for *Antony and Cleopatra* and on her play. In the evenings she and Phil wrote letters to their friends announcing their marriage. She wrote to her students that she missed them and was trying to visualize what they were doing. "Perhaps," she added, "in this environment I should subsist entirely on Theocritus." It was a hint, though only a slight one, that an environment of ancient ruins was beginning to pall. While Hallie was entranced by the beauty on Delos, she also felt a stranger in Philip's world, and the doubts she had had about marrying entered a new phase. In her journal she wrote:

> Day after day, sitting alone through the clear mornings or the heat-throbbing afternoons on Delos, looking out across marble columns and shattered temples to the sea, I think about the Delos of the past twenty-seven centuries. I'm filled at times with a sense of the past so strong that for a moment I am landing with the Syrian merchants at the long line of shops, I am walking through the portals of Cleopatra's house, a guest at some dinner party; I am with the processionals carrying torches and singing hymns to Isis; I am celebrating the Dionysos festival in the great theatre. Once, on the roof, looking out at night over the strange city, I had a complete sense of the day when this was a holy island, when nothing was here except the huge monolith of the god, with scarlet and purple flowers sweeping up in waves to the feet of the god . . .

Curious that part of me, on Delos, can be so animal like—bathing in the good salty sea, eating the strong earthy food—fish and herbs and rabbit and octopus and sheep's butter and goat's cheese and hard bread and red wine and onions and peas in the pod and lamb—sleeping in the silence so complete, so unbroken; and yet part of me be millions of stars away in time and in space. *Millions of stars.*

Each time Hallie entered the small museum adjoining the house where Philip worked, she learned something new about Delos. Philip pieced stones together and read their inscriptions. He translated as he read and told her what archeologists had discovered about the island's past. Each stone or fragment of stone he discovered added a bit of knowledge about ancient history. In the earliest centuries, thousands of celebrants had come to Delos from all over Greece to lay offerings and sacrifices at the foot of the shrine to Apollo. Men bearing gifts for Apollo came with dancers and wrestlers to entertain the populace. One, Nikias, came with a bridge of boats "built in Athens, adorned with gold, overlaid with dyed stuffs, garlanded, tapestried, joined with ropes of silver," as Hallie wrote in the long poem "Chorus for the Delian Apollo." Nikias also brought, as an offering to the god, a hundred bulls carved out of marble and mounted on columns. Others brought silver wreaths, gold crowns, lamps, painted bowls, and precious stones. Later in the island's history, various factions in Greece fought for possession of the island; and still later Delos was plundered for its archeological treasures. Hallie began imagining these later invasions as male assaults on the island's virginal purity. In her poem (later published in *Theatre Arts Monthly*) she imagined Delos as a symbol of female aloofness and inviolability. It was a symbol she had often used before.

> They all wanted Delos—
> Wind swept, wave bitten,
> Fitter for gulls, they sneered than for horses.—
> Yet they all wanted Delos.
> Most of them got her one way or another—
> Got her by a league and traded for a treaty,

Got her by accident and traded for a song,
Got her in a sea fight and sold her to a land lubber,
Hung her for a flag on a pirate ship.
Yes, they got her but they never had her.
Delos somehow never was had.
Never was a soft one,
Never was a kept one,
Never would promise to honor and obey.
Even when they hacked her up,
Cut her into pieces,
Dragged her off to Venice—those Venetian palaces—
Hauled her off to Tenos—all those little churches—
Hung her up in Paris,
Laid her down in Oxford,
Made her into turbaned tombstones for the Turks.—
Still they never had her.
Delos always stayed herself,
Delos had a self to be.

Philip's preoccupation with the island's history apparently brought back memories that Hallie had half forgotten. Her earliest experience of loneliness with a beautiful but unapproachable mother who submerged herself in order to serve her husband had faded. But it still lurked in the shadows, as memories do. Hallie's insistence that Delos "had a self to be," "never would promise to honor and obey," makes one think of the feelings she must have struggled with: her longing to be loved by an idealized mother versus her need to escape the bondage of loving and discover her own destiny. There is no other way to understand the terrors Hallie felt on Delos.

Every day is a cycle with me emotionally—the dawn about four is terrifying. I feel that this place and this marriage are driving me mad. Why did I do it? I have lost my life, my measured ordered life for which I've fought for ten years. I've lost in a way my identity. I'm no longer Hallie, but Philip's wife. He must increase and I must decrease. His work, strange, incomprehensible, I can never really grasp. I believe it is wonderful because it is reclaiming part of the past, adding to the sum total of human knowledge. But it is

of the past—and I am chiefly concerned with the present
and the future. Here is this language which I can never learn.
I feel a powerful sense of the Greek world, the Greek theatre,
Greek plays, Greek art—but it doesn't come through the
language. I have put myself in a position where, with Phil's
friends and work I must always be an outsider. All these
things rush through my mind, together with a sense of absolute terror at the new way of life and whether I will be equal
to it. I know that I changed the whole course of my life when
I married and I feel that only tragedy will result.

In striking contrast to these early-morning terrors was the
happiness Hallie felt when Philip stopped working and they walked,
lunched, and read together. At noon she would go into the museum
and, finding him there, regain a sense of peace. They would swim,
lunch, and take a brief siesta. Philip would read Euripides or
Theocritus, and Hallie would feel "perfectly happy in a deep and
complete content almost like death."

> Then afternoon—Phil goes, I try to work, I get in a panic
> again—and our sunset walks are a combination of anguish
> and ecstasy. I am afraid—of the place—of Phil—of all that
> is to be. I feel fatality. I think of suicide until it is almost
> madness . . .

Hallie must have conveyed some of these fears to her husband.

One morning Philip told her he had dreamed that she had lost
her head. At first this seemed terrible, he said, but then he found that
she could speak and hear and so it was all right. "Is this a sign?"
Hallie wrote in her journal. "Am I going crazy?" Fortunately, she
was able to summon a sense of humor. In one journal entry she
composed this brief poem:

> What will we have for dinner?
> —maybe trout.
> O light the lamp and shut
> the strange gods out.

At dinner, with the lamps lit and Philip beside her reassuring her that
he had never in his life felt so happy, the cycle of her day came to an
end. She felt "happy again." She knew "love and peace."

*   *   *

Back in Athens, Hallie settled into a more rigorous writing schedule. She was unhappy at having to spend their first days in Philip's old room at the American School, but there was nothing to do, as they had not yet found their own apartment. Although feeling that the people at the school were "strange beyond words," she made an effort, for Philip's sake, to be friendly, and after they moved into their own apartment she entertained his colleagues on several occasions.

Hallie's feeling of not belonging drove her to write a humorous short story somewhat in the manner of Anita Loos. The narrator is an American girl who has been invited to spend a weekend on Delos with a "Greek gentleman." "I was really quite pleased," the girl muses, because, "after all, Athens is almost all history and ruins and there is practically nothing to interest a girl after a few days. So I said, if Delos was an island like Capri it would be very pleasant . . . The gentleman said I would like it much better than Capri because it was a holy island with a statue of Apollo sixty feet high, and a theatre . . . So I had a manicure and packed four bags, even though the gentleman said it would be a quiet weekend and to bring nothing but heavy shoes." The story continues with the girl continually being surprised by the gentleman's preference for "uncivilized living." The boat they take from Mykonos to Delos contains people who do not wear shoes and stockings, and the gentleman is "coarse enough" to say that he is "going to get some wonderful squeezes on this trip." At the landing place, there is "not even a wharf or taxis or houses or even a hotel," and this is "very peculiar for a girl who always likes the Ritz and places like that." While the gentleman goes off to study stones, the girl takes a walk about the island and discovers that there are lots of flowers, "only they do not seem natural because they are spread out all over the whole place and not arranged in any kind of a garden." "Also there are crocodiles, I mean lizards that look like them hiding under the rocks with orange heads. All of the bugs seem to eat the red flowers and turn red. The worms turn purple, and everything, even the ocean, is very brightly colored and not what a person would expect." When she eats dinner with the gentleman, she is served by an "old man and his son with a fierce look like Douglas Fairbanks."

So then after dinner the gentleman said wasn't this the life and I said what about the theatre. So he said oh yes of course and on the way we'll stop in at a few shops and maybe pay a call on Cleopatra. So I went in and got dressed and felt quite cheered up, because I thought perhaps I have only seen one side of the island. Only I did not care so much to call on Cleopatra, because I always think it is better and simpler not to have too many ladies in a theatre party with only one gentleman. But she turned out to be a statue on the outside of her house which was also ruined. So we walked along the street and my worst fears were realized because the shops also fell down before Christ.

The theatre too turns out to be ruined, "everything lying around on its side and all extremely broken to pieces." And then Lorelei gets her biggest surprise of all—the gentleman says they are going to "ride the lions in the moonlight." Her motto being "never to let a gentleman know whether or not it is the first time you have gone for a lion ride," she acts calm and puts on her riding clothes. But she discovers that the lions are made of stone and were constructed before Christ was born. "I seem to think it is quite a strain on a girl to try to converse with a gentleman whose mind is full of things people were talking about before Christ." Her gentleman friend has turned out to be an epigraphist. "He takes broken pieces of stone and squeezes them together and reads what people were writing on them before Christ." Hallie never finished this story. She wrote it apparently simply to entertain her students.

Hallie had greater ambitions for the play she wrote in Athens, though it was never published or produced. *The Lost Aphrodite* is a more serious, though also humorous attempt to portray the scholarly world Hallie feared and from which she felt so alien. In it, the heroine, Pat, the wife of an epigraphist, wins out over her husband's erudite colleagues by discovering the statue that all of them have been trying to find. Pat, like most of Hallie's heroines, is pretty, flirtatious, used to being admired by men, and somewhat scornful of people who do not share her interest in the present and future, but she loves her husband and, though unhappy about living in Athens, determines to help him find the statue, the lost Aphrodite, because this is what is important to him. To his dismay, and that of his colleagues, she decides to dig, to put on old clothes and get down in the trenches and search. Though she breaks all archeological rules in the process, she discovers the Aphrodite and wins the respect of her husband's previously skeptical colleagues. Along the way, however, she manages to make her husband's work look ridiculous. When he declares that they must stay in Greece until the Aphrodite is found, she replies, "And when she is found, this Aphrodite, she'll look just like all the others—just like the miles and miles of Aphrodites on the shelves of museums—flat faced, with dents for eyes—another flat piece hacked in at the waist—a third flat piece with points sticking out for toes." When her husband says he wishes she would make "the slightest effort to understand Greek or archaeology," she is revolted. "A lot of full-grown men and women standing around panting with ecstasy every time a piece of baked clay is hauled out of a cess pool. There are too many ugly things in the world now without digging them out of the ground—too many things to be read in the world here and now without trying to squeeze ideas out of stones."

Pat's speeches sound like some of the sentiments Hallie expressed to Esther Porter a month later:

> My experience in Greece makes me know how great Russia is. This is the end of a civilization just as Russia is the beginning of one. It is valuable for me but I shall not come back here—my life is not in the past but in the present and future. Phil can do the past for the family and together we can try to relate it to the present.

A Nation in Crisis

HALLIE'S mood changed totally when she returned to Pough-keepsie. Back in her own world, among students and friends, she was still Mrs. Philip Davis, but, more important to her need for independence, she was still Hallie Flanagan. The new couple was warmly welcomed at the college. When President MacCracken, at a spring convocation of students and faculty, read aloud an announce-ment of their marriage, "all bedlam broke loose," according to Philena Lang, who recalled "screams and cheers of delight. They were both so popular." Hallie and Philip were wined, dined, and feted. They were seldom at home.

For the first few months of their marriage, home was a spacious Victorian house in downtown Poughkeepsie that friends of Hallie's allowed them to use while they looked for something more perma-nent. Hallie fell in love with the neighborhood, with its large, old houses, broad lawns, and carriage houses all testifying to a former era of prosperity. The Beale house was in a part of town that had once housed some of Poughkeepsie's most prominent citizens, though by 1934 at least half of these once grand houses were empty and in shambles. A few had been taken over by the local bank. Hallie went to the bank to inquire about rentals. One of the first she was shown, a modest but by no means small Victorian house, had a large brick barn out back with wild pink roses climbing the walls. The lawn and garden were both overgrown with weeds, and the summer house was filled with garbage, but Hallie saw at once what she could make of it. The inside, with its fading wallpapers and dark woodwork, was also in need of repair, but Hallie saw this too as a challenge. If the bank would pay for repairs, repainting, and repapering, she said, she and Philip would plan and oversee the renovations. The bank agreed to this and to a rental of $75 a month, and Hallie at once went to work to make the house light, airy, and modern. She had the woodwork painted white. She tore down walls and installed graceful archways to separate the living room from the library behind it. This was to be her study, and she had a desk built to fit into its large bay window. She outfitted a study for Philip in the room behind her own and turned the large garden room at the back into a playroom for her stepchildren. She bought modern furniture, including a dramatic semicircular couch for the living room to complement the pieces she and Philip already owned. 12 Garfield Place, when Hallie had finished remodeling it, was a modernized version of the spacious house her parents had occupied at 1421 Broad Street in Grinnell.

There were two differences. Hallie's parents had shared a bedroom and had made no division between adults and children. Hallie wanted a bedroom of her own and privacy from the lives of her children. She chose the largest upstairs room, the only one with an adjoining bath, for herself and the next largest for Philip. She divided the house into two separate living quarters, one for the adults, the other for the children. Since the house had two sets of stairs, this was easy to arrange. Frederic, like Philip's three children, had a bedroom near the back staircase for the times he came home from the Pawling School. The cook and nurse had rooms above. Everything was arranged to meet Hallie's needs. Not that she meant to isolate herself from life at the back of the house. She took a leading role in organizing birthday parties and holiday festivities, and when she had time she involved herself in her children's lives. But she knew that she needed time and space for her creative work. Philip had apparently agreed to this during the months when Hallie had agonized over the marriage.

A couple of years later, when Hallie was asked if she believed that marriage and the home interfered with women's achievement, she answered: No. "A woman must of course learn to balance these two elements," but she thought "that a shifting from absorption in a profession back to absorption in a home enables a woman to regard both home and profession with a fresher point of view."

"Really, it's some undertaking!" Gordon Craig wrote her. "In America that juggling as you call it is easier than it would be here in Europe." Craig thought Hallie would find her role as wife and mother the more important. "Oh I know, I know, what you will say but for all that, one thing is always in front of the other." He advised her to take care of her health and "rest whenever you can. That way, you give yourself twenty more years instead of fifteen." Craig did not know Hallie as well as he thought. Hallie's career came first. Though she was to regret this later when she was alone and in ill health, she must have realized at the time that she could not have acted otherwise. Theatre was her life after she married Philip just as much as it had been before.

After they had settled into Garfield Place, Hallie and Philip gave a housewarming party. Lester Lang contributed a wine press, and a week before the party he and Philip made wine. At this party, as at many which followed, Clair Leonard of the music department and Christine ("Tina") Ramsey, a former student of Hallie's who was currently teaching speech, were the entertainers. "Sometimes we turned up the rug and danced," Patsy and Bill Walsh recalled. Patsy, who had acted in *Hippolytus* as an undergraduate and afterward married a Poughkeepsie lawyer, remembered Hallie and Phil's parties as "not like twenties' parties where everybody had to have a drink. Hallie would say, All right, Clair, let's go to the piano. Christine would have a German or French or Italian costume and Clair would invent an opera. Tina would sing it. They had a whole repertoire. They created spontaneous farces." Tina remembered a game that was played at parties which took place a year or two later. "It was called Social Justice. We had to write on a paper who we would kill from the point of view of social justice, and who should remain living. You'd consider a whole bunch of people and you'd have to decide who you would throw out first." "Philip," said Patsy, "always came out on top. He would be saved because of the breadth of his concern for people." Christine added, "We didn't get personal. At least we tried to think we didn't. All of us were concerned with the state of the world."

Hallie and Philip's marriage—their home, their life together, and the parties they gave—seemed an idyll to many of their students. "I can still remember the magic!" one of Hallie's students recalled. "Their home seemed the epitome of what we all dreamed of—a daffodil in a vase, lightness and air, and books, books, books!"

Hallie had decided she wanted to produce *Antony and Cleopatra* when she visited Rome in 1927. The Ludovisi Aphrodite, the same statue that inspired her production of *Hippolytus,* also turned her thoughts to Antony. Later, on Delos, she concluded that heat had done Antony in. There was too much sun on Delos, she told Philip's sister. It robbed one of will power. In Rome Antony had been master of his faculties, but in Egypt he had behaved as though he were under the influence of drugs.

She began making notes for the production shortly before her marriage. In Tripoli she wrote in her journal:

> North Africa is full of Italian soldiers and it is amazing to see the subtle difference between them and their brother officers all through Italy and Sicily. In Rome or Syracuse the omnipresent soldiers were erect, stern, military, always drilling, marching, all apparently bent on emulating Mussolini. Here in Africa . . . the tropical heat has gotten into them.

Watching the soldiers lounging about the hotels and bazaars in their loosely worn white fatigue uniforms, she thought about color and movement. Later, in Paris, where she went to the Louvre to study Egyptian wall paintings, she noted that colors for the production "should be green and terra cotta, with much blazing white. The scenes in Egypt might show officers with white fatigue uniforms, with attendants in Arab or Turkish costumes . . . Soldiers in Rome could have green uniforms, and when Antony and his men came north they could put on blue-green capes over white . . . The women should look of no particular time, rather like terra-cotta figurines. Cleopatra's costume might be subtle blue-green with lapis jewels and anklets."

Louisa Fischer and Frederic Ferguson, about 1883

Hallie Ferguson with her parents, about 1892

Hallie Ferguson, age eighteen, starring in a high school production of *The Little Princess*

Kenneth, Hallie, and Gladys Ferguson, about 1903

Murray Flanagan, about 1908

Murray Flanagan, about 1915

Hallie Flanagan, about 1915

Hallie Flanagan with Jack and Frederic, about 1921

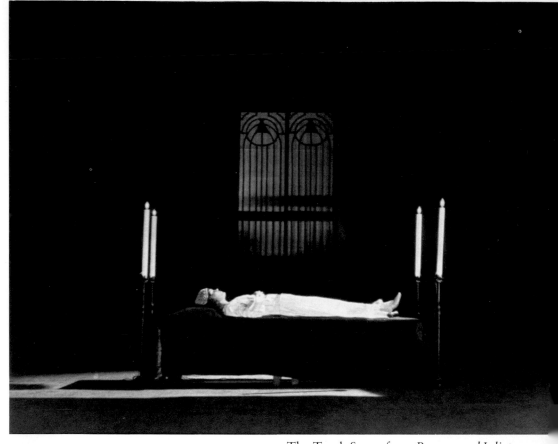

The Tomb Scene from *Romeo and Juliet,* 1925

Howard Wicks in 1925

Three versions of Chekhov's *The Marriage Proposal*, 1927

Dr. Horsley Gantt in Russia, 1930

Frederic Flanagan in 1928

Philip Davis on Delos, about 1925

Scene from *The Hippolytus of Euripides*, 1931

Scene from *Sweeney Agonistes* in *Now I Know Love*, 1933

Joanne, Hallie, and Philip Davis in the garden at 12 Garfield Place, Poughkeepsie, about 1938

Hallie and Philip Davis in their car, about 1938

Hallie Flanagan Davis and Harry Hopkins in 1935

Scene from *One-Third of a Nation*, New York production, 1938

Hallie Flanagan Davis, 1935

Scene from Muriel Rukeyser's *Middle of the Air* at the University of Iowa, 1945
Hallie Flanagan Davis, about 1937

ABOVE Hallie and Helen
Davis on the terrace of the
Northampton house, 1943;
LEFT Robert Schnitzer in 1943;
BELOW Hallie Davis with her
grandchildren, Frederic and Hallie
Ann Flanagan, 1943

She read what Plutarch had to say about Antony and commented:

> Plutarch is hard on Antony but all he says should be
> reflected in the playing of the role—his wastefulness, arro-
> gance (he believed himself to be descended from Hercules),
> his amours, his drinking bouts, his familiarity with his
> soldiers and with actors . . . His cruelty is important: not
> content with having Cicero killed, he had him butchered.
> Just the same, he was a born leader. His men preferred
> death with Antony to life with anyone else.

Antony, she decided, was "a divided person. He wants to eat his cake
and have it. Caesar knows what he wants and goes after it and is not
led astray by powerful appetites," as Antony is. Cleopatra also
knows what she wants: "She is absolutely cold, with the kind of
coldness that engenders flame . . . Her greatness lies not in nobility
but in fire, subtlety, childlike innocence, laughter, infinite variety, in
short, power." Hallie conceived her production in terms of opposites:
Rome on the one hand, Egypt on the other; Antony's indecision
against Cleopatra's decisiveness.

She wrote Quincy Porter of the Vassar music department asking
him to compose a score and detailing her ideas. There should be two
motifs: "the Egyptian motif, Cleopatra's motif, something not only
sensuous but haunting. Antony's Roman thoughts should be the
opposing motif, growing into battle sounds when needed."

By the time Hallie returned to Vassar, her conception of the play
was complete. She was ready to begin casting and planning the set
and lighting effects with Lester Lang. Casting for the most part
consisted of asking the people she had already decided would be right
for the roles. Gordon Post, a professor of political science, was the
tallest, most imposing figure on campus. He liked acting and readily
agreed to play Antony. President MacCracken, by this time a regular
in Hallie's shows, agreed to play Enobarbus. Several other professors
and some actors from town filled the other male roles. And in
November Hallie found "two real wrestlers and two coal-black and
very handsome Nubians for the street scene—People materialize
when needed for a play." She gave the role of Cleopatra to Kalita
Humphreys, a tall, handsome girl from Texas.

Hallie began training her students by having them read the play
rapidly and often, getting them to feel it "not as a succession of
scenes but as a rush of life and passion to an inevitable end." Her
conception was cinematic, just as her conception of *Romeo and Juliet*
had been.

> We all agree that the opening scene must strike the keynote
> of the whole production. We doubt more and more the
> usual stately procession ... If this was the way the lovers
> usually appeared before the public ... why would Philo
> say, "Look where they come: Take but good note and you
> shall see in him the triple pillar of the world transformed
> into a strumpet's fool." Also, Cleopatra's first line, "If it be
> love indeed, tell me how much," would seem very flat if she
> is merely being borne along on a litter fanned by eunuchs.
> The opening should give us the heat, languor and erotic
> excitement of Egypt, and a sense of the power pulling this
> man who bestrides the world like a colossus to the enchant-
> ing queen.

Hallie's scenic ideas were in keeping with her notion of the play
as pulling in opposite directions. Lester Lang designed a set that
consisted of sharp geometric shapes on one side of the stage,
sensuous curves on the other. "This is the design the audience sees on
entering the theatre. Lights change and in the darkness the design
becomes a place."

> To an accompaniment of street sounds, cries of the water
> boys and sweetmeat vendors, the stage begins to fill. Philo
> and Demetrius stroll in. A girl with a water jug comes
> around the corner and meets a soldier who laughs and
> draws her aside. Another soldier and two girls cross the
> stage laughing and talking. The soothsayer greets Mardian,
> the eunuch stands fanning himself. Other soldiers and girls
> lounge about and make love while Philo and Demetrius
> look on with disapproval ... Then when the heat and
> voluptuous quality of life in Egypt are established, excite-
> ment runs through the crowd. Philo makes his speech now,

"Look where they come," about Antony being transformed
into a strumpet's fool.

Antony, laughing, leaps into view at the top of the
ramp, looking back at Cleopatra, who appears in silhouette
against space, a vivid, imperious figure, a whip in her hand.
To the accompaniment of shouts and laughter from the
crowd she lashes him down the ramp. Antony, still laughing, takes the whip, breaks it across his knee and flings it
aside. Mardian comes up bowing and points to the wrestlers
who run down the ramp, turning handsprings. The crowd
shouts approval. The wrestling match starts. Cleopatra
watches, Antony looks only at her. She becomes excited.
Antony is jealous and sharply orders the wrestlers to stop.
The crowd is hushed. Mardian motions the athletes off.
Cleopatra, furious, whirls on Antony. He laughs, catches
her up in his arms and kisses her. From this embrace she
gives her first line, "If it be love indeed, tell me how much."

Shakespeare's stage directions for the opening scene suggest
nothing more than a stately entrance for his two principal players.
Nothing in the text gives any idea of Cleopatra lashing Antony with
a whip or of Antony's jealousy when Cleopatra is intrigued by
wrestlers. There is not even any indication that wrestlers are present.
So it was inevitable that some of the Vassar scholars would react
with surprise and annoyance on opening night. "At this point,"
Hallie recalled, "one of the members of our audience, a professor of
psychology, got up and left, saying audibly that she felt as if she were
in a brothel." Another professor present, a Shakespeare scholar who
did not get up and leave, was also critical of the opening scene. The
"brilliant street revel preceding the entry" she thought "justifiable
elaboration from the text," but Antony and Cleopatra should come
into it "set apart in dignity." The lovemaking ought to be public and
processional, "not wantonly personal." Hallie's reaction to this was
to point out, "Look at what the Romans thought about Antony's
behavior in Egypt."

Most reviewers wrote favorable notices. Even the Shakespeare
scholar who criticized the opening scene admitted enjoying the
production thereafter. She praised the acting and, even more, the

creation of place. "We were never at a loss to know where we were when it mattered. We were never troubled by a thought of where we were when it didn't. The triumph of the scene was the beauty of its colors, its masses, its lights and shadows." Another Shakespeare scholar, this one at Princeton, wrote Hallie that he had been studying and teaching *Antony and Cleopatra* for years. "I imagine you will have many people write you about the beauty of the acting and staging, but I want to write about the illumination of the play itself. The production was the most lucid, most brilliant exposition of Shakespeare's play that I have encountered. It explained certain obscure passages in a way which gave me a shock of pleasure. I must mention one thing particularly: the element of heat, of the tropical climate and its effect on the soldiers. This was something that had never struck me. Now, on rereading I see that you have indisputable evidence. I suppose it is important to you that your students speak the language of the stage so splendidly. For me it is even more important that they know what they are talking about." Coming from the scholarly world of which her husband was a part, this letter must have especially pleased Hallie.

She would have been amused by what President MacCracken later wrote about playing Enobarbus. "When I was impersonating Enobarbus in Shakespeare's *Antony and Cleopatra,* I was drawn in by Mrs. Flanagan after the first act one evening and given a pep talk. Mrs. Flanagan on such occasions excels all the football coaches I have ever heard in the variety and picturesqueness of her vocabulary, and in the resulting emotional reaction. This evening she wanted speed and was dissatisfied with our slowness of delivery. We went back to the stage determined to do or die for Hallie. Never was Shakespeare so speeded. We dashed from speech to speech. In the midst of the great purple patch of the play, when Cleopatra in her golden barge 'pursed up the heart of Antony,' the thought suddenly came to me, I am talking so fast Hallie will be pleased with me. This thought completely blocked the memory paths with the result that that night Cleopatra was left languishing upon her barge and never did get ashore." But MacCracken also recalled "Mrs. Flanagan's serenity in rehearsal, and her ability to wait for results." He thought her "that rare being in the theatre, a scholar and philosopher who thinks in theatrical terms. Every rehearsal of a play with her was a training in the logic of dramatic thought, as well as a delightful recreation."

Gordon Post later reflected: "If Hallie did not help me to overcome a dreadful shyness, she at least gave me a capacity to hide it. I thoroughly enjoyed working under her direction—and what a superb director she was!"

Hallie's assistant director, Anne Oliver, was less enthusiastic. The rehearsals exhausted her.

Hallie was a great one for notebooks. She wanted us all to keep notebooks. She wanted our interest in D.P. to spill over into our own lives. While working on *Antony and Cleopatra,* she said we should be scanning magazines we read for bits of information that had to do with the play. When the set was designed, she asked, Now what colors? knowing perfectly well what colors there were going to be. When we came up with black and white and sepia and peacock blue, she asked for proof. What museum had we found that in? What room? There had to be dates. It had to be absolutely right.

Those of us who had other interests found that our patience was tried at the end of a rehearsal. We would rehearse, getting the flow of the play and not stopping for details. Afterwards there'd be a break and we would sit down and she would start her endless notes, and after about five or six pages, you'd think, I can't stand one more, but there'd still be more pages. This would be 12, 1 or 2 o'clock. She saw things in such detail. She wanted every detail perfect.

We were all put to designing costumes. We looked at clothes of the period and abstracted from them. They were done with very little money. We had to improvise. Lots of us went to the Metropolitan Museum to study what was there.

Hallie kept saying, the speech must be colloquial, it must be hot. You've got to give the feeling of sweat pouring down . . . When we studied the play, we had to know every variation of every word in the text . . . Hallie wanted us to know how the play was done in its own time. That is the way she approached things. You were to find the equivalent in the present time for what Shakespeare was writing in his time.

She had a genius for casting. Kalita Humphreys was not a finished actress. She was not beautiful. She was a big, awkward girl from Texas, but she did the role beautifully . . . Hallie had tryouts, but you felt that it was already decided. She did have favorites.

Another backstage worker, Alison Murphy, recalled, "When Hallie would talk to us in the greenroom, I think we would all have gone out to slay dragons for her. Fatigue left and excitement took over."

Antony and Cleopatra, which was produced in December 1934, was the last play Hallie directed that season that did not focus on the economic crisis of the time.

In January President Roosevelt proposed a gigantic relief program of emergency public employment. Previous relief programs had proved insufficient to meet national needs, and the Democratic landslide of the November congressional elections gave the President the support he needed to push through a much larger spending program. Hallie, who had earlier criticized the President for doing too little, became an increasingly enthusiastic supporter of the New Deal from then on.

Clifford Odets's radical tour de force, *Waiting for Lefty,* which opened in New York on January 5, 1935, would later be called "the birth cry of the thirties." American playwrights in increasing numbers would henceforth focus their dramas on a world in crisis. Hallie had been one of the first non-Communists in America to use the stage to rouse public opinion against poverty and unemployment. She was to be joined by hundreds more in the coming four years.

In the last week of February, when the Nunan bill, which would have required every student entering a college receiving public funds to take an oath of allegiance, came before the New York State legislature, a group of Vassar students marched to Albany to protest. William Randolph Hearst responded by publishing an editorial in the New York *American* which he titled "Keep the Faith of Our

Fathers." The Vassar students, Hearst declared, were ridiculous and immature; they should be sent to bed on bread and water. As for Vassar's "authorized disseminators of Communist propaganda such as Hallie Flanagan," what was to be done with them? Hearst implied that they should be sent to Russia.

"Many on the Vassar faculty were Norman Thomas Socialists at the time," one student recalled. "Hallie was not more Left than others on campus." But she was more in the public eye. Through *Shifting Scenes* and the articles she had written about Russia for *Theatre Arts Monthly* she had become known as an authority on Russian theatre. By producing *Can You Hear Their Voices?*, *American Plan*, and *Miners on Strike* she had come to be known as a theatrical propagandist for leftist causes.

Hearst's editorial, reprinted in newspapers across the country, brought a flood of mail to Hallie's office. To most inquiries Hallie replied, "You and Mr. Hearst are equally in error. I am not a Communist and I cannot give you the information you seek." To her former Grinnell student Junius Wood, she answered in more detail:

> No, my dear Junius, I am not a Communist. Things aren't as simple as that to me and perhaps I lack the apostolic zeal. At the same time I have no intention of teaching drama in a teacup or running a theatre as a pick-me-up at a time when, as you so eloquently put it, "ten million can't get work, those who have saved through their lives are impoverished by sumptuary legislation, and others have incomes of a million a year."

At the end of her letter, Hallie suggested that if Junius wanted to know what the Vassar theatre was doing, he should come to Poughkeepsie to investigate. Like President MacCracken, Hallie believed in motivating students to become involved in the world around them. She had more interest in raising problems than in solving them. American college students, MacCracken went on record as saying, had been censured for showing indifference to political realities and had been represented in novels and plays "as mere children playing at life." Colleges teaching politics, economics, and history, he thought, must expect their students to participate in the political movements of their day "just as colleges which teach music expect to have a glee club that amounts to something in the way of serious music." That had been President Main's philosophy also. So when a student in Hallie's playwriting class and her boyfriend wrote a play that raised the question of what relationship should exist between a liberal arts college and the economic disturbances around it, Hallie was naturally interested. She decided to produce it.

"Herb Mayer and I," Doris Yankauer recalled later, "got the idea of writing a play together in order to have a legitimate excuse for spending lots of time together. Those were the days when Vassar students were allowed to have boys visit their rooms on Sundays between four and four-thirty, with the door open. Herb came from a middle-class Jewish family like my own. Like many of us, he was a rebel against the society which had so much poverty in the midst of wealth. He had lost his job in a publishing house in the depths of the depression and was doing such things as organizing longshoremen." Their play, *Question Before the House,* opens with a college president urging his students to take part in the life around them. In subsequent scenes students participate with workers in a strike at a downtown factory. Many picket, one is injured, and one falls in love with the young strike leader.

"The play has its faults," the *Vassar Miscellany News* editorialized, "but it is nevertheless an honest attempt to grapple with a very pressing problem ... Its action may not have been uniformly dramatic, but it was swift enough and pointed enough to have caught the attention of Vassar. Several good friends have already come to blows over the issue it raises, and that really was its purpose, to raise an issue, not to solve it." Following the proposed Nunan bill and the protests organized at Vassar against it, the production was timely.

Doris Yankauer recalled an embarrassing first-night incident: "Hallie thought Herb was a genuine representative of the working class. It was a long-established custom that after the first night of a new play there was a very elegant party for the cast and all concerned at Hallie's house. Evening dress was always worn. Hallie, without telling me, had explained to everyone that in order to be tactful to our young working-class representative, everyone should wear ordinary clothes. Meantime I had persuaded Herb to dig up evening clothes. It turned out that we were the only people there in tuxedo and long dress!"

Yankauer felt she never quite knew where she was with Hallie. "Hallie was rather easily offended and might lash out at someone who had generally been in her favor." Hallie did not like a critical review that Yankauer and Mayer later wrote for *New Theatre* magazine about one of her shows, and wrote to the editor about it. As a result, Yankauer and Mayer were never asked to write another review. "And yet years later," Yankauer said, "after I had decided to try to get into medical school and Hallie was Dean of Smith College, I wrote a cautious letter asking if she'd be a reference for me, but please to tell me if in all honesty it would have to be lukewarm. She wrote me a lovely letter and sent a superlative one to the medical school. Her anger didn't last long, and she certainly didn't bear grudges."

Although Hallie was eclectic in her tastes (the same season she produced the propagandistic *Miners on Strike,* she also did Pirandello's *The Man with the Flower in His Mouth*; the season she did *Can You Hear Their Voices?* she also produced *Groceries and Notions,* a lighthearted comedy written by one of her students), it was her left-wing theatrical experiments that caught the public eye. Many young people interested in the arts began to regard Hallie as an authority in this field, among them the future historian Arthur Schlesinger, Jr. Schlesinger wrote Hallie that he was preparing an article about left-wing theatres for the May Day issue of the *Harvard Advocate*. He had heard that she was doing a better job with propaganda plays than anyone else and hoped she could help him in his research. "We are not a propaganda theatre," Hallie wrote back, "though we have done plays on social justice." She added that audiences at Vassar had shown less interest in workers' plays than in plays like *Question Before the House,* where the issue focused on the right of students to participate actively in economic affairs. Hallie wanted to set the record straight: she was a theatre person with radical beliefs, not a radical intent on using the stage to disseminate propaganda.

Around this time—the spring of 1935—the American Communist Party adopted a new, more tolerant policy toward non-Party leftists. Before 1935, Communist Party members had labeled Socialists, Roosevelt supporters, and other liberals as Fascist reactionaries.

The new Popular Front policy fostered unity among formerly divided groups and brought new middle-class members into the Communist ranks. Communists and non-Communists now saw themselves united in a just cause.

The play Hallie chose to direct as the climax of the six-week theatre workshop she organized in the summer of 1935 came as no surprise to those aware of her interest in experimenting with new and unusual works. When Hallie had seen W. H. Auden's *Dance of Death* in London the previous year, she had thought the production frowsy, muddled, bungled, and confused. "You know I once wanted to do it," she wrote her students, "as a geometric design visually, and as a study in conflicting rhythms. Now I never want to see or hear of it again." But several months later she changed her mind. Auden's play had not been produced in America. It represented a challenge.

Dance of Death, which Hallie retitled *Come Out into the Sun,* may have become exciting under Hallie's direction, but it remained somewhat confusing. That, anyway, was the opinion of local critics, who considered the poetic drama too erudite, not right for a popular theatre. One such reviewer thought the play was not even intended to communicate a message. Hallie disagreed. The reviewers, she decided, *did* understand but "didn't like what they understood. For the play is not a pleasant play."

Hallie decided to interpret Auden's poetic drama not as a struggle between capitalist and working classes "but as the picture of all of us who think and talk about a better life for more people, but secretly like our own comfortable way of life . . . We take refuge in retreats from reality—the night club, various mystic cults, war, hatreds and persecutions, anything to avoid facing the truth—that the new life will come about only when we desire it enough to do away with these evidences of death."

"I do not pretend that Auden is clear in the tell-everything-three-times manner," Hallie later wrote. Auden in this play often escaped from the deeper meaning he meant to convey into twenties-style parodies and pure tomfoolery. He enjoyed playing with language; he was no propagandist. To Hallie, though sometimes a propagandist herself, this was a relief. Auden's combined use of twenties' frivolity and thirties' social concerns appealed to her. She too liked to alternate between the lighthearted and the serious.

Reviewers, even those who claimed not to understand Auden's meaning, were mesmerized by the production. Clair Leonard, who had quickly become a favorite of Hallie's after he joined the Vassar music department, wrote the score. Lucretia Barzun, who taught at the Wigman School of Dance and had recently married the Columbia historian Jacques Barzun, directed the dancers. Both, under Hallie's guidance, helped to give the production its "gay, merciless" tempo. One reviewer compared "the one lonely dancing figure of Death played against choruses in bright odds and ends of costumes" to the "acid precision of the sharpest Picasso." The "modernistic" setting, flexible enough to become at one moment a reviewing stand, at another a ship at sea, at still others an airport or night club, was considered effective.

As the lights dimmed, the Announcer, in silk hat and scarlet sash, ran up the ramp, a part of the abstract set, to call on all interested in celebrating to "come out into the sun." The chorus, composed of playboys, belles, "gents from Norway and Ladies from Sweden," and all others wanting excitement and reform, gather to chant:

> We shall build tomorrow
> A new clean town
> With no more sorrow
> Where lovely people walk up and down.

At this "moment of high resolve," Death comes onstage from the audience. "Do not be mistaken for a moment about this stranger," the Announcer says,

> The lives of many here are already in danger.
> He looks on the just and the unjust as he has always done.
> Some of you think he loves you. He is leading you on.

Death, as the play proceeds, takes away the scarfs of the chorus and replaces them with epaulets and chains. Auden's point is clear enough, and it is curious to note that some people ignored it. William Rose Benét, writing in the *Saturday Review of Literature,* saw in it what Hallie had seen: "the irony of the time and the panic of pleasure," the wish on the part of the middle classes to go on living for pleasure at a time when their compassion and understanding were sorely needed.

Hallie's son played a role in the chorus. Frederic, who had finally managed to get himself expelled from Pawling School for smoking, had come home in the spring to become part of the Garfield Place household, where he found himself the much-admired elder brother of Philip's three children. For the first time in years he had a family, but it was a family that would soon be disrupted. His mother, he learned, was in the process of taking on a new job, which would keep her away from home for weeks at a time.

PART

II

The Federal Theatre
1935–1939

Launching the Project

THE Emergency Relief Appropriation Act, which Congress passed in the spring of 1935, allocated five billion dollars to create jobs for the unemployed. Roosevelt's belief in work relief instead of handouts for the unemployed had won the day. "I am not willing," he said in his famous speech on this subject, "that the vitality of our people be further sapped by the giving of cash."

One of the men who had worked hardest to persuade the President to this way of thinking had been Hallie's old school friend, Harry Hopkins, and it was Hopkins who got the huge task, through the hastily created Works Progress Administration, of putting the jobless to work.

Although Hallie and Harry had met infrequently since leaving the small Midwestern town where they had grown up, they had followed each other's career with interest. Harry knew of the plays Hallie had been directing at Vassar, and Hallie knew of the work Harry had been doing for Roosevelt—first as head of the New York State relief program and then as head of the Federal Emergency Relief Administration. A year earlier, when Hopkins was setting up this first federal relief operation, he had phoned Hallie to ask her advice about a small theatre project he was creating in New York City. At the time Hallie, who was preparing to sail for England, had told Harry she might take a job at Dartington Hall. She was to recall his reply—"I don't know what an American wants to do in an English theatre"—because she came to feel the same way.

In high school and later at Grinnell College, Hallie and Harry had been friends but never close friends. Harry was later to recall that he had once held hands with Hallie, but Hallie had no such recollection. Harry, she said, was full of hokum. He was also a practical joker, on one occasion leading freshmen on to drop stink bombs on sophomores during the annual sophomore-freshman class battle. Harry was high-spirited and ambitious, but his ambitions were hidden. Most of his classmates recalled only his rowdiness just as Hallie's classmates mainly recalled her enthusiasms. Harry thought Hallie would make some track or football star a great wife. She used to "stand on the backs of people," he said, "to cheer on Grinnell's teams." Neither had any idea that they would one day be working together to put into action the philosophy President Main had espoused at Grinnell. Neither had any idea of the extent of the other's commitment.

What Hallie and Harry did have in common was their love of the arts. Grinnell fostered that interest. The arts were not just taught at Grinnell, they were a focus of campus life. Everyone went to hear music at the college chapel on Sunday evenings. Classes and clubs put on plays and other forms of entertainment. Poets and dramatists came to lecture and to read their works aloud. Everyone who knows anything of Hopkins will recall that he began his career as a social worker. Few know that when he went on Keats' Walk on Hampstead Heath, he felt exalted, as though he could "reach out and touch the poet—quite like a dream." He never lost his love of poetry, music, and theatre, even after he became Roosevelt's closest confidant, even after he dedicated his life to helping America win the Second World War. His love of the arts led to the creation of the four WPA Arts Projects.

The first small projects Hopkins set up under the Civil Works Administration were widely criticized. The public, Hopkins soon learned, did not share his concern for unemployed painters, musicians, writers, and theatre folk. "Hell," he replied, "don't artists have to eat like other people?" He thought violinists, painters, and actors should not have to build bridges and highways to keep their wives and children from starving. They should be given a chance to preserve their skills. They were a part of America, just as bridge builders were. Brusque and outspoken in his comments, sometimes rude, Hopkins discovered that although he was becoming a target of the conservative press, he was also winning the President's confidence. Roosevelt too wanted unemployed artists included in his new relief program. A few months after the WPA came into being, Hopkins phoned Hallie to ask her to meet him in Washington.

Hallie meantime had read of the President's intention to pour several million dollars into four Arts Projects—one for painters, another for writers, a third for musicians, a fourth for men and women of the theatre. Hopkins's phone call could only have meant one thing to her: he was looking for people to run them. To say that she leaped at the idea of heading a nationwide theatre would be overstating the case. She had not yet been offered the job and had no idea what it would entail. But she was excited and immediately went into action. After telegraphing several people, she spoke on the phone with Elmer Rice, who said he would meet her anytime, anyplace to discuss the future project. Rice, a successful Broadway playwright and producer, told Hallie he had already formulated a plan that involved leasing theatres in one hundred large cities, putting a permanent stock company into each, and using the theatres for art exhibits, concerts, and dance recitals as well as plays. Subsidized by the government, these centers would be free from the commercial considerations that dominated Broadway. Commercialism, Rice thought, was murdering the American theatre. It was the enemy of experiment, innovation, and everything artistically worthwhile.

By the time Hallie and Elmer (the latter, in Hallie's words, looking "very unpressed, rumpled, rosy and rather unkempt") reached the Pennsylvania Hotel in New York at five the next day, their elation had grown. Over cocktails they talked "very rapidly, often in unison." After Roosevelt's intentions became known, said Rice, a lot of New York theatre people had gone to Washington to ask Hopkins for money. Eva Le Gallienne wanted financial help for her Civic Repertory Theatre, the president of Actors' Equity wanted money to subsidize the commercial theatre, one Broadway producer asked the government to establish a million-dollar fund to subsidize producers. Rice admitted that he too had gone to Washington to ask for $100,000 for a pet project of his. "Oh God," Hopkins told him, "all of you people are driving me crazy. Don't you know someone with no axe to grind?" "Whereupon," said Rice, "I mentioned you." Hopkins got up and shook Rice's hand. Hopkins too had thought of Hallie but did not want to be accused of favoring a friend.

In Washington Hallie found Harry much as she remembered him—"nice, brown and humorous," and to the point. The job he wanted her to do, he said, was a "tough" one. Was it even possible? Would people go to the theatre to see plays put on by actors on relief? Hopkins must also have been wondering if people would go to concerts to hear musicians on relief or read books by writers on relief. To Hallie this problem was no problem at all. Talent, she was sure, existed wherever one sought it. It needed only to be unearthed; artists out of work were no less artists. Employees wouldn't be workers on relief after they started, she said. "They'd be theatre workers again. People would come if the plays were good and wouldn't come if the plays were bad." It was a point of view Harry very much wanted to share and he told her to draw up a plan.

At the White House later that afternoon, Hallie found Mrs. Roosevelt just as eager to discuss the artistic merits of a federally funded theatre project as Hopkins had been. Recalling the ambitious productions of Shakespeare, other classics, and modern plays that Hallie had put on so inexpensively at Vassar, the First Lady asked if it would be possible to do something similar for the Federal Theatre. And would a federal theatre be accepted if in the process of entertaining people it also taught them (as so many European theatres did) something about the world they lived in? Naturally Hallie thought this was worth trying. Mrs. Roosevelt's ideas were in tune with her own.

But back in Hopkins's office, as she read reports on the arts projects Hopkins had set up in 1934, Hallie began to wonder if the job she was being offered was for her. The purpose of these early projects had been to provide relief, nothing more. The job, she told Hopkins, was humanitarian. What he needed was a social worker, not an artist. Hopkins persuaded her to withhold her decision until after she had met and talked with the other three directors of the Arts Projects: Henry Alsberg, a journalist and former anarchist, who was to head the Writers' Project; Nikolai Sokoloff, former conductor of the Cleveland Symphony Orchestra, who was to head the Music Project; and Holger Cahill, an expert on American folk art, who was to head the Art Project.

At Alsberg's house that evening, everything seemed possible. Everyone had a plan: Cahill wanted to send artists to various states to photograph early functional art for an Index of American Design, Sokoloff wanted symphony orchestras all over the country, Alsberg had an idea for producing state guides, Hallie suggested dramatizing contemporary events in a series of Living Newspapers. None of the four doubted that talent existed among people on relief. They talked about grouping inexperienced and experienced artists in apprentice-master relationships and about the audiences they hoped to find. All four had lived in small communities and were convinced that such communities would be interested in concerts, plays, and art exhibits offered at affordable prices. Millions of Americans, they told one another, had never seen a living actor on a stage. Millions of children had grown up all over the country with no opportunity to see or hear anything of artistic merit. The vision the four directors shared that evening was not just a vision of artists developing their skills while audiences nationwide became more receptive to good art, though that was part of it. The Arts Projects, Hallie concluded, could be "part of a tremendous re-thinking, re-building and re-dreaming of America." They would represent "the new frontier in America, a frontier against disease, dirt, poverty, illiteracy, unemployment, and despair." Her dream and that of the others was the dream of the New Deal rooted in the ideals of the Progressive era—the era that had shaped liberal thinking earlier in the century.

Hallie returned to Poughkeepsie in a state of elation. Philip, she knew, would support her in whatever she wanted to do. He always did.

But it was 1935. Women were expected to stay at home, or if they did work they were expected to return home at night. The job Hopkins was asking her to do was going to mean living in Washington during the week. It was going to mean taking trips and staying away from home for weeks at a time. Even if Philip agreed to all of this, he was not going to like it. Hallie was well aware of how much her husband needed her, so after she told him about everything that had happened to her in Washington and about Mrs. Roosevelt's hope that she would take the national job, she added firmly, "But I'm not going to do it. You, Fred, and the children all need me. And I need all of you, and nothing is as important as that."

Philip listened in silence; perhaps he smiled a little. Hallie's roundabout way of tackling a subject when her conscience troubled her was something he was familiar with. Hallie did not allude again to the topic until after she and Philip had had dinner, read to the children, and gone outside to sit in the garden. But finally she did. Years afterward—long after Philip had died—she was to recall his response: "You know, darling, don't you, that you will *have* to take that job. All the forces of your life have led to it." Wanting then to be cavalier, he added, "It will be all this and heaven too." Despite the gallantry Philip understood—as did everyone who knew Hallie—that when she wanted something badly enough she allowed nothing and no one to stand in her way.

Hallie never minimized an opportunity. She set her sights on the stars. So when Hopkins asked her to find jobs for unemployed theatre workers, she decided she would also lay the groundwork for a national federation of theatres that would continue to function even if federal subsidy was later withdrawn. After formulating a tentative plan, she told Jacob Baker, who was Hopkins's assistant, that the government would be doing more than caring for the unemployed, it would be "creating a national theatre and building a national culture." The challenge, as Hallie saw it, was to organize theatrical enterprises "so excellent in nature, so low in cost, and so vital to the communities involved that they would be able to continue indefinitely."

The idea of a national federation of regional theatres had been in the minds of many people for several years. In June 1931 Hallie had met in Chicago with leaders of community and university theatres from all over the country to formulate such a plan. Members of what came to be known as the National Theatre Conference, many inspired by the example of George Pierce Baker, were dedicated to providing America with quality theatres not dominated, as Broadway was, by the profit motive. Most members also believed the theatre had an important social and educational contribution to make to American culture. These rebels against the commercial New York theatre included, among others, Jasper Deeter, director of the Hedgerow Theatre near Philadelphia, Gilmore Brown, director of the Pasadena Community Playhouse, E. C. Mabie, teacher and director at the University of Iowa, and Frederick Koch, who headed the theatre at the University of North Carolina. *Theatre Arts Monthly* under the leadership of Edith Isaacs had been publicizing their work for years. Isaacs, in fact, had been the chief organizer of the National Theatre Conference, and she was one of the first people Hallie got in touch with after Hopkins asked her to go to Washington. But it was Mabie who was to contribute most to Hallie's plan for a Federal Theatre.

In June, Hallie wrote Mabie that she was thinking of organizing one hundred community theatre centers across the country. Mabie's reply was exultant: she was going to "change the entire course of American drama for years to come." Thus encouraged, Hallie asked for his help, and within days his letters, filled with an unending supply of "wonderful ideas," began arriving in Poughkeepsie.

Working at top speed while also running a summer theatre at Vassar, Hallie had soon hatched a plan encompassing five production centers. New York, Los Angeles, Chicago, "possibly Boston," and "possibly New Orleans" would each house a professional company and also act as a retraining, playwriting, and research center. Resident companies would do new plays, classical plays, and other kinds of dramas that commercial theatres could not afford to try. Touring companies would play a circuit of smaller theatres, and university or civic theatres in each of the regions would develop playwrights and conduct theatrical research. Hallie would mandate general policy from Washington, but each region would develop its own drama in its own pattern. It was an ambitious, all-encompassing plan, and Hopkins was enthusiastic. He suggested announcing her appointment as Federal Theatre director at the National Theatre Conference meeting that was to take place at Iowa City in July.

On a train headed west, Hallie and Harry talked excitedly about what was uppermost in Hopkins's mind—the role government had played in building America. Hopkins saw his new work program as a cooperative venture: the unemployed would receive wages from the government and in return help build a stronger America. Suddenly he asked Hallie, "Can you spend money?" Hallie laughingly replied that an inability to spend money was not one of her faults. But Hopkins was serious.

"It's not easy. It takes a lot of nerve to put your signature down on a piece of paper when it means that the government of the United States is going to pay out a million dollars to the unemployed in Chicago. It takes decision, because you'll have to decide whether Chicago needs that money more than New York City or Los Angeles. You can't care very much what people are going to say, because when you're handling other people's money whatever you do is always wrong. If you try to hold down wages, you'll be accused of union-busting and of grinding down the poor. If you pay a decent wage, you'll be competing with private industry and pampering a lot of no-accounts. If you scrimp on production costs, they'll say your shows are lousy, and if you spend enough to get a good show on, they'll say you're wasting the taxpayers' money. Don't forget that whatever happens you'll be wrong." He was preparing himself, as it turned out, for the questions he was to hear from the next night's audience.

Farmers from all over Iowa gathered on the University of Iowa campus to hear what Roosevelt's administrator of relief, was going to tell them about the WPA. "He was never above a certain amount of hokum," Hallie recalled, "and on that occasion he pulled a piece of business that would delight any stage manager. It was a hot night and the farmers were in their shirtsleeves. Harry painted the picture of poverty and desolation before work relief had come along, launched the work theme, built up a thrilling story of what it could do. He came to a climax and at that point someone in the crowd called out, 'Who's going to pay for all that?'

"That was the question they had been waiting for. Harry looked out over the crowd. He took off his coat, unfastened his tie and took it off, rolled up his sleeves. The crowd got perfectly still. Then he said, 'You are.' His voice took on urgency. 'And who better? Who can better afford to pay for it? Look at this great university. Look at these fields, these forests and rivers. This is America, the richest country in the world. We can afford to pay for anything we want. And we want a decent life for all the people in this country. And we are going to pay for it."

The next day, addressing members of the National Theatre

Conference, Hopkins spoke of the "new kind of theatre" he hoped would emerge as a result of federal subsidy: "I am asked whether a theatre subsidized by the government can be kept free from censorship, and I say, yes, it is going to be kept free from censorship. What we want is a free, adult, uncensored theatre." In mid-1935, with the New Deal riding high, Hallie had every reason to believe that Hopkins could keep such a promise. She was to spend the next four years doing everything within her power to hold him to it.

When the newspapers announced Hallie's appointment the following day, reactions were mixed. The favorable articles described Hallie as a "practical idealist" and a producer of plays "vitally related to modern life." She was said to have the "confidence of important people in the professional theatre" while remaining outside it. And *that*, murmured several Broadway professionals, was exactly what was wrong: how could a college professor from a fancy girls' school find her way through the labyrinths of the commercial theatre? Such a gigantic undertaking as heading Federal Theatre should have been given to one of them. And then from England came a point of view which in its generous appraisal of Hallie's talents was in sharp contrast to all the rest. "Almost any routine production of the theatre workshop at Vassar," said Alistair Cooke in an English broadcast, "makes half the productions of the West End or Broadway look like the village concert."

Hallie took the oath of office on August 27, 1935, her forty-sixth birthday, in the Old Auditorium, a vast hulk of a building in Washington that was under reconstruction to accommodate several thousand WPA, PWA, and other government workers. Gray partitions divided the hot, airless hall into cubicles, and in one of these, under the glare from overhead lights, Hallie began the task of learning government procedure while putting ten thousand theatre people to work. She had the help of the statistical and legal divisions of the government, Lester Lang and Esther Porter, whom she had brought from Vassar, and a curly-headed young man named Mr. Bowser who (Hallie told her husband) "loves the theatre and is very excited at being connected with anything so great." His enthusiasm, she confided, "is rather nice since there is such a lot of gloom, with Lester sitting head on hand and talking about the pain of it all."

Up to this point in her life, Hallie had managed to accomplish a good deal using little more than the enthusiasms, energies, and youthful talents of amateurs. She liked working with inexperienced young people, because it gave her a chance to mold them. Besides that, she realized, as many theatre people have before her, that amateur talent, properly focused and directed, can often produce professional, or near professional results. But talent in the theatre is not the same as talent in managing a government bureaucracy, and Hallie did not seem to understand this. Even with the best will in the world, and with a willingness to learn, her former Vassar associates would have had a difficult time coping with the vast machinery that was necessarily involved in setting up a federal project. Lester Lang became discouraged early and resigned after a few months. Esther Porter, who made a persistent effort to learn government procedure, was slower in realizing that management was not her métier. As for Hallie, she often—and from the beginning—became so impatient with government procedure that she simply side-stepped it. While some people rejoiced at her tactics, others uttered cries of dismay.

The obstacles in her path were more numerous than she cared to admit. Even such simple matters as getting desks and secretarial help for her regional directors could be held up for weeks by state administrators accustomed to dealing with road crews and building supervisors but not with artists. Often these administrators refused to endorse Hallie's appointments. All she could do was register protest. But when a situation arose which gave her the opportunity to override government procedure, she seized it. The earlier theatre projects Hopkins had set up in several cities were due to end in late September. Just before that time Hallie learned that hundreds of people who had been hired by these projects were about to lose their jobs because Federal Theatre procedures for transferring them had not been worked out. Reacting impulsively, Hallie wrote a memo to a WPA official asking if she could keep these people on the government payroll. Then, without waiting for approval, she wired her regional directors to do it. When the WPA official in charge learned what she had done, he "raised hell. So now he is answering," Hallie wrote Philip, "God knows what. I suppose Go to Hell, until our statisticians get their commas right. I am trying very hard to keep from exploding with rage at the damnable stupidity of it."

Fortunately, there were days when the frustrations seemed more amusing than infuriating. After one such day Hallie and Holger Cahill "took refuge in the smokey lounge at the Powhattan Hotel." Hallie said they "must not let Sepsis have the advantage." Cahill said "hopefully" that maybe the government would liquidate the Arts Projects as they had the National Recovery Administration and then he could go back to writing his book on American folk art and Hallie could go back to directing plays at Vassar. But Hallie did not want to go back to directing at Vassar. Despite the difficulties, she was finding her job in the national arena an exhilarating challenge. For some time she had been looking for an opportunity to expand her horizons. Now that she saw the possibility of imposing her artistic vision on theatres across the nation she wanted to keep on.

The difficulties did not stem just from government bureaucracy. Hallie had been given a few lists of theatre workers who were on relief. An administrative organization for labor projects was in existence, but there was no organization for anything as complicated as a theatre, with all the necessary interlocking departments needed to fashion sets and costumes, choose plays, assign parts, and issue publicity. No policies had been formulated on how to lease theatres or pay royalties; agreements with unions had still to be made. Hallie had appointed some regional directors, but more were needed. Above all, she was faced with the task of funding projects and getting actors on the payroll. A friend and author, Barrett H. Clark, to whom she turned for advice, wrote Hallie saying he wished she could delay action for at least a year to "clarify our ideas." But there was no time to clarify anything. The pressure from Washington was for quick action. Some twelve or fifteen thousand people had to be put to work at once. Hallie was "comforted by the thought that these dots and lines we work with all day may really turn out to be human beings who will actually go back to work."

She wrote to Philip every night. "Oh darling," she told him, "I hope I can do it. I can only do it with and through you." That Hallie could only have done the job with and through Philip was also the opinion of those who knew them best. "She was always asking his advice," recalled Vernon Venable, one of Philip's closest friends. "He called her every night." "She depended on him completely," said Patsy Walsh, a good friend of both. "She was a big person but she made mistakes, and she would have made a lot more without Phil. She shared everything with him, the frustrations, everything."

In mid-September the four Arts Projects moved from the Old Auditorium into a Florentine mansion, the former house of the owner of the famed Hope diamond, Evalyn Walsh McLean. Elegant chandeliers hung from elaborately painted ceilings, the walls were papered with silk or paneled in mahogany. There were huge bathrooms with Roman tubs and gold faucets. Gold-tasseled ropes were draped along the stairways, and a marble court was "presided over by a horrible gigantic Neptune and rows of baffled looking busts." Despite her amusement, Hallie did not fail to notice that the Music and Art projects got the "choice outside rooms" and the Writers' Project got the handsome ballroom, while the Theatre Project was assigned what she considered the ugliest room in the house—the dining room, "a huge, dark tomb in the middle." Sokoloff, Hallie was told, had been given preferential treatment because he was sensitive to noise and distraction. With "Titian babies goggling down at us," as she put it to Philip, she began negotiating union contracts.

Officials representing at least twenty unions (among them Actors' Equity, the Dramatists' Guild, the International Alliance of Theatrical Stage Employees, and the Workers' Alliance) had been invited to Washington from cities across the country to talk about wage scales, hours of work, and touring regulations. Hallie met first with the stagehands' representatives. She had always liked stagehands, she told Philip, and stagehands had always liked her. She apparently felt she would have no trouble getting them to agree to WPA wages, which were lower than union rates. But she was wrong. These "successful-looking men in business suits, derbys and diamonds" delighted Hallie by chewing on cigars and asking "intelligent, hard-boiled questions," but in the end told her that unemployed union stagehands would not sign up for relief (a prerequisite for all WPA workers in the nonsupervisory category), would not accept WPA wages for full-time work, and would never, under any circumstances, work with nonunion stagehands, whom they described as amateurs. "Their demands," Hallie wrote Philip, would "have to be gotten around." They never were. As a result, all union stagehands had to be assigned to the supervisory category. They worked fewer hours than those who signed up for relief.

A second kind of problem arose at Hallie's next meeting with unions. This time representatives from at least twenty different unions were present. According to Hallie's legal counsel, Irwin Rubinstein, Actors' Equity president Frank Gillmore led off by stating that no union leader present would participate in the talks until the representative from the Workers' Alliance had been asked to leave. The Workers' Alliance, which had been set up in 1934 to represent unemployed persons with no other union affiliation, had no business, said Gillmore, at a meeting of professional unions. This narrow-minded view incensed Hallie, who replied that the Alliance represented many Federal Theatre workers and therefore had a right to be present. When Gillmore threatened to absent himself and to take all the other union representatives with him, Hallie insisted she would not ask anyone to leave. According to Rubinstein, there was a mass exodus. "But she won her point," he added. "The professional unions had to return and work things out with the Alliance."

A more pressing problem from Hallie's point of view was finding the right person to run Federal Theatre in New York City. New York had more theatrical workers than any other city. There was more theatrical talent there than elsewhere. Hallie guessed, rightly as it turned out, that the unit in New York would become the showcase and inspiration for others in the country. After reviewing names suggested by friends and advisers, she approached Sidney Howard.

Howard had recently dramatized the story of Walter Reed's search for the cause of yellow fever in a play called *Yellow Jack*. *Yellow Jack* was part documentary, part melodrama, and as such not unlike the plays on social themes Hallie had produced at Vassar. In choosing Howard, Hallie hoped he would adapt the documentary form to the needs of Federal Theatre, which, on express instructions from Hopkins, was not to compete with the commercial theatre. But Howard, who was busy with his own affairs, turned her down. Her second choice was Elmer Rice, a more feisty personality than Howard (one critic said he devoted his life to dissent) but, like Howard, a middle-of-the-road liberal. Rice told Hallie he would consider her offer, and in time he said yes.

As Rice's assistant Hallie appointed Philip Barber, one of the young playwrights she had studied with at Harvard, who had since that time worked with the Group Theatre and Theatre Union. Barber was later to say he thought Hallie had given him the job to "keep an eye on Rice," because Rice was considered unpredictable by Washington WPA officials.

In the New York office of *Theatre Arts Monthly,* with the assistance of Edith Isaacs and her associate editor, Rosamond Gilder, Hallie was trying to find people able and willing to run Federal Theatres in other parts of the country. Those chosen to head the regional projects would have to be willing to deal with the miles of red tape the WPA insisted upon. They would have to be energetic, dedicated, and visionary if they were to see the creative possibilities, under stringent government regulations, of administering huge theatrical centers, each employing a thousand or more workers. They would have to accept small salaries and cope with monumental frustrations. The men Hallie hoped to find, Sidney Howard predicted, could not be found. Indeed, Hallie sometimes felt this herself. Her letters to Philip in the fall of 1935 alternate between hope and despair. It was her humor and sense of fun, as always, that came to her rescue.

After appointing actor Eddie Dowling as her national adviser on vaudeville, variety, and circuses, she wrote her husband that she had found him to be "an absolutely new character in my experience." Dowling at their first meeting discoursed "earnestly and effusively, interspersing all his remarks with explosives. . . . Listen," he told Hallie, rising out of his seat and hitting her on the shoulder, "know what I think when people say to me, Eddie, why in Hell are you mixed up in this relief stuff? I say, Listen, the man in the White House is a swell guy. Listen, do you know anyone else paralyzed, a cripple, denied the pleasures of life, making good to that extent? Me, I'd have crawled under cover to die somewhere." He elaborated a plan: he would get Masons in various cities to loan Shriners Halls for road company shows. . . . But in fact Dowling did nothing of the sort. As soon as he found Federal Theatre more of a headache and a challenge than he had bargained for, he resigned. Hallie registered no complaint when he did. By that time resignations had become the order of the day.

In her search for sponsors, Hallie asked the Urban League if it would help launch a Negro Theatre. She asked the Dramatists' Guild if it would contribute space or money or both for a playwrights' theatre. She asked Actors' Equity about the possibility of supporting a unit with rotating companies in three New York boroughs. Some of these ideas worked out, some did not. When she met with members of the League of New York Theatres to ask if they would sponsor a managers' tryout theatre she felt at first that she was getting nowhere. Martin Beck, whom Hallie described as "very bitter and very antagonistic," led off with a series of questions as to why *real* theatre people had not been consulted before Federal Theatre was set up. Other League members told her that no talented people would be found among actors on relief and that Federal Theatre, if it did produce good shows, would be competing with Broadway. Hallie pointed out that these two views were contradictory and was pleasantly surprised when Lee Shubert, disagreeing with his colleagues, declared that Federal Theatre might actually *help* Broadway. "If people who can't pay for *our* theatres," he told Hallie, "go to *your* theatres, then they'll want more and they'll come buy our cheap seats." This thought changed the tone of the meeting. Before it ended, Hallie had managed to win personal support from several members, and she got her tryout theatre. As *The New York Times* put it the next day, "The managers arrived in no very sympathetic frame of mind. They left saying she would do. And that, if you know your old-line managers, is praise."

Others in the New York professional theatre world were not so sure. "Frankly," Eva Le Gallienne remarked to members of the Town Hall Club, "I am terrified by the large sums of money being given by the government to assist dramatic work in this nation. . . . It is a vast mistake to feed the people of the nation upon very malnutritious and downright bad food when they can get the best food."

Through it all, and despite the resignations, delays, and frustrations, Hallie found pleasure in what she was doing. And it was not all work. One afternoon Katharine Cornell invited her to tea in a "long, mirror-filled room with gorgeous red curtains at one end and the river seen over a balcony at the other." She then "went over to Mr. Altman's store" and in two hours bought her entire winter wardrobe—a moss-green dress, three-quarter ocelot-lined coat to match, a soft brown afternoon dress, and a brown and green felt hat. She wrote Philip she hoped he would think she looked "fascinating as hell." Martin Beck, whom she now considered a crony, capped her day by sending her two tickets to Maxwell Anderson's *Winterset*.

By October 8 Hallie had a staff: regional, city, and state directors gathered together for the first time around a long conference table in the McLean Mansion. While the Hearst newspapers complained about how much money was being spent by the federal government to lease the mansion, Hallie pointed out to her new directors the irony of meeting in a place which had been built when art was "a commodity to be purchased by the rich, possessed by the rich, and shared on occasional Wednesday evenings with the populace."

She pushed the point further. "During my first days in this house," she said, "I was haunted by a sense of having gone through this experience before." She remembered a theatre meeting in the Great Hall of Mirrors in Leningrad. "Stalin, Litvinov, Lunacharsky, Petrov, and other leaders of political, educational, and theatrical life" sat in chairs once occupied by the Empress and her officers. Their purpose? To discuss how "the theatre could serve in educating the people and enriching their lives."

A year, even a few months, later Hallie would have hesitated before associating Federal Theatre's purposes with those of the Soviet Union. Such statements provided ready fuel for those newspapers which hated Roosevelt and all his innovations. In early 1936, however, Hallie was not yet aware of the lengths to which the press would go. Nor was she aware of how little Stalin really cared about "enriching" the lives of Russians.

Who were the people who sat round her table? For the most part they came out of noncommercial, regional theatres. When Hallie had tried to appoint commercial theatre people, she had met with some curious reactions. One story she told was of approaching a young, enthusiastic Broadway producer. "But how," he wanted to know, "can I manage on $200 a week?" She had had to explain that she was talking about $200 a *month*. Her early appointees did, of course, include some people from the commercial theatre. Rice was one, Eddie Dowling another; the actor Charles Coburn had hesitantly agreed to be director for New England. But these were exceptions. Jasper Deeter, who had left the Provincetown Playhouse to found the

Hedgerow Theatre, agreed to take charge of Pennsylvania; for the Midwest there was E. C. Mabie; for Chicago, Thomas Wood Stevens, who had established a department of drama at Carnegie Institute in Pittsburgh before taking over the Goodman Memorial Theatre in Chicago; for Ohio, Frederic McConnell, director of the Cleveland Community Playhouse; for the western region, Gilmore Brown, who directed the Pasadena Community Playhouse; for the South, dramatist-director John McGee and Frederick Koch, creator and director of the North Carolina Playmakers; for the Bureau of Research and Publication, Rosamond Gilder. It was an impressive group—though some members had already told Hallie their collaboration might be part-time or temporary.

Jacob Baker began the meeting by explaining that the regional Arts Projects, though directly responsible to the national directors, would operate through state WPA offices. He went over regulations: 90 percent of all employees must come from relief rolls; one nonrelief supervisor could be hired for every twenty employees on relief; production costs could amount to no more than 10 percent of labor costs. Other officials explained financial policies (for example, forms must be submitted in triplicate before funds could be applied for), outlined procedures to be followed when sending reports to Washington, and described how audition boards were to be set up and projects established. As the explanations went on and on, Hallie looked around the table and "felt that there was nothing such a staff could not accomplish." She could not, of course, know what her directors were thinking nor anticipate that Charles Coburn, who appeared to be "in a fog," would resign immediately after the meeting adjourned. Several others, it would transpire later, were beginning to wonder how anything good could come out of so many complicating and limiting government stipulations.

Hallie's colleagues might have been cheered by knowing how much worse things could have been. Two weeks earlier she had been shocked by a mandate coming from the army: a Washington official, Colonel Westbrook, had decided that "all appointments in the arts were to be stopped, including secretarial help, until political endorsement was secured." Without waiting to hear what anyone else might think about this latest frustrating interference, Hallie went straight to Hopkins, who responded by telling Jacob Baker that the Arts

Projects were special and should be treated as such. The upshot was that Federal Theatre got a "declaration of independence." "The new procedure," she wrote Philip, "gives us complete and almost terrifying power. Let us hope we won't be hoist by our own petard. I feel it is magnificent, especially the note signed by Hopkins and Roosevelt saying that each federal director is free to appoint personnel without any political endorsement." She obviously enjoyed her conspiratorial role, for she added that the "best part" was that "the others" did not know how the original limitation had come to be changed.

"We live," Hallie told her staff, "in a changing world. Man is whispering through space, soaring to the stars, flinging miles of steel and glass into the air. Shall the theatre continue to huddle in the confines of a painted box set?" The movies were experimenting, so must the stage. "If we have six thousand people on relief we all know that probably four thousand of them are not of the calibre to experiment. However, we must keep steadily in mind that we do not work with the six thousand alone." Others could be chosen to lead them—and must be. In her mind, Hallie had already carried Federal Theatre far beyond the confines of a relief project. She was later to say, and to be criticized by WPA officials for saying, that Federal Theatre had been set up to give quality productions to the people of America. Herein lay the difference between the WPA officials Hopkins appointed to regulate the Arts Projects and Hopkins himself. Hopkins hoped Federal Theatre would contribute to the national culture. Most WPA officials had no sympathy with this purpose. The Arts Projects, they believed, had been set up solely to provide jobs. The Workers' Alliance, which represented the unemployed, agreed. It was left to Hallie, as artistic director, to try to balance relief needs with artistic achievement.

The men Hallie addressed, those who sat round the McLean dining room table, had helped lead American theatre out of the nineteenth and into the twentieth century. Most were leaders in the fight to build appreciation for the arts beyond the narrow confines of Broadway; all knew what Hallie meant by experimenting and expanding horizons. But being leaders, most were too busy with their own jobs to take on the exacting task of organizing federal projects.

Not these people, then, but others—younger and not yet known for their achievements—were to contribute most to building Federal Theatre.

An office on the mezzanine of a bank that had closed near Times Square served as Hallie's headquarters when she was in New York. Here, overlooking 44th Street, or in the public banking room below, Hallie spent hours questioning the people who lined up each day at the tellers' windows to fill out applications. Here she met men and women of every age and degree of talent. Some, retired from the days when stock, road, and vaudeville had flourished, had worked under famous actors like Sarah Bernhardt and Edwin Booth. Others had spent their lives walking briefly onto stages to announce, "Madame, the carriage waits" or "Dinner is served." Hallie was not surprised to find desperation in some of these faces—in the early days she saw a man "go mad, beating his head against the wall" when he did not immediately get work—but she was taken aback to discover how many of these people had lost pride in their work.

Under earlier relief projects in the city, plays that did not require royalty payments because no one wanted to do them were produced after two weeks' rehearsal in schools, hospitals, and settlement houses. Troupes toured Civilian Conservation Corps camps and army posts, but there was never any money for settings, properties, or costumes. When Hallie tried to suggest that things would now be different—that she valued these actors' talents and meant to produce good shows—she was told, "The theatre may be art to you, but to us this project is a bread-line." Her first job, she realized, must be to give these people back their dignity. "Please bear in mind," she told them, "that you are not being offered relief or charity but *work*. . . . Write me if you have any complaints about the way your application is handled." She herself had many complaints about the way things had been handled under the old regime, though she did not say so to those on relief.

The man who had taken charge of the Civil Works Administration theatre project in New York was a Colonel Booth, and he was still on hand when Hallie arrived there. Hallie and Booth clashed at once on what kind of people were to be hired by the Federal Theatre. Booth said all that mattered was what Broadway roles an actor had played. Hallie said everything, including an actor's education, was important, and told Philip that her "thoroughly amateur point of view incensed the Colonel to the point of frenzy, but I overrode him." She was determined to attract vigorous new blood, people like those who had joined Theatre Union, Group Theatre, and the Provincetown Players. When she wrote Philip that "my one qualification for this job is my housewifely instinct," she did not mean her impulse to tidy up but rather her determination to "rake out all the dead leaves." Sidney Howard told her that "the greater part of our unemployed actors should be hurried out of acting as quickly as possible . . . and relieved of the constant misery of encouragement in a profession for which they are not qualified." Hallie agreed.

The difficulty in getting qualified theatre people was time. The WPA administration in Washington could not understand why an arts project should differ from any other WPA project. When, for instance, a road project was decided on, administrators called for *any* two hundred unskilled laborers; they did not requisition by name. Hallie pointed out that for a Theatre Project audition boards were needed so that those most qualified should be selected. But WPA administrators kept pressing Hallie to hire people and get going, and the press demanded to know why setting up Federal Theatre was taking so much time. Where were the plays the theatre was supposed to be producing? "It was a struggle," Hallie admitted, "in which all of us were trying to bend government machinery to the needs of show business."

Elmer Rice was meanwhile feeling harassed. Telling Hallie there was no time for auditions, he hired large numbers of people without knowing whether they had talent or experience. Some, it would turn out, had neither. Rice had an answer: they could be fired later. Hallie, who was also feeling harassed, let Rice have his way. There were other matters to think of, some more troubling even than the hiring of actors.

Where, for instance, were her producers going to put on their plays? Equity and other union leaders set up cries of unfair competition when project officials suggested leasing theatres in the Broadway area. Meantime, weeks went by while Hallie and Rice tried to discover why the Treasury Department had still not released money for theatre rentals. Who was responsible? Everyone she talked to passed the buck. Finally, in a rage, she phoned Baker in Washington.

"Well, Hallie," Baker replied calmly, "why are you so upset? You don't want to get upset over these things, they're all part of the game."

"These Arts Projects," said Hallie, "are becoming a joke; they're being ruined by stupidity, inefficiency, and delay."

"Whew!" said Baker. "That's quite an accusation."

Most of the unions were adding to the turmoil. Equity officials said WPA salaries should equal prevailing union wages; Actors' Forum insisted that Federal Theatre ought to maintain a closed shop; Workers' Alliance sent delegations to Hallie's office to complain of discrimination against their members, and all the unions set up howls of protest when Washington decreed that no one who had not applied for relief by November 1 would be eligible for a job in any of the Arts Projects. And while all this was going on, *Variety* was informing its readers that Federal Theatre was headed by a "pedagogue" and that some of her appointees, like Elmer Rice, had "distinct radical leanings." Of course no curtains had gone up, *Variety* exulted: Federal Theatre was just another of Roosevelt's ill-advised boondoggles.

"*You* try getting up a few curtains," Hallie flung at the newspaper's editor in an imaginary soliloquy. "I'd like to see you sign a thousand requisitions in triplicate without going to Alcatraz. I'd like to see you satisfy at once the demands of governmental procedure and of ten different theatrical unions, every one with a different wage scale. I'd like to see you break this contract jam without breaking heads and landing in jail." "The number of editors and critics thus profanely apostrophized," she was to say, "would have staffed our much needed and nonexistent promotion department."

Elmer Rice continued to feel equally frustrated. "Do you enjoy working for the government?" he asked one supervisor before launching into an attack against the "lousy red tape," the "piddling details," and the number of times he had to sign his name. "It used to be worth a hundred. I must have signed it down to a nickel in just about three weeks." He said he was about ready to cry quits. But in fact he was no more ready to than Hallie was.

When she got discouraged, and sometimes so exhausted she felt ill or "in such a state" that one of Philip's letters made her weep, she would remind herself of "the Ferguson clan cry—Nothing has defeated us!"

Imagining Philip weeding the garden, teaching a class, or writing in his study, she gained the reassurance she needed to keep on living a hotel existence. "Did you have a nice day, Angel?" she inquired in one of her October letters. "When I call you Angel, I do not mean with white wings and a halo like Christmas cards, but dark and slightly frowning at the entrance to a garden. I have always meant to explain this to you, but we never have time to talk."

On weekends Philip played a double role: chauffeur and nurse-maid. If Hallie was unable to get away, he went to Washington to be with her. If she was in New York, he drove there to pick her up. When she needed rest, he ordered her to bed and made sure she stayed there. Anyone who threatened that rest, he banished. Hallie's characterization of her husband as the angel standing at the entrance to a garden was apt. But more than an acknowledgment of his protective role, her description served to keep him playing the part. If Hallie took Philip's ministrations for granted, she was always careful to express her pleasure and gratitude. "What fun this weekend, darling," she wrote, thanking him for taking such good care of her. "I love the car, the house, the four assorted children, our entire strange and beautiful marriage"—strange because Hallie had reversed the roles as they existed in most marriages. Philip's support enabled Hallie to go on believing that Federal Theatre was "vast, exciting, discouraging, but still potentially superb."

As 1935 drew to a close, she told Rice that his "belief and fortitude" would soon be justified, and she sent similar messages to her other directors. In New York she had finally obtained six theatres—the Biltmore, the Manhattan, Daly's, the Lafayette in Harlem, the Willis in the Bronx, and the Shubert-Teller in Brooklyn. To run New York's units she had hired five directors. She also had a *Federal Theatre Magazine* and a Bureau of Research and Publication. Her first four months' work had borne fruit. She began to pack for a trip across the country that would take her to theatre centers being set up in Chicago, San Francisco, Los Angeles, Dallas, and New Orleans.

Hallie had high hopes for Chicago and the Midwest, but the plans she had made were proceeding slowly and under difficult conditions. A few weeks earlier she had suggested to her regional directors that they make "courtesy calls" on their WPA state administrators. Mabie discovered that Iowa's administrator was interested only in exercising control by making political appointments (which made it impossible to get good people in key positions), and both he and Stevens, in charge of the Chicago theatre, had experienced many other frustrations, including the usual delay in getting actors on the payroll. They were thoroughly discouraged. Remembering how she had felt only a few days earlier, Hallie tried to encourage them, but it was not an easy task.

Hallie seized on the few encouraging signs. Stevens had organized an experimental unit which was preparing to produce Meyer Levin's *Model Tenements,* a play about housing in Chicago, and arrangements were under way for putting several vaudeville units in the parks. Meeting with the vaudevillians, Hallie explained Federal Theatre and was delighted when one of them, a tap dancer and contortionist, got up and said it was a "proud moment" in theatre history. "I certainly like these human beings better than the Opery crowd," Hallie wrote Philip, wishing he had come with her because she thought he would have liked the "big crudeness and tremendous maleness of Chicago . . . Everything is violently colored—the influence of Joseph Urban."

There was a press conference at which Hallie found herself "on the spot" with antiadministration reporters who made valid criticisms about the project's slow progress ("though needless to say," she assured Philip, "I did not betray the U.S." by agreeing). And Harry Minturn, a Chicago director, amused her by telling her how theatre used to be in the Windy City: Al Capone, he said, bought sixteen tickets for every show he attended, two for himself and the rest for his bodyguards. You never knew when you might get mixed up with a "first-class shooting."

She went on to San Francisco wondering if she would find her California directors as downhearted as Mabie and Stevens. But the contrast between the Midwest and West was heartening. Gilmore Brown, in charge of the western projects, and J. Howard Miller, who headed the one in Los Angeles, had the situation "well in hand." Miller, who had directed a theatre-choral-music project under the State Emergency Relief Administration, was an experienced administrator. In Los Angeles he had workshops, offices, rehearsal halls, and a research bureau in a six-floor building in the garment district.

Plans were going forward for a vaudeville theatre, a Yiddish theatre, a Negro theatre, an experimental group, and marionette and dance theatres. The California Project, part in Los Angeles, part in San Francisco, was one of the largest in Federal Theatre. Scores of theatre people who had formerly worked in stock had settled there hoping to get into movies.

There was only one major difficulty: the WPA administrator for Southern California, a Colonel Connolly, wanted to have nothing to do with any of the Arts Projects unless he could have "complete authority over them." Meeting with Hallie, Miller, and Brown over dinner, he told them he had been trained in the army and believed in military discipline. If the government wanted to set up Arts Projects it was no business of his, but they either came under him, in which case they would be operated exactly like every other WPA project, or else they didn't, in which case he washed his hands of them. When Hallie reminded the colonel that Hopkins wanted the Arts Projects directed nationally, he said every state administrator had told Hopkins it wouldn't work. "Is that good army discipline?" Hallie asked. "Isn't Mr. Hopkins your superior officer?" When Connolly laughed, she felt reassured. The evening ended well, Connolly gave Brown and Miller total control.

It was getting close to Christmas. Hallie had spent more time in Los Angeles than she had originally intended, but she decided to make one stop, in Dallas, on her return trip. But Dallas turned out to be an unfortunate choice. The WPA administrator in charge had recently seen a production of *Waiting for Lefty,* done by the man Hallie had appointed to run the Texas project, and he decided as a result that Hallie's appointees were dangerously radical men who might corrupt the values of Texans. "Do old plays here," he was to tell her some months later. "We don't want to get into the papers. Do plays that people won't notice."

Hallie's overall supervisor for the South was John McGee, who had studied with her at Grinnell and then directed the Birmingham, Alabama, Little Theatre. He recommended starting theatre units where there was community support for them—New Orleans, Birmingham, Jacksonville, Tampa, Miami. This Hallie was to do, but Federal Theatre in the South, as she admitted later, was slow in getting started.

She returned to Washington with a bird's eye view of her projects across the nation. In preceding months she had gone to Hartford, Boston, Philadelphia, and other nearby cities. She now had some idea of which projects might meet her ideal of the new, the vigorous, and the outstanding and which would probably not. New York would lead the way, primarily because production groups like Theatre Union, Group Theatre, the Workers Laboratory Theatre, and the Provincetown Players had been trying out new plays in new ways for years. When these groups came to an end, many of their members became eligible for relief and went on to Federal Theatre. They and others like them were to provide the bold, inventive leadership that Hallie sought.

She reached Poughkeepsie just in time to spend Christmas with her family. Although during the past weeks Hallie had occasionally worried about her children—had they forgotten her?—she quickly dismissed this thought in the rush of preparing for Christmas. Of all celebrations Christmas was the high point of Hallie's year. She planned for December 25 as though she were planning a major production. 12 Garfield Place vibrated with her comings and goings during the preceding days. Philip bought and set up the tree. He and Hallie decorated it together. Philip bought presents, and Hallie wrapped them, each with a special message. She decided on the menus and on the silverware, glassware, and linens for the Christmas Eve and Christmas Day dinners. The centerpiece for the table on Christmas Day was the last but not the least thing she thought of. There was always something to be found in the garden, some evergreen, branch or twigs with berries, which she set into one of her favorite vases or bowls and intermingled with angels blowing trumpets or flowers floating in a transparent dish. The focus of Hallie's Christmas dinners was never the food, though that was good (usually a stuffed chicken for the main dish). It was the setting—the pale pink or silver cloth laid on the long mahogany table, candlelight reflected in glassware, freshly polished silverware, and handwritten place cards, everything combined to look elegant but simple in the dining room which, though modest in size, invited (after Hallie had finished arranging it) talk, laughter, and a tremendous feeling of celebration.

Early Crises

Before accepting the job as head of the New York project, Elmer Rice asked Hallie a number of questions. Even if he put thirty actors into each show he produced and had twenty shows running at once, this would still not take care of all the actors who needed jobs. How were they to be employed? Then there was the problem of sets and costumes: both cost money, but the production budget was small. Hallie told Rice what she had already told Hopkins: "We could do Living Newspapers. We could dramatize the news without expensive scenery." Reminding him of the documentary dramas she had produced at Vassar, she pointed out that the sets in every case had been simple and easy to build; props and costumes had been minimal; the shows had cost next to nothing to produce; and many actors had been put to work.

Rice was familiar with the Living Newspaper. In Russia, where illiteracy was widespread, staged dramatizations of current issues served to publicize the new regime's sweeping social reforms. Why not, Hallie thought, use a similar form to make Americans take a good look at what was happening in their own country? Later, after she had been accused of being too interested in Russian theatre, she was to say—with justification—that although Living Newspapers borrowed from many sources, including Russian, they were "as

American as Walt Disney, the March of Time, and the *Congressional Record*."

Rice, who was as enthusiastic an advocate of theatrical experiment as Hallie, seized on her idea at once. The American Newspaper Guild, he said, had many unemployed journalists. He would ask the Guild to sponsor a Living Newspaper unit. He then went ahead and appointed the Guild's national vice president to head the unit.

Morris Watson's appointment was not a step Hallie had anticipated. Watson was a newspaperman, not a theatre person. He "knew less about the theatre," Hallie later said, than any other person in charge of a Federal Theatre unit. And, as Hallie was soon to learn, Watson's first loyalty was to furthering the aims of the American Communist Party. When the Party wanted demonstrations to protest WPA policies, Watson helped organize them. His allegiance was to become an embarrassment not just to Federal Theatre but to Hallie personally. Nevertheless, in 1936 his ideas were not as divergent from Hallie's as they would later become.

Mussolini had just invaded Ethiopia. The events surrounding the invasion were exactly the sort of material Watson and Rice were seeking. They began looking for writers with dramatic ability, urging them to submit sketches which might be put on a stage. One young writer, Arthur Arent, submitted a sketch which so excited Rice that he asked him to expand his work into an hour-long show. This became *Ethiopia*, a documentary with an outspoken point of view: *Ethiopia* asked why the democracies had not put a stop to Mussolini's brutal invasion.

Given the temper of American public opinion, the subject of the Ethiopian invasion was an unfortunate first choice. Yet in the light of what was to follow, no topic could have been more timely or important to air in the public arena. The threat of fascism abroad was to hang over all the years of the Depression. It was a threat, however, that at first most Americans chose to ignore; crises at home were all too real and too absorbing. Moreover, many leaders of public opinion, historians as well as journalists, felt that America had been drawn into World War I unnecessarily. If another war was to be avoided, went one common argument, Hitler and Mussolini should be accommodated. Although Roosevelt never shared this point of view (and in fact vehemently opposed it), he felt he had to conciliate the isolationists who dominated Congress. His private opinion was that the Ethiopian invasion was an outrage—"This is war," he told Hopkins. But the sanctions he imposed against Italy were minimal.

Roosevelt's disapproval of Mussolini's action was shared in this country by Communists, fellow travelers, and many others. But whereas the President's actions were shackled by isolationist sentiment, theirs were not. Watson, Rice, and Arent saw the invasion as an opportunity to speak out against the dangers of fascism. So did Hallie, who immediately gave her approval to the plan of putting Arent's documentary drama before the public. However, when Roosevelt's secretary, Steven Early, learned that actors in a Federal Theatre show were to impersonate Mussolini, Haile Selassie, Pierre Laval, Anthony Eden, and other foreign dignitaries, he became worried about the effect this might have on American foreign relations. "We are skating on thin ice," he told Jacob Baker, who was administering the Arts Projects under Hopkins's supervision. Baker called Hallie to his office for an explanation. Reminding Baker first that he and Hopkins had both applauded the idea of Living Newspapers, Hallie then assured him that *Ethiopia* was carefully documented and free from political bias. She was, in fact, side-stepping Early's points, for although Arent's script was not biased in favor of either Democrats or Republicans it did take the internationalist stand that Roosevelt had feared to take publicly. Baker said he would send a copy of the script to Early's office. But Early, who had no intention of reading it, was adamant: any play dealing with foreign relations, he insisted, was "dangerous" and the impersonation of foreign dignitaries "particularly dangerous." A press agent who was present when Hallie received this news by telephone recalled later that he had "to hold her hand. She was in tears."

That night she wrote her husband: "it all means that I have stuck through this incredible agonizing business only to find that there is a joker at the bottom of the pile"; and she worried that she might never be able to "operate anything worth doing." But during the night she thought of a course of action. The first thing next morning she dashed off a letter to Eleanor Roosevelt. "I have the gravest fears," she wrote, "that if [*Ethiopia*] is closed, schools, universities, and newspapers will regard it as a political move." She asked the First Lady to get in touch with her "if there is anything you can do." Mrs.

Roosevelt responded by inviting Hallie to the White House and assuring her that she would talk with Steven Early. Buoyed up by this promise, Hallie boarded a train for New York, where Elmer Rice, she learned, was threatening to resign and where a unanimous cry of *censorship!* had gone up from one end of the project to the other. All might still be well, Hallie told her workers; Mrs. Roosevelt had expressed interest. Somehow she managed to keep Rice from exploding.

But bad news awaited her when she returned to Washington: Mrs. Roosevelt had not changed Early's mind. In a telephone conversation with Hallie, the First Lady said she had discussed the matter with the President, who felt the production could open if no foreign statesman was represented in person. A memo from Jacob Baker repeated this directive: "No issue of the Living Newspaper shall contain any representation of the head of a foreign state unless such representation shall have been approved in advance by the Department of State."

Although Hallie later came to see this decision as a reasonable compromise (despite the enormous amount of rewriting it would involve), all she could see at the moment was that Rice would probably resign and that the whole New York project would take his side. *She* would be blamed as the one who had let it all happen. She did not like this part of it at all. Her workers' support was essential. What should she do? It was the first major crisis of her administration. She could side with Rice and resign with him, or she could stay and face the opposition. To give herself time to think things over, and to avoid meeting reporters, she spent the evening at the apartment of her assistant, Esther Porter.

"She told me she wanted to go into hiding," Porter recalled. "But I didn't want to be the only one to advise her. I asked Baker and his aide to come to the apartment to discuss the situation. They did, and it was a long evening. Baker and his aide told Hallie, 'It's your choice. This is probably the last moment you can leave with integrity.' If she walked off that night, she'd be like Elmer Rice, untouched. If she stayed on, it would happen again. 'If you care so much about your integrity,' Baker said, 'leave . . . Look, this is gonna happen again no matter what Hopkins has said' . . . Well, they talked her into staying."

When the news of Baker's directive reached New York, the uproar Hallie feared became a reality. Rice said publicly that he would never under any circumstances submit to censorship by the United States government. If *Ethiopia* closed, he would indeed resign. He phoned Baker, who agreed to meet him in New York. The majority of workers on the New York project stood firmly behind him. Rice had become the hero of the hour.

Back in New York once more, Hallie tried to persuade Rice that the government's position was not unreasonable. The script could be changed, foreign dignitaries eliminated. Roosevelt had said the production could still go on. But Rice was adamant. Washington, he said, never intended Federal Theatre to produce a play which said anything; all it wanted was "pap for babes and octogenarians."

He did not really expect Baker to accept his resignation, however. After all, he was a person of some influence. What he seems to have hoped was that his public stand against censorship would change the government's mind. But Baker had other plans. When Rice repeated his threat in Baker's office, Baker reached for a statement he had already prepared and read the following: "When difficulties have arisen in the past in connection with the operation of the Federal Theatre Project, you have proposed either to resign or to take the difficulties to the press. Now that a problem has arisen in connection with a dramatization that may affect our international relations, you renew your proposal of resignation in a telegram to Mr. Hopkins. This time I accept it."

"It was one of several occasions," Hallie recalled afterward, "when homicide would not have surprised me."

Rice had a final say. He invited employees, guests, and members of the press to a final dress rehearsal of *Ethiopia*. At its conclusion there was an explosion of applause. Spectators leaped to their feet yelling "Encore!" "Bravo!" and "To hell with Washington!" Then Rice strode to the stage and held up his hand for silence.

"It seems to me," he said, looking out over an audience that included Hallie, "that for me to try to present a play called *Ethiopia* without presenting any of the chief officers, ministers or members of foreign governments is a lot like trying to put on a performance of *Hamlet* with the Melancholy Dane left out."

It must have been a difficult moment for Hallie, who believed, as

much as Rice did, that the democracies' stand against fascism had
been inadequate, and that *Ethiopia*'s message needed to reach the
public. But she was beginning to think (as she would soon hint to her
project workers) that Rice's insistence on keeping the script exactly
as written was self-destructive. The play, Hallie thought, could still
be effective and *almost* as hard-hitting without the foreign dignitaries. (This was a view that would not prevail. Morris Watson, who
sided with Rice, was in no mood to compromise.)

Rice had more to say that night, all of it directed against his
employers in Washington. "The government's decision to censor the
Living Newspaper did not come until after I had outlined some of the
other productions which were being planned. These include a play
which deals realistically with unemployment and the handling of
relief. Our second edition of the Living Newspaper was to handle the
situation in the Southern States, touching on such vital subjects as
lynching, discrimination against Negroes and the plight of the share-
croppers. In other words, hitting a number of our political friends
where they live. In short, we are confronted here not only with
evidence of the growth of fascism which has always used censorship
as one of its most effective weapons, but with the resolute determination of a political machine to re-elect its own underlings at all
costs."

At Hopkins's request, Aubrey Williams, deputy administrator
of the WPA, wrote to Mrs. Roosevelt: "You can see from this that
they intend to present only those things which are highly controversial."

Newspaper reaction was widespread. The New York *Mirror*
headlined its attack on Federal Theatre, "How the Alphabet Government Laid a Million Dollar Broadway Egg." Brooks Atkinson in
the *New York Times* thought the cancellation of *Ethiopia* proved
"how utterly futile it is to expect the theatre to be anything more
than a sideshow under government supervision."

Hallie disagreed. "We are not dropping the Living Newspaper,"
she told her regional directors. "We are finding out something about
the relationship of the government to the theatre. Let us proceed on
the assumption that by exercising care we can do the sort of plays we
want to do." In a private conversation with a young employee she
was more explicit: "Don't think we're lowering the flag. Our next

one will have plenty to say. There'll be impersonations of Congressmen . . . Let Washington try and stop it!"

She had weathered her first major crisis. She came out of it, in time, with most of her project workers firmly behind her. Those members of the New York project who had so recently lumped her with "those bureaucrats down in Washington" came to realize that the stand Hallie had taken, though not as firm as Elmer Rice's, had saved the Living Newspaper—at least for the moment. As one project supervisor would later put it, "Hallie's name began to flare like a torch . . . She became our protagonist."

The censoring of *Ethiopia* was just the first in a series of setbacks Hallie faced in early 1936. Further instances of censorship, the resignations of many of her supervisors, and a disastrous press reaction to New York's opening production followed.

First, Chicago's Mayor Kelly, on the advice of a local priest, forced the closing of Meyer Levin's *Model Tenements,* a play suggesting the need for sweeping social changes. Then Maxwell Anderson's *Valley Forge* closed in Plymouth, Massachusetts, because a town selectman considered it obscene. Just previously, Hallie had had dreams of sending this play on tour throughout New England with a band in colonial costume playing colonial tunes in front of the theatre before curtain times, "just as the old touring companies," she told Philip, "used to do when we were kids." She hoped the audiences, which hadn't seen "a drama in flesh and blood for ten years," would rise to the "challenge of a revolutionary hero and leave the theatre pondering the lines, 'This liberty will look easy by and by when nobody dies to get it.' "

But Hallie's wish to set her audiences thinking was not shared by her bosses. In his Washington office Jacob Baker, "looking very grave," told her he was beginning to wonder whether he could continue to run the Theatre Project. On top of everything else newspapers were attacking John McGee's *Jefferson Davis,* a play sympathetic to the Confederate president, which was due to open in New York in mid-February. Hallie, who had wanted to like this play by her former student, did not agree that it was inflammatory but was dismayed when she attended a rehearsal. "When I think that this is our first Broadway show," she wrote Philip, "I am ill. If I were a reporter I would pan the life out of it." A newsman who spotted Hallie coming out of a dress rehearsal looking "the picture of dejection" got her to admit that rehearsals were not going well and that many of the people she had appointed were resigning. She looked him straight in the eye. "But I am going to stick," she told him. "And I am going back into the theatre to try and make a play out of *Jefferson Davis*." She did not succeed. The play was panned.

Her regional directors were dropping out rapidly. Citing un-cooperative state administrators in Iowa and minimal theatrical talent throughout the Midwest, Mabie had resigned in early January. So had Koch in North Carolina, for different reasons. In Pennsylvania, Jasper Deeter's complaint was that political interference by district officials made a program impossible. Hallie, who had intended to create strong regional and community centers throughout the country, found herself in February in charge of three huge metropolitan centers—New York, Chicago, and Los Angeles—and several small, struggling units in various cities and towns.

One thing was encouraging. That was the coming New York production of T. S. Eliot's *Murder in the Cathedral*. Three years earlier, after Hallie had directed Eliot's *Sweeney Agonistes* at Vassar, the author had promised her his first full-length drama. He was working on it at the time: it was to be about Thomas à Becket, the twelfth-century archbishop and martyr.

Murder in the Cathedral is not a play for every taste, nor is it an easy play to put across. Many people have disliked it or thought it undramatic. Not Hallie. When she and Philip read it aloud, they felt it had the stark simplicity of a Greek drama. Although Eliot's protagonist is not a flawed Greek hero but a Christian martyr beset by worldly temptations, the action of the play, as in Aeschylus and Sophocles, moves relentlessly toward the doom one senses at the beginning. Hallie felt particular sympathy for the women of Canterbury, who make up the central chorus. She saw them as women "concerned with the business of children, homes, crops, and harvest," wanting peace and an ordinary life but "disturbed by a sense of doom in the air. They do not want anything to happen." She conveyed her ideas to the show's producer, saying she wanted a director who knew how to work with choruses and could create brilliant lighting effects. He was found at Yale.

Halsted Welles had studied design and directing at the Yale Drama School. He had worked with Donald Oenslager and had recently directed a Russian play for the Yale Dramat with great success. When he read Eliot's play, he thought it dull but felt he could make it look good. "I'm not a good director," he recalled later. "I don't like actors. I'm no good at digging characters. But I'm a hell of a good prose choreographer."

He was given one accomplished actor, Harry Irvine, to play Becket. Irvine, Welles remembered, "spoke beautiful English. But a lot of the other actors were old bags off the street. They hadn't worked for twenty years. So I said to them, I don't want to hear beautiful poetry. Just give me your good whiskey voices. The lines took on a great vitality."

He conferred with Lehman Engel, who wrote a score. "We had a full orchestra." Welles now claims he had "no concept of the play." He just decided to do "some flashy things, and it worked . . . It was great working on Federal Theatre. You could get whatever you wanted. When I decided I wanted a chorus of knights to come onstage with their swords flashing, sure enough, we got them." A problem arose with the sets. Aline Bernstein was to have designed the scenery, according to Welles, but "every time I turned up at her apartment she was vague. She didn't have them. 'I design in the bathtub,' she told me—and once when I arrived she was *in* the bathtub. But she was still vague." So Welles designed the sets himself.

Whenever she was in New York, Hallie attended rehearsals. She sat at the back of the theatre taking what she later described as "fiercely critical notes," although her producer and director were the only people who saw them. Then came opening night. "Many people," Hallie recalled, "went into the theatre believing that they were going to see a murder mystery . . . They stayed on, listening humbly with the rest of us . . . For this was one of the plays in which Federal Theatre actors attained stature because they knew what they were talking about." They were talking about "tribulation" and about "living and partly living." All had had (in Eliot's lines) their "private terrors," their "particular shadows," their "secret fears."

When New York's critics acclaimed the show as a "moving and triumphant performance" and "one of the most notable theatrical offerings of the winter," Hallie wrote rather wistfully to her husband,

"I can't help wondering sometimes what they would have thought of *Antony and Cleopatra, My Country Right or Left,* or the Aphrodite chorus from the *Hippolytus* . . . but I do like what the critics say about the women of the chorus knowing what they were singing about."

During the 1936 fall season Federal Theatre produced one other smash hit. This was *Triple-A Plowed Under,* a Living Newspaper about the history of American agriculture. Through a rapid succession of pantomimes, skits, and radio broadcasts, the audience learned how mortgages were foreclosed, farms auctioned, and crops deliberately destroyed. They learned about the devastating effects of drought, the organization of farmer-consumer cooperatives, the creation of the Agricultural Adjustment Administration and how the Supreme Court had declared it unconstitutional. Actors portrayed Henry Wallace, secretary of agriculture, the nine justices of the Supreme Court, and Earl Browder, the head of the Communist Party. The terrible difficulties farmers faced throughout the twenties and thirties were the focus of the show.

Who suggested the idea of doing a Living Newspaper about agriculture's struggle with the courts is not clear. It may have been Hallie, whose earlier documentary drama had addressed the problems of farmers. It may have been Watson or Arent. But once the idea had been decided on, a group of reporters and dramatists under Arent's supervision put the material into dramatic shape. Hallie then invited Arent, Watson, and Joe Losey, who was to direct the show, to Poughkeepsie to "pool our ideas." Losey, like Hallie a Meyerhold enthusiast, had ideas for staging which Hallie liked. But as rehearsals got under way, some of those participating in the production, in particular a group of older actors, complained that the set, which used ramps and projections, was strange and that the play had no plot. "Who in New York cares about farmers and about wheat?" they demanded.

After a late-night rebellion, Hallie and Losey urged the cast to stay with it. If the public disliked the play, they promised, there would be no more Living Newspapers. "We then proceeded," Hallie recalled, "to screw our courage to the sticking point, and we had need of it." A veterans' group threatened to stage a demonstration on opening night on the grounds that the play was unpatriotic. By the time the night arrived the actors were full of misgivings, the audience full of tension, and the lobby full of police.

But the threat everyone feared turned into a farce. The veterans in the audience waited for the scene when the loudspeaker announces, "January 6, 1936 . . . Supreme Court invalidates AAA in Hoosac Mills case" and the actor playing Earl Browder counters, "The constitution of the United States does not give the Supreme Court the right to declare laws passed by the Congress unconstitutional." A veteran at this point rose from his seat and began singing "The Star-Spangled Banner." But the police at the back of the theatre, who had been warned to be on guard against communist activity, misunderstood what was happening and evicted the veteran.

The production was a tremendous hit. Brooks Atkinson, who had been complaining that the Broadway theatre had "no convictions and, in the midst of vast social upheaval, no comment to make," called *Triple-A* "hard hitting" and "frequently brilliant." Night after night spectators were moved by one scene in particular: the loudspeaker declares, "Summer 1934 . . . drought sears the midwest, west and southwest." A light focuses on a farmer kneeling in a field while the voice on the loudspeaker continues: "May first: Midwest weather report, fair and warmer." As the forecast is repeated for May 2, 3, and 4, the music grows in intensity and the farmer who has been examining the soil straightens up, lets a handful of dry soil sift through his fingers, and speaks just one word: "Dust!"

Norman Lloyd, an actor in Federal Theatre, later recalled that "a lot of people who saw that show had never been to the theatre before. And they would talk back to the people up there. Most of all they would talk back to the Supreme Court justices . . . And if a justice got up to speak and someone in the audience didn't agree with him, that someone would shout him down . . . People felt very partisan about things in those days, they really participated."

Richard Lockridge wrote in the New York *Sun,* "It is an engaging audience. Its face is not frozen, it is not sitting on its hands; when it hisses, it is not self-conscious, and when it cheers, it means it. It is young, lively and I suspect, hard up." Hallie was pleased. "We want an audience," she said, "which revolves in a large orbit. We prefer the four million to the four hundred with their jewels, furs, and town cars."

The "four hundred with their jewels, furs, and town cars" were not so pleased. Republicans on the whole were outraged: "pure and unadulterated politics," said one congressman; "the most outrageous misuse of the taxpayers' money that the Roosevelt administration has yet been guilty of," declared the Hearst press. The *Saturday Evening Post* went even further, noting a similarity between the play's message to farmers and laborers to unite and the Communist Party's plea for the formation of a Farmer-Labor party.

The calmest surveyor of the scene was Eleanor Roosevelt, who in one of her daily columns wondered if Communists occupied in producing plays were not "safer than communists starving to death."

By the end of March, the Federal Theatre New York project had three hits on its hands. (The third hit, *Chalk Dust,* about bureaucracy and intolerance in a high school, had been produced by the Negro Theatre in Harlem, which was under the direction of John Houseman.) The nationwide project was no longer the gigantic fiasco Hallie had thought it just a month earlier. Her determination to stick it out had paid off.

Hallie got so caught up in production plans she sometimes failed to see political intrigues taking place under her nose. She was also, Philip Barber thought, susceptible to flattery. One day Barber, who had replaced Elmer Rice as head of the New York project, noticed "an ugly, cross-eyed woman" approach Hallie to ask for a job. "Hazel Huffman got a job sorting Hallie's mail," Barber recalled "because Hallie felt sorry for her and because Huffman called her the most wonderful woman living . . . I told Hallie she was putting a rattlesnake in the office. I was sure she was a spy, but Hallie said, 'Oh, I'm sure that's not true. She said the loveliest things.'" Sometime afterward Hazel Huffman informed the Hearst press that Hallie's mail was "incendiary, revolutionary, and seditious." She had been paid, it transpired, by rightists in the local WPA office, who wanted Hallie replaced by a conservative.

Even a more politically astute person than Hallie might have had trouble heading off all the plots and counterplots within the New York project. The rightists kept the Hearst press informed about leftist activities and on occasion sold Federal Theatre scripts to the press. As for the leftists, a small number were more interested in organizing grievance committees and picket lines than in putting on plays, and often they got others to join them. "Sometimes we'd all get to the theatre," one actor related, "and somebody would say, Let's go someplace and agitate." Such activity increased as workers increasingly found reasons for agitating. After one particularly frustrating day Hallie sent a telegram to her husband: "Had seven various delegations of complaining actors. Attended a meeting of complaining dancers. Am all for abolition of all art, especially theatre. Feel it is essentially absurd. When does ship sail for Sicily?"

Hopkins had told Hallie when he hired her, "We're for labor first, last and all the time. Don't forget that. We're going to cooperate with all these unions." But the unions, in particular the Workers' Alliance, more often than not did not want to cooperate with the government. Alliance leaders tended to regard Hallie, as they regarded their WPA bosses in Washington, as enemies.

When the Communist Party got control of the Workers' Alliance in 1936, many members did not know it, or, if they did, made no objection. The Communists, after all, had been the first people to protest against unemployment and demonstrate for jobs. "Anyone who did not flirt a little with Marxist ideas in those days must have been pretty insensitive," Irwin Rubinstein thought.

In the Bureau of Research and Publication, where Hallie spent much of her time when she was in New York, the lines from the first were drawn between the militants and those who, however sympathetic to the leftist cause, believed Federal Theatre should not be made into a political battleground. Rosamond Gilder, who headed the Bureau in its earliest days, recalled telling the militants: "This project is to help people. If you picket it and keep sending delegations to Washington to protest everything you dislike about it, then little by little you will get Congress to close it out and hundreds of thousands of people will have nothing to eat." Gilder had been given the stupendous job of setting up the most difficult bureau in Federal Theatre. Playreaders in one room searched for suitable plays. In another room playwrights started work on new scripts. "The trouble was," said Gilder, "you'd have to take whoever was in line for the job, and then you couldn't fire anybody, you had to inveigle somebody to take them off your hands if they were particularly insane." While Hallie was hoping to bring audiences face to face with the great economic problems of the day, Gilder was coming face to face with the problems of people who had felt helpless a short time before and now, having been helped a little, were beginning to reassert their dignity and power in militant ways.

Gilder resigned after seven months, confiding to a friend that she was glad to think of returning to editorial work—the protests and "incredible red tape" were exhausting just to think about. An assistant in her office agreed that "the whole thing was chaotic" but had a different feeling: "It was fun because we were young and had so much hope about it and we'd come out of such a hopeless situation."

Around the time that Gilder resigned, Harry Hopkins decided that Hallie needed a strong administrative assistant. He had chosen her for her artistic vision and theatrical know-how, but Federal Theatre, like the other Arts Projects, was proving to be more than an artistic venture. He thought he knew just the right person. William Farnsworth, a young lawyer who had helped organize the National Recovery Administration, had also produced a couple of shows on Broadway and run a stock company in Baltimore. Hallie liked his experience, and she liked him. Two days after meeting him, she was exulting that at last she had a "sense of the whole administrative end being in very competent hands." Bill, Hallie told Philip, "is a large, brown person with a pipe and a sense of humor. Plots and counter-plots don't faze him at all. In the midst of all the storms he remains absolutely calm." Farnsworth thought, "You always have tempera-ment in the theatre. If you didn't have temperament, you wouldn't get a performance that was worth a damn. So you just kid people out of it. Because you know nobody is really gonna stick a stiletto in anybody."

Bill and Hallie hit it off. He thought she was a "real swell guy. She didn't follow channels, but that wasn't Hallie's nature. She'd get on the phone and call Aubrey Williams and say, God damn it, Aubrey, we can't do this! And then she'd phone Harry Hopkins. If she *had* followed channels, she wouldn't have got anything done."

Others were less tolerant of "Hallie's nature." Some people in the WPA Washington office—it is not clear who—wanted her replaced. One day in the early spring Hallie heard a rumor that Alsberg and Cahill were to be retained as directors of their Arts

Projects but that she and Sokoloff were to be fired. Jacob Baker was to take over the management of music and the theatre. "I can scarcely give my mind seriously to the contemplation of Baker dictating the art policies of the nation, but of course it is no madder than the whole situation," she wrote Philip. She added that she was being very guarded in her comments, giving no criticism of WPA. "It speaks for itself." A few days later, in a dismal mood, she wrote to her husband that she wanted her directors to begin doing some really good things—"sort of a death dance before we all make an exit." Nothing came of the rumors. No one was fired. It is not even clear why officials in Washington objected to Hallie at this point, but probably political reactions to *Triple-A Plowed Under* had something to do with it.

Even if she was to lose her job, Hallie was determined to run Federal Theatre the way she believed it ought to be run. When she met with her largely new national staff in mid-March (only eight of her original twenty-four regional directors remained) Hallie launched into future plans as though nothing threatening had happened. Acknowledging that the theatre units were not yet as effective as they should be, she urged her staff to give better plays in more exciting ways. "I realize," she said, "that in the beginning many of you found it necessary to do such plays as *The Old Soak* and *Broken Dishes* [standard stock company plays] because you were testing your material, and letting the actors regain confidence by playing in parts to which they were accustomed. But from now on I hope you agree with me that there is no particular justification for continuing to give federal funds for plays which at best can be no more than stencilled copies, becoming dimmer with each countless repetition."

In the spring of 1936, with conservatives in Congress looking for ammunition with which to bombard Roosevelt, the latest Living Newspaper became an easy target. When Hopkins went before the House Committee on Appropriations in early April, he was asked whether he thought federal funds should be used to produce propagandistic plays like *Triple-A Plowed Under*. The show, Hopkins replied, was just a dramatic version of the news, "something like the March of Time in the movies." But this did not satisfy Representative Robert L. Bacon from Long Island, who insisted that in an election year it was especially important not to use taxpayers' money for political purposes. "Oh," said Hopkins easily, "if you knew the kind of people who are administering this for us, you would know they would not tolerate for a moment any enterprise of a partisan propaganda nature."

A few days later James J. Davis of Pennsylvania took the floor of the Senate to inform his colleagues that the current administration was allowing relief money to be spent by a woman who was infatuated with Russia and the Russian theatre. He read letters that he had been sent by the Veterans' League and by an Equity member complaining of Communist infiltration into the New York project. Why, he wanted to know, had the administration appointed a woman who after visiting Russia wrote, "I became absorbed by the drama outside the theatre, the strange and glorious drama that is Russia"? Although Senator Robert Wagner of New York later read telegrams from project officials countering the charges of Communist infiltration, and although Hallie issued a statement saying her interest in Russia was theatrical only, the damage had been done. Most newspapers were interested in printing only what Davis had said.

Meanwhile, in Washington, Jacob Baker was trying to convince Hopkins that the Arts Projects would be more efficiently run if they were put into the hands of state administrators. Since Hopkins did not immediately counter this suggestion, Baker on April 17 asked Hallie and the other three directors to come to his office. "Well, folks," he told them, "we are having a weekend meeting of our field staff, and I want you to get ready to show them the lowdown, because they are the folks who will be running the projects next year." Money for the projects was to be divided among the states and control handed to local WPA officials.

Hallie was not one to take this news lying down. After the meeting adjourned she tried to reach Hopkins without success. When she finally did reach him, he told her he owed all four directors an apology. "I should have fired Baker long ago, and I am doing that now." He added that he hoped she would stay on as director for another year—if there *was* another year. He thought it possible that the House, when it passed the coming appropriations bill, might eliminate the Arts Projects altogether. But "if you go out under charges of Communism, certainly I will too."

With troubles mounting in Washington, John Houseman and Orson Welles prepared to launch—in Harlem—a Negro *Macbeth*. The idea of doing a nineteenth-century *Macbeth* laid in Haiti, with the witches as Voodoo priestesses, had come from Welles's wife, Virginia, after she learned that an African witch doctor and his troupe of drummers had been stranded in America and were therefore eligible for relief. John Houseman, one of the first producers Hallie hired in New York, had brought Welles onto the project along with a wide variety of other talented young people—Virgil Thomson to compose music, Abe Feder to create lighting effects, Nat Karson to design the set. They came on, Houseman recalled, "certainly not for the thirty dollars a week" but for the "excitement of the whole new venture." His cast and crew, he added, were "a mishmash of amateurs and professionals, church members and radicals, adherents of Father Divine and bushmen from Darkest Africa."

Despite Harlem rumors that the production would be a "vast burlesque intended to ridicule the Negro in the eyes of the white world," rehearsals proceeded, news of the production spread throughout the city, and theatregoers began buying tickets. By mid-April every seat in the theatre had been sold for opening night and every first-string drama critic planned to attend. On April 14, while ten thousand people milled around the Lafayette Theatre, dozens of police, including two on horseback, tried to keep order. "All northbound automobile traffic was stopped for more than an hour," the *New York Times* reported the next day, "while from trucks in the street, floodlights flared a circle of light into the lobby, and cameramen took photographs of the arrival of celebrities." When the curtain fell, the spectators cheered for fifteen minutes, many standing on their seats. The witches' scenes, Brooks Atkinson wrote in the next day's *New York Times,* had always worried people. "The grimaces of the hags and the garish make-believe of the flaming cauldron have bred more disenchantment than anything else that Shakespeare wrote. But ship the witches into the rank and fever-stricken jungle, stuff a gleaming naked witch doctor into the cauldron, hold up Negro masks in the baleful light—and there you have a witches' scene that is logical and stunning and a triumph of the theatre art." Martha Gellhorn wrote that she would henceforth think of *Macbeth* "as a play about people living in a Haitian jungle

. . . Macbeth wore military costumes of canary yellow and emerald green . . . Women came on and off the stage in salmon pink and purple. The impression was of a hot richness that I have almost never seen in the theatre . . . the audience sat and watched and listened as if this were a murder mystery by Edgar Wallace, only much more exciting."

Critics were enthusiastic, with one notable exception. Percy Hammond, writing for the city's leading Republican newspaper, the *Herald Tribune,* described the production as "an exhibition of deluxe boondoggling." Citing the brightness of the costumes and the loudness of the music as evidence of criminal extravagance, he proceeded to ridicule the whole idea of a popular theatre supported by government funds. Although Houseman and Welles were undisturbed by what they recognized as "not so much a review as an attack on the New Deal," the witch doctor and his African drummers took the review to heart. Was it "the work of an enemy"? the doctor asked Houseman. Houseman agreed. "He is a bad man?" "A bad man," said Houseman. That night, according to Hallie, the basement of the theatre was filled "with unusual drumming and with chants more weird and horrible than anything that had been heard upon the stage." When Percy Hammond caught pneumonia and died a few days later, the story became a Federal Theatre legend.

In the April issue of *The New Yorker,* Robert Benchley wrote that Federal Theatre was putting on "darned good shows." Five he had seen were "definitely worth doing, which is more than I can say for five consecutive shows on the Broadway." The New York project now had, besides the large units producing the hits, a circus in Brooklyn, an experimental theatre, a marionette theatre, a retraining center for community directors, a radio unit, a bureau of research and publication, a magazine, a dance theatre, and a municipal theatre providing free entertainment for schools, hospitals, and city parks. Some of these units, the circus and municipal theatre included, which WPA had inherited from relief projects set up under the Civil Works Administration and the Federal Emergency Relief Administration, needed improving, and Hallie urged her producers to re-think and redesign them. "Here we are," she said, "limited in some respects because we are part of a federal program, but freed financially from many other pressures . . . Within reason we can do any plays we wish in any way we wish."

She took a special interest in *Federal Theatre Magazine,* which she had originated to act as a link between New York and the rest of the country. The Rockefeller Foundation, at Hallie's request, had provided funds for a multilith offset press. Tony Buttitta, who had edited *Contempo,* a lively literary magazine, had been Hallie's first choice for editor, but Buttitta lived in North Carolina and WPA red tape made it almost impossible to move people across state borders, so she had hired instead a man she knew nothing about who had been recommended by Vice President John Nance Garner.

Pierre de Rohan, who, according to a colleague, was arrogant and "looked like something out of Noel Coward," produced a first issue of the magazine that caused Hallie to explode. To illustrate an article entitled "Men at Work," he attached photographs of Seminole Indian squaws holding babies beside a lonely creek. All of his ideas, in Hallie's opinion, were sentimental and out of touch, and she told him so. "They had a terrible fight," Rosamond Gilder recalled. "Hallie just tore his ideas to pieces." Although two thousand copies of the magazine had already been printed, Hallie ordered them destroyed.

At this point Buttitta arrived in New York. Having come north on his own, he could now call himself a city resident. "Let's gang up on him," Hallie told *Contempo*'s former editor. She got Buttitta a job working for Rohan and asked his help in editing something "with lively articles, lots of photographs, and a cover that's as smart as *New Theatre* . . . We want no chummy house organ but a first-rate magazine."

This budding conspiracy was stopped quickly by Rohan himself, who, instead of resenting Hallie's criticisms, went to work to improve the magazine and won her over. Before long, Hallie was instructing him on editing, writing, and even on how to behave to win the support of his staff. "I'm not quarreling with people anymore!" Rohan wrote Hallie delightedly in midsummer. When Hallie liked his reviews, even when they were critical of Federal Theatre shows, she told him so. When she thought he was uttering criticisms for the sake of being critical, she told him that also. Hallie won Rohan's allegiance by being tough but fair, and she kept it as long as Federal Theatre lasted.

New York and California had got off to good starts, Hallie felt, but elsewhere, it sometimes seemed, there was nothing but trouble.

When Hallie went to Chicago in April, she found the project no better than it had been in December. The Chicago reviewers were calling Federal Theatre shows "feeble, futile, and foggy," and Hallie herself admitted feeling aghast at the administrative setup. Her regional supervisor, "asleep on the job," had not brought his project supervisors together even once. The plays being done were "old hat," nothing better was being planned for the future, and her directors were listless and discouraged. When Harry Minturn, in charge of a repertory unit, blamed the state of affairs on his employees' lack of talent and on the meager fifty-dollar-a-week royalty that playwrights received, Hallie disagreed. What was needed, she told him, was bold and vigorous leadership.

Hoping to attract new talent, she persuaded Susan Glaspell, an original member of the Provincetown Players, to set up a Midwest Play Bureau in Chicago. The best acting, she thought, was going on in the experimental unit. She encouraged this group to rewrite their project and apply for further funds. With those in charge of the eight vaudeville units playing in the parks, she discussed ideas for portable stages and new routines. And when Thomas Wood Stevens resigned as head of the project, she chose a New York producer, George Kondolf, to replace him.

Making improvements in other regions, particularly New England, proved more difficult. "We have not one thing to show for a quarter of a million spent in Massachusetts," Hallie said despairingly in August, "not a decent show, no equipment, no shop, no morale, no press, no research. The state director, under orders to keep peace, has been flabby and afraid." Part of the problem was political. Early on, Hallie's regional director for New England had written her, "The newspapers down Boston way don't like us. One office has a sign on the reporters' call board, *Soak the Raw Deal*." Another problem was that state WPA administrators did not want a theatre project but only an inconspicuous relief project. Consequently, whenever local criticism arose (against *The Merchant of Venice* in

New Britain, Connecticut, and against Maxwell Anderson's *Valley Forge* in Plymouth), the WPA took the side of the protesters without weighing issues. Despite all Hallie's efforts—she sent a new director to the region and leased a downtown Boston theatre for WPA shows—audiences in towns and cities remained small.

The South presented other difficulties—fewer actors, fewer professionals with theatrical experience—but Hallie never gave up the hope of starting lively southern theatre companies. Though she did not achieve everything she wanted, her confidence eventually proved justified. Her plan, when she went south in the spring of 1936, was to find some way of collaborating with Frederick Koch, who was training playwrights in North Carolina, and with Paul Green, whose *The House of Connelly* had been the first play produced by the Group Theatre.

Green later said that when he first met Hallie she was "the cutest person you ever saw. When Hallie walked into a room wearing one of her jaunty little hats, the men all looked!" Hallie found Green a charming southern gentleman, and their friendship was to last for years.

Green told Hallie he was writing a play—a "kind of celebration"—to commemorate the first English settlement in America, on Roanoke Island, off the coast of North Carolina, and that he wanted the island people to participate. "I was interested," he recalled later, "in the people's theatre. I'd just read a book by Romain Rolland called *The People's Theatre* and I was very much taken with it." Hallie urged him to finish writing the play and promised to send Federal Theatre actors for the production. "So," Green said, "we started building an amphitheatre on Roanoke Island. We had one old mule and a scoop—and we had about two hundred CCC camp boys with shovels."

In 1587, twenty years before the founding of Jamestown and thirty-three years before the landing at Plymouth, a small group of English settlers had landed on this island, built a fort, and tilled the ground. But four years later, when Sir Walter Raleigh sent a company to relieve the colonists, his men found only an abandoned fort and houses overgrown with melons. No one discovered what had happened to the colonists. This was the story Paul Green retold in *The Lost Colony*. Produced in collaboration with Federal Theatre a little over a year later, the play was an immense success. For the next three years, during the summer months, a thousand people a week poured onto the island to see the play. Mrs. Roosevelt went down to watch rehearsals. The President joined her, and six thousand people went over to hear him talk. This was the kind of theatre the Roosevelts had hoped would blossom all over America—art evolving out of a particular region, about Americans and for Americans.

The poverty Hallie saw in the South made her want to do something special to help. En route to North Carolina, she had passed a CCC camp, observed gray unpainted buildings, a few dejected boys in dirty clothes lounging about, and learned that there were 300,000 boys in such camps throughout the United States. When she returned to Washington she wrote her directors that these boys needed theatrical entertainment: couldn't someone evolve a technique for putting on camp shows that would involve members of the audience? In response Grace Heyward wrote the *CCC Murder Mystery,* a play that required eight actors and numerous spectator volunteers to play the roles of witnesses and members of the jury. The show proved so popular with the boys that nine companies were formed to tour the Atlantic coast with it during the next two years. Eventually, the play was put on in 258 camps.

One other innovation evolved from Hallie's trip south. Herbert Price, a young actor-director, told Hallie he wanted "something hard to do." She sent him into rural areas and the poor districts of southern cities. Every place he went, Price got some church or club or school to donate space. His object was not to put on established plays but to get plays out of the people who came there. Old people would start reciting stories about their experiences, and the stories would be resumed week after week. In a West Virginia coal camp, Price encouraged some miner to begin. Others chimed in, adding details, arguing over what happened next. When a story assumed shape, Price called in others to help—to build, paint, rig up a stage. "Their feet are still in the mud," Price told Hallie. "They live in indescribable want . . . Their one entertainment is an occasional revival meeting." He persisted despite getting chigger bites, because, as he put it, "I have never seen one of these plays where there was not a tremendous strengthening of human values."

Although Hallie did not have time to visit all the theatres that

Federal Theatre was establishing in the southern states, she kept in touch with the people who were running them and tried to instill in them a belief in what they were doing. Many of her supervisors, not only in the South but all over the country, continued to feel bewildered and discouraged by the lack of talent. "Is this social work or theatre?" one supervisor wrote to ask her. "Oh Lord," another complained, "if I could only find more directors to raise the standard of acting!" In many places the actors who signed up for relief work were old and dispirited, in need of support but short on talent. Where she had sufficient staff, Hallie was able to set up retraining centers, but in the smallest places this was not possible. When she was lucky, she found capable, dedicated people like Herbert Price. Where such men were not available, the small units suffered and eventually went under.

In May, when the House of Representatives passed the appropriations bill without disbanding the Arts Projects, Hallie and Hopkins celebrated by lunching together on the roof of the Washington Hotel. Looking out over the city she had come to think of as beautiful, Hallie told Hopkins that she and Philip had talked things over, and that, much as the House decision pleased her, she had decided she needed more time at home. She would have to leave the job. "Hell, Hallie," Hopkins replied, "I wish we could have Phil down here and talk this over because I don't see how we can get along without you." He said he thought Federal Theatre the "best thing in the WPA—said so," Hallie related to Philip, "very unemotionally, eating raw carrots as he did so."

Hallie and Philip had another talk. Hopkins, she said, had promised that, if she stayed on, she could have more weekends at home. She may have put this to Phil as a question—What did he think? She probably added, as she had at the outset, But I'm not going to do it, because this was her way: to insist she was not going to do what she knew would distress her husband. Although Philip never complained of feeling neglected, he had managed to let Hallie know he was missing and needing her. In one letter he had written, "I fear I sent the last letter by mistake to Mrs. Philip Davis." Although Hallie had reassured him, "That was no mistake, my love," she had not missed the message. But she was in conflict over a decision whose outcome was predictable. By this time the task absorbed all her energies. She could not turn back, and Philip knew that as well as she.

In the months that followed, Hallie made several efforts to reassure herself and her husband that she had made the right choice. One of her letters, detailing her reactions to Martha Gellhorn's novel *The Trouble I've Seen,* read: "I can't possibly tell you how true it is, or how terrible. It is about people that are old and afraid, people that are middle-aged and know they are just ready to do their best work and can't get a chance, and people that are young and want to go to school and have nice clothes and make love and get married, and can't. How [the book] can be made into a play I don't know, but it has got to be, because it would do more to make people care than all the speeches in the world. I want nothing now except to sit in the garden with you and do this into a play . . . None of it could be done without you. Because, my dearest love, nothing can be without you. How much you are the core of my life I am just beginning to know. How terribly I need to keep coming back to you."

Hallie probably did not know what some members of Philip's family had begun to notice. To blot out the loneliness he felt in the evenings, he had gone back to drinking. Late at night, after everyone else had gone to bed, he kept himself going at his desk with glasses of wine. In the morning the housekeeper would find him asleep on the floor of his study.

Hallie did not make Gellhorn's tale into a play. She did not give up her job. And Philip continued to be supportive. That was his nature—as Hallie had known when she married him.

11

Federal Theatre at Midpoint

ALTHOUGH Hopkins had been criticized by Republicans in Congress for allowing the Federal Theatre to present New Deal propaganda, there had been no serious consequences. The Committee on Appropriations had refunded the Theatre Project. Emboldened by this, Morris Watson and those he worked with in the Living Newspaper unit decided in the spring of 1936 to launch a militant attack on the Supreme Court. The "nine old men" of the court, as Roosevelt scornfully called them, had invalidated first the National Industrial Recovery Act, which sought to regulate procedures, hours, and wages in industry, and eight months later, the Agricultural Adjustment Administration Act, which levied a tax on crop processors in order to aid the hard-hit farm population. In the court's opinion, Roosevelt's attempts to solve social, industrial, and agricultural problems by legislating what farmers, middlemen, and factory owners could do was unconstitutional. Its decisions set the stage for the clashes between the President and the judiciary that were soon to follow.

According to Arthur Arent, who supervised the writing of the Living Newspaper *Injunction Granted,* some "young Turks" turned the script into "a militantly pro-labor account of the working man's fight for liberation through unionization." In style and tone it has much in common with the agitprop and cabaret satires of the twenties. While truthfully dramatizing the history of labor from indenture to the formation of the CIO, it satirizes everyone except the workers as fools or villains. Joe Losey, who directed the production, invented a clown figure to mimic and parody the judges and industrialists, who are repeatedly shown foiling every attempt the workers make to organize in their own interests. The Clown, played by Norman Lloyd in tennis shoes, wide-sleeved jacket, patched trousers, and a Harpo Marx hairdo, at one point presents H. J. Heinz with a large pickle. At another moment he hands John D. Rockefeller a huge dime. He blows up a balloon while a reactionary demagogue addresses a crowd of enthusiastic supporters, and, when the demagogue has finished, pulls a bouquet out of his sleeve and gives it to him. "I had a little piano that I carried about to play tunes on," Lloyd later recalled. "Somebody would ask for a higher wage. I would pop up through a trap door with a big cigar."

Apparently Hallie was not disturbed by what she saw the first time she attended a rehearsal. Her husband and her legal counsel, Irwin Rubinstein, who were with her, advised, "You're going to be attacked anyway. If you feel this is the right thing to do, do it." Hallie liked Joe Losey's imaginative direction. A couple of years earlier, before Losey left for a trip to Russia, Hallie had given him letters of introduction to directors whose work she admired there. Losey's set for *Injunction Granted,* inspired by what he had seen on that trip, was the sort of thing Hallie might have done herself—a fluid arrangement of runways and platforms providing ten playing areas which could be spotlighted for a rapid succession of scenes. Virgil Thomson had provided an inventive score calling for ratchets, bells, sirens, and trombones. And Hallie liked Norman Lloyd's acting. She asked Watson and Losey to "clean up the script and make it more objective." Then, busy with other matters, she did not involve herself further.

Watson and Losey did not take Hallie's advice. They changed nothing. Soon afterward, Hallie heard from Philip Barber and Bill Farnsworth that in their opinion the show was "radical propaganda from beginning to end," a view later echoed by Richard Watts in the *Herald Tribune,* who called it a "bitter and sardonic cartoon chronicle of organized labor against reactionary opposition." Barber and Farnsworth wanted Hallie to scrap the show, but Hallie replied that she had asked those in charge to make the script more objective. Believing they would follow orders, she had allowed rehearsals to continue.

Up to that time Hallie had had no experience with outright defiance. She expected that those she placed in positions of authority would follow her orders. Her method of putting directors in charge and allowing them their freedom had worked to her advantage: much creative work had come from it. But Hallie failed to realize that Watson and Losey were totally committed to the radical point of view expressed in *Injunction Granted*. To them, the script was as objective as it ought to be; it told The Truth about the struggle between labor and the Supreme Court.

She got a shock on opening night when she discovered that the script had not been changed. Although it was after midnight when she reached Poughkeepsie, Hallie sat down at her desk to write Watson and Losey a letter. The production, she wrote, was "special pleading, biased, an editorial, not a news issue." She singled out a scene in which the Supreme Court justices are shown asleep. "Whatever my personal sympathies are," she said, "I cannot, as custodian of federal funds, have such funds used as a party tool. That goes for the Communist Party as well as for the Democratic Party. To show the history of labor in the courts is appropriate; to load that document at every turn with insinuation is not appropriate." She described the climax of the play as "the old cliché of calling labor to unite in the approved agitprop manner" and suggested that the script would be improved by presenting the Republicans' and the Democrats' differing stands on labor. "There would then be a question mark end, the only true end." When Watson replied that the show was drawing crowds, Hallie retorted, "Everyone knows that those crowds are being sent by their unions. And let me say that I am informed that [a radical pamphlet] is being hawked in the lobby. Will you please give orders that this be stopped at once?"

Obviously Hallie had been given a political education by her bosses in Washington. Newspaper reviews like those by Watts must have added to her political awareness. In her next letter to Watson and Losey she was even more emphatic. "I took your word," she wrote, "that Federal Theatre would not be used politically. I think you both let me down. As you very well know, the avalanche of un-favorable publicity on [this play] is ammunition against the project, to say nothing of being added ammunition against me personally." The play closed in October, and Losey left the project when it did. "I broke with the Living Newspaper," he was later to say, "over the withdrawal of *Injunction Granted*. I was not fired and at no time was I under any pressure from Morris Watson. I was under considerable pressure from Flanagan and Barber, which was disagreeable . . . Flanagan found my militancy increasingly inconvenient." He decided she was "terrified of confrontation . . . As you probably gather," he wrote this author, "I didn't have a very high opinion of her."

The militants on the New York project, Hallie was discovering, were often able to exert a force far in excess of their numbers. Their power, though Hallie did not realize it at first, had two sources. First, they were organized, and second, because liberal New Dealers shared many of their views, they were often able to persuade the liberals to join them. This situation was nowhere better illustrated than in the Play Bureau, where Hallie was soon to find herself in even greater conflict than she had been with Watson and Losey.

Many Federal Theatre employees were later to describe the Play Bureau as a political battlefield. In fact the Bureau was a microcosm of all the units in the New York project: the personnel represented every political persuasion from conservative, to liberal, to militant pro-Communist left.

In early summer, after Rosamond Gilder had resigned her position as Bureau supervisor, Philip Barber appointed a younger woman to take her place. Katharine Clugston had Hallie's enthusi-astic endorsement. She was young, hardworking, and conscientious and, like Hallie, had studied playwriting with George Pierce Baker. Her political views, Barber thought at first, were liberal. He told Hallie she was "good friends with all the factions." Using the detailed instructions Hallie sent her from Washington, Clugston set to work to make the Bureau more efficient.

It was not an easy task, particularly since one of Clugston's closest friends, an outspoken member of the Play Bureau's Commu-nist cell, kept urging her to get off her high horse and make Federal Theatre more responsive to workers' needs. Although Clugston was often dismayed by Communist rhetoric (in her words, "so happily, so obstinately sure that everybody down in Washington was pigheadedly wrong"), there were other times when she felt energized by its fervor. Years later she was to say: "It was so easy to fight in those days. Things were never true *and* false, they were true *or* false, with radical members of the project always in secure, authentic possession of the truth."

The "radicals" had ways of discovering what plans were being formulated inside the local WPA office before these plans were made public. In June, Clugston heard that the WPA was about to make some drastic changes. There would be cuts—employees would be fired unless something was done. She let herself be persuaded to join a delegation of supervisors intent on taking their grievances to Washington. Hallie and Aubrey Williams, Hopkins's second in command, were the targets of the delegates' complaints.

Rumors of cuts and the constant changes in WPA policy were as discouraging to Hallie as they were to her workers. She did what she could to countermand policy when it threatened her workers' jobs, often taking her protests to Hopkins, but there was a limit to what she could do. Moreover, her artistic ambitions for the project made her primarily concerned with the choice of plays and the quality of the productions. The constant demonstrations and protests staged by the "radicals" threatened those ambitions because they drew public attention away from Federal Theatre's achievements and onto the dissatisfaction of its employees. When Hallie saw her young, newly appointed supervisor among the protesting delegates, she was astonished, and her astonishment quickly grew to anger. Clugston's credentials had made Hallie feel that the young woman would be an ally. She needed an ally in the politically troublesome Play Bureau, for it made decisions about plays that affected Federal Theatre units across the country. After the delegates had registered their complaints and Aubrey Williams had tactfully promised to do what he could, Hallie summoned Clugston to her office. She did not ask her to sit down, and Clugston, who later wrote about this confrontation, correctly interpreted the omission as a sign of her administrator's disapproval.

Hallie led off by saying that she was hurt and disappointed. When this brought no response from Clugston, who could see that Hallie was not so much disappointed as angry, Hallie erupted. "How dare you come down here with all those tiresome radicals? What are you trying to do—ruin me?" Hallie, of course, had no way of knowing that Clugston's friends in the Bureau had been warning her for months to "be on your guard when you talk with Mrs. Flanagan." She was "most dangerous," they said, when she was "being most charming." Nor did Hallie know how deeply her Bureau supervisor had been affected by talk against "those bosses down in Washington." Clugston's friends blamed Washington for every change in policy, and Hallie, since she announced these changes, was lumped with the enemy. She accepted that frustration as part of her job, but to have her Play Bureau supervisor, someone she had hand-picked, turn against her was infuriating. The interview ended with bad feelings on both sides.

WPA officials in Washington did often blunder. Sometimes they gave directives, then changed their minds and issued contradictory orders. In July they announced that all Federal Theatre supervisors could take vacations. Shortly afterward they announced that the vacations had been canceled. Clugston promptly joined with those filing suit against Hallie, Hopkins, and Aubrey Williams. They won their case. "So keep up the protests," a friend of Clugston's remarked, "but don't say I didn't warn you if you find yourselves out of a theatre someday." His words were wasted. Clugston by this time had joined the rebels. In midsummer someone in the Bureau persuaded her to attend a Communist cell meeting. She was curious at first, then dismayed when "one of the better playwrights promised to change a whole act of his current script" because a member objected that he "hadn't stuck close enough to the latest Party line." A few days later Philip Barber, who had meantime learned of her attendance at the meeting, asked her if she had "gone loony . . . Maybe you actually are a convert. I hope not." He warned her not to associate exclusively with members of the Workers' Alliance. It would only, he said, make "somebody down in Washington" say she was being run by the Party.

Washington officials meanwhile were telling Hallie that she was catering too much to the militants' demands. Despite berating Clugston in private, in public Hallie's statements had so far not reflected dissatisfaction with the leftist activists in her New York project. The officials' criticism was one Hallie was hearing with increased frequency, and it was one that at times she inclined to agree with. "I think you and I," she wrote Rohan that summer, "have an unfortunate tendency to romanticize the workers."

When the WPA administrator for New York, Colonel Brehon Somervell, made inquiries into the Play Bureau in September, he found several members who were willing to sign complaints against Clugston on political grounds. Hearing of this, Hallie decided she ought to make one last attempt to warn Clugston of the danger she was in. It was not her supervisor's sympathies which distressed her so much as Clugston's determination to ignore what Hallie termed Federal Theatre politics. On one of her trips to New York she invited Clugston to lunch. But she had little stomach for confrontations and her manner, Clugston noted, was "stiffly strained."

Suddenly, in Clugston's recollection, Hallie launched into an angry attack on the delegations which had been pestering her and everybody else in Washington. "People like you," Hallie told her, "were given supervisory jobs to take the burden off us down there." The picket lines, she said (picket lines as well as protests were a common feature in New York during the days of the WPA) were "deadly, demoralizing, a menace." Officials were talking of disbanding the Arts Projects, "especially this Federal Theatre hotbed." Clugston blurted out, "So disband us!" She then pointed out that it had been Hallie herself who had urged workers to fight for their rights, Hallie who had said this was the only way to get things done. "Don't be stupid," said Hallie. "We give all we can. Then when somebody important makes a fuss, of course we're compelled to take some of it back ... So long as you remain in Federal Theatre, particularly as a supervisor, you're in politics whether you like it or not." More angry words were spoken on both sides, and then Hallie rose, abruptly ending the luncheon.

Two weeks later, while Clugston was vacationing in Maine, she got a phone call from Hallie. Twelve charges had been brought against her by WPA investigators. Several Bureau employees had signed complaints stating that Clugston had mishandled government funds, employed government workers for private ends, and permitted Communist propaganda to be distributed in the Bureau during working hours. She suggested that Clugston resign. Hallie knew even then that the twelve WPA charges were unfounded—when Clugston insisted on a meeting, Hallie referred to them as ridiculous. But she had decided that Clugston must go, and the easiest way to have this happen was to let the WPA proceedings take their course.

Clugston did not resign without a fight. A week later Hallie wrote Philip that the City Projects Council (a white collar branch of the Workers' Alliance) had taken Clugston's case and was demanding a hearing. Hallie said, "She threatens to go to her office, barricade herself, and make me eject her with police." Hallie and Bill Farnsworth spent that day talking with WPA administrators. Farnsworth told Hallie the case was the most important one the union had raised. "But I think," Hallie told Philip, "the important issue is: *Where are all the plays for the new season?*"

Despite all the efforts of the City Projects Council, Clugston was not reinstated, although all charges against her were dropped. It was some time before Hallie admitted the real reason for her supervisor's dismissal. "Some supervisors," she went on record as saying, "cannot manage to get on with the person or persons next higher up. That has been Miss Clugston's difficulty."

Hallie's confrontations with Kate Clugston, Morris Watson, and Joe Losey, though they increased her awareness of the difficulties posed by militants within Federal Theatre, did not deter her from bringing current issues before the theatregoing public. During the summer of 1936 she urged her supervisors and directors to suggest ideas that would make the theatre more responsive to "an age of expanding social consciousness." What she meant (for one thing) was an age that was just beginning to understand the dangers of fascism. In Spain, Franco had declared his resolve to overthrow the Spanish Republic. In America, Sinclair Lewis's anti-Fascist novel, *It Can't Happen Here,* had become an immediate best-seller. At a Play Bureau meeting in New York, Francis Bosworth, who had replaced Katharine Clugston as supervisor, had a novel idea: why not ask Lewis to dramatize his book for Federal Theatre? Farnsworth suggested opening the play in theatres all over the country on the same night to celebrate the first anniversary of Federal Theatre. Hallie, who liked the idea, wanted it to happen two weeks before the November elections.

It Can't Happen Here made the point that fascism could happen

anywhere, including America. It had characters modeled on Father
Coughlin and Huey Long, two men considered potential dictators by
everyone with leftist views. For a time the book was considered for
a Hollywood production, but MGM eventually concluded that
Lewis's views would offend too many people, particularly those who
wanted to keep America out of world affairs. Lewis agreed to do a
dramatization for Federal Theatre. Another writer, Jack Moffitt,
agreed to help. They settled into two suites in Essex House in New
York and went to work. Hallie was later to recall the busy days that
followed as the "funniest, craziest and most exciting" of her life.

"Lewis had frequent tantrums," Phil Barber recalled. "Night
after night I'd get waked; it would be after two o'clock. Lewis would
say, 'Phil, better get over here. I'm stopping the whole thing' . . . So
I would trot over and Lewis would go over what was wrong and say
how it was falling apart and how nobody liked him, and it was
hopeless. I'd say, 'But it isn't true. Everybody loves you. They're
saying how great it is.' So he'd say, 'Well, all right, we'll go on for a
while.' " By the time Hallie entered the fray, Lewis and Moffitt were
not on speaking terms. She tried to mediate. While Barber, Bosworth,
and others supplied Lewis and Moffitt, in their separate Essex House
suites, with coffee, ice water, and Fanny Farmer candy to keep Lewis
sober, Hallie went back and forth carrying messages, making suggestions, and in moments of utter frustration wondering why she had
ever agreed to such an insane idea. "At intervals determined by the
agents, we would emerge from the debris to meet the press and Mr.
Lewis would say that he loved the federal government and I would
say that I loved the works of Mr. Lewis, and Mr. Moffitt would say
that he loved living drama. Then I would go to my office and try to
cope with frantic messages from the field." Chicago complained that
the revised version of act three made no sense; Los Angeles wanted
no more revisions; New Orleans said the play was not appropriate
for a city where many people still revered the memory of Huey Long;
Missouri authorities wanted to change the message of the play;
Birmingham asked permission to stage the play in the mood of a
political rally.

Meanwhile, stories began appearing in the newspapers: The
play, some writers claimed, was election propaganda for Roosevelt;
others said it was anti-Roosevelt; it would antagonize Hitler; it was

Fascist; some even claimed the play was pro-Communist, though Lewis was an outspoken anti-Communist. Brock Pemberton, a Broadway producer, told the press: "It's funny that the WPA can tackle something which the films cannot," to which *The Nation* replied, "We think it's funny too, for different reasons . . . As for Mr. Pemberton's charge of radicalism . . . there is nothing to prevent him from putting on a rousing pro-fascist drama, *It Can and Should Happen Here.*"

The conservative press was doing its best to equate the New Deal with communism. Some papers warned that if Roosevelt was re-elected, the American Way of Life was doomed. Would the WPA continue? No one could be certain. Hallie felt that the Lewis dramatization, though not as good as she had hoped, would contribute to "keeping alive the free, inquiring, critical spirit which is the center and core of a democracy."

October 27 was the day chosen for the simultaneous openings of the twenty-one productions. As the date approached, Hallie's biggest worry became the production scheduled to open in New York at the Adelphi. Philip Barber and producer Edward Goodman wanted more time. "Let the other productions open," Goodman told Hallie. "They will only be regarded as tryouts in hick towns anyway." "This was one of several times," Hallie later said, "that I was furious with the provincialism of the New York project and its lack of any sense of the theatre we were trying to build." *Variety* next day quoted her as saying that the show would open on time in every single theatre, "even if the actors have to walk around the stage reading their parts and wearing signs identifying themselves."

Then one morning while she was weekending in Poughkeepsie she got a phone call from Lewis. "I haven't slept all night," he told her. "It is all terrible—everybody has gone into a coma . . . I want you to get right on the train and come to New York and postpone the play a week and get new people to do everything, or do it yourself." Lewis was particularly distraught by the living room set, which looked "like a cheap boarding house on Second Avenue."

When she reached the Adelphi, Hallie discovered that everyone, except the technicians and stagehands, was in "a state of jitters." Allying herself with the few people who had remained calm, she sent the others home to bed, then, locking the theatre doors, started in to change what she could. "We got into our warehouses and secured different furniture and draperies and lamps and pictures." Somehow the show was pulled into shape. And two nights later the curtain rose on twenty-one stages in sixteen states. The 78,000 lines the press had devoted to the play had its effect: thousands of people bought tickets. Hallie watched the first act at the Adelphi, noting that "the power of the idea was there," despite the play's faults and production weaknesses. Then she taxied to the Biltmore to see the second act of the Yiddish version. "On the whole," she thought, "a better show." (She was unable to see a third version at the Jewish Center on Staten Island.) Returning to the Adelphi before the third act, she found the lobby crowded and everyone there talking over the show.

"Any New York manager," Lee Shubert told her, "would give his hat to have thought of this idea first." Dr. Henry Moskowitz, president of the League of New York Theatres, called the evening "the most thrilling first night" he had ever attended. And Hallie herself, deeply impressed by the attentiveness of the audience during the final scenes, was swept along in the current of enthusiasm.

After a late-night party at the Plaza hosted by Lewis and his wife, Dorothy Thompson (at which Ernst Toller told Hallie he wanted to write a Living Newspaper for Federal Theatre and call it *Europa— Last Edition*), she returned to Essex House to ponder the reviews.

The play had been far from meeting her own high standards, and New York's critics agreed with that judgment. Richard Watts's review in the *Herald Tribune* was typical: "It has its chilling and effective moments, but does not make the attack on fascism as bitter and angry as it should." Critics outside New York were less critical. In a syndicated column in the Chicago *Tribune,* Burns Mantle reported favorable reactions in Denver, Chicago, Boston, Cleveland, Tacoma, Seattle, Miami and Newark.

Audience interest kept the show running for months. In New York, the three productions played a total of 314 performances. Companies in Boston, Newark, Detroit, Los Angeles, Miami, and Tacoma went on tour. By the time the last curtain had come down, performances had reached a total of 260 weeks.

In Hallie's opinion, what counted most was that hundreds of thousands of people all over America had seen a play "which says that when dictatorship threatens a country, it does not necessarily come by way of military invasion but may arrive in the form of a sudden silencing of free voices."

When Roosevelt won the election in a landslide victory over Alf Landon, Hallie, along with the millions of other people who had helped return him to office, felt jubilant. Whatever the Republican-dominated press might continue to say against the President and his schemes, the people had come out overwhelmingly to show their approval. Hallie was also pleased to think of the part, however small, that Federal Theatre had played in FDR's reelection. During the spring her regional director for the South, John McGee, had helped to write and produce a pageant celebrating the history of the Southwest. It had been the sort of gigantic creative collaboration that Hallie particularly enjoyed—"all the forces of the centennial, the WPA, the Federal Theatre and Music Projects, many civic and educational bodies, together with some 16,000 participants," uniting to produce a huge spectacle that honored the President and which 40,000 spectators went to see and hear in the Little Rock amphi-theatre.

In short, Hallie had become a dedicated partisan of Roosevelt and his New Deal. She had not always been as wholeheartedly pro-Roosevelt. In an earlier year, when the President announced his intention of balancing the budget, Hallie told Philip she hoped he had not forgotten the workers who had elected him. No one knows how she voted in 1932, when many liberals came out for Norman Thomas. By late 1936, however, her allegiance was firm, a fact that made it difficult for her to accept what happened after the election.

On the day following the victory, Hopkins called a meeting of his four Arts Project directors to give them some bad news. Since the WPA had used up funds to aid drought victims during the previous summer, it must now reduce the number of its employees by 20 percent. For each director this meant firing two thousand workers. "Unessential" persons not on relief were to be fired first, then those "least useful." "It is a tough assignment," said Mr. Hopkins. "It has got to be done."

Hallie had known the cuts were coming. She knew how her

workers would feel. They had done good work; and they were now going to feel betrayed. And of course they did. Protests erupted across the nation, the fiercest of them in New York City.

Hallie described the scene in a letter to Philip: "Picket lines with banners, *Mr. Roosevelt, What Do You Mean?* . . . Men and women screaming and fainting . . . People barricading themselves behind desks when the police break in . . . Police clubbing people, people spitting in the faces of the police." Eleven members of the dance unit were arrested for picketing outside the Nora Bayes Theatre. Demonstrators who participated in a sit-down strike outside the building where Hallie had her New York office had to be dragged away by policemen. WPA officials promptly fired all of them. Although Hallie sympathized with the demonstrators' cause, she was not happy with their methods. Aware that some of the more militant groups were inciting riots for their own purposes, she told her husband, "There is a lot of chicanery in it too. You can't get too sentimental."

But Hallie was equally unhappy with the methods of New York WPA administrator Colonel Brehon Somervell, who not only fired many of the demonstrators, but also threatened to fire everyone who protested in any way. On more than one occasion he was quoted as saying all protesters should be shot. In the late winter and early spring of 1937 he became one of the most hated men in New York City.

Everyone agrees that Somervell was a martinet. He had no patience with disorder and no sympathy with the sufferings of workers who had lost their jobs. He had very little interest, even, in the Arts Projects that he supervised. Hallie in his opinion, one rumor went, was a "number one Stalin agent." What he *must* have, he told Washington, was complete control in New York. Unless he got that control, the cuts Hopkins ordered would never be made. Hallie's way of dealing with protests was entirely different. You don't make cuts, she told Hopkins, and then slap people down for objecting. You listen to the complaints, you sympathize, and you explain why the cuts are necessary. Her workers, she said, had become demoralized— and no wonder. If Federal Theatre was to continue doing good work, what was needed was morale-building.

The battle for control of the New York project, which *Variety* called the "contest between the army and the artists," hung in the balance for several weeks. In the end, Hopkins (as was often the case during the first two years of Federal Theatre) sided with Hallie. In late February he removed its administration from Somervell's jurisdiction and put it under Hallie's. No more cuts, he assured her, would be made for at least six months.

Meantime, to comply with Hopkins's order, Hallie had closed some small projects outside New York. Not surprisingly, she made choices on the basis of *her* definition of good theatre. Projects doing "old plays in old ways" were the first to go. She closed down some efforts in Texas where the WPA administrator continued to insist on doing noncontroversial plays. *Triple-A Plowed Under*, he said, had evoked criticism. Hallie had replied that it was impossible to predict what critical response a new play would bring. Before there was a necessity for cuts, she had put up with his ways, feeling she had no choice. But when cuts became necessary, she naturally decided against the policies of a man with whom she vehemently disagreed.

When Hallie made a public statement early in 1937 that the "Federal Theatre had been established to provide a high type of theatrical entertainment for the people of America," WPA officials jumped on her. No, they said, Federal Theatre had been established to "provide employment for needy theatrical people." Interestingly, the WPA and the militant leaders of the Workers' Alliance, so far apart on most issues, were in agreement on this one point: Federal Theatre should concentrate on providing relief. Fortunately for Hallie, she still had Hopkins's support. He was enthusiastic about the shows Federal Theatre was producing in New York, not because he shared all of Hallie's tastes, but because his education had made him appreciate whatever was lively and well done. And he trusted Hallie's judgment. She had proved herself right artistically more often than not. So he listened to her when there was opposition to what she was doing.

In February, Robert Schnitzer, Hallie's director in Delaware, decided to produce a modern *Julius Caesar*. As Schnitzer put it, he "had a lot of vaudevillians on his hands." He needed a play with a large cast. Realizing that "these old boys would look silly in togas," he decided to dress Caesar's men in black shirts and Brutus's in khaki. Schnitzer belonged to no militant group and was in no sense a believer in leftist dogmas, but he was keenly aware of the Fascist threat abroad. When the press zeroed in on the political implications of his costume innovation, there was an uproar. The priest of a large Italian Catholic congregation in Wilmington complained to Hopkins, who asked Hallie if she would be willing to discard the black shirts. When she said no, she would close the show first, he dropped the matter. "She won that fight with Harry," Schnitzer recalled, "and we had a very successful run."

From the start of her career, Hallie had been careful to nurture friendships with the men who had positions of power above her. The men who picked Hallie to run theatres at Grinnell and Vassar and for the WPA—President Main, President MacCracken, and finally Hopkins—backed her wholeheartedly, not solely because she brought acclaim to the institutions they headed, but also because she asked their advice and kept them apprised of her plans. Although there is no record of any conversation between Hallie and Hopkins regarding *Power*, the next production of the Living Newspaper unit, it is safe to assume that such a conversation did take place. Hallie had been thinking about electrical power for more than a year. While still at Vassar she had started to write a play about the private electric companies and the public need for electricity. This was soon after Roosevelt had created the Tennessee Valley Authority. Her play, she told *Theatre Arts Monthly* editor Edith Isaacs, was called *Power*. She was spending all her free time working on it and was excited about producing it. But then the Federal Theatre had come up and Hallie put the script aside.

Electricity—and the companies that generated it—was a big issue in the early thirties. Ninety percent of America's farmers still had no power, because the electric companies would not spend the money to build lines in rural areas. Roosevelt was incensed by this. So were many other people, Hallie and Hopkins among them.

Sometime during the fall of 1936 Hallie must have given Morris Watson the idea of doing a Living Newspaper about electricity. Whether or not she showed him the play she had been working on is not known. But Arthur Arent did go to work to turn this potentially dramatic material into a Living Newspaper. By Christmas he had a draft ready. Hallie then asked Watson to have the regional director of the Federal Power Commission check the draft for factual accuracy. Learning soon afterward that the commissioner had been visited by a young newspaperman seeking "facts which would fit in with a preconceived idea of power," she called Watson on the carpet. *This* time, she told him, there was to be no "twisting of facts."

The script that finally emerged was pro–New Deal. It favored the government creation and sponsorship of power companies, pointed out the advantages of government ownership to consumers, and demonstrated how private companies were attempting to prevent public ownership. Hallie wanted the production to start with "a projection of Niagara Falls completely filling the proscenium arch and seeming to spill over into the audience." She hoped to demonstrate the power of machines in contrast to the powerlessness of those who manned them, an idea Charlie Chaplin had recently dramatized in *Modern Times*. In a conference with the director and designer, she described what she wanted for the opening scene: "one factory worker against a long vista of machines . . . one man at a switchboard against a background of a switchboard enormously elongated." Believing that those in charge would carry out her scheme, she turned her mind to other matters.

As often happened when Hallie left a project to her subordinates, her directives were not followed. She had not yet moved to New York (this was shortly before Hopkins gave her administrative control of the New York project), so she did not get to see a runthrough until rehearsals were well under way. Her impression at the first rehearsal she attended was that the show was "the most bungling and inept piece of work Federal Theatre had done." Hallie never spoke moderately when she disliked what was happening on stage. If something was not right, it was "terrible," "dreadful," or "the worst" she could imagine. Instead of the gigantic machines she had visualized and the "comic scenes . . . in the nature of cartoons," she found a stage "jammed with realistic properties, . . . infantile paintings of such properties as desks," and a badly timed first scene. Did the director and designer, she asked Barber's assistant, have "any concept of the play"?

What happened during the next few days may be imagined, but last-minute changes were made and the production opened to unanimously favorable reviews. *Variety* called it "as timely as tomorrow's headline"; *Newsweek* declared that the Living Newspa-

per had "grown up as a dramatic form," and the English critic James
Agate reported in the *Times* of London that the acting was "far and
away the best we have seen in this country."

Norman Lloyd was the Consumer, a meek-looking individual
who, knowing nothing about electricity except that his bills are too
high, wanders through the play asking questions, getting confused,
and becoming increasingly angry. He pays 17¢ for a kilowatt-hour,
he says, but what is a kilowatt-hour? And why can't he shop for
electricity in the same way he shops for groceries? Reports, announce-
ments, and news headlines heard over a loudspeaker carry the play
through a rapid succession of scenes that dramatize the history of
electrical power from the time when men first worked on the
problem of generating electricity to the time when the government,
through the TVA, began generating and distributing it and private
companies began fighting this competition through the courts. The
audience sees nineteenth-century entrepreneurs bidding against one
another to sell power in towns and cities, then forming monopolistic
holding companies to keep prices high. They hear consumers in 1905
complaining that "only one sixth of the population of any given
territory" has electricity and learn that municipally owned power
plants charge consumers much less than the private companies do.
The play ends, as Hallie insisted Living Newspapers should, with a
huge question mark: "What will the Supreme Court do?"

No one was more enthusiastic about *Power* than Hopkins. "This
is a great show," he told the company when he went backstage. "It's
fast and funny, it makes you laugh and it makes you cry and it makes
you think—I don't know what more anyone can ask of a show. I
want this play and plays like it done from one end of the country to
the other." Acknowledging that people would call it New Deal
propaganda, he said the big power companies had spent millions on
propaganda. "It's about time that the consumer had a mouthpiece."
As he and Hallie left the theatre to discuss the next Living Newspaper
over supper, he told her, "I guess I stuck my neck out." "You're
certainly on the record," said Hallie.

When Hopkins, at the time cuts were being made, told Hallie he
wanted the New York project run more efficiently and economically,
she suggested some ideas for cutting expenses. "Go ahead," said

Hopkins, "and put them into action. Just keep Ellen Woodward informed." Ellen Woodward, who succeeded Jacob Baker, held the post of Assistant Administrator in Charge of Women's and Professional Projects of the WPA.

Before taking up residence in the city in early 1937, Hallie had decided on a course of action. With Bill Farnsworth's help, she would consolidate all production services in one central place. "From offices, rehearsal halls, and other job locations all over the city," she later wrote, "we moved the project, aside from shops, warehouses and theatres, into the Chanin Building at 42nd Street and Lexington, establishing for the first time an efficient plant in which it was possible to see operations in all departments and rehearsals in many studios every day. We emphasized the necessity for concerted effort in which every division was to play a part. Each day in addition to working with administrative and theatre heads, either Mr. Farnsworth or I saw one big group, such as the telephone operators, guards, maintenance workers, outlining their part in Federal Theatre; in every case we met with enthusiastic cooperation." Philip Barber continued to oversee the twelve producing units, but these units no longer controlled their own personnel or publicity. Philip Barber's assistant, Walter Hart, took charge of production services, including a new casting bureau that Hallie set up under Madalyn O'Shea at the Provincetown Theatre. This innovation pleased Hallie especially. Actors on the payroll not currently engaged in shows, she decreed, would now take O'Shea's course in fundamentals of acting. "God knows, all of our people need it," she wrote Philip.

Naturally there was an outcry. Watson, Houseman, Goodman, and Geddes—the "Big Four" among the New York producers—did not want to relinquish control over their units. They must continue to have their own designers, press representatives, and lighting and costume people, they said, if they were to continue to produce such hits as *Macbeth, Murder in the Cathedral, Triple-A Plowed Under,* and *Power.* But Hallie was adamant. If they will not give up their demands, she wrote Ellen Woodward, there is "no place on the project for them." She could be tough; given Hopkins' directive to economize, more than usually tough.

The few months Hallie spent administering the New York project were among the happiest of her four years in Federal Theatre.

She loved New York: the crowds, the skyscrapers, the busy comings and goings of people, even the noise. Above all, she could now see plays every night. Those she particularly liked she could see not only once but often. Her favorite was Houseman's production of Marlowe's *Dr. Faustus,* directed by Orson Welles.

If Welles, as Houseman claimed, was "always at heart a magician," so was Hallie. The way Welles and his lighting technician, Abe Feder, used overhead spots—vertical "stabs of light"—to punctuate the almost total darkness of the stage intrigued her. Objects and actors appeared and disappeared as though by incantation. "Faustus, emerging out of darkness on a platform thrust boldly out into the audience, drew us into his imaginings of living in voluptuousness, of resolving all ambiguities, of being on earth as Jove is in the sky. Tragedy lay in seeing the Seven Deadly Sins reduced to the stature of lewd and nauseating puppets flopping about at Faustus' feet." The production, which won almost universal acclaim, played to eighty thousand customers during a four-month run. Its only critics were a handful of militants who canceled their seats because the play was given no "social" slant. "I suppose," Hallie wrote Philip, "they wanted Lenin's blood streaming from the firmament."

The militants had also objected to Houseman and Welles's first production of the season, a zany extravaganza based on the French farce *An Italian Straw Hat* by Eugène Labiche. Houseman recalled choosing *Horse Eats Hat* to give work to a "very peculiar bunch" of actors on relief—"clowns and eccentrics and old comedians, and character ladies." Welles invited Joseph Cotten, Paula Lawrence, Arlene Francis, and Hiram Sherman to play lead roles. He got the clowns and eccentrics cavorting across the stage "in carriages and cars, tricycles and roller skates." The acrobatics of the show were, in Hallie's word, "unrestrained." In one wild moment Cotten leapt from a sofa to a table to a piano top to a chandelier. As he vanished into the flyloft, a three-tiered fountain flung a giant stream of water at the seat of his pants. Probably no show Welles ever directed had so much of what Hallie called "inspired lunacy." Although reviews were mixed, Hallie had the satisfaction of knowing that she was building audiences. *Horse Eats Hat* drew large crowds and became a fashionable Broadway hit. She felt during this second New York season that everything was possible.

One day, in a burst of enthusiasm, Hallie wrote Hopkins to suggest that "we build a theatre modeled on Epidaurus." It could be built of wood at first, in North Carolina "or some warm place." Later, if successful, it could be constructed of marble. "Then we will do the first Gigantic Backgrounds of the Modern Theatre ever done on this continent—or any other place for that matter." She told Philip she was "crazy about the idea, and I have not been drinking anything."

Everything at this point was going her way. Hallie had Bill Farnsworth to take charge of administrative details. She had a chauffeur to drive her about and two secretaries to handle work in the office. While she ate breakfast in bed in her suite at the Mayflower, her executive assistant Mary McFarland took dictation and made phone calls. When she left to attend rehearsals or confer with supervisors, McFarland remained behind to take and relay messages. Hallie told a friend, "My secretaries don't mind how hard they work. They say they have fun." Her chauffeur, Joe Celani, became so fond of her that he periodically presented her with a large box of chocolates. Her legal counsel, Irwin Rubinstein, often drove her to Poughkeepsie in the middle of the night. "During the first year of Federal Theatre," he recalled, "when Hallie was in Washington, she wrote me notes asking questions. Then she would rush into town in time to grab a sandwich and go to an opening. I'd be at the opening with her, but you don't talk business during an opening. So I'd drive her to Poughkeepsie to discuss certain points, and then I'd drive back to New York to be ready for work the next morning. I never needed more than four hours' sleep . . . I remember one night— it was around 2 A.M.—my car broke down and I was terribly embarrassed. It was pouring with rain but that didn't disturb Hallie at all. When things happen, she said, that I can't do anything about, I don't worry about them."

Once more Hallie had about her a nucleus of hardworking admirers whom she treated as family. And just as she had done previously, with a nucleus of admiring Vassar students, she backed what they were doing, listened to their problems, and, on occasion, when she felt they needed to expand their horizons, encouraged them to do something more, even if it meant leaving Federal Theatre. Robert Schnitzer thought Hallie succeeded as an administrator because she supported those who worked under her. She did not please everyone, of course, and those seeking an excuse to attack her did not have far to look. Hallie, in her desire to be helpful, was not always honest. Philip Barber, who wanted it understood that he was "not one of Hallie's lieutenants," recalled a time "when Hallie and I went backstage after a dance show. Hallie told the dancers she was particularly happy to report that I had fought to keep fifty dancers on the project at a time when Washington wanted to dismiss them, although it was *she* who had done that. She thought I would like to have that credit, but I felt like telling her she was a liar."

No matter what else she was doing, Hallie was always looking for plays. When she traveled she took scripts with her. She read them in taxicabs, on trains, and in hotel rooms late at night after finishing other work. She soon discovered that the best plays being written were often not available to Federal Theatre. Broadway paid higher royalties. When she discussed this difficulty with Irwin Rubinstein on one of their late-night drives to Poughkeepsie, he suggested asking authors she liked to release a series of plays. Or she could promise to do one play in several places, thus ensuring the author of substantial royalties. Which authors? What plays? Hallie wanted to know. Rubinstein suggested Shaw and O'Neill, and Hallie quickly answered, "Let's do it."

O'Neill consented at once. So did Shaw, but his reply was longer. Beginning by sympathizing with what Hallie was up against—"useless to hope that you can find groups with a high degree of skill in acting and direction everywhere. You may not be able to find them anywhere"—he went on to comment that plays are "murdered more or less barbarically all the time." He said Hallie should ignore the protests of the Theatre Guild, whose "object is to prevent anyone except themselves doing my plays." Finally he got down to business:

> They tell me that your theatre, being a Federal institution, is unable to move without miles of red tape being consumed, and that money can be extracted from it only after signing nine receipts. They also seem to think that every production will be a separate transaction involving a special license and weekly payments and acknowledgments. That will never do for me. As long as you stick to your fifty-cent maximum for

admission, and send me the accounts and payments quarterly, or half yearly if you prefer it, so that I shall have to sign only four or two receipts a year, and forget all about you in the meantime, you can play anything of mine you like unless you hear from me to the contrary.

Any author of serious plays who does not follow my example does not know what is good for him. I am not making a public spirited sacrifice; I am jumping at an unprecedentedly good offer.

Shaw's welcome letter came at a high point in Federal Theatre affairs. In May Archibald MacLeish, in a long article for *Fortune* magazine describing the Arts Projects, named Federal Theatre the most "spectacularly successful" of the four and a "roaring success." The New York *Daily News* printed a story calling Hallie "the biggest boss of show business the world has ever known," and Donald Kirkley in the Baltimore *Sun* reported that Federal Theatre's "significance as a social force [was] just beginning to be understood"; it was succeeding "beyond the wildest dreams of its sponsors." Yet Kirkley was worried: its success in "restoring drama to millions who cannot be reached by the commercial theatre" was overshadowing its "original purpose" of bringing relief to persons unable to find employment in the profession.

Although Hallie saw no contradiction between her artistic ambition and "the original purpose," there were many besides Kirkley who did. Washington officials had shown how little they cared for artistic aims when they proposed to turn the projects over to WPA state administrators. If Hopkins, who had shared Hallie's goals from the start, had not been in charge, officialdom would have triumphed. For different reasons, radical leaders of the Workers' Alliance likewise had no patience with Hallie's artistic goals. As already noted, what they wanted was more jobs, more relief, larger congressional appropriations. Needless to say, conservatives in Congress who wanted to cut the appropriations made up a third group that opposed what Hallie hoped to achieve. All of these groups played their part in ending Federal Theatre. For the moment, however, Hallie still had Hopkins' support—and she had Mrs. Roosevelt's.

12

Relevant Theatre

ROOSEVELT'S popularity, at high tide all through 1936, reached a peak when he gave his second inaugural address in January 1937. But a month later, when he proposed to enlarge the Supreme Court, remarking that some judges continued on the bench "far beyond their years of physical or mental capacity," he not only lost some of his staunchest supporters, he gave those who opposed him a *cause*. The fracas that ensued destroyed the unity of the Democratic party and helped generate the antagonism in Congress that Hopkins faced when he went before the Committee on Appropriations in the spring. A greatly strengthened anti–New Deal coalition proposed to cut WPA spending by 25 percent.

Even before the reduction was voted through, rumors of impending cuts began circulating in New York. Although WPA officials denied the rumors, most workers knew better than to believe the denials. Faced with the prospect of losing what little security they had gained, they were quick to join any and every activity that promised to bring their plight before the public. Demonstrations and protests became everyday occurrences. One of the most prominent took place on May 19, when a Federal Theatre dance company staged a sit-down after a performance of *Candide* at the Nora Bayes Theatre. Charles Weidman, who had danced Candide, came onstage to ask the audience to join the dancers in protesting the proposed cuts. A great cheer arose, and more than five hundred people remained in their seats until they were ejected by the police at dawn the next morning.

Observing that the city was in a fever of anxiety, Hallie tried to reach Hopkins and Mrs. Roosevelt by telephone. Neither was reachable, but she did get through to Bill Farnsworth. "All of us," she said to him, "should be on the side of the workers." After learning that the Workers' Alliance planned to call a one-day citywide strike of all WPA workers on May 27, she got in touch with the Washington administrator, David Niles, to ask permission to cancel all performances that evening. The Alliance people, she said, were going to picket the Chanin Building unless she announced the cancellation in advance. But Niles, convinced that such an announce- ment would be tantamount to cooperating with the strikers and putting pressure on Congress, asked her, "Are you going to abdicate and let the Workers' Alliance tell you how you can run your performances?" He instructed her to proceed as usual: as a govern- ment official she was duty bound to carry out government policy.

Hallie obeyed. But on the day following the strike, in a speech before the American Theatre Council convention, she told her listeners that whatever they might think of the strikers' methods, they should ask why the workers had staged the protest in the first place. Did anyone, she asked, have another method to suggest? No one did. She had made her point. Nevertheless, on June 10, Hallie had to tell her project workers that appropriations for the coming year would be 75 percent of what they had been. Once more she was faced with the painful task of deciding which workers would have to be fired.

To meet Washington's demand that the cuts result in a propor- tion of 95 percent workers on relief to 5 percent not on relief, Hallie decided that many stagehands would have to go. The stagehands' unions had refused to let their members apply for relief status, which meant that stagehands made up a considerable proportion of those in the nonrelief category. Cutting this class of workers also meant dismissing some of the people Hallie valued most. "We hate to lose Herbert Price," she told Farnsworth, who was helping her make the decisions. In Hallie's opinion Price had done more than anyone to help destitute people in rural areas of the South. She also lamented having to drop all service to the CCC camps. As she put it to an assistant, "Those in charge have done a swell job." But she had to cut somewhere and do it quickly.

The decisions were even harder on those people who had to do the actual firing. "It was up to the head of each unit to make his own cuts," a Play Bureau supervisor recalled. "You were given an arbitrary figure that you must get rid of, say, fifty people. Unfortunately you knew the background stories of all these people . . . So it was horrible. Whoever you cut, he was either going to starve or go back on Home Relief . . . People used to line up in front of me to announce their names, and I would say Cut. I never dared look at their faces."

Hoping to prevent further disturbances, Hallie remained at her desk to listen to the delegations and grievance committees that poured into her office after the dismissal notices had been given out. She asked Farnsworth and Charles Ryan, her personnel director, to do the same. Ryan stayed in his office all night to hear the stories and pleas of those who felt they had been discriminated against. As Hallie had hoped, sympathetic listening did much to reduce tensions. Federal Theatre workers staged fewer riots and hunger strikes than their fellow workers on the other Arts Projects. But her tactics won Hallie no sympathy in Washington, where Aubrey Williams complained that sympathy might be interpreted by the public as encouraging rebellion.

The country's attitude toward labor was changing. Labor was gaining power. In the Midwest the CIO under John L. Lewis had launched a drive to unionize the auto industry. In late December 1936, General Motors employees in Flint, Michigan, began a series of sit-down strikes; in early February, General Motors surrendered. Other industries, after strife and violence, followed suit. The movement to unionize blue-collar workers, which was to culminate by the end of 1937 in a decisive victory for the workers, dominated the press during most of the year, but it also alienated a segment of middle-class America. As William Leuchtenburg was later to say, "While initially sympathetic to the cause of labor, much of middle-class America took a less tolerant view than Roosevelt of the sit-downs. Property-minded citizens were scared by the seizure of factories . . . Foes of the sit-down strikes believed that Roosevelt, in refusing to employ force, was condoning an assault on property rights by lower-class rebels at the very moment he was attacking the sacred institution of the Supreme Court. Throughout 1937, these two issues—court packing and the sit-downs—were repeatedly linked." The reaction of New Dealers trying to salvage middle-class support for Roosevelt was predictable, and Hallie was caught up in it.

Back in the national capital in late June, Hallie learned that a new series of sit-ins in New York had culminated in workers' holding two WPA officials hostage. The incident, she told Philip Barber, made Washington want to "close the New York project immediately." She asked him to make an appeal to the workers to "refrain from that type of action." She might as well have asked for the moon.

However, except for the one day in May when all WPA activity stopped, the New York unit continued to function. Employees who demonstrated or joined grievance committees by day turned up at Federal Theatres at night to perform, work backstage, or do the chores necessary for production. Audiences made up of the poor and unemployed and the fashionable Broadway crowd continued to fill the theatres to cheer, boo, or otherwise express what they felt about what was happening on stage. Most of the shows receiving critical acclaim at the time addressed themselves to social issues. The dance group under Helen Tamiris had choreographed *How Long Brethren*, which dramatized Lawrence Gellert's *Negro Songs of Protest*. *Professor Mamlock*, by German Communist playwright Friedrich Wolf dramatized a Jewish surgeon's experience in Nazi Germany and was acclaimed as the best anti-Nazi drama to reach America. Two plays by Paul Green, *Unto Such Glory* and *Hymn to the Rising Sun*, were also on the boards. *Hymn*, about chain gang brutality in the South, was closed by a WPA administrator in Chicago who called it immoral, but was well received in New York, where critics found it beautiful, moving, and a "deadly indictment." They were less happy with a play a young director, Elia Kazan, had done for the children's theatre. *The Revolt of the Beavers* by two militant writers, Oscar Saul and Lou Lantz, is a fairy tale that pits oppressed beavers against their exploitative chief. When the chief threatens to replace the oppressed beavers with scabs, a revolution, which ends with the cruel chief going into exile and the worker beavers living happily ever

after, ensues. Brooks Atkinson called the play "Mother Goose
Marx" in the *Times,* and the *Daily Mirror*'s critic, Robert Coleman,
agreed. Hallie, who had told her husband that it was "very human
and amusing though also class conscious," reiterated her belief that
the play was only a fairy tale. All fairy tales, she said, have villains
and heroes. She cited the reactions of children who attended: they
thought the play was about good and bad beavers. Her reasoning did
not stop Federal Theatre enemies from distributing copies of Atkinson's review to every congressman in Washington.

John Houseman and Orson Welles had meantime begun rehearsing Marc Blitzstein's *The Cradle Will Rock,* a witty, derisive musical
drama pitting villainous capitalists and cops against heroic union
organizers. Blitzstein's inspiration had been Brecht and Weill's *The
Threepenny Opera.* Blitzstein told Brecht he wanted to write an
American *Threepenny.* Brecht suggested: "Make prostitution a dramatic symbol for overall prostitution—contemporary man's sellout
of his talent and his soul to the powers that exploit mankind." From
this advice came a brilliant, sardonic musical, a first of its kind in this
country. Aaron Copland was later to say that Blitzstein's achievement
made indigenous opera possible.

Hallie recognized the superb theatrical qualities of the work the
first time she heard it. Blitzstein played it for her at John Houseman's
apartment after the closing of the Actors' Repertory Company,
which was to have produced it with Orson Welles as director.
Houseman then thought of Hallie, and Hallie had no hesitation in
saying, Yes, Federal Theatre would do it. It was timely, exciting
drama, and this fact took precedence in Hallie's mind over every
other consideration. She probably did not even pause to wonder
what her bosses in Washington might think.

The Cradle Will Rock turned out to be more timely than Hallie
suspected. As Houseman wrote in his autobiography,

> The day *The Cradle Will Rock* went into rehearsal there
> were riots in Akron and Pontiac and strikes halted work in
> the Chrysler and Hudson auto plants. That same week the
> CIO under John L. Lewis started a drive to unionize the
> steel industry.
>
> By May the main battleground had shifted from autos

to steel; five mills of Republic Steel were struck and picketed. At Canton and Massillon, strikers prevented night-shift workers from reaching plants . . . On May 29th in South Chicago, a thousand steel workers marching on a mill of the Republic Steel Company were beaten back by police after a sharp fight . . . Two days later ten people were killed and eighty-four hurt as strikers again battled police in Chicago . . . During the first week of June, as we were starting our technical rehearsals, five thousand CIO sympathizers invaded the business section of Lansing, Michigan, forced the closing of factories and stores and blocked all traffic in protest against the arrest of pickets.

Blitzstein's opera was due to open at the Maxine Elliott Theatre on June 16. As the date approached, the question grew in everyone's mind: *would* it open? Rumors began circulating, those in the know predicting that Washington would never allow it.

Then, on June 12, Hallie, Alsberg, Sokoloff, and Cahill all received what looked, on the face of it, like a routine memorandum. "Because of impending cuts and reorganization," the memo stated, "no new plays or musical performances or art gallery shows" were to open before July 1. Hallie at once telephoned Houseman to ask how he felt about the delay. When he said he would not accept it, she called Washington, cited the adverse publicity that the postponement was bound to provoke, and asked for an exception to the ruling. When this move failed, she appealed to Archibald MacLeish, who flew to Washington to speak with David Niles. So did Orson Welles. But Niles insisted on the postponement. He did want it understood that Washington was postponing *Cradle,* not canceling it. Welles did not believe this and said that if the government would not let him open *Cradle* in June he would launch it privately. "In that case," said Niles,"we would no longer be interested in it as a property." That ended the interview. Welles and MacLeish returned to New York to confer with Hallie, who agreed with Welles that this was "censorship under a different guise."

But the news depressed her. If Welles and Houseman carried out their threat to launch the show privately, she was going to lose her most imaginative director and producer. She realized they had been roused to a spirit of mutiny. Houseman, who later admitted that under other circumstances "we would almost certainly have postponed the opening," went forward with plans to disengage himself from Federal Theatre. He invited a group of distinguished guests, including Moss Hart, George S. Kaufman, and producer Arthur Hopkins, to see a final runthrough. It might be their only chance, he said, to see Blitzstein's opera.

The next day a dozen uniformed WPA guards arrived at the theatre to prevent actors and stagehands from removing props, costumes, and stage sets belonging to the government while Houseman and Welles, installed in the basement, prepared to transfer their show to another theatre. The WPA notified organizations with tickets that the show would not go on. Houseman notified the same organizations, as well as the press, that the show *would* go on, even if Blitzstein himself, without scenery, costumes, or actors, had to sing all the roles. Those who had tickets, he later recalled in *Run-Through,*

> needed no urging. They were all part of that new left-wing audience that had sprung up with the Depression—the crowds that filled the houses on *New Theatre* nights and made *Lefty* and *Bury the Dead* and *Stevedore* the thrilling theatrical events they became. The Federal Theatre, with its half-dollar top, had further expanded this audience. Fifty percent of our public came from organized theatre parties, mostly of the Left-prejudiced and semieducated but young and generous and eager to participate in the excitement which the stage alone seemed to offer them in those uncertain times.

On the evening scheduled for the opening, Houseman and Welles announced that *The Cradle Will Rock* would be presented at the Venice Theatre, twenty-one blocks north of the Maxine Elliott, at 9:00 P.M. At the last moment a piano was rented and transported to the large, run-down, little-used theatre at Seventh Avenue and 58th Street, and the crowd of New Yorkers who had bought tickets for the opening, plus hundreds more who wanted to share the excitement, began the long march north. No one, least of all Houseman and Welles, knew what sort of performance the audience would see— perhaps only Blitzstein singing at the piano and three or four actors singing from their seats in the auditorium—for Equity had warned the actors that they could not perform, onstage, for a new management, without getting permission from Federal Theatre. And although Houseman had discovered that there was no Equity ruling forbidding actors from performing from positions offstage, he suspected that those performers who were wholly dependent on their government checks might withdraw. Most of the lead players—Will Geer, Howard da Silva, Hiram Sherman, and Paula Lawrence—were not on relief, but everyone else in the cast was.

The one lead player on relief was Olive Stanton, who played the prostitute. Welles had discovered her on the project. With her fresh, innocent looks, she fitted his conception of the role: an ordinary American girl driven to sell herself because of the Depression. She was to sing the first song, but no one knew whether she would. If she sang, would she lose her job with Federal Theatre?

By nine o'clock every seat in the Venice Theatre was filled, every inch of standing room taken. Blitzstein, in shirtsleeves and suspenders, had taken his place stage center at the untuned upright piano behind the curtain. After some preliminary remarks by Welles and Houseman, the curtain rose and the composer, looking pale and tense in the glare of a spotlight, announced, "A street corner—Steeltown, U.S.A." He then began to play and sing. "It was a few seconds," Houseman later recalled, "before we realized that another voice, a faint, wavering soprano," had been added to Blitzstein's. All heads in the audience turned as the spotlight moved offstage and onto the lower left box, where Olive Stanton, dressed in green and with hair dyed red, was standing. At first her voice was barely audible but she gradually gained courage. After she had finished, a second actor, also on relief, stood up. From the front row of the orchestra he made his rejoinder. The first scene took place with the actors positioned thirty yards apart. Most of the other actors took up their cues. From orchestra, balcony, and box seats, they rose to sing or speak their lines. As the play progressed, they moved into the aisles, they improvised movements. It was an evening no one who was present forgot and one that Hallie, perhaps more than anyone, would have cherished. But she was not present. Next morning the *New York Times* decreed that Blitzstein's opera was "the best thing militant labor has put into the theatre yet."

When Hallie first heard *Cradle,* she had suggested doing it on a bare stage, but Welles, wanting scenery, had overruled her. In the end she got the bare stage she wanted, but not in the theatre of her choice nor in the way she had anticipated. The evening's event, so brilliantly successful for Houseman, Welles, and Blitzstein, was for Hallie a bitter disappointment. The play she had championed succeeded, but for Federal Theatre itself the evening signaled a defeat. Although she did not know it at the time, the confrontation about *The Cradle Will Rock* marked a turning point for government-sponsored theatre. In Houseman's words, the "honeymoon of the New Deal and the Theatre was over."

The honeymoon was not *quite* over. Shortly before Blitzstein's opera opened, Hallie returned to Poughkeepsie to begin work on *One-Third of a Nation.* This latest Living Newspaper, which was to become Federal Theatre's biggest hit, was at first simply called *Housing.* Like every Living Newspaper before it, it had a history. In 1935 the Public Works Administration had published a pamphlet about housing. The publication, which concluded that one-third of Americans were inadequately housed, made national headlines. It advocated a program of clearance, building, loans, and code enforcement. If all citizens had a right to adequate shelter, the author argued, then the government had a responsibility to guarantee that right. When Roosevelt told the country in his second inaugural address that he saw "one-third of a nation ill-housed, ill-clad and ill-nourished," he was borrowing from the pamphlet's conclusion. His words started Hallie wondering what Federal Theatre could do to dramatize the plight of the ill-housed; eventually they provided *One-Third of a Nation* with its title.

After *Power* opened, Hallie invited New York City's Housing Commissioner, Langdon Post, to see a performance and dine with her and Hopkins. They talked about the difficulties people had finding adequate shelter, and Hallie said she would ask Morris Watson to collect material. Senator Robert F. Wagner was drafting a housing bill. Hallie thought the time was ripe for directing public attention to the issue. Then other plans absorbed her attention. She was thinking about the summer and about a summer theatre workshop that would bring together actors, designers, and directors from across the country. She had too little contact, she told Hopkins, with Federal Theatre professionals in the South, West, and Midwest. The workshop would be a six-week retraining session, with all participants helping to plan and produce a play that Hallie would choose. When Hopkins gave the idea his enthusiastic approval, Hallie went to David Rockefeller to ask for a grant to cover transportation and living expenses. President MacCracken agreed to house the participants and to give them the use of the Vassar theatre.

By mid-May Hallie had chosen a staff: Howard Bay was to teach design, Abe Feder lighting, Madalyn O'Shea acting, Helen Tamiris dance, Mary Merrill costuming, Clair Leonard music. Harold Bolton, who had directed *Professor Mamlock,* would direct. But Hallie had still not chosen a play. Though the Living Newspaper unit had collected a vast amount of material on housing and Arthur Arent had begun work on a dramatization, no script was ready. Then, suddenly, Wagner's housing bill was big news. The public was discussing it, Congress was debating it. It was at this point that Hallie decided that *Housing* was the play she wanted. Pierre de Rohan renamed it *One-Third of a Nation,* Arent hastily put together a first act, and the forty people who had signed up for the summer workshop converged on the Vassar campus.

How were all these people, strangers to each other and accustomed to working in very different ways, going to get on? Hallie wondered. Would they come to know each other in six weeks, to say nothing of being able to produce a play together? Eight theatre professionals came from the Midwest, six from the far West, three from the South, but the majority were Easterners. The staff members Hallie had chosen, with the exception of Clair Leonard, all came from New York City. "That didn't sit well with the California delegation," Colorado delegate Michael Slane recalled later. "You had on the East Coast people interested in experiment and new plays . . . The people from California were a different kind of cat." What they wanted was "to preserve the status quo, to continue with the old well-lighted box set." Everyone took a class in the Stanislavsky Method with Madalyn O'Shea. "At the very first meeting," according to Slane, "she wanted us to become couches." In the dance class, Tamiris got everyone tossing imaginary balloons back and forth. In the evenings the Westerners went into Poughkeepsie to drink beer, then returned to the campus, took off their shoes, and on the lawn outside the dormitory did burlesque versions of passing a balloon from hand to hand. "The people who were supervising didn't think it was funny," said Slane, "and many of us got calls to come to the office about this unseemly behavior."

Some supervisors also complained about the Westerners' behavior at mealtimes. Josselyn Hall's dining room was somewhat intimidating. Slane remembered chairs "so heavy it would take a man and a mule to move them," a huge portrait of Mrs. Russell Sage "scowling down on us with a faint smile of disapproval," maids in black uniforms and white caps, and a hostess who "wore a different colored evening dress every night, all made exactly alike." The situation eased a bit after the hostess revealed that Josselyn Hall had been named for a family that made its money selling a gonorrhea cure through pulp magazines. But one situation was never resolved. The theatre group shared the dining room with a group of parents who had come to the college to study eugenics. Somebody from the eugenics group, in Slane's words, "was always getting up, tinkling a spoon against a glass and announcing that tomorrow there would be a scenic trip to Bear Mountain, or some other place. They'd go into great lengths about this, and then sit down amidst a round of modest and polite applause. At which point somebody from the theatre group would get up, clank a spoon against a glass, and say, I would like to announce that I have three good lots in Mill Valley, California. If anybody's interested, please see me after dinner. It got to the point where everybody on our side of the room was breaking up and everybody on the other side of the room was getting their noses out of joint."

Hallie was not one of those who objected to the Josselyn Hall antics. When she got frantic messages from various members of the staff that the theatre was getting out of hand, she replied that it was up to the staff to use all this energy. "And once we got underway we certainly used it," she said later. She was on hand during the first days of the session to lead discussions and help formulate production plans. She asked Howard Bay to create a design that would point up the worst aspects of slums: the leaky faucets, the sagging beds, the crumbling walls, the broken stair rail, the roach-infested sinks, the unusable fire escapes. Bay's set showed people living under the shadow of these objects. Above the stage he hung a huge toilet seat, a sagging bed, a broken fire escape, a cockroach, a leaking faucet. The audience was to be shown a nightmare.

Act one—the only act presented at Vassar—begins with a fire breaking out in a tenement. "This might be 397 Madison Avenue, New York," the Loudspeaker announces, "or 245 Halsey Street, Brooklyn, or Jackson Avenue and 10th Street, Long Island City"—all places where fires had actually occurred. The audience sees investigators trying to determine the cause of the fire. It hears the Tenement House Inspector complaining that "if that building is a firetrap, then so is every old-law tenement in New York City." It hears the Landlord say he does not have enough money to fix up the tenement because the tenants do not pay him enough rent. His investment is in the land on which the tenement stands. "You'll have to go back into history," he says, "and blame whatever it was that made New York City real estate the soundest and most profitable speculation on the face of the earth." As in other Living Newspapers, the point is made that human misery results less from personal greed, which is taken for granted, than from a lack of proper social legislation.

To illustrate the point about real estate, the Landlord becomes an earlier version of his present self. He unrolls a grass mat, dons eighteenth-century attire, sets up a stanchion marked "Broadway and Canal Streets," and another one marked "This is mine. Keep off!" and sits down. Tenants arrive and sit on the mat with him as the years pass. Each tenant pays the Landlord larger and larger rents for smaller and smaller parcels of land. By 1850 there is not a blade of grass showing and the tenants are squeezed so tightly together they can hardly move. Then the Landlord leaves to buy another piece of property uptown. The tenants, he says, will somehow manage, because "a man's got to have a place to live." This line recurs repeatedly throughout the play.

Act one ends with a cholera epidemic in the year 1854. The New York City Health Inspector says that the main cause is the "crowded and filthy state in which a great portion of our population lives." The Landlord says, "Listen, we'd all like to live in a marble palace but we can't—so we take what God gives us and we're thankful." He addresses the tenants: "If you don't live here, where are you going to live? In the park? In the street? In another place that's no better than mine and maybe a hell of a lot worse? Because in case you're forgetting . . . you've got to have a place to live." Act two was still being written when this act was shown at Vassar.

A reporter from *Variety* who attended the opening night thought the show "tremendously effective." Eleanor Roosevelt, who was also present, told Hallie the play "achieved something which will mean a tremendous amount in the future, socially, and in the education and growing-up of America . . . far more than any amount of speeches that Langdon Post or I, or even the President, might make." A neighbor of Hallie's described the moment he liked best: "When the Trinity church wardens came to collect their rents, they weren't attired in knee britches and buckles. They were dressed in black and white. What you noticed was the gauntlet glove, the hand out-stretched for the rent, the one outstretched hand. That was Hallie's style, her kind of thing. It was a tremendous appeal to the imagina-tion." One of the points the play made is that the tenements owned by Trinity Church were among the worst in the city. Every time laws were passed to improve conditions, Trinity found ways to sidestep them.

Naturally Hallie hoped that her vision of the play would carry over into the New York production. The Adelphi Theatre was to present a full version in mid-January 1938. But Philip Barber had a conception that was fundamentally different from Hallie's. He wanted realism—a real tenement and period costumes. As producer, he got his way. Arent and Bay went along. Bay designed a forty-five-foot-high tenement house out of steel-pipe scaffolding that no one who saw the show ever forgot. To this structure he attached real objects from tenements—tin cornices, balustrades, and other such pieces that he was able to rescue from tenements being demolished. Rhoda Rammelkamp, who designed the costumes, spent hours in the public library studying newspapers and magazines to get "a realistic look." "If a fabric from the shop was too bright for the period," she recalled, "we dyed it."

When the curtain rose on opening night, the audience, amazed at the sight of Bay's towering tenement structure, burst into applause. Barber, who was standing next to Bay at the back of the theatre, felt triumphant. "Hallie," he was to recall, "had done something creative with the play and I had rejected it. In her eyes, my production was old-hat because I used flats." When the audience applauded once more as the tenement burst into flames, Bay turned to Barber and commented, "I hate every minute of it." In Barber's opinion, Bay was simply being loyal to Hallie. Later Bay was to say that he preferred the set he did at Vassar, but "it wouldn't have been right for the larger New York stage."

The climax of act two was lifted straight out of the *Congressional Record*. Since it caused a furor in Congress, it is worth recording. The time is spring 1937. Wagner's housing bill is being discussed on the floor of the Senate. Southern Democrats have just joined the debate.

Loudspeaker: Senator William E. Borah of Idaho.

Borah: Is [Senator Wagner] going to discuss the question of causes of slums? Why do we have these awful degraded conditions?

Loudspeaker: Senator Robert F. Wagner of New York.

Wagner: I think it is a very simple matter. It is because of the low incomes received by the individuals who live in the slums. That is the fundamental difficulty. If overnight we could increase their incomes by a more fair distribution of the wealth of the country, we would not have any slums!

Loudspeaker: Senator C. O. Andrews of Florida.

Andrews: Mr. President, I should like to ask the Senator from New York where the people who live in the slums come from.

Wagner: A great many of them have been here a long time. What does the Senator mean by, Where do they come from? Whether they have come from some other country?

Andrews: I think we ought not to offer any inducement to people to come in [to New York] from our country or foreign countries or anywhere else and take advantage of our government in supplying them with homes. For instance, if we examine the birth records in New York, we will find that most of the people there in the slums were not born in New York, but the bright lights have attracted them from everywhere, and that is one reason why there are so many millions in New York without homes.

Soon after the play opened, Senator Josiah W. Bailey of North Carolina commented acidly during a Senate session that the government was paying to do extensive research into "this sort of thing . . . How many more," he wondered, would follow their example? "This activity is a fine thing for us," he told his colleagues with pointed sarcasm. "Our little brief authority here will not go very far. We shall soon be forgotten; but it is a great thing to know that we have this [Federal Theatre production] for which we may appropriate money, and which will make us all actors on the stage forever."

If the production had gone unnoticed, the senators might have been less concerned. But *One-Third of a Nation* got rave reviews. Brooks Atkinson in the *Times* called it a "rabble-rouser of uncommon eloquence . . . aggressively New Deal . . . a caustic and vibrant piece of theatrical muckraking." In the *Daily Mirror,* Robert Coleman said the show was "a swiftly paced, exciting pageant." The *Sun*'s critic thought it "a vivid, coherent report, often deeply moving, and almost always forceful." As Walter Winchell put it, the critics "used their best Sunday adjectives."

That was the trouble. As the *Herald Tribune* pointed out in a front-page story, certain senators felt they had been made into villains. Senator Andrews wrote to Hopkins, enclosed the *Tribune* article, and asked, "Who is responsible for this play, and what action, if any, has been taken by your department to have these particular scenes eliminated?" He demanded to know the names and addresses of every actor, writer, and producer associated with the production, as well as their weekly salaries. Senator Harry Byrd of Virginia joined him in demanding detailed financial information. "We all pay taxes" was Senator Bailey's comment. "Why not have some Baptist, Methodist, Seventh-Day Adventist, and Mormon plays as well?"

When Aubrey Williams appeared before the Senate Appropriations Committee considering supplementary funds for work relief in late February, Georgia Senator Richard Russell asked him to explain the Theatre Project. How did plays originate, he wanted to know. Some "very dangerous precedents," he argued, were being set. Other senators agreed that when taxpayers' money was involved, plays should be "very carefully censored" so as not to hold anyone up to ridicule.

One-Third of a Nation, Hallie later conceded, made enemies as well as friends. But when Aubrey Williams asked her what she meant by insulting senators, Hallie replied that the play had simply reproduced material from the *Congressional Record,* which as she understood it was in the public domain. "If senators and congressmen oppose an increase in appropriations for housing and say so in Congress, why should they object to being quoted?"

Was Hallie politically naive, as some of her critics contended— one administrative official later commenting that she "convicted the senators right out of their own mouths. They deserved it, God knows, but you just don't do that to senators"—or was something else at stake? As administrator of the Theatre Project, she was bound to think of consequences, and in time it no doubt did occur to Hallie that "you don't do that to senators," especially senators who have the power to vote appropriations. But in the thrill of an opening— and, typically, she responded to the moment—the play was the thing. The Senate scene was not just theatrical, it made people sit up and think. It even gave some spectators apoplexy, and giving apoplexy to conservatives, as she was to say in a speech, was in her view one function of the theatre. Hallie had acted in accordance with her nature.

Years later, after the project had closed and Hallie had had time to reflect, she had something more to say. "Living Newspapers made enemies that were very powerful and instrumental in the closing of the project. I think of this fact at times and wonder whether it would have been better for our people to have remained aloof from all subjects controversial. Then I realized that this would have barred from our stages, judging by the plays which involved us in censorship, Aristophanes, Shakespeare, Ben Jonson, Maxwell Anderson, Elmer Rice, Paul Green, and many other important authors classical and modern."

One-Third of a Nation, altered to meet local conditions, was also produced in Detroit, Cincinnati, Philadelphia, Hartford, New Orleans, Seattle, Portland, and San Francisco. There were repercussions in these cities as well. As Esther Porter Lane, who helped produce *Nation* in Seattle, put it, "We found what so many projects found. You go and photograph property in the community and you find that the most powerful church in town owns it . . . All these dirty, unsightly garbage dumps are owned by people whose names you can't mention."

Esther Lane had a strong sense of what could and could not be done. The Seattle production mentioned no names.

CHAPTER

13

Mounting Opposition

IN the spring of 1937, while protests against the appropriations cut had been getting under way, leaders of Actors' Equity and other professional theatrical unions had asked their members not to participate. It was a bad time, they warned, to risk antagonizing Washington. A bad time indeed! With Roosevelt's popularity on the wane and conservative reaction against his New Deal policies beginning to gather momentum, the WPA was in jeopardy and the union leaders' advice was no more than practical. Having learned to live with Federal Theatre, the professional unions did not want to see the project abandoned. But leaders of the Workers' Alliance saw things differently. Always less concerned with immediate consequences than with long-term political goals, they urged their members to demonstrate, protest, and in every possible way oppose the congressional action.

Faced with the differences of opinion that developed among her workers, Hallie wavered. Her natural inclination to scorn the conservatives led her to sympathize with Alliance strategy, but practical sense and an allegiance to Hopkins led her in the opposite direction. Hallie knew that violent protests accomplished nothing. She had been clear in her instructions to Philip Barber to urge workers to "refrain from that type of action." What she seems not to have realized was that the protests were being led by people to whom upheavals were a welcome step toward a new social order. If someone had told Hallie that a handful of Communists decided Alliance policy, she might have thought the charge a piece of Red-baiting, and she had been too long a victim of Red-baiting herself to condone it. She saw her workers as one. She knew there were extremists among them—"tiresome radicals," as she had more than once called them, people like Morris Watson and Joe Losey who had angered her by inserting Communist dogma into a Living Newspaper script. But she saw these people merely as having gone too far. Was this simple-minded? Her Washington bosses certainly thought so when Hallie told an American Theatre Council audience to ask itself what other method workers had at their disposal.

Hallie was one of the many people caught up in Popular Front ideology, a leftist umbrella so broad that it blurred all distinctions. Communists, Socialists, liberals, and fellow travelers all declared themselves in favor of social reform. Their opponents saw them as one. While politically sophisticated people understood the differences, many others, including large numbers of artists and intellectuals, did not. News of the Stalin trials and purges, which was soon to disillusion many people on the left, was just beginning to be heard. Most of the people Hallie worked with still believed that the Soviet Union was going to usher in a more just social system.

In mid-1937 Hallie had no way of seeing what was coming. She did begin to sense that WPA officials would have welcomed her resignation. If some among them had once rejoiced in Federal Theatre as a New Deal showpiece, none of them did now. The Arts Projects, which had inspired more demonstrations than all other WPA efforts, had become a liability to the parent body, and Federal Theatre, the most visible and controversial of the four arts, had become the number one liability.

For a time Hallie seems to have thought that she could still turn to Hopkins, that no matter what those in his office might dictate, Harry would continue to help her keep Federal Theatre "free, adult, and uncensored." When he was suddenly less easy to reach there was reason: Hallie knew he was ill and that his wife was dying of cancer. It was several months before she became aware that Hopkins's thinking had changed.

Hopkins's first loyalty was to Roosevelt. It was an unwavering loyalty. Even when the President did not take Hopkins's advice, Hopkins fought for the President's interests. Roosevelt responded by making Hopkins a close confidant. In 1937 he did more. He urged Hopkins to consider himself a presidential candidate in the 1940 Democratic primaries. Hopkins, who had never before felt a need to play party politics, who indeed until this time had enjoyed his role of maverick, suddenly found himself in a new situation. Once his ambitions had been aroused, he began to listen more attentively to what officials inside his own bureau were saying, with predictable results: Hopkins the Crusader became Hopkins the Realist.

Hallie got a first clue when she read in *Variety* in July that at a meeting of theatre-union representatives in New York Hopkins had "at long last" shown sensitivity to the charge that leftists were running Federal Theatre. Within a month, *Variety* was reporting that the line of command had changed drastically: Hallie, who had always before done business "directly with Hopkins," now had to go through Ellen Woodward and her assistants.

It had been this group who had postponed Blitzstein's opera, and its members had not been slow to take further steps. In the spring, they had asked Hallie if Pierre de Rohan, the editor of *Federal Theatre Magazine,* was a Communist and why the magazine printed so many pictures of shirt-sleeved crowds in city parks. When Hallie pointed out that Rohan, far from being a Communist, had been recommended by the archconservative vice president, John Nance Garner, it made no impression. Despite a marshaling of facts and the support she garnered from prominent people in the New York theatre, the magazine had been discontinued.

While Hallie was still trying to fathom this turn of events, Washington made a move that, in the view of almost everyone in New York, was even more unexpected and shattering. A finance expert from the national WPA office was sent north to administer the Arts Projects. Hallie was not consulted about this change, nor were any of the other national directors. Paul Edwards simply arrived in New York, and Bill Farnsworth, who had previously managed such matters as employment, labor, and supplies, was told to go. When Hallie subsequently tried to install Farnsworth as artistic director for the New York project, she was told that the appointment would have to be approved by Hopkins, who was not available. *Variety*'s comment that the "Flanagan influence" was waning ranked as one of the understatements of the year.

Although Hallie did not know it at the time, Hopkins had already decided on the man he wanted as artistic director for New York. This was George Kondolf, who headed the Chicago project. Hallie had appointed Kondolf at a time when the Midwest was not doing well, and Kondolf had made a success of it. One of his big hits had been *O Say Can You Sing,* a musical satire on the New Deal. Hopkins had gone out to Chicago, seen it, liked it, and, in Hallie's words, laughed inordinately at its corny jokes. Subsequently Hopkins had returned to Chicago to sound out Kondolf about taking charge in New York. Hallie learned all this after the fact.

According to Philip Barber, who found himself kicked upstairs to make room for Kondolf, Hopkins told Hallie that he wanted a Catholic for the top job, because Roosevelt believed there was going to be a world war and had issued instructions to unify the country. Catholics represented a strong opposition bloc to the President's international policies. Kondolf was Federal Theatre's most prominent Catholic. Although Hallie liked him personally, he would not have been her choice for top position in New York. His views, both political and artistic, were at odds with those prevailing in the city. George Kondolf was an old-time showman with a preference for the sort of play that stock companies had been producing for years. He had little interest in political matters and no ties at all with the experimental theatre movement of the thirties. He was, in fact, the perfect embodiment of the noncontroversial theatre that Hallie had fought from the start.

Wasting no time, Paul Edwards and George Kondolf set about reorganizing New York. Their mission, as they saw it, was to return Federal Theatre to its original aim of providing relief for professionals. Many in New York who had hoped for more resigned at this time. As Barber's assistant, Walter Hart, explained to Hallie in his letter of resignation, this latest reorganization, coming on top of the "barrage of constantly changing WPA rules and regulations," was one too many. He had fought, he said, for more than a year to enable Federal Theatre to "function, not as a road-building project, but as a theatre." Yet every time a play was produced it meant a "miracle" accomplished, and at long last he was tired of creating miracles. He concluded his letter by saying that his enthusiasm for the ideal Hallie had set remained "undampened," but he could not continue.

Hart was correct in perceiving that Washington's wish to rid the New York unit of its "radical" tendencies would soon result in a more bureaucratized theatre. Officials, not artists, began making the important decisions. Right then, Hallie could have chosen to resign. But, as she was soon to tell Hopkins, the work had become her life's blood. Having invested so much in creating a national theatre, she could not now desert it. She chose to stay—to fight what was to be a losing battle. She tried to salvage what remained. Those among her co-workers who saw Federal Theatre as an instrument to fight injustice were disappointed by her next moves. Hallie did everything she could to save "her" theatre. The curtailed funds, she told her supervisors at a regional staff meeting in the fall, made it necessary to revise plans. "We are being watched by everyone," she warned, "by our friends, our enemies, our audiences, the press, and above all by Congress, to see whether we justify continued allocation of federal funds." In a hard-hitting speech to her New York producers, she made the point that choices of plays had been "too limited, too unbalanced, too uninformed." There had been too little effort to study audiences, on the one hand, and "our angel, the United States government," on the other. There had been a "dangerous overemphasis on left-wing plays," which now threatened the theatre's freedom of expression. She did not want to withdraw from plays dealing with current American problems, but other sorts of plays— classical, religious, and historical—should be given consideration. She mentioned a pageant that several actors had performed in honor of the sesquicentennial of the U.S. Constitution, noting that it had done more "to help the continuance of Federal Theatre than all the marchers in all our picket lines." She wrote Hopkins that the appointment of Kondolf had probably been a good thing, as it might serve to contradict the charge of radicalism.

She went further. She appointed a Poughkeepsie neighbor and former playwriting student, a one-time lawyer who had become a popular Catholic playwright, to head the Play Bureau. This, of course, brought her into conflict with Francis Bosworth, the current Bureau head. "Emmet Lavery ingratiated himself with Hallie,"

Bosworth thought. "He got the job because he was more conservative." Hallie would have had a different explanation. The truth was,
Lavery had turned up at the Poughkeepsie summer session, and the
moment had been opportune. Hallie, under pressure from Washington, saw Lavery's moderate views as advantageous. Besides, he was
a devoted friend. He was invaluable at a time when Hallie was feeling
vulnerable and in need of reinforcements.

Accommodating others' wishes when those wishes were at odds
with her own did not sit easily with Hallie. Although she gave in to
Washington when she saw there was no alternative, her state of mind
as the summer season eased into fall was by no means as compliant
as her actions might suggest. Writing Philip in mid-October that
Ellen Woodward had been admonishing the project directors to
remember that Congress was in session, Hallie added, "Whether this
means that we should prostrate ourselves every time we pass a fat
man in the elevator, or what it does mean, none of us know. But it
bodes no good to anyone. I'm glad I'll be gone when they begin to
rant around."

Hallie's fall plans included a second inspection of her western
units. She planned to visit Michigan, Illinois, Oregon, Washington,
and California and, enroute, to confer with Eugene O'Neill in
California. She was to look over work being done, assess needs,
confer with supervisors and WPA administrators, and, where necessary, make changes. Her trip got off to a flying start. Philip took their
children to the train station to see her off, and Jack ran down the
tracks to wave good-bye. A few minutes later Hallie began a letter to
her husband: "Dearest, I want very much to do a good job on this
trip—to work hard and help my beloved, big, funny Federal
Theatre." Her beloved theatre was now more dream than reality, but
the dream sustained her, as did her conviction that she had the best
of all possible marriages. Hallie wrote that she would think of Philip
through everything she did. And had he known that while she was
painting the kitchen chairs and changing the linoleum she was really
making love to him? (This was a reference to a remark Philip had
made about gardening: that weeding was one of his ways of making
love to her.)

Hallie made her first stop in Detroit to visit her mother, who was now almost totally blind. Her view of her mother as the embodiment of all the stoical virtues had not changed. Louisa Ferguson, in Hallie's words, was "intrepid, proud, and neither too childishly rebellious nor too resignedly sweet." She had hoped to view the Detroit theatre in a similarly positive light. The city, she felt, was dramatic: grand houses and industrial slums. She was disappointed that Federal Theatre had discovered no playwright to point up the contrasts. "I do wish we had a real project here," she wrote Philip, "instead of a half-baked group doing *Boy Meets Girl*." But when she saw *Boy Meets Girl* she surprised herself by finding it hilarious. Out of a hope that something even better might come from Detroit, she dissuaded the local WPA office from closing the unit down. Eventually, she arranged to send in talent from out of state, and Detroit improved.

Because of the reduced appropriation, many Midwest efforts had ended. Federal Theatre still had small units in Des Moines, Springfield, and Peoria. There was a children's theatre in Gary, Indiana, and theatre groups in Cincinnati and Cleveland, though it had taken a flood to make the Ohio undertaking acceptable to the state. Before rains flooded the Ohio River valley in the spring of 1937, many in the state had felt that the government should stay out of the arts business, because art is a medium of propaganda and the government might use it as such. Then came the deluge, and Federal Theatre actors danced, clowned, and performed magic tricks before thousands of cold and homeless people. Feelings changed and public support rallied.

The Omaha project was one example, Hallie thought, of a unit that could have developed into a good one, given more federal support. Directors in Nebraska were local men with stock company experience. In 1936 they had directed plays for schools and outlying villages, and though Hallie thought these shows rather crude, they reached people who had never before seen live drama and brought in full houses. After Omaha had been in operation for five months, a newspaper reported that the center had entertained "more than 50,000 persons with dramatic comedy and variety bills as well as minstrel shows and vaudeville." The June cuts had meant firing almost all the actors not on relief, and the shows had ceased. In Hallie's words, she "let Omaha down." The loss hurt. Omaha had been Hallie's first home.

At her next stop Hallie discovered a vigor and variety that was in sharp contrast with her Nebraska experience. Chicago had grown. It had seasoned directors, and though many of them were doing the kind of stock company plays that Hallie called "Old Hokum," they were doing them well. There was a good Negro company, and Ruth Page and Katherine Dunham were the choreographers for some expert dance units. Friends met Hallie at the station and rushed her off to see *Monesh,* a Jewish spectacle that she pronounced a "little too florid but very swell." She liked O'Neill's *The Straw* rather more. She saw it, she wrote Philip, with Kay Ewing, a former student whom she had made a director. "We wept in complete unison, and the usual gum-chewing Chicago audience sniffled and sobbed in an unbeliev-able manner. Even a hard-boiled critic cried and had the decency to say so in his column. We're sold out for weeks, so evidently tears are a pleasure to lots of people." Hallie was once more among her own kind. She was probably, she confessed, "incurably Midwest."

Then she was off to Seattle. The train trip west was to be her reward after work. The shows she saw had relaxed her, but she had spent most of her time conferring with supervisors. Among natural beauties seen from the train's windows she recaptured a serenity. "I've had such a day of looking, of absolute quietness," she wrote Philip. "Remember Paul Green saying he didn't want just a little bit of music but a whole mess of it? That's the way I feel about quietness—and about nature—and there certainly is a whole mess of it, and all kinds. The great plains of yesterday changed by this morning to hills with cactus and sage brush, and then began oil wells and oil fires, and then Montana with great cattle ranges, rivers, blazing yellow trees, strange little gray towns in the midst of brilliant-colored rocks and mountain torrents. All afternoon we've been going through this breathtaking continental divide . . . It is dusk now and we are sliding down the most terrific grade, with enormous mountains on either side, great crags, gray and purple, with a dark embroidery of pines. The train is way up ahead and you can see it moving perilously up the mountains." She had been out on the observation deck all afternoon, she added, alternately looking and writing a piece about Federal Theatre, in which she concluded that the theatre she headed, like the airplane, the radio, the French Revolution, and the Gothic cathedral, made little sense. (In moods of ecstasy Hallie was capable of linking the most unlikely things.) "Neither do I probably," she admitted.

Seattle, with its seven hills and dramatic views of distant mountains, enchanted her as few cities had. Her hotel room, with a large bay window looking out over the city's grandeur, inspired her to fire off a telegram to Philip the morning after she arrived saying: "We should live here." But Seattle's Federal Theatre unit, as she was soon to learn, did not match the city's natural splendor.

The Living Newspaper *Power,* which had been produced in Seattle the previous June, had created a public sensation. It had sold out all five performances, but its popularity had caused alarm among conservatives, who felt that it "assailed, satirized, ridiculed, exposed, attacked, and condemned" private utilities. The state WPA had been upset, the directors of the play had resigned, and the project director had resolved to do noncontroversial plays. Then came the cuts, and many supervisors, directors, and technicians had been fired. When Hallie arrived she found a Negro unit, a white unit, and a vaudeville unit with only one dingy out-of-the way movie house for all of them to perform in. She was further dismayed to discover what was going on in the theatre at the University of Washington. Hallie had appointed one of its leaders as a regional consultant. She had hoped that the university would collaborate with her own people, but the university, it turned out, had used WPA funds only to build up its own theatre department. The campus had three theatres operating every night, each in a beautifully constructed building. Satisfied audiences did not attend Federal Theatre shows, especially after the furor caused by *Power* resulted in lackluster programs. The contrast between her own theatre and those of the university was a blow.

After seeing her Negro unit perform in a poor production of Shaw's *Androcles and the Lion,* Hallie wondered if the fault was hers. Perhaps the company was poor because she had neglected the region. She at once sent off a letter to Esther Porter Lane, asking if she would be interested in starting a children's theatre in the city. Esther was a good choice. Like Hallie, she realized that actors, no matter how discouraged, could be retrained if given the proper incentive. Using the vaudeville group, she started a theatre for children that was well received. One vaudevillian she rehabilitated had been a skilled roper. "He had only performed in burlesque houses," she recalled, "so all he knew besides rope tricks was how to tell filthy jokes." Esther taught him to substitute nursery rhymes for the jokes. "It took ages to teach him, but he did learn. He recited while he roped."

Portland, Hallie's next stop, was a high point of the trip. The WPA administrator in Oregon had had the idea of using WPA laborers to build an inn six thousand feet up on the slope of Mount Hood. Timberline Lodge had an outdoor theatre, which the local theatre director used for a series of dance performances. Hallie was so delighted with the beauty of the lodge that she asked the state administrator to build her a year-round theatre. "We should be building theatres," she wrote Philip. "If the WPA blew up tomorrow, the Federal Theatre would be forgotten in a year, but Timberline will exist for centuries. I want five regional theatres, each taking on the color of the region. That is my present dream." Later she wrote: "Of all the states in the country, Federal Theatre had its most perfect working conditions in Oregon under Mr. Griffith. He ran the business and administrative end completely but left program and artistic personnel to us. Under this arrangement, there was no censorship in Oregon in spite of the fact that we did a strong program, including three Living Newspapers."

Portland was fortunate in having Bess Whitcomb as its theatrical director. Whitcomb had attended the Vassar summer session and returned to Oregon intent on using her thirty-five vaudeville actors to create Living Newspapers. She had two Living Newspapers in rehearsal when Hallie arrived. One, *Flax,* was being prepared for a festival of flax growers in the Willamette Valley. The other, about the Bonneville Dam, used the troupe's dancing talents. Hallie thought *Flax* crude, but the character of the attempt absolutely right. She decided to expand the Oregon program. She phoned Yasha Frank, a Los Angeles director who was using vaudevillians to create children's plays, and asked him to meet her. Frank promptly arrived, accompanied Hallie to Timberline Lodge, and, during a blinding snowstorm on the return down the mountain, got her so excited about doing children's shows in Oregon that she almost forgot the danger they were in. She elaborated this incident into a highly dramatic tale in *Arena*.

The car they were in careened down the mountain pass in the growing dusk, lost its way, and came to a halt. Two passengers went for help while Hallie and Yasha Frank continued their discussion in the freezing dark. All passengers were eventually rescued by a vehicle which, in Hallie's words, "crawled down the mountain and hauled us from what proved to be the edge of a precipice." Whatever the truth of the matter, Hallie's talk with Frank had substantial results. Frank promised to work out some plans for Portland. To begin with, a production of *Pinocchio*, which would have real acrobats for the circus scenes.

A year and a half earlier, Hallie had received a report that Federal Theatre in San Francisco had more misfits, neurotics, and worn-out performers on its rolls than any other California outfit. So the night she got there she was surprised to see a well-done show in a freshly painted theatre. It was a miracle, she wrote Philip, to see actors who had been frightened, anxious, and insecure on her first visit now performing professionally. But she was feeling exhausted. The administrative part of her job—particularly visiting state offices—got her down. Howard Miller, whom Hallie had recently promoted to deputy director in Washington, was traveling with her and was sure she needed a break. He decided to take her to a matinee at a burlesque house. She had never been to a burlesque show, he recalled, and she loved it.

Two marionette shows she saw in San Francisco, *Alice in Wonderland* and *Twelfth Night*, made her "long for the children." She wrote Philip that they would have "loved the twitching of Malvolio's mustachios." But the zenith of Hallie's California trip was the day she spent with Eugene and Carlotta O'Neill.

Mrs. O'Neill drove into the city to pick Hallie up. Hallie was always impressed by beautiful women. Her hostess, she reported, was one of the "most beautiful creatures" she had ever seen: "black hair, enormous black eyes circled with purplish shadows, and an aroma of strangeness." During their ride through the mountains, Mrs. O'Neill repeatedly warned Hallie that when they arrived Mr. O'Neill might have decided that he would not see her. "She told me at least three times that I must not stay more than half an hour and that she would give me the signal when to go." Her husband, it was explained, needed complete seclusion. The last time they had been in New York, he had been "almost torn to pieces by celebrity hunters and autograph hounds."

The O'Neills lived at the top of a mountain, in a long, spread-out house. There was a large living-room facing a garden and a view of distant mountains. Hallie thought O'Neill was "more human" than she had been led to believe. She sized him up as "very simple, quiet and shy, with not a trace of the pose of a great man." This was her badge of approval. O'Neill asked her about the productions Federal Theatre had done of his plays. They talked about these for a while, and then Hallie, having received the "unmistakable sign" from Mrs. O'Neill, rose and said she must leave. But O'Neill quickly said she must stay to lunch. He wanted to discuss his work in progress, a cycle of nine plays about an American family, their ancestors and descendants. He wanted a company that would study the plays for at least a year before producing them. He was thinking of the Theatre Guild. Hallie said if for any reason the Guild did not want to do them, Federal Theatre would like the opportunity. "Would you take them sight unseen?" O'Neill asked. Hallie said, "Absolutely." She could promise to produce them in at least three places—East Coast, West Coast, and Chicago. O'Neill commented that Federal Theatre was becoming a "great force in the life of American writers and the history of our stage." Afterward, thinking over the day's events, Hallie kept thinking of the relationship between the O'Neills. "They seem to live together in that strange, remote place as if they were held together by one of those repulsion-attractions which he often describes. I got a very definite impression that he needs to see people more, and that she does not wish him to."

There was more variety in Los Angeles, the second-largest of all the centers, than in other places. Hallie liked everything she saw. There was a dance-drama about pioneers crossing the plains, which Myra Kinch and her dance group had created in response to Hallie's plea for native material. There was *Ready! Aim! Fire!*, a musical satire on dictatorship that two local writers had got up for the vaudevillians and that was taking in $1,000 a week. To start off a new international cycle, there was *The Weavers*, which Gerhart Hauptmann had written in 1892 about a weavers' revolt in the

Silesian mountains. Hallie thought it "the most exciting and probably the most revolutionary play we have yet done." The experimental unit under the direction of Virginia Farmer was developing a cycle of plays about California. A Negro unit was doing *Androcles and the Lion*. A marionette group was doing *The Emperor Jones*. A classical group was rehearsing a cycle of nativity plays to be done in churches during the holidays. The two plays Yasha Frank had put together for children, *Hansel and Gretel* and *Pinocchio,* were Hallie's favorites. "Yasha Frank," she wrote Philip, "is a genius." She began making plans to move his productions to New York.

But the people in Los Angeles, like the people in New York, were facing political difficulties, as Hallie discovered when a delegation met her as she emerged from a matinee. Wasn't *The Weavers* subversive? she was asked. And weren't some members of the experimental troupe living immoral lives? Hallie replied that *The Weavers* was a classic about events that had taken place in the 1840s, which, of course, did not answer their question. The delegation also complained that Federal Theatre had put on a show in which a girl was unrolled from a carpet. That happened, said Hallie, now on more certain grounds, in Shaw's *Caesar and Cleopatra*. She told the delegates they would probably enjoy seeing it. But other allegations soon followed, and Hallie, fed up with hearing so many accusations and realizing they could be damaging, decided to ask the Washington bureau to investigate all charges. In time, according to Hallie, they proved unfounded. But the truth or untruth of the charges was not the real issue. Reaction against Federal Theatre was building on the West Coast as it had on the East, and for similar reasons. Hallie had been all too successful in developing the kind of theatre she believed in, a *relevant* theatre.

She got further indications of trouble to come on her trip to San Diego. Hallie had one day off, a Sunday. Howard Miller and the local music director persuaded her to spend it in Mexico. It was "typical," Hallie wrote Philip, that on her one free day of the trip Washington phoned. After sightseeing, Hallie went to bed. Suddenly, she heard a loud banging on her door and a Mexican saying that there was a phone call for Mr. Miller. Hallie said she did not know where he was and went back to sleep. An hour later, Miller came in to say that he was terribly sorry, but Lawrence Morris, Ellen

Woodward's assistant, was on the phone from Washington saying
that Federal Theatre was being maligned in the *New York Times*.
"What does Larry want us to do about it," Hallie retorted, "in the
middle of Mexico in the middle of the night?" Morris, it turned out,
wanted Hallie in San Diego by nine the next morning to meet press
representatives. This meant they would have to leave at once. Hallie
refused: to drive through the mountain roads at night was insane.
But they did get up for the trip early the next morning.

Miller later recalled that he and Hallie had a "wonderful
relationship. We had great ups and downs and many differences of
opinion. She used to get damn mad at me and vice versa, but I was
very fond of her." And Hallie was fond of Howard, almost as much
as she had been of Bill Farnsworth. Both men were efficient,
down-to-earth, knowledgeable about the theatre, and more worldly-
wise politically than Hallie. She needed their counsel, knew it, and
was grateful to get it. Howard could also humor Hallie in a way that
delighted her. One day when she felt particularly discouraged by the
news from Washington, he composed a poem for her:

> The United States flag flies over our plant,
> said Hallie Flanagan gaily,
> Red for the liberals, white for the virgins,
> and blue for the way I feel daily.

She had another blue day after the evening she and Miller spent
with Max Reinhardt and his wife. During their discussion, Reinhardt
asked Miller to be the business manager of a school he was starting.
"I am so afraid he is leaving," Hallie wrote to her husband. Having
lost Farnsworth, John Houseman, and Orson Welles, she felt she
could not continue in her job if Washington kept refusing to help her
hang on to the "few good people I have. Howard does not want to
leave, but he is furious at the attitude of Washington." Washington
had turned down Hallie's request to raise Miller's salary.

Her job and her mood changed from one day to the next. At a
farewell party in Los Angeles, twelve hundred of her workers
foregathered to present her with bunches of violets, corsages of roses,
boxes of candy, and a woolly dog. "No one can help loving this
project," she concluded. "It is unquestionably the best."

Traveling back east, Hallie tried to reassure herself about what was happening on the West Coast. She had substantial backing. Her audition board included the well-known movie stars Boris Karloff and Edward G. Robinson, and she was sure that neither could be accused of fostering subversion. She had the support of Robert Montgomery, president of the Screen Actors' Guild, and of John Howard Lawson, the playwright, both of whom had voiced the opinion that the California project was too cautious and ought to be doing more controversial plays. Hallie was not aware that Lawson ruled the Hollywood Communists. She might not have cared if she had known, though she would have been more cautious in claiming his allegiance to Federal Theatre. To her way of thinking, caught up as she was in Popular Front ideology, Communists were for justice. Even when tiresome, they were on the "right side."

She was feeling homesick—for the children, the house, and most of all for Philip "holding a cigarette, looking at me suddenly, reaching out as I pass to touch my dress." She told him she would soon be home.

Howard Miller did not resign, but that was the only good news Hallie was to hear during an otherwise bleak December. She returned to Washington to discover that the Arts Projects had moved from the decayed splendor of the McLean Mansion to a dowdy structure known as the Ouray Building, a place, Hallie promptly told a friend, which one reached after walking "through a fringe of dismal slums and through the unappetizing red-light district." Writing Philip that her new office had dull tan walls and dull brown woodwork, she added that she would never be able to think anything in such an atmosphere except dull brown thoughts. Her first idea, which she later admitted came from a failure to recognize the full significance of the move, was to try to make the place more homey. How about acquiring some of the Venetian blinds that employees on other WPA projects had made? she asked WPA officials. Or one of the rugs she had seen at Timberline, also made by WPA workers? Absolutely not, she was told. Hallie decided she was being treated like a child who makes unreasonable demands. "Apparently the sight of Timberline Lodge had gone to our heads . . . There was not to be any of that nonsense in the Ouray Building." She, Sokoloff, Alsberg, and Cahill had suddenly become "the poor relations of the WPA."

She soon got a clearer notion of the reasons behind the refusals. President Roosevelt's determination to balance the budget had thrown the WPA into panic. As the *New York Times* put it on December 12, the future of the entire WPA hung in the balance. One budget proposal for the fiscal year 1938–1939 would cut half a billion dollars from relief funds.

In the midst of this latest crisis Hallie was summoned to Hopkins's office. She found him alone, looking out the window. When he turned to greet her, Hallie was shocked. The man who had hired her and who had been, with Philip, her most constant supporter, looked thin, haggard, and terribly ill. "I have got something I want to get off my chest," he told her. "Sit down."

What Hopkins told Hallie that day in December was that he had cancer—"some damn thing wrong inside me," as he put it. He was on his way to the Mayo Clinic to have it "cut out." "It is the devil and all to go just now and leave you all up against this new order to add more people when we haven't got enough money to take care of what we've got." Roosevelt had just asked Hopkins to add 350,000 people to the payroll without additional funds. "Anyway, I sent for you to say good-bye. And to say I'm sorry about the mistake of not seeing you oftener. You've done a big job—nobody knows how big—and I'm grateful. I wanted you to know it. And if you possibly can stand it, I want you to keep on during the hard days coming. We can't lose what we've gained."

It was all the encouragement Hallie needed. No matter how she felt about his administrators, no matter how often she heard later that Hopkins had sacrificed Federal Theatre to his own political ambitions, Hallie's loyalty to the man remained firm. The hard days Hopkins predicted were to come, but Hallie did not blame him. If Hopkins was ambitious, so was she. What counted were the goals he had worked all his life to achieve. They were Hallie's too, and she did not let him down.

She had need of his support. On January 12, the four directors of the Arts Projects were summoned to Ellen Woodward's office and told that because of criticism in California their projects would henceforth be managed by Colonel Connolly. When Hallie pointed out that investigators had found no foundation for allegations of immorality and Communist activity on the West Coast, she was told the decision was final. Woodward assured Hallie that the decision did not mean she would lose control of policy and play selection. It was aimed rather at winning local support for the arts. Hallie had no choice but to take this directive at face value. Writing Colonel Connolly that she would cooperate, she went on to explain how plays were chosen. She enclosed letters to her regional and state directors urging them to go along. She also reminded Connolly that Hopkins had entrusted all decisions about policy and program to her.

She got no answer. What followed struck Hallie, if only in retrospect, as a satire on bureaucracy, a California musical comedy. West Coast directors and supervisors were told that they could not communicate with Hallie except through Colonel Connolly. Every letter she wrote went to him first. Plays scheduled to open were scrutinized, and *Judgment Day*, an antitotalitarian drama by Elmer Rice, was canceled.

Hallie reported the situation to Lawrence Morris. Morris said there was nothing he could do without Mrs. Woodward's authority, and she was ill. Hallie had to stand aside while the California press denounced Federal Theatre for censorship and while Actors' Equity, the Screen Actors' Guild, and the American Civil Liberties Union added their own protests. The Washington *Post* made the point that Federal Theatre was repeating itself. First it had canceled *The Cradle Will Rock*. Now it was canceling an antitotalitarian drama. What would it do next? Was it at long last turning timid?

Hallie hit the ceiling. Woodward had reneged on her promise to leave play choice in Hallie's hands. Now she was giving Hallie the run-around, expecting her to sit back while the press criticized Federal Theatre for Washington's decisions—for Connolly's decisions. It amounted to the same thing. Hallie did not take easily to sitting back. When she was angry, she acted. Now it seemed the only recourse was to write Hopkins a letter. She was reluctant to do so, since Hopkins was still recuperating from his recent operation. But when Woodward continued to be unavailable, Hallie drafted a letter. "Harry, I know you have been ill." She apologized for disturbing him, adding that she had tried unsuccessfully to reach Mrs. Woodward. She thought he ought to know that Federal Theatre was being attacked as "too timid to produce any controversial play." She felt that the postponing of *The Cradle Will Rock* had been a "tragic mistake." She had heard Blitzstein play the score "long before anybody knew who Marc Blitzstein was . . . We spent seven months and thousands of dollars on it, and sold 25,000 seats in advance. Then, in spite of my protests, the whole thing was stopped." Houseman and Welles had gone, and Federal Theatre had lost "the praise currently being heaped upon the new Mercury Theatre." All of this was past, but was it too late to stop the censorship and intimidation in California? She assured Hopkins that she had tried to be cordial and cooperative with Connolly, but it had not worked.

Hallie's letter, a last-ditch attempt to regain control, reveals how little she understood Hopkins's state of mind. Her concluding words were the desperate plea of a discouraged but not yet defeated leader. "Only you," she told Hopkins, "are powerful enough to end this petty dictatorship of the arts . . . Harry, you know my devotion to you personally and you know that my very life is bound up with this project. I believe in you, in the project, and in the magnificent future of both. Please help me in carrying out your own order to create a free, adult, American theatre."

Hopkins also received telegrams from Burgess Meredith and Henry Fonda on behalf of Actors' Equity and the National Council of Freedom from Censorship.

There is no record that Hallie ever received an answer to her letter.

CHAPTER

14

Further Crises

WITH the crisis in California still in limbo, Hallie, Alsberg, Cahill, and Sokoloff were told they should prepare to appear before a congressional committee that was considering a bill to establish a federal department of science, art, and literature. David Niles assembled the four in Woodward's office a few hours before they were to appear. The briefs they had submitted describing their projects, Niles told them, had been approved. What he now wanted was to be reassured that everything they said before the committee would reflect their loyalty to the WPA. For instance, if they were questioned about specific situations, they should forget whatever minor irritations they might be feeling.

Hallie's brief stressed the successes of her project. She made light of the difficulties. Federal Theatre, at its peak, had employed over twelve thousand people. At the present time, despite cuts, almost eight thousand employees were still on the payroll, nine-tenths of them from relief rolls. Theatre companies still existed in forty cities in twenty-two states. Some of the plays produced had been controversial, but the whole enterprise, after undergoing some local pressures, had been remarkably free from censorship. Niles was pleased with what she had written. But he was worried about what she and the other directors might say if questioned about the situation in

California. When he asked her how she would reply if asked about the canceling of Rice's play, Hallie said she would reply that there was censorship. When Niles's assistant asked what *Judgment Day* was about, Hallie said it depicted corruption, oppression, and intimidation in an unnamed totalitarian state. Niles insisted that the canceling of *Judgment Day* was not censorship but "selection." Alsberg stood by Hallie. Didn't the play present "the position of our democracy toward dictatorship?" Cahill went one step further: if state administrators who knew nothing about the arts were henceforth to decide what art was to be exhibited and what music was to be heard, censorship *was* involved and he would have to say so. At this point Ellen Woodward withdrew to make a long-distance phone call to Colonel Connolly. Niles meanwhile kept insisting that it would be fatal for everyone concerned if the public learned of this "family difficulty."

The directors then won a minor victory. Woodward returned to announce that she and Connolly had come to a complete understanding: the national directors were to keep artistic control of their projects and *Judgment Day* would go on as planned. Later, Hallie pointed out that when the play did go on, no one thought it radical. In future, she added, any theatre operating with public funds would have to decide whether it wanted plays chosen by nonpolitical people, in which case there would undoubtedly be some politically unwise choices, or a theatre that would "die of yawning."

During the congressional committee hearing, Burgess Meredith, who as Actors' Equity president had also been summoned to testify, denounced the WPA for placing people in charge of theatre projects who had little sympathy with them. Morris Watson, no longer in charge of the Living Newspaper unit but still national vice president of the American Newspaper Guild, was equally outspoken. In New York, he said, it was an "open scandal" that the project had been permitted to do only one major play in more than six months. Hallie was more tactful. "Despite local problems of censorship," she said, "this Federal Theatre has probably been one of the freest theatres ever subsidized by a government in the history of the world."

When the arts directors gave their testimony, there were two bills under consideration in the House. One, introduced in early 1937 by Representative William Sirovich, proposed that the government

build a fine arts building on Capitol Hill to house a new department
of Science, Art, and Literature. The other, introduced by Representative Coffee, provided for a Bureau of Fine Arts with a commissioner
appointed by the President and six arts directors and specified that
the Bureau carry over all persons at present employed by the WPA
federal arts projects. When Burgess Meredith asked Brooks Atkinson
what he might do to help build support for the Coffee bill, Atkinson
replied by publishing a lengthy article in the *New York Times*. His
reply, however, was not what Meredith had hoped for, as Atkinson
took the opportunity to give his own assessment of the successes and
failures of Federal Theatre.

The proposed Coffee bill, he wrote, while admirable in its intent,
had one very objectionable article: the one providing for the continued employment of present personnel. "The melancholy fact," said
Atkinson, was that many of those presently employed on Federal
Theatre "have outlived their usefulness to the modern theatre," and
others "are more interested in politics than in the theatre." Atkinson
once more raised the question: Was Federal Theatre a relief project
or an arts project? Hallie, he wrote, when she had had total
authority, had "come as close as anyone could to balancing the two
objectives." She had almost succeeded in "making a people's theatre
out of an emergency relief project." But certain obstacles had proved
insurmountable. "An insurgent element in the ranks" had called
incessant sit-down strikes, and this element continued to use Federal
Theatre "to practice the technique of revolution." Such tactics had
caused repercussions, as a result of which Federal Theatre had
become unpopular in Washington. "It is noisy out of all proportion
to its size. Unlike the WPA labor projects, which employ people by
the hundreds of thousands and are scarcely heard from, it meets
millions of Americans across the footlights." By treading on political
toes, it endangered the whole WPA program. "Before Congress sets
up the Federal Theatre as a permanent organization inside the genial
conditions of the Coffee bill," Atkinson concluded, "it should try to
find out why the Federal Theatre is next to moribund now. Most of
all, it should decide whether a permanent Bureau of Fine Arts is to be
a relief organization or the home of the free inquiring spirit that
keeps art vital in a democracy."

If Hallie agreed with Atkinson about the insurgent element

inside Federal Theatre, she never said so: it would have been tantamount to dividing her workers, and that was something she would not do. When she had fired people, Kate Clugston, for instance, she had done it because she believed they lacked the cooperative spirit needed in a theatre. That a sizable group in Federal Theatre might have been working not for the good of the theatre but to further the goals of a political party, was not something she acknowledged or wanted to acknowledge. She agreed with Atkinson that a Bureau of Fine Arts should have its own beginning and not be tied to Federal Theatre. She subsequently admitted that many of the most needy theatre professionals "were not of the caliber to operate a strong program." When she and Hopkins met later to discuss these questions and Hopkins suggested she draw up a plan, Hallie produced several ideas that went beyond anything she had thought of for Federal Theatre. A government department of the arts, she thought, might be financed by existing federal amusement taxes. Such a department could underwrite artistic activities in twenty-five to one hundred cities. The theatre branch could provide free performances for underprivileged groups and maintain touring programs, training centers in the largest cities, and an annual theatre festival "showing the best of the work being done." Fifty percent of the personnel might be chosen from professionally qualified people who were in need. There was precedent for such a scheme: "Chile had been taxing all theatre and motion-picture seats for the benefit of a national theatre, as had Bulgaria, Denmark, Greece, Estonia, Yugoslavia, Latvia, Rumania, and Iceland."

Just before Federal Theatre ended, the WPA allowed Hallie to present her ideas to Mrs. Roosevelt. The First Lady commented, "I wish very much that the President had seen this earlier." When he read Hallie's plan, Roosevelt remarked, "I do not believe we are yet ready for so advanced a plan as that which Mrs. Flanagan suggests."

Her plan, Hallie reflected, was a "blueprint, a memorandum for tomorrow."

By February 1937 Federal Theatre workers in New York had lined up into two opposing camps. Most objected to Paul Edwards's administration; a few stood by him. Nonpolitical people who only wanted to get on with the show got lost in the scuffle.

When Edward Goodman, one of Hallie's most valued producers, resigned in early February, the Supervisors' Council, which he had headed, seized the opportunity to print and circulate a lengthy attack on Edwards's administration entitled "Murder in the Federal Theatre." Cleverly combining valid criticisms of Edwards's reign with praise for Federal Theatre accomplishments, it went on to make propaganda points for the Workers' Alliance. Our chief enemies, stated the writer, are those who stand to "profit by the depressed wages of cheap labor," and Edwards's administration uses "unfair labor practices." The author cited an instance where seven workers on relief, "who were guilty of nothing more than the peaceable exercise of the fundamental right of workers to protest the conditions of their employment," had been dismissed.

In his letter of resignation, Goodman told Hallie that he felt he would no longer be able to do the kind of work they both believed in. He cited the demoralization of the vast majority of her people owing to broken promises, dismissals "for the avowed purpose of economy," and a "general picture bearing an extraordinary resemblance to the Spoils System." The new administration, Goodman charged, was antiunion. He believed there was a plan to "sabotage the project with a view to its liquidation." The outcome would be a "doing to death of one of the most forward achievements our government has ever made." In resigning, Goodman wanted Hallie to know "how much your leadership, your insight and your vision have meant to me, as I know they have to a vast majority of those who have worked with you." She had "worked valiantly" for the "great dream of the Federal Theatre," and he wanted to offer any assistance he could toward the future realization of that dream.

Hallie, who had tried to keep Goodman from resigning, penciled in at the top of her copy of "Murder in the Federal Theatre": "File as ancient history." Internecine warfare did not concern her now; that was Edwards's business. It was a continuing problem at a time when she was trying to keep artistic standards from collapsing altogether. But George Kondolf, in the middle of the battles, had no such choice. Goodman's resignation, he was later to say, was a "godsend." He would not elaborate. "This is the sort of thing I don't want to get into."

In one respect Goodman was wrong. The new administration

under Paul Edwards was not antiunion. It continued to support Actors' Equity and other unions representing theatre professionals, but it was anti–Workers' Alliance. And it had Hopkins's support.

After Hopkins had partially recovered from his operation, he made a trip to New York to confer secretly with Kondolf. No one, not even Hallie, knew Hopkins was in the city. The WPA chief wanted Kondolf's view of the New York scene. Kondolf told him that many people had got into Federal Theatre illegitimately. He had learned that someone from the Workers' Alliance was always posted outside the office where people signed up for relief. Whoever wanted to join the theatre project was told he would have to join the Alliance first. The Alliance would then work to place him, whether he was a theatre professional or not. Others have testified that this was indeed Alliance procedure. Brooks Atkinson had understood all this when he wrote his article in February, but others on the left were slower to perceive it. Malcolm Cowley, who was rather sympathetic to the Communists at the time, later wrote: "The Communists on the project worked harder for the revolution than for the theatre. That was their duty as they conceived it."

Kondolf did what he believed he had been hired to do. Whenever the Alliance lodged a protest because one of its members had been laid off, Kondolf consulted the records. "When I found that someone on the project had never done anything in the theatre, I would fire him. I would say to myself, How in hell did this guy get on? When I investigated, I would find that he had been a clerk in a grocery store or something." Burgess Meredith, who also believed that the Alliance had smuggled in too many nonprofessionals, urged him to hire more legitimate actors. Confrontations multiplied and were often violent. Kondolf had a hard life. "Many times when I would go to a theatre to see a rehearsal, a political meeting would be going on; a local commissar would be there working with the actors and directors. It infuriated me that they would do it on government time, and also do it instead of working and rehearsing." In retrospect, Kondolf was "amazed" that the project lasted as long as it did. "I don't blame Hallie for it. She may not have realized the degree of it. They may have been too powerful for her. They were powerful enough for me, I can tell you that . . . They used to picket my apartment. Sometimes a whole street had to be closed off." Once—it happened to be Washington's Birthday—"I was buried in effigy with a big coffin. I would come home certain nights and I'd see this mob. I had World War I guards who would have to break a path for me to go through." When Kondolf arrived at his office in the morning he would often find people carrying placards reading "Kondolf's a Fascist." "They always had grievance committees, very carefully selected, with every ethnic group represented . . . Apparently the technique is to present a few demands that are perfectly reasonable, but then it goes on to things that are just impossible."

"The worst morale we ever had on Federal Theatre," Hallie later said, "and the most unsatisfactory labor agreements" happened in New York during the Federal Theatre's last two years. Although Edwards, not Hallie, was now in charge of New York, the chairman of the Alliance, Willis Morgan, often appealed to Hallie directly. He phoned her and wrote her whenever he had a grievance. In May he concluded a grievance letter with the comment, "I would like to conclude by saying that I have an uneasy feeling that there is a growing tendency on your part to keep away from meeting committees." Morgan's complaint was that Alliance members were not being hired to fill regional touring posts. Hallie replied that there had been "no discrimination against any class or group" and that Kondolf was the "final judge." She concluded by saying, "I have no intention of avoiding meetings with workers." She would look forward, she said, to a time when she could meet with Alliance members "in regard to forward-looking plans for Federal Theatre's future."

Edwards did not often seek Hallie's advice, but on one occasion he asked her to meet with Meredith and Morgan. He needed her help in getting the unions to cooperate, so Hallie agreed. "As I studied the two men," she later said, "I wondered whether they would ever get together on anything. Burgess, volatile, emotional . . . and Morgan, hard as nails, square jawed. He kept referring to Kondolf as Korndolf, which irritated Burgess. After correcting him several times, Burgess finally lashed out, 'You want to be a leader of men, well, learn to pronounce. Get a dictionary and learn to *pronounce!*' 'Take it easy,' retorted Morgan, 'don't use up your energy acting when you're not on the stage.' " Hallie's advice was to forget it, get the unions to back Edwards, stop the internal fighting, and "restore the morale of 1936."

Hallie's letters to Philip, which had arrived in Poughkeepsie in a steady stream all through 1936 and 1937, suddenly decreased in number. Her letters during the first two years had been almost unfailingly optimistic. In writing Philip, Hallie had felt she was recording a chapter of unusual interest in the history of the American theatre, as indeed she was. After 1937 she no longer saw record-keeping as an essential task. From 1938 onward she was not creating a project so much as trying to keep it from going under. Now she needed Philip less as a supportive audience than as an active adviser. After Shaw gave her permission to produce his plays, she wrote her husband to ask if he thought *On the Rocks* "too dangerous." *She* thought it was a "swell play" but worried because the Theatre Guild had turned it down. The play reflected Shaw's conviction that parliamentary democracy in the 1930s was on the rocks, not a revolutionary idea, in Philip's opinion, and he gave it his enthusiastic endorsement. The play was given its first American production during the 1938 season.

It is interesting to speculate what turn Federal Theatre might have taken had Hallie married a man of conservative views. Philip was a liberal caught up, as Hallie was, in Popular Front ideology. During the period of the Fascist threat in Europe, he presided over the local chapter of the League for Peace and Democracy, an organization which the Communist Party, unknown to most League members, was manipulating for its own ends. Even moderates joined the League, which was certainly not viewed then as communistic. Phil's friend Vernon Venable recalled that "Phil had been appointed president because he was widely accepted in the community. I was more abrasive, so Phil became the front man. We used to go about the town trying to persuade the merchants to boycott Italian and German and Japanese goods."

One of the plays slated to open in New York during the 1937–1938 season was *Trojan Incident,* a dance-drama based on Euripides' *The Trojan Women,* which Philip had adapted with Hallie's encouragement. Hallie had at first tried to get Herman

Shumlin interested in producing the play. When Shumlin turned it down, she assembled some of the best people she had. Helen Tamiris did the choreography and danced the role of Cassandra, Howard Bay designed the set, and Harold Bolton, who had directed the Vassar version of *One-Third of a Nation,* directed. The production, Bolton recalled later, "was an experiment. We had dancers speaking dialogue for the first time." But despite the innovation, the talents of the performers, and the play's strong stand against war, *Trojan Incident* failed to win critical acclaim. Hallie had tried to use her influence to fill the theatre. A few days before its opening she wrote Kondolf, "Everything will depend on a packed house the first few nights. Can't Tamiris get the whole dance league or some such organization to turn out on some pretext?" Even this had not worked, and there was further annoyance: Hallie was criticized for trying to promote her husband. It was a disheartening time for both of them.

Other openings that spring fared better with the professional critics, though not with the growing number of congressional critics. E. P. Conkle's *Prologue to Glory,* which opened in March and was about the young Abe Lincoln, was considered sentimental by some reviewers, but most agreed with Burns Mantle, who declared in the *Daily News* that "no citizen in these United States should be permitted to miss it." Unfortunately for Federal Theatre, the House Committee on Un-American Activities was just then being established and Representative J. Parnell Thomas, who became one of its leading members, decided that this was an opportune moment to attack the WPA. In a widely publicized interview he stated that *Prologue to Glory* portrayed Lincoln battling politicians and was "a propaganda play to prove that all politicians are crooked." It was nothing of the sort. Even those most critical never called the play anything other than a politically mild love story.

On the Rocks got mixed reviews. Many called it long and talky. (Shaw had refused to let Hallie cut it, tersely cabling her, "No, Hallie, no.") Set in London during the early 1930s, the play portrays a nation in crisis. England's Prime Minister advocates nationalizing the land and making labor compulsory. The workers reject this idea and stage riots and protests, but never reach the point of revolution. Shaw steers clear of giving victory to either side. Although a witness for HUAC would later label the play Communist propaganda, the

Communist press was unenthusiastic. In the *Daily Worker* a reviewer accused Shaw of slandering the proletariat and advocating a Fascist tyranny. Shaw ought to know, the reviewer stated, that there is a "distinction between a personal dictator and the dictatorship of the proletariat."

The House Committee on Un-American Activities was set up in late May 1938, soon after Roosevelt decided to ask Congress to embark on a new large-scale spending program. Budget trimming had not worked to invigorate the economy, the recession of 1937 was in its seventh month, millions of people still needed jobs. Thanks to the President's initiative, Hopkins received more than a billion dollars for the WPA. But if there was rejoicing in some Washington circles, the joyous mood was by no means universal. Roosevelt's determination to rid the Democratic party of its right wing had roused an equal determination among the right-wingers: *they* wanted to rid the Democratic party of Roosevelt. Both factions were looking to the primary elections in 1940. HUAC was thus created in the midst of a fight for control of the Democratic party. And Hopkins, who had never been popular among conservatives, became one of their targets. From the right-wing point of view, nothing was more dreadful than the huge expense of the WPA, and within the WPA no project was more dreadful than Hallie's "relevant" Federal Theatre.

Martin Dies, the first chairman of HUAC, was a Democrat from Texas who believed, or professed to believe, that the crisis of the thirties had been caused by Communist conspirators and that the nation could be restored to normal only if this conspiracy was put down. It was a politically opportunist position to take. The Red-baiting Hearst press had been saying the same thing for years. Those opposed to Roosevelt's spending could take refuge in the thought that unemployment was not the problem, Communism was.

Hallie, as usual, tried to focus on the future she still thought possible. Political infighting, she might have said, would pass. And then what? One of her most cherished dreams for Federal Theatre was architectural. After Congress had voted its appropriation for the WPA, her ideas took on more definite shape. "If the WPA can build schools, playgrounds, and airports throughout the country," she told a group of supervisors in the spring of 1938, "why should it not also build theatres?" Shortly afterward she spent two weeks visiting theatres in the South. In talking with Paul Green and Frederick Koch in Chapel Hill, she discovered that they had building plans of their own. The University of North Carolina had donated land for a regional southern theatre. Local sponsors and the Rockefeller Foundation had promised funds. Hallie proposed that the WPA furnish the labor to erect the building, which would then become available for "retraining our theatre leaders in the South." When she returned to Washington, she conferred with David Stevens of the Rockefeller Foundation about the possibility of establishing an architectural commission to advise on designs for other regional theatres.

An amphitheatre did eventually get built in Chapel Hill with WPA labor, though it did not become the southern retraining center Hallie had envisioned, for Federal Theatre ended before the building was completed. When Hallie, Green, and Koch deliberated about the setting, they were, of course, unable to predict what would happen. Koch wanted the building set on a slope that reminded him of the Bankside Theatre, where he had worked in North Dakota. Green thought this was "the worst place in the world for an amphitheatre" because of nearby roads, and he appealed to Hallie to dissuade Koch. In her "quiet, sweet way," Green recalled, Hallie tried to convince Koch that another spot might be more appropriate, but when Koch wouldn't listen and Green became angry, Hallie took Green aside and advised him to let Koch have his way. Not many people who worked with Hallie would have described her as quiet or sweet. Yet Green, himself the embodiment of the southern gentleman, perhaps perceived something that others sometimes failed to. Where her own plans for Federal Theatre were concerned, Hallie could be fiercely determined. With friends she was advising, she was more apt to use methods of quiet persuasion.

Hallie's architectural plans were just one small part of a much larger program which she and Hopkins agreed was necessary if Federal Theatre was to win broader public support. While Hopkins was recovering from his operation in mid-February, he told a press conference that Federal Theatre had concentrated too much attention on the larger cities. In the future it was going to focus its efforts on towns where the stage had disappeared. To do this, Hallie told him, she would need the support of the national office. Experience had taught her that local WPA administrators often counteracted orders from Washington. Federal Theatre had focused its activities in large cities not solely because actors on relief were more numerous in places like Chicago, Los Angeles, and New York but also because of the expense and complications involved in transporting actors from one state to another. Some touring had been done, but many of Hallie's plans for tours had failed. Political issues had also become an obstacle. Hallie cited a situation encountered by a Midwest supervisor in 1937: businessmen who at first offered to contribute nonlabor costs to bring Federal Theatre productions into the state were quickly dissuaded when a group of citizens, quoting an article that had appeared in the *Saturday Evening Post,* objected that the government theatre was a mouthpiece for the New Deal. Without his all-out backing, Hallie told Hopkins, none of their plans for touring could be accomplished.

At a reception for the directors in May, Hopkins made a public promise of support. As long as he was relief administrator, he said, the Arts Projects would remain under federal supervision. But the occasion was not a solemn one and Hopkins, only partially recovered from his near fatal illness, was feeling playful. He decided to indulge what Hallie called his talent for hokum. Two hundred actors, writers, artists, and musicians had gathered for the occasion. Hopkins introduced Hallie with the words: "This girl I am going to introduce to you now, I was brought up with her. I went to grade school with her, then to High School. I used to hold her hand when I was sixteen . . . [When I got this job] I remembered how nice Hallie Flanagan used to be when she was a little girl."

"Mr. Hopkins's flights of imagination and romanticism," said Hallie in reply, "are superior to anything the Federal Theatre has yet produced." But she too had planned a personal tribute, and she went on to make it. On a recent trip to New York, she said, she had had a free night. She had gone to Harlem to see scenes from the opening of *Haiti,* then downtown to see a part of *Prologue to Glory.* Finally she had looked in on the second act of *One-Third of a Nation,* which was still playing to record crowds. "I looked at the lines outside the theatre," she said, "and remembered the long lines of dejected men and women I saw three years ago in every city where these projects were being set up." What happened in the interim had happened because of Hopkins's "forethought and daring and revolutionary mind"—revolutionary because in America it *was* revolutionary to believe "that artists made up a part of the national wealth."

The occasion marked the last time Hallie and Hopkins appeared together publicly. Henceforth Hopkins became engrossed not simply in his own political ambitions but also in the battle being waged inside the Democratic party. In June the President began a campaign to support New Dealers in the coming primary elections. By distinguishing between liberals and conservatives, Roosevelt hoped to win support for a liberal Democratic party. He made his strongest attacks on conservatives in the South, where newspaper reporters responded by accusing the President of becoming a Fascist dictator intent on purging the party of its right-wing dissidents. This southern retort proved effective propaganda. Roosevelt's attacks on conservatives came to be viewed as Hitler-like moves made to reinforce his own power. Hopkins too was attacked, for similar reasons. The relief administrator, the press declared, was "using the WPA to build a national New Deal political machine." Meantime, the *New York Times* reported, Representative J. Parnell Thomas called the Federal Theatre a "link in the vast and unparalleled New Deal propaganda machine" and a branch of the Communist Party.

Even before she read this, Hallie confessed to feeling dispirited. When an actor wrote to her in June to say how much Federal Theatre meant to him, and how it had helped him grow as an artist, Hallie replied that his letter meant a lot, especially since it had come "at a time of great physical weariness, a time when I often feel that we cannot make Federal Theatre realize our high dreams for it." Other tributes pleased her. The English writer Anne Freemantle made a survey of Federal Theatre on a trip to the States and wrote Hallie that the undertaking was "a complete answer both to fascism and communism . . . only a free people could do this." But even this praise could not divert Hallie's thoughts from what was to come. She had begun at last to see the handwriting on the wall.

15

HUAC

T HE House Committee on Un-American Activities began its
hearings in August 1938 with seven members representing seven
widely scattered states. One member, J. Parnell Thomas, Republican
from New Jersey, would later go to prison for defrauding the
government. The other six included a second Republican, Noah M.
Mason, of Illinois; three conservative Democrats, Martin Dies of
Texas, Joseph Starnes of Alabama, and Harold G. Mosier of Ohio;
Democrat John J. Dempsey of New Mexico, who was a not very
enthusiastic New Dealer; and one New Deal Democrat from Massachusetts, Arthur D. Healey, who was clearly outnumbered.

A month before the hearings began, Committee chairman Martin
Dies announced to the press that he was determined to conduct the
investigations on a "dignified plane." He would maintain a "judicial
attitude" throughout. There would be no "character assassination or
any smearing of innocent people . . . The chair is more concerned
with facts than with opinions, and with specific proof than with
generalities." This announcement would turn out to be a tragic joke.

Chairman Dies's extreme nationalist views were well known to
his colleagues. Elected to Congress in 1931, he immediately launched
a campaign to restrict immigration and prevent America from
becoming the "dumping ground" of Europe. He had also quickly

become the self-appointed president of the Demagogue Club, an informal group of House members who, in the words of one observer, were "addicted to flamboyant speeches saturated with hokum." The large, powerfully built Texan had more than a touch of the ham actor about him, and at first this made him and his Committee seem ridiculous to WPA officials. As Hallie put it, it was "the fashion at that time" to laugh at HUAC, "but it never seemed funny to me."

In July, when Representative Thomas fired his first shots against Federal Theatre, calling it a branch of the Communist Party and announcing that his committee would ask Hallie to explain why applicants for project jobs had first to join the Workers' Alliance and why the only plays authorized were those with "Communist leanings," Hallie made an immediate public denial. Some of Thomas's statements, she said, were "obviously absurd." The plays he attacked, *Prologue to Glory* and *One-Third of a Nation*, were not Communistic. Furthermore, she had not written and produced a Communist play in Soviet Russia, as Thomas had alleged. Hallie refrained from commenting on the Workers' Alliance. Later she was to say that she had no way of knowing whether the Workers' Alliance was a Communist front organization. Workers' Alliance leaders had consistently denied this, and the Party's role within the union was still far from clear to the public.

WPA officials immediately told Hallie she had broken a cardinal rule: only the information division in Washington was authorized to answer charges in the press. In the future, she was to keep silent until given permission to speak. Meantime HUAC began hearing witnesses, and the press gave increasing space to all allegations. Assuming she would be subpoenaed, Hallie drafted a letter to Dies saying she would be available to testify on August 11, when six regional directors would give evidence about projects throughout the country. Dies's reply to her letter was curt: "If your presence is required, it will be several weeks after August 11, as we already have a heavy schedule of witnesses."

Thomas had no trouble finding witnesses willing to testify against the Theatre Project. In New York, Hazel Huffman, the mail division employee who had earlier informed the press that Hallie's mail was inflammatory and seditious, was only too willing; she became a star witness. Mrs. Flanagan, Huffman testified, had been known "as far back as 1927 for her communistic sympathy." Her book *Shifting Scenes* had eulogized Soviet Russia and the Russian theatre. Also, she had written a play, *Can You Hear Their Voices?*, which the Communist press had praised, and a laudatory article in *Theatre Arts Monthly* about the Communist-dominated workers' theatres. As director of Federal Theatre, she had allowed the Workers' Alliance to make policy decisions. Project supervisors "worked hand-in-glove" with the Alliance and its white-collar division, the City Projects Council. Naturally, Communist plays had become "the rule" in Federal Theatre. Huffman listed twenty-eight, among them *One-Third of a Nation, On the Rocks, It Can't Happen Here,* and *The Cradle Will Rock.* Throughout her testimony the congressmen listened attentively and without interruption. When it was over, the many newspapermen present rushed off to file their write-ups.

Other witnesses spoke the following day, but none of them interested the press as much as Hazel Huffman. William Humphrey, the actor who had played Earl Browder in *Triple-A Plowed Under,* told the Committee he had no facts to give, he had simply turned up because he thought people should know the role he had been asked to play. Another witness, Francis Verdi, testified that Hallie had asked him to investigate employee complaints that Workers' Alliance members managed to hold on to their jobs during the 1937 cuts while members of professional unions were fired. Hallie, he added, had never, "by implication or by word, encouraged the Workers' Alliance and its communistic tendencies." But this was not a point of interest to the Committee, and he was soon asked to step down. Many witnesses blamed the Workers' Alliance for the troubles of Federal Theatre. A former stage manager testified that Alliance members got preference when plays were cast. Another described them as nonprofessionals who lived in garrets below Fourteenth Street and spent most of their time "fighting for their jobs rather than working at them." Mrs. Huffman's husband pointed out that Alliance members had circulated petitions, sold Communist propaganda literature, solicited funds for the Spanish Loyalists on government time, and were forever comparing the bounties of Russia with the very bad conditions existing in the United States. A Viennese-born actress said Alliance members hobnobbed "indiscriminately with Negroes as part of the communist program for social equality and race merging."

All this, later described by an historian as "one of the weirdest collections of evidence ever permitted before the Committee," was bad enough. What most newspapers made of it was worse. Hallie was called a "WPA RED" on the front page of many papers. Her picture appeared all over the country, in one case with the word RED emblazoned in huge letters above it. Hazel Huffman's testimony was recounted in detail and summarized in ways that made it sound even more sensational than the witness herself had made it. An entry in the Boston *Herald* for August 19 is typical:

> With few exceptions, the plays produced by Federal Theatre have been filled with ridicule of the government and of various institutions of the existing order, the witness testified, and have held out Communism as the solution for the nation's economic problems.
>
> "Do you mean to say that public funds have been used for the purpose of spreading Communism in the United States and to build up a Workers' Alliance?" Chairman Dies asked.
>
> "Yes sir," she replied emphatically.

Although a few papers carried editorials denouncing the Committee for its Red-baiting tactics, no writer attempted to refute any of the witnesses' assertions. Truth, half-truths, and downright lies were allowed to stand. The impression left with the public was that Hallie was using Federal Theatre to promote a Communist takeover of the United States government and that the Committee was performing a service in making this known.

Hallie was shattered. One weekend, when her friends the Strelskys arrived at her house for a visit, they found her in tears. "She was not a weeping person," Kay recalled, "so it was shocking." Nik promised to write a letter to the *New York Times* saying he had fought the Bolsheviks during an attempted counterrevolution and could assure the world that Hallie was no more a Communist than he was. Philip helped him write the letter, which was printed and appeared in papers throughout the country. Of course, it did nothing to deter HUAC.

Other friends rallied round. Emmet Lavery, who was in charge of clearing play contracts for Federal Theatre, wrote Dies, saying he was a Catholic, that he had never authorized a communistic play for the project, and that he wanted to testify. He got no answer, and the attacks in the press continued. On the first of September, Congressman Thomas told a *Herald Tribune* reporter that "practically every play the project had produced was clear, unadulterated propaganda." Again Lavery wrote Dies asking to testify on the production record, and again he received no answer.

Meantime the WPA office in New York began making inquiries of its own. In surveying personnel records, Paul Edwards discovered that almost all the people who had testified before HUAC were "disgruntled employees" who at some time or another had been "refused promotions because of lack of ability." Personnel officials signed affidavits stating that they had never furnished the Workers' Alliance with lists of available jobs nor consulted Alliance representatives about filling jobs. The charge that the Alliance controlled appointments was untrue. None of this information helped Hallie, for the national WPA office stuck to its policy of maintaining silence.

"Day after day," Lavery wrote Hallie, "hearsay testimony floods the newspapers of the country, so that slander and libel thrive on the simple fact of their constant repetition." Furious that Hallie was still forbidden to speak out on her own behalf, Lavery demanded to know: "What is the WPA going to do?" When Hallie forwarded his letter to the national office and the situation still remained unchanged, Lavery became convinced that the WPA itself wanted Federal Theatre abolished. Many agreed, but not Hallie. Inclined to believe that everyone, even bureaucrats, had their reasons for not responding, she was no doubt thinking of Hopkins. Where was the relief administrator in the midst of all this? Hallie could not believe Hopkins would let her perish. She decided to counter the Committee's attacks indirectly by sending Hopkins an annual report detailing Federal Theatre's past achievements and current plans and by making sure that copies of this report got to mayors, WPA officials, drama critics, newspaper editors, columnists, playwrights, actors, and other persons of standing in the theatrical and literary world. The report was glowingly optimistic.

Congressman Thomas meanwhile was getting more publicity

than ever before in his life. Loath to let go of the audience he had so recently aroused, he proceeded with a fresh attack. Over Station WQXR he once more inveighed against the "shameful and invidious" Theatre Project, calling it a "veritable hotbed of un-American activities" and describing the plays as ridiculing American ideals and inciting rebellion.

This time, however, a Democratic congressman came to the defense. At a meeting of the American Theatre Council, Emanuel Celler of New York spoke out against the Committee's attacks. With no one except a handful of editorial writers publicly joining him, it was a singular act of courage, and Hallie was quick to tell him how much she valued his support.

For reasons that were never clear to Hallie, the WPA continued to do nothing until mid-September, when Thomas and his fellow committeeman Joseph Starnes began hearing witnesses describe Communist activity in the Federal Writers' Project. The project director, Henry Alsberg, was known to be an anti-Communist. Yet he too was slandered by witnesses, and the slander went unchallenged by committee members. This hearing was as ludicrous as the previous one. At one point, Thomas said the *New Jersey State Guidebook* had been guilty of making statements about labor "as if there had been trouble between labor and capital." It was the sort of ignorance combined with malice that was to mark so many HUAC hearings.

This time, perhaps because of Alsberg's record of anticommunism, Ellen Woodward reacted. She wrote Dies a respectful letter expressing surprise that he had not yet called any of the officials in charge of the projects to testify, despite their willingness to do so. "I believe," she wrote, "that it is the American practice that all parties should be given an opportunity to be heard when an investigation of this character is under way."

Hallie later said: "I have often been asked why we did not demand to attend the hearings, insist that the project record of the witnesses be examined by the Committee, and above all, why we did not bring libel suits against some of these Congressmen . . . The answer is that citizens are not able to insist on the same measure of due process of law in Congress that they receive in the courts . . . At a trial an accused person may demand that accusing witnesses be cross-examined, that evidence be relevant; the accused may summon expert witnesses . . . These are rights granted at the bar of our courts; but congressional committees operate as quasi-judicial bodies which are a law unto themselves; and a congressman is immune from libel suits for statements he makes while engaged in his official duties."

Finally, in late September, Martin Dies wrote Hallie that she and Ellen Woodward would be allowed to testify, although he could not say when. Emmet Lavery and the New York director of information, Theodore Mauntz, with assistance from the legal division of WPA, at once began preparing a brief to answer the Committee charges. The brief analyzed, among other things, the content of each play the Committee had attacked. It also made the points that even though no person in charge of policy was a Communist, the political affiliation of employees was by law not subject to scrutiny and the large majority of Federal Theatre workers did not belong to the Workers' Alliance. Whether or not the Alliance was a Communist front organization, the authors could not say. Hallie's statement that she was not and had never been a Communist, had never engaged in any Communistic activity, or belonged to any Communistic organization, was added to the brief.

About this time Hallie received a letter from Mrs. Roosevelt saying that she and the President "never worried much" about such charges. This was little comfort. (Later the First Lady told an interviewer that Roosevelt regarded the Committee hearings as part of a campaign to undermine his programs and that he did not feel he could afford to take them seriously.) Yet the President's tolerance did not last indefinitely. Although he could afford to sit back while the least popular of his programs, the Arts Projects, were attacked, perhaps feeling that a large part of the public regarded artists as idlers and dreamers, he could not afford to look on philosophically when the Committee began attacking, first the Michigan governor, Frank Murphy, and then the California Democratic candidate for governor, Culbert Olson. At that point Roosevelt delivered a scathing condemnation of the Committee and its methods.

Hallie rejoiced, as did Philip and all their friends. At long last, it seemed, Hallie was going to be allowed to make public the brief she had so assiduously prepared. She was going to be given a chance to tell the public her side of the story. But if what had gone before had failed to make Hallie aware of Hopkins's thinking, the WPA's next move must have. In early December, Hopkins ordered Ellen Woodward to present Hallie's and Alsberg's briefs to the Committee. She, not they, would answer all charges. Bitterly disappointed, Hallie reminded herself that at least the pertinent facts would reach the public, and that was what mattered most.

Ellen Woodward was not as well prepared to defend the Arts Projects against charges of communism as the previous witnesses had been to label them communistic, and she was handled in an entirely different manner. Whereas the friendly witnesses had been allowed to make sweeping statements without rebuttal, Woodward's remarks were challenged at every point. When she insisted that she knew of no Communist activity in either the Theatre or the Writers' Project, she was pushed to admit that this statement was based on subordinates' reports, not on her own personal knowledge. When she tried to refute accusations that Federal Theatre audiences were composed almost entirely of Communist or radical groups, she was criticized for making a "broad, sweeping declaration." When she read favorable reviews of plays which witnesses had attacked, she was told she was not answering charges of communism. A favorable review, said Dies, "simply means that the dramatic critic believes that this play . . . is a good play; he is not charged with the duty of deciding whether or not the play spreads propaganda." Questioned about her familiarity with the plays under attack, Woodward had to admit that she had read or seen only half of them. When she was asked if she knew anything about the authors' backgrounds, she had to admit that she did not. When she made an attempt to find out whether the Committee members had ever read the criticized plays, she was compelled by Congressman Starnes to apologize to the Committee. "You are not here to ask the Committee questions," he said. "You are here to answer questions. You and every other witness are here to answer questions, not to ask them . . . I must insist that you be respectful to this Committee." Finally Chairman Dies announced that the Committee would adjourn until the following morning when Mrs. Flanagan would be asked to testify.

Hallie was prepared. She was also alert to the drama of her surroundings. Great chandeliers hung from the high ceiling of the

Committee room. Two long tables in the shape of a T dominated the center. There was a chair at the end for the witness, more chairs for reporters, stenographers, and cameramen alongside. Exhibits from the Theatre and Writers' Projects lined the walls. The audience sat in the balcony. Frederic and Philip were there, as were Hallie's closest associates. Appearance, Hallie had often told her casts, makes the first impression. She had decided to wear a plain dark dress, highlighted by a brightly colored scarf. She always wore a hat. Five feet high, she was the smallest person in the room. Her size, though, told the congressmen nothing about either her determination or the amount of work she had done to prepare to meet them.

By the time Hallie appeared before HUAC on December 6 she had spent three months acquainting herself with the facts she would need to know: exactly how many socially conscious dramas the Federal Theatre had produced; exactly what it was that each of these dramas had advocated; how many religious dramas and classics and marionette shows and circuses the Theatre had also produced; how many actors had been employed and how many subsequently hired by Broadway. She and her helpers had gathered these facts with the same thoroughness and attention to detail that she had previously shown in producing plays for the Vassar Theatre. Her conviction that most of the Committee charges were false gave her confidence.

The congressmen were equally confident. Having so easily demolished Ellen Woodward's testimony on the preceding day, they had reason to believe that Hallie, too, would be an easy target. Although President Roosevelt had recently condemned their Committee, neither he nor Hopkins had lifted a finger to save Federal Theatre, and this silence had allowed the public to conclude that HUAC's attacks were justified. The politically astute congressmen were further aware that insinuations, not facts, would decide the day. All they needed to do was provide material of a sufficiently dramatic and inflammatory nature to ensure its publication.

After swearing her in, Chairman Dies asked Hallie who had appointed her to head Federal Theatre. When Hallie replied, "Harry Hopkins," Dies asked if the appointment was Hopkins's own idea or if someone else had put him up to it. Hallie said she had no knowledge of any recommendations made on her behalf.

"Now," said the chairman, "will you just tell us briefly the duties of your position?"

"Yes," Hallie answered. "Since August 29, 1935, I have been concerned with combating un-American inactivity."

"Inactivity?" asked the astounded Dies.

"I refer," said Hallie, "to the inactivity of professional people who, at the time when I took office, were on the relief rolls." She elaborated. The proceedings had got off to a flying start, but it was not the sort of start that Thomas had anticipated, and he hastened to interrupt. "I think," he put in, "that it is of great importance that we know something about her history."

"We are going to get to that," said Dies. Less in a hurry and more subtle than his colleague, the chairman had decided to preserve an appearance of fairness. He allowed Hallie to continue. Since all the witnesses against Federal Theatre had come from the New York project, Hallie proceeded to emphasize the national scope of Federal Theatre and to point out how many theatre professionals had returned to private industry. But Congressman Starnes became impatient at this listing of Federal Theatre successes and turned the conversation to one of Hazel Huffman's chief charges, that Hallie had been more interested in the artistic aims of the project than in providing relief and that many of her orders to supervisors had followed that policy. Hallie read from letters Huffman had described to show that the witness's testimony was inaccurate.

Hallie's background became the next focus of attention. Was it true, she was asked, that she taught at Vassar? Yes. Was it true that she went to Russia in 1926? Yes, and to twelve other countries, at a time when she was studying European theatres on a Guggenheim Fellowship. But hadn't she spent more time in Russia, Congressman Starnes insisted, than in other countries? And had she not made the statement that theatre in Russia was more vital and important than theatre in other countries? She had, and she thought other dramatic critics would agree. And what was it about Russian theatre that made it so much more vital and important? "If we are to go into this," said Hallie, obviously not pleased at having to do so, "the Russians are a very gifted people . . . temperamentally equipped for the stage." She began to describe the variety of theatres she had seen in that country, was repeatedly interrupted by Starnes, who wanted to know what moral lessons the Russians inserted into their productions, and was finally told she was not answering his question.

But "you are interrupting her all the time," said Thomas. Congressman Dempsey agreed, and Hallie was allowed to continue. She pointed out that when *Shifting Scenes* came out in 1927, not one newspaper critic found anything in it that was subversive or un-American. Hallie then asked if the Committee would like her to read quotations from the press clippings. "No," said Starnes, "because that is not responsive to my question." Another minor altercation then ensued between the congressmen, Thomas accusing Starnes this time of interrupting the witness whenever he did not like her answers. Dempsey and Dies agreed that Starnes's tactics were objectionable.

Starnes then switched to the subject of Hallie's second trip to Russia. Had she been a delegate to the first Olympiad of the theatres of the U.S.S.R. in 1930? Hallie said she had been an observer, not a delegate. Had she written about that trip in a series of magazine articles? Yes, said Hallie, and again not one critic saw anything subversive or un-American in what she wrote. Had she made other trips to Russia? No, she had been to Greece recently, and to Italy. She tried to make the point that theatre, not Russia, was her primary interest.

Thomas next asked Hallie about her affiliation with the International Educational Board, which had proposed an exchange of professors between American universities and the University of Moscow. This occurred "just after we had recognized the Soviet Union," said Hallie. The idea behind the plan was "that we should know what it was that we had recognized." This line of questioning, obviously aimed at discovering that Hallie was implicated in international communism, failed, since she was not. The questioning then returned to Federal Theatre, with Starnes once again the chief questioner.

Was it true, he asked, that the *Daily Worker* and other communistic propaganda had been circulated on the project, on project time? If so, said Hallie, it had been done against her own express orders forbidding such distribution. If it had been done, it had been done without her knowledge and consent? Yes, that was absolutely true. She could not say that it had not been done? No, she could not. (Hallie as a matter of fact had been told many times that such propaganda *was* being distributed. She had made efforts, whenever she heard this, to stop the distribution but had not always been successful.)

"All right," said Starnes, now coming to the point he had been trying to make for some time, "do you believe that the theatre is a weapon?"

"Shall I discuss the American theatre," Hallie asked, "or talk about the Russian?"

Starnes replied, "I refer to the theatre generally. Do you believe that the theatre is a weapon?"

"I believe," said Hallie, "that the theatre is a great educational force. I think it is an entertainment. I think it is excitement. I think it may be all things to all men."

But Starnes was not to be so easily deflected. The Russians, he insisted—and would she not agree—used theatre to teach "class consciousness." Hallie agreed. Starnes then labored to make the point that the Russians, as part of their objective, sold tickets at reduced prices to the working classes and that teaching class consciousness was also Hallie's objective in setting up Federal Theatre. He referred to an article Hallie had written about the American workers' theatre movement, in which she had said that its object was to create "a national culture by and for the working class of America." Hallie pointed out that she had written the article as a reporter and that it described *facts*. "Mr. Starnes, let us not get into a controversy over this because it is so simple. At that time, in 1931, the workers' theatres were being set up in mines and schools and all sorts of places in America. The *Theatre Arts Monthly* asked me if I would go to one of their meetings and report on it." Hallie's article, in Starnes's opinion, was one of the most damaging pieces of evidence the Committee had. For the moment, however, he decided to drop this subject and bring up a related matter, which was the propagandistic nature of twenty-six plays the project had produced. He asked Hallie to limit her comments to those twenty-six.

"To the best of my knowledge," said Hallie, "we have never done a play which was propaganda for communism, but we have done plays which were propaganda for democracy." She cited

One-Third of a Nation as being "propaganda for better housing" and *Power* as being "propaganda for a better understanding of the derivation and the scientific meaning of power and for its wide use." She also thought *Prologue to Glory* could be called a propaganda play because it emphasized the "value of sturdy American qualities and simple living."

"How about *Injunction Granted?*" asked Starnes. Wasn't that play an "attack against our present system of courts"? Didn't it teach class consciousness?

"I do not believe that it fosters class hatred," said Hallie.

Starnes returned to the article Hallie had written in which she had said that the theatre—if it was to be "of use to the worker"— must be divorced from expensive buildings, painted sets, and elaborate costumes so that it might become as it had at times in the past, a place where ideas were "so ardently enacted" that they became the "belief of actors and audiences alike."

"Well," said Hallie, "that is a better article than I remember."

"You subscribe to that? You agree with it?"

Hallie asked Congressman Starnes to read the passage again. She wanted to know whether others at the table might not also "subscribe to it."

But Starnes was not to be sidetracked so easily. He went on with his attack. Repeatedly Hallie pointed out that what he was reading was a report. Finally he got her to admit that she had approved of the workers' theatre. But when he made the point that many workers' theatre groups were communistic, Hallie insisted that the only reason he was reading the article was "to show that it has to do in some way with the Federal Theatre Project; and I claim that it has nothing whatsoever to do with it."

"You do not believe," asked Starnes, "that plays in America should have the social significance that you say the plays of Russia have?" By a socially significant play, said Hallie, she meant a play "that has something to do with the world today." "It is a changing world, isn't it?" asked Starnes, who had obviously borrowed this phrase from another of Hallie's articles. "It is," said Hallie, "and the theatre must change with it, Congressman, if it is to be any good."

Dies had meantime decided that a more gentlemanly approach

might better serve the Committee's needs. He asked Hallie how many people had seen Federal Theatre plays, and after Hallie had answered, "Twenty-five million" and inquired if she could elaborate, he very courteously replied, "Yes, ma'am." Hallie wanted to discuss audiences, she said, because Mrs. Huffman had alleged that Federal Theatre "couldn't get any audiences for anything except Communistic plays" and that was absolutely false. She summarized lists of organizations which had supported Federal Theatre, noting that "every religious shade," "every political affiliation," and "every type of educational and civic body" was represented.

This exchange was not tolerated for long by Starnes, who was impatiently waiting to read again from Hallie's article. When he got the chance, this was what he read: "The workers' theatres intend to shape the life of this country, socially, politically, and industrially. They intend to remake a social structure without the help of money—and this ambition alone invests their undertaking with a certain Marlowesque madness." Starnes then commented, "You are quoting from this Marlowe. Is he a Communist?"

There was a silence, then laughter from the spectators seated in the balcony. Hallie laughed too, then quickly apologized. "I am very sorry," she said. "I was quoting from Christopher Marlowe."

Starnes was adamant. "Tell us who Marlowe is, so we can get the proper reference, because that is all we want to do."

"Put it in the record," Hallie replied when the laughter had subsided, "that he was the greatest dramatist in the period immediately preceding Shakespeare."

The Alabama congressman carried this off as best he could. He echoed Hallie's words. "Put that in the record because the charge has been made that this article of yours is entirely Communistic, and we want to help you."

"Thank you," said Hallie. "That statement will go in the record."

But Starnes, before numerous spectators and in the hearing of newspaper reporters, had momentarily given the impression of being an ignoramus, and he could not allow that impression to stand. "Of course," he added, "we had what some people call Communists back in the days of the Greek theatre."

"Quite true," said Hallie.

"And I believe Mr. Euripides was guilty of teaching class consciousness also, wasn't he?"

"I believe that was alleged against all of the Greek dramatists."

"So we cannot say when it began," Starnes went on.

"Wasn't it alleged also of Ibsen," Hallie asked, "and against practically every great dramatist?"

"I think so," Starnes conceded. So ended a conversation more curious than anything that had gone before. For one brief moment a member of HUAC had seemed to concede that the entire business of making Communist allegations against free-thinking writers was a farce. Or perhaps he was making the point that writers are dangerous and should be suppressed. In any case, his remark about Marlowe would go down in history and be quoted in his obituary.

Thomas took up the questioning next. He asked Hallie if she remembered the testimony relevant to *The Revolt of the Beavers,* the play Brooks Atkinson had called "Mother Goose Marx." Hallie said yes, and she was sorry the play had disturbed Atkinson, whose skill and learning she valued, and sorry it had disturbed a police commissioner, "but we did not write this play for dramatic critics, nor did we write it for policemen." She asked if she could read into the record what children had thought about the play, explaining that she had had a survey conducted on children's reactions. One child had said the play taught "that it is better to be good than bad," another that "it teaches us never to be selfish." "I think their reaction is very interesting," said Thomas, "but at the same time what was the reaction of Mr. Atkinson?" Hallie once more attempted to distinguish between adult reactions and reactions of those for whom the play had been performed. She insisted there was "nothing subversive in it." This was probably the only defensive line Hallie could have taken about a play that has been called the one purely Marxist play Federal Theatre produced.

Thomas proceeded on to *Injunction Granted,* another Federal Theatre production that had been criticized for its political implications. He asked Hallie whether she did not think it an improper use of government funds to produce a play that criticized the New Jersey legislature for failing to provide adequate relief for the unemployed. "I happened to be a member of that legislature at the time and I happen to know that there was nothing [inactive about the legislature]," Thomas stated. "If you had written to us at that time," said Hallie, "and given us material, we would have tried to get that into the play." She was having a more difficult time now but still was not willing to concede that she or Federal Theatre was at fault. "You see," she explained, "in the Living Newspaper, everything is factual . . . In the three years of the existence of the Living Newspaper, not one allegation has been made that the news presented was untrue. Nobody has ever proved that we misquoted." She was, of course, side-stepping the issue, and Thomas was quick to tell her, "I want an answer to my question." Did she think this was the "right kind of propaganda to put out against the government of a particular state, against the legislators who were elected by the people of that particular state"?

"I think," said Hallie, "that plays dealing with real problems facing all of us as Americans today may be one phase of the work that the Federal Theatre should do."

Thomas again insisted that she was not answering his question, and that, in his opinion, representatives of the Arts Projects who had come before the Committee had "evaded question after question." Hallie insisted that the play in question was "not propaganda against the elected legislators," it was "propaganda for fair labor relations . . . intended to prove that during the time when there was this mass need and this mass unemployment, unemployed people were not getting sufficient help from their legislative bodies."

"Then you will admit," replied Thomas, "that we should use the Federal Theatre Project, through their plays, to encourage mass movements? That is practically what you just said." Hallie would not agree that she had said anything of the sort.

Representative Mosier next questioned Hallie. Had she ever produced an anti-Fascist or an anti-Communist play? Shaw's *On the Rocks,* said Hallie, had been called both. She went on to say that she did not think it was fair to denounce plays as subversive when characters who opposed "our own political faith" appeared. Did anyone, for instance, think that the March of Time, because it quoted Stalin, was Communistic? or that Marlowe's *Dr. Faustus* was evil because it presented the Devil's point of view? Mosier asked if Federal Theatre had produced any antireligious plays. "We certainly have not," Hallie declared. "On the contrary, we have produced more plays religious in character than any other theatre or organization." In every city where projects existed, she added, religious scenes had been given at Christmas "on the steps of libraries, on street corners, in trailer camps, and churches."

As best she could, Hallie had managed to sidestep the allegation that Federal Theatre had a bias in favor of labor and against capitalism. She had taken the same position she always had: a government-sponsored theatre should present "relevant theatre." The only other line of defense would have been to make a distinction between herself and the workers on the project who from the beginning had worked primarily to champion their own political position. She had not interfered, and perhaps now she regretted her permissiveness. Having permitted them leeway, however, she was not going to turn against them.

During the last half-hour of the session, Starnes summed up his position by saying, "The statement has been made in the testimony that you are in sympathy with Communist doctrines." Hallie replied, "Congressman Starnes, I am an American, and I believe in American democracy. I believe the Works Progress Administration is one great bulwark of that democracy. I believe the Federal Theatre . . . is honestly trying in every possible way to interpret the best interests of the people of this democracy. I am not in sympathy with any other form of government."

Dies began to wind up the session. There were certain points he wanted emphasized, certain issues he wanted the reporters to take back to their newspapers. And being a master at theatre himself, he wanted these issues developed in the most dramatic way possible. He asked Hallie what she thought should be the primary purpose in producing plays: amusement or "the presentation of facts or material in a way to leave a definite impression?" Hallie thought that "a good play must always entertain" but that it could also teach. "Along moral lines, or along social lines or economic lines, isn't that a fact?" Hallie agreed. The chairman inquired if she thought it was "correct to use the Federal Theatre" to educate people along social or economic lines. "Among other things, yes," she answered. But since Federal Theatre was an agency of the government, supported through all people through their tax money, "people of different classes, different races, different religions, some who are workers, some who are businessmen, don't you think," asked Dies, "that no play should ever be produced which undertakes to portray the interests of one class to the disadvantage of another class?"

"I think," said Hallie, "we strive for objectivity." She also thought that any "dramatist holds a passionate brief for the things he is saying." She agreed with the chairman that if every Federal Theatre play expressed the same class opinion, it would be a "loaded theatre and quite out of keeping with a theatre subsidized by government funds." Dies inquired if she did not think she was treading on "dangerous ground" to produce *even one* socially biased play. Hallie insisted once again that she was not doing plays to stir up class hatred. Dies wanted to know if she could name "a single play" among those she had produced on social issues which did not give the impression that organized labor had "the best of the other fellows." "Why, Congressman Dies," Hallie exclaimed, "I could sit in this room until the end of the day and give you such plays." She proceeded to name and discuss several. She would go back to her "original premise," her standard: a play should be "a good play, a powerful play, preferably of native materials ... In at least ten percent of the cases, I feel we should do a play that has something to do with modern life."

"Then," said Dies slowly, to give the reporters plenty of time to take his statement down, "this Federal Theatre is a very powerful vehicle of expression, isn't it, and of propaganda, because as you say, it reaches twenty-five million people. It therefore can be used or abused." Hallie agreed. Again Dies asked whether she did not think it improper to use taxpayers' money to present plays "which champion one side of a controversy." Hallie had now reached the point of admitting exactly what Dies wanted her to admit, what the Committee wanted the taxpaying public to hear her say. She had side-stepped many questions while the chairman pushed doggedly on. She had finally to say what she herself believed about this matter of the taxpayers' money.

"No, Congressman Dies," said Hallie. "I do not consider it improper ... Ten percent [of our plays] do hold a brief for a certain cause in accord with general forward-looking tendencies." But who was to determine what a forward-looking tendency was? he asked. "Our play policy board chooses these plays," said Hallie. *They* were the ones who had the idea that public ownership of utilities was a forward-looking tendency? the chairman countered. (Just a few minutes earlier they had discussed the Living Newspaper *Power*.) Did Hallie really think that because the Board had that idea, that Federal Theatre should champion it? Hallie replied in the affirmative. "All right," said the chairman. "Now would the same thing be true with reference to the public ownership of railroads?" And what "if someone came with a play [championing] the public ownership of all the property in the United States?"

"Well," said Hallie, "that is a very clever move on your part to maneuver me into a certain position." Having been so maneuvered, she was forced to say no: "We would stop with that because that would be recommending the overthrow of the United States government, and I do not want that, gentlemen, whatever some of the witnesses may have intimated."

"In other words, you would favor doing it [nationalizing industry] by degrees, but not all at once, isn't that right?" Dies had got Hallie to admit that her one criterion for choosing a play was that it be a good play, "an entertaining play," as he put it. She had said that "if someone came up with a very good play proving that the *private* ownership of railroads was the best possible thing," she would do it, but had then had to admit that if a good play "proved that the public ownership of railroads was a good thing," she would do that also. The chairman had made his point. The implications were vast, and for Hallie, in her present position, ruinous. Dies reiterated his question, asking her once more if she would put on a play that championed "the public ownership of other forms of private property."

"I came up here," Hallie answered, "under the distinct understanding that I was to refute testimony given by witnesses before your Committee. You are proposing a long series of hypothetical questions." She insisted that she wanted to take up testimony of the witnesses, "charge by charge." "I see," said the chairman. "But you have already stated that you did not know of any of these Communistic activities, you did not see it." Therefore, he added, she was not in a position to answer charges dealing with Communistic activities on the project. When Hallie insisted, however, that she *was* in a position to deny statements made by witnesses, Dies allowed her to continue.

During the next few minutes Hallie lost ground. Although she pointed out false statements certain witnesses had made (one having been that the Federal Theatre director of community drama in New York was her cousin), these corrections did nothing to prove or disprove Communist activity within Federal Theatre. They proved only that the witnesses before the Committee had often made unreliable statements. That, of course, was a good point to make, but it did not satisfy Dies, who repeatedly asked Hallie to refute, if she could, any witness's testimony that Communist activity had taken place, that pamphlets had been distributed, and that Communist Party meetings had been held "on the project during pay time." Hallie had once more to say that she had "not been present" and could not answer such charges.

The session was almost over. During the remaining few minutes of the hearing, Dies conceded Hallie's point that Federal Theatre plays had not been subversive. He did not, however, concede that Communists did not exist on Federal Theatre. When Hallie said it was untrue that the Workers' Alliance was "in charge of the project," Dies countered, "You would not undertake to disprove that six of your supervisors on one project were Communists, would you?" Hallie had to admit that she had no evidence as to whether or not this was true. The chairman had again made his point. Reporters had written down his allegations. He had succeeded in making Federal Theatre look like a hotbed of Communism. But Hallie, even at the last moment, was unwilling to give up.

At one-fifteen the chairman announced, "We will adjourn for one hour."

"Just a minute, gentlemen," Hallie said. "Do I understand that this concludes my testimony?"

Said Dies: "We will see about it after lunch."

"I would like to make a final statement if I may," said Hallie.

Dies repeated, "We will see about it after lunch."

There was no after-lunch meeting.

As the hearing broke up, Hallie suddenly thought (as she wrote later):

of how much it all looked like a badly staged courtroom
scene; it wasn't imposing enough for a congressional hearing on which the future of several thousand human beings
depended. For any case on which the life and reputation of
a single human being depended, even that of an accused
murderer, we had an American system which demanded a
judge trained in law, a defense lawyer, a carefully chosen
jury, and above all the necessity of hearing all the evidence
on both sides of the case.

Yet here was a Committee which for months had been
actually trying a case against Federal Theatre, trying it
behind closed doors, and giving one side only to the press.
Out of a project employing thousands of people from coast
to coast, the Committee had chosen arbitrarily to hear ten
witnesses, all from New York City, and had refused
arbitrarily to hear literally hundreds of others, on and off
the project, who had asked to testify.

Representative Dempsey approached Hallie after the hearing to say
he thought her testimony had been "completely satisfactory."
Thomas also approached Hallie, to say, "You don't look like a
Communist. You look like a Republican." Hallie told him that if he
still thought Federal Theatre was Communistic, she wanted to come
back and testify further. "We don't want you back," said Thomas.
"You're a tough witness and we're all worn out."

Henry Alsberg's testimony before the Committee that afternoon
was in stark contrast to Hallie's. Although a staff assistant had
assured him that he had heard Hopkins say, "As far as I am
concerned, Hallie and Henry have my permission to go up and spit
in the faces of the Dies Committee," Alsberg appeared nervous and
anxious. His testimony at first could barely be heard, and Dies had to
ask him to raise his voice. Alsberg's experience with communism had
been totally different from Hallie's. His attitude toward the Communists on his own project was therefore also different. In 1925
Alsberg had edited a series of letters written by Russian political
prisoners. At that time, he told the Committee, his series, which had
run in Sunday papers all over the country, was considered a

"devastating attack," and as a result he had lost most of his liberal friends, who branded him as an arch-anti-Communist. He explained that in 1925 many liberals "felt there should be nothing said about Russia that was not completely favorable." Since then, many of them had "changed their minds," but he had suffered. He had been blacklisted, he had not been able to get his articles published. When asked if he was considered pro-Fascist by his liberal friends, Alsberg said no: "They call me a poor liberal who has slipped, and that is the term that is applied to a great many liberals who do not go the full way." Alsberg went on to say that he had tried to maintain his "independence of judgment as to what people and governments do," but that had been difficult. Nevertheless, as director of the Writers' Project, he had demoted or transferred all the radicals who made trouble. "We will not tolerate another rumpus in New York City," he assured the Committee.

Alsberg had noticed things Hallie had not wanted to discuss. He told Dies about the "constant pressure" in New York from union delegates. "Every time we drop a man there are delegations, there are protests . . . They have had street picketing," with banners denouncing project supervisors. Kondolf had experienced all this and Hallie knew about it.

Dies grew more and more benign as Alsberg's testimony continued. He summed up: "You, as an administrator, are absolutely opposed to Communistic activities, or any other subversive activities on the project." Alsberg agreed that this was decidedly so. He also agreed with Dies that it was "wrong" to put into the project guidebooks "things which seem offensive, unfair, prejudiced, or partisan, or from a class angle." The session ended with both men patting each other on the back. "The chair wants to commend you," said Dies, "for your frankness, for your desire to give the committee the facts and for the attitude you have assumed."

No one else gave Alsberg high marks for his witness stand behavior. The New Dealers realized, wrote a member of Alsberg's staff, "that Alsberg was no reactionary . . . but when they measured his performance against that of Hallie Flanagan . . . their initial reaction to his testimony was harsh. Some of them knew what Alsberg was soon to discover, that the Dies Committee, by its very nature, could not be appeased by acts of cooperation." Nevertheless, the House was soon to appropriate $100,000 to continue the Committee inquiry. During the first four months of HUAC's existence, the hearings had dominated the press. A Gallup Poll indicated that more than half of all voters were aware of the hearings, and that, of those, 75 percent wanted the investigations continued.

At the end of December 6, Hallie had one major concern: that her brief rebutting the charges be made available to the public. Although the secretary of the Committee promised to include her brief in the transcript, Hallie was skeptical. She went to David Niles, who told her not to worry. "They'll have to include the brief," he said. "They can't suppress evidence." He promised that in case the Committee did not print it, he would see that 500 copies were distributed to the Senate and a number of representatives. Hallie had the 500 copies printed and sent to Niles's office. Her brief was not included in the Committee transcript, and the 500 copies were never distributed. Thus it was not just the general public that got a one-sided account of the hearings but members of Congress as well.

When the Dies Committee Report was filed in early January 1939, it included much information condemning the Federal Writers' Project. In the case of Federal Theatre, "six months of sensational charges," as Hallie put it, "tapered down to one short paragraph":

> We are convinced that a rather large number of the employees on the Federal Theatre Project are either members of the Communist Party or are sympathetic with the Communist Party. It is also clear that certain employees felt under compulsion to join the Workers' Alliance in order to retain their jobs.

When the two New Deal members of the Committee, Dempsey and Healey, read an early version of this report, they threatened to submit a minority report unless Dies qualified his charges. A paragraph was then inserted stating that much of the witnesses' testimony had been "exaggerated" and "biased."

The press, however, took no notice of this inconspicuous paragraph.

There was a conference in Hallie's office after the hearings. "Hallie was greatly disturbed," Howard Miller remembered, "as were we all, because you don't lower a congressman's image when he's among his peers." And she had done that. She had laughed when Starnes asked her if Marlowe was a Communist. Of course, "she was under a lot of emotional pressure," and that was why she had seized the opportunity to show Starnes up "as a dullard."

It was important to Hallie to maintain an attitude of dignity throughout this difficult time, and she soon acted to repair what her own staff regarded as a tactical mistake. A few days later she wrote Congressman Dies inviting him to the opening night of *Pinocchio,* which Yasha Frank had first launched in California and just brought to New York. "I feel you might be especially interested in this production," she wrote, "not only because it represents one of our major efforts in the field of children's theatre but because [it shows] what we have been able to do in rehabilitating professional theatre people and retraining them in new techniques. In *Pinocchio* we use fifty vaudeville people who were at one time headliners in their profession" but then found themselves "without a market." Hallie extended this invitation to every member of the Committee, but none of them responded, a slight which prompted her to comment that the "Committee proceeded to its final deliberations with its theatregoing record intact: officially it never saw a production of the project under examination."

CHAPTER

16

Final Fight

PINOCCHIO was among the last of Federal Theatre's big successes. In California, Walt Disney and his staff attended eight performances, and Disney decided to make the story his next cartoon feature. Yasha Frank, who had had the idea of dramatizing the much-loved fairy tale, started his career as a psychologist working with street gangs. He got them to create something, then challenged them to tear it down. Of course they refused. He used his psychological training in working with vaudevillians as well. Hallie, who had written David Stevens of the Rockefeller Foundation, "I once told you that I either had or intended to have on the Federal Theatre before I got through, the best theatre brains in the United States," cited Yasha Frank as "proof that the thing is really happening."

The show at New York's Ritz Theatre sold out every night of the week. Reviewers turned in rave notices. Scalpers reacted by buying up fifty-five-cent tickets and selling them for $6.60. The theatre critic for the New York *Telegraph* enthusiastically described the "beautiful undersea fantasy," the "charming marionette sequence," the dogs, cats, foxes, and goldfish that came to life on the stage, enchanting adults as much as children. Even the *Daily Worker* and the *Wall Street Journal,* so far apart on most issues, agreed the show was a great tribute to Federal Theatre. The *Wall Street Journal* reviewer, who was particularly delighted by the lead player's performance wrote, "One can only wonder at the obtuseness of the theatre business which leaves men like this to find their outlet on WPA." Hallie was amused. She was never surprised by the talent she and her producers unearthed on WPA.

New York boasted other Federal Theatre successes that 1938 Christmas season. Two marionette shows, *The Story of Ferdinand* and *String Fever,* played to full houses at every performance. The New York *Daily News* printed a photograph of a little girl bursting into tears at the box office when told that no more tickets were available. Shaw's *Androcles and the Lion* at Harlem's Lafayette Theatre was equally popular. Brooks Atkinson and John Mason Brown both thought it better than the production done earlier by the Theatre Guild. Theodore Pratt's *Big Blow,* a new melodrama about life in Florida's "cracker country," was voted a "big hit" and "one of Federal Theatre's finest." A revival of Clifford Odets's *Awake and Sing,* produced by the Yiddish group, was called "a more trenchant domestic drama than the Yiddish stage has witnessed in some time." Meanwhile neighborhoods throughout the city watched troupes of Federal Theatre players reenact the birth of Christ. The other two big metropolitan centers were also having successes—Los Angeles with a variety show called *Two-A-Day,* Chicago with a new version of Gilbert and Sullivan's *The Mikado.* The Negro company's adaptation of this classic light opera had by January become the hit of the season, breaking all previous attendance records in the history of the Great Northern Theatre. The show became so successful that Michael Todd, in competition with Federal Theatre, soon launched his own *Hot Mikado.* But none of this news buoyed the spirits of those running the WPA.

With Congress moving aggressively to dismantle the New Deal, many employees felt their jobs were in jeopardy. Hallie, who was temporarily opposed to thinking in terms of defeat, made up her mind to resist the pessimism she found in Washington as long as she could. But she was not blind. In an attempt at light-heartedness, she wrote to her friend Burns Mantle, "Please keep the Dies brief in case I am whisked away by the American Cheka on some dark night. It *can happen here*—but only after you and I and quite a few others have done all in our power."

A few days later, all WPA administrators once again received orders to cut the number of their employees—no explanation. Some people speculated that the order anticipated the determination in Congress to slash relief spending. Another explanation is just as likely: alarmed by events abroad, the President had begun to think of rearmament. There was a need to free funds. During 1938 Hitler had moved into Austria and parts of Czechoslovakia. War now seemed more and more likely.

In late January 1939 Hallie met with Mrs. Roosevelt to discuss Federal Theatre. Afterward she wrote: "We are trying in every way to develop a program which will meet wide community needs and sponsorship. This is the only way we have of combating the false statements circulated by newspapers which choose to play up the garbled testimony of incompetent witnesses before the Dies Committee." In a speech to her New York supervisors, she stressed the importance of gaining wider public support by touring and loaning personnel to the field.

The need for greater support was still in Hallie's mind when she wrote to Senator Claude Pepper of Florida, an ardent New Dealer. At the time, the Senate was considering Hopkins's appointment as Secretary of Commerce. Roosevelt had offered Hopkins this job as a preliminary step to promoting him for the presidency. At the hearings Pepper had pointed out the dangers involved when the press was allowed to injure the reputations of individuals. Hallie described to Pepper her own ordeal with the press, then added: "If you and some of your colleagues could continue the line of reasoning you so brilliantly launched in the Senate . . . you would be doing a great service for American Democracy."

Gaining more support for Federal Theatre at this moment in its history was probably not possible. Even Hallie must have known how slight the chances were. Her plan of decentralization had been blocked from the start, not merely because of official difficulties and the concentration of actors in large cities, but also because of Hallie's own priorities. It was the big cities that had given Federal Theatre its great successes.

Before Hallie left for her last trip to the West Coast, two events occurred, neither of them auspicious. In late January, the House passed a bill that reduced the President's request for relief spending by one hundred and fifty million dollars, and the Senate, after a dramatic and bitter struggle, upheld the House. About the same time Roosevelt appointed a new relief administrator. Colonel F. C. Harrington, although an able administrator, lacked Hopkins's interest in the arts. Nobody expected him to become a strong supporter of Federal Theatre, and, indeed, he did not.

When Hallie stopped in Detroit, as she always did on her trips to the Coast, she learned that the district WPA office wanted "no loan of personnel" and "no social plays." When she pointed out that there had been only two social plays in three years in all Michigan and that they had been the "biggest box office successes," she was told to make an appointment with the state administrator. The state administrator was not interested. But at her next stop, Hallie was cheered to discover that the University of Chicago wanted to sponsor a Federal Theatre company for a summer training session. The president of the university and many of his colleagues thought the Theatre Project "the great living force in the theatre today." Here, at least, was one group that did not believe everything it read in the newspapers. Chicago editorialists had been extreme in opposing the New Deal. Even when Federal Theatre put on shows that hardly anyone considered controversial, even when theatre critics praised them, the editorial writers found something to criticize. The Chicago *American* had recently urged readers to see for themselves the deplorably dangerous and disrupting plays being produced by Roosevelt's theatre groups. These "dangerous" plays included a children's play, *Little Black Sambo,* a variety show, *Bandbox Revue,* and a revival of *The Copperhead,* a Civil War piece. The attacks, as Hallie noted in *Arena,* were based on the "policy of the paper rather than on common sense."

In Seattle she watched a rehearsal of *Spirochete,* a Living Newspaper about syphilis that state and county medical associations were sponsoring. Arnold Sundgaard, a play reader in Susan Glaspell's Midwest Play Bureau, had written it at Glaspell's suggestion. Hallie had seen a first draft, liked it, and recommended it for Seattle. She could hardly believe the company she had seen a year earlier was responsible for the wonderful staging. One of the actors, Toby Leach, a former circus performer whose legs had been broken in a barrel act, impressed her particularly. Leach was still lame and played his scenes sitting down. "Our company members," she was told, "may not be so good in drawing-room comedy, but they were trained in the art of timing." Leach was written up in a special edition of the Seattle *Times*. His stamina, Hallie thought, was "Federal Theatre in a nutshell."

At Timberline Lodge on Mount Hood, Hallie got the "most complete rest, interspersed with sledding," that she had had for three years. Most people who knew Hallie would have found it difficult to imagine her on a sled. She was not in the least athletic, but sledding was the order of the day. She participated whenever she was not meeting supervisors to plan a Paul Bunyan festival at the lodge for the coming summer. There were to be wrestling matches and horseshoe pitching at the foot of the mountain, and at the lodge a performance of E. P. Conkle's *Paul Bunyan and the Blue Ox*.

"I want it to be a production that will say for the West dramatically what Timberline says for the West architecturally," Hallie told the Oregon director. He replied: "The Federal Theatre can do it. To tell you the truth, I thought the company was hopeless at first, but now I go to everything they put on. I take all my friends. I'm amazed at the whole thing. After the Bunyan festival, we're going to build a civic center, and that's going to include a theatre to house the federal company." Such ideas kept Hallie going, at times even made her forget what was happening in Washington.

The Dies committee might have been surprised to know that Hallie was not only not un-American, she was unreservedly patriotic. The technical achievements of twentieth-century America never failed to impress her. One of those achievements was the Golden Gate Bridge spanning the entrance to San Francisco Bay. When this bridge was completed in 1937, excavated soil was used to create an island in the bay, which was then designated as the location for the Golden Gate International Exposition, what Hallie called the "great patriotic event." Many buildings went up, among them a federal building containing a theatre. The money to finance the theatre had been raised from Federal Theatre admission funds to give the project a rent-free location for future productions. Hallie enthusiastically approved the modern steel-and-glass theatre when she first saw it on Treasure Island but was dismayed by the architect's color scheme, which she immediately labeled "in the worst tradition of Greenwich

Village 1920." Her housewifely instincts aroused, she dashed off a memo to her Washington bosses:

> On the morning I arrived I was rushed to the grounds and shown the samples of wall paint—three shades of rose, banded at the top by sky blue and at the bottom by purple. We all disliked them . . . I did cut out the blue and purple and left only the three tones of rose . . . After the paint was on, the carpet came in blue. This made a rose and blue theatre, certainly not my idea of 1939 functional art. And on top of that, the seats arrived, in the worst horrible mottled orange leather—an eye-splitting color which with the rose walls was so outrageous that everyone got really ill . . . It makes the walls look like raspberry sherbet . . . I wired [the architect] to come at once . . . but the color will never be right.

Some of the colors got changed, and the shows, which were brought to the island from Federal Theatre units in Los Angeles and San Francisco, went through their last rehearsals. Hallie spent the day making numerous improvements. "We spent all Friday until 2 A.M. on Treasure Island," she wrote her husband, "and got back to San Francisco at 3 A.M. so tired we all hated each other, Federal Theatre, and even the thought of the Golden Gate Exposition." But at the opening, Hallie was as happy and excited as a young girl attending her first fair. "Darling, it was wonderful," she wrote Philip. "The flags went flying up and everyone made speeches, bands played, a Cossack choir sang, and cowboys strummed Home on the Range." Afterward the official in charge gave a luncheon, and "I sat next to Elsa Maxwell."

A reporter for the San Francisco *Chronicle* sent to interview Hallie was surprised by her size. She was "almost frail-looking," he decided, and "not at all the type you would expect to be chief administrator for so vast a concern" as Federal Theatre. After a while, however, he concluded that she was "ideally fitted" for the work she was doing. She had "the enthusiasm of a true zealot." Hallie told the reporter that she liked the Treasure Island program because it exemplified what Federal Theatre was working toward. "She would like to see festival centers established all over the country."

One innovation that particularly pleased her was the flexible light board her Los Angeles lighting director, George Izenour, had created for the Exposition. Izenour was one of Hallie's discoveries. "She took a hell of a chance," Izenour thought, "when she appointed me lighting director for the Los Angeles project." At the time, 1937, he had little to recommend him. Fresh out of college, with a background in physics and some experience in lighting college shows, he was new to California and could not qualify for state relief. But Hallie, after reading a paper he had written on lighting, cut through the red tape and gave him the job. Izenour survived in Los Angeles despite the resentment of stagehands who disliked him for his youth and new ideas. Later, with Hallie's encouragement, he went to Yale, where he eventually built a revolutionary lighting system for the Yale University Theatre. "If I had not gone to Yale," he said, "I would probably have left the theatre. The greatness of Federal Theatre was that it gave young people a chance."

But even Izenour's achievement, great as it was, could not compensate Hallie for the political climate she found in California in February 1939. Not all papers were as friendly to her as the *Chronicle*. When she opened the San Francisco *Examiner* one morning, she was faced with the caption "Federal Theatre Communist Trend Must be Eradicated." This was exactly what the state WPA office was now determined to do. A new state administrator had replaced Colonel Connolly. Without consulting Hallie he appointed a new artistic director who had no knowledge of the project. A general reorganization that usurped Hallie's control in the state followed. The Los Angeles project, Hallie later wrote, "with its proud record of accomplishment, its classical repertory, its dance productions, its shops, laboratories, research bureaus, its productions which for several years had been strong enough to keep three or four theatres open simultaneously—all this came to a close. It did not take an Act of Congress to end Federal Theatre for southern California. It ended the day the local WPA took it over."

Returning to New York in mid-March she took heart in the discovery that "four major triumphs" were showing: *Pinocchio, Androcles and the Lion, Swing Mikado,* and *Big Blow,* the last two imported after successful Chicago runs. "If we go out," she wrote a

friend "it will be at least with a major conflagration lighting the sky."
Except for *Androcles,* the four plays had all been written specifically
for Federal Theatre.

Although Hallie was determined to stand by "until the last gun
fired," even she came to admit that moment might come "by June if
not before." This time her judgment was realistic. By March,
President Roosevelt had abandoned all efforts to press Congress for
additional relief legislation. Democratic conservatives hoping to see
Vice President Garner as the Democratic candidate were rallying
round a bill proposed by Senator James Byrnes of South Carolina,
which would consolidate all relief agencies under a Department of
Public Works and eliminate white-collar programs such as the Arts
Projects. When Colonel Harrington called this last step a "serious
omission" in hearings before a Senate committee investigating relief,
he was told that the WPA theatre was competing with private
enterprise. That was to be the new line against Federal Theatre. In
preparation for a new relief bill, the House in late March decided to
make a sweeping inquiry into the WPA. Special investigators were
sent to New York, Los Angeles, and Chicago with instructions to dig
deep into the Arts Projects, particularly the Federal Theatre.

New York at the time was concluding rehearsals of *Sing for Your
Supper,* a musical revue about unemployed actors, singers, and
dancers who find work with the government. Although its songwrit-
ers had turned out some good songs, among them *Ballad for Uncle
Sam,* which was later popularized by Paul Robeson as *Ballad for
Americans,* the show had been widely criticized for its lengthy
rehearsal period. George Kondolf had a political explanation for the
delay. Rehearsals, he said, often became rallies for those on the left.
"One day I went to see a runthrough and I noticed a brilliant young
dancer in the show. I suggested to those in charge that we do
something about this man, surround him with more material because
he was so good. They agreed, but several weeks later when I again
saw a runthrough, he was no longer in the cast. I asked why. Well,
he hadn't worked out, wasn't cooperative, something like that. It was
Gene Kelly. Later he told me that he had been fired." Kondolf
thought that *Sing for Your Supper* mixed art and politics in a way
that "hurt the project terrifically."

Those caught up in the excitement of producing *Sing for Your*

Supper were naturally unprepared for the vehement, distorted attacks
the show evoked in Congress. That Hallie was equally unprepared,
despite her previous experience, is shown by the letter she wrote to
one of her directors shortly before the show opened. *Sing for Your
Supper,* she told him, was the "narrow thread on which the fate of
the entire Federal Theatre hangs. There is no question at all but that
a successful production here could turn the tide of a great deal of
congressional wrath." But in 1939 nothing could have turned the
tide of congressional wrath.

By May 1, a special investigator of the House Subcommittee on
Appropriations had returned to Washington with the damaging
information that Federal Theatre was costing too much. He cited
Sing for Your Supper as a case in point. It was playing at the Adelphi,
which rented for more than two thousand dollars a month. Rehearsal
time, he said, had been too long. Furthermore, Negroes and whites
were in the mixed cast and "dancing together." After committee
members had discussed this interracial issue for a time, they got
around to discussing "lewd lines" in the show. Chairman Clifton
Woodrum of Virginia suggested that these lines would be "rather
embarrassing with ladies and gentlemen present," and Representative
Burton of Indiana agreed, saying they should be included in the
record without being read. He wanted only to read one example, a
line from a song which went "I don't want to be intellectual, I want
to be sexual." The committee then launched into the kind of attack
already established by the Dies Committee: the New York Arts
Projects were "largely controlled by the Workers' Alliance and its
Communist affiliations." The Woodrum Committee had taken up
where the Dies Committee left off, with the same mixture of truth,
half truth, and outright untruth and an equal degree of histrionics,
which again captivated the press.

A month later, Representative Woodrum, in a style foreshadow-
ing the McCarthy hearings, told his colleagues: "I have here the
manuscript of *Sing for Your Supper*. If there is a line in it or a passage
in it that contributes to the cultural and educational benefit of
America, I will eat the whole manuscript."

Hallie was later to say that Federal Theatre unfortunately
symbolized all the characteristics of the New Deal: "it cost money; it
represented labor unions, old and new; it did not [until 1938] bar

aliens; and it did not bar members of minority parties." Congress, she added, could have decided to bar members of any specific minority party. Instead, it "punished us for failing to take action which was its exclusive prerogative. It was scarcely necessary to tear the house down to get at a mouse in the cellar." This oblique reference to the Communists as mice in the cellar was as close as Hallie ever came publicly to criticizing the militants who had caused her so many headaches.

The Woodrum Committee investigations were once again followed by sensational headlines in the press, and once again Washington refused Hallie permission to launch a counterattack. With few exceptions, the same type of witnesses appeared before the Woodrum Committee as had appeared before the Dies Committee. But this time the attacks focused almost as heavily on Federal Theatre expenditures as on its "subversive activities." The Augusta *Chronicle* in Maine, among other newspapers, waxed indignant over the "wild extravagances" of WPA. When Brooks Atkinson, in the *New York Times,* pointed out the difference between regulations affecting a government-sponsored theatre and those affecting a commercial production, his voice was lost in the uproar. No one was present at the hearings to point out that Federal Theatre had been set up by Congress to spend money. No one was present to point out that box office receipts were paying much of the cost for scenery, costumes, theatre rentals, and royalties.

Representative Clarence Cannon of Missouri was the one member of the committee who worked hard to make the hearings more objective. When Charles Walton, a New York stage manager for the Theatre Project, quoted informants to prove that the New York project was nothing more than a "clever fence to sow the seeds of communism," Cannon objected that "we are going pretty far afield. This is the most extraordinary testimony—who said this or that; it would not be admitted in any court in the country." When Walton said he had been demoted by the project because he had testified before the Dies Committee, Cannon replied, "Here is a man with a grouch. He says this man said this or that. What is the fact?" Walton, who had no facts, went on to make further allegations and finally cited an instance where an audience had hissed a policeman in *Life and Death of an American,* a play Federal Theatre had taken over after Theatre Union closed. "So because in a play an audience gets up and hisses a policeman, you think that is sowing the seeds of communism?" Cannon demanded. "That is the most ridiculous thing I ever heard of. If that is sowing the seeds of communism, then we have communism all over this country."

Cannon's valiant attempt to bring common sense into the hearings went unheeded. Walton went on to say that he had been asked for his opinion and he had given it, and although Cannon retorted that his opinion, unless supported by facts, was worthless, the evidence was allowed to stand. Hallie, though not allowed to answer charges, was given permission to write Woodrum a letter. The hearings, she said, gave a "distorted picture." Communists might well be among the forty million persons who attended the plays, but so were people of every other political faith. As for the allegations of Communist employees, congressional statutes did not allow inquiry into a relief client's loyalty.

Hallie was in New York, watching an Ibsen production in a high school auditorium, on the day she heard the news she had been dreading. When she emerged, an employee handed her a newspaper which reported that the Woodrum Committee had submitted a bill to the House eliminating funds for Federal Theatre. The employee watched her read, then asked, "They can't do that, can they?" "I'm afraid," said Hallie, "that they can." She went to a phone and called the WPA office in Washington. A Mr. Hunter answered, confirmed the report, and added that his superiors were out of town. Hallie asked if he would see her. When he said he would, she boarded a train for Washington. Who, she wondered, had been put in charge of the fight to save Federal Theatre? But Mr. Hunter looked at her regretfully. "There isn't going to be a fight to save Federal Theatre."

Hallie was glad at least that his answer was honest. No straight talk had come out of the WPA office for some time. "From the moment when Mr. Hunter told us the truth," Hallie said later, "we ignored WPA and all WPA rules." But first she went to see Hopkins. "It's your baby," Hopkins told her. "Fight for it." She needed no other encouragement.

Now she was on her own, free at last to launch a counter-offensive. The House was to begin debating the relief bill in a day or two. Hallie and her Washington staff went to work to line up congressional support. Representatives Sirovich, Celler, Coffee, and Dempsey agreed to speak for the defense. Mary Norton offered to introduce an amendment restoring the Theatre Project to the bill.

The debate took place at night. Hallie later commented: "Our Federal Theatre staff sat in the gallery of the House and watched a scene which, if dramatized on one of our stages, would have resulted in a charge that we were libeling the legislative branch of the government. Every mention of a so-called salacious title—and apparently every title that had the word love in it impressed the congressmen as salacious—was greeted with howls and catcalls." Friendly representatives who spoke in favor of Federal Theatre were shouted down, as were favorable statements telegraphed in from Burns Mantle, Wolcott Gibbs, and John Gassner. Brooks Atkinson had written an article which was read into the record, but this too received a hostile hearing. "Art seems like boondoggling to a congressman who is looking for a club with which to belabor the administration," Atkinson had written, "and there is always something in the Federal Theatre that can be blown up into a scandal. But for socially useful achievement, it would be hard among the relief projects to beat the Federal Theatre, which has brought art and ideas within the range of millions of people all over the country . . . It has been the best friend the theatre has ever had in this country." The congressmen were not interested.

Facing the hostile House, Representative Norton rose at last to say that she did not believe anything that anyone could say was going to change the temper of the House, but she hoped the representatives would consider what this bill was "doing to 9,000 men and women on this project . . . I beg of you tonight, before you go to your comfortable homes, to think twice before, by your vote, you deprive 9,000 persons of their right to a home. This is the sort of thing responsible for communism." Norton was shouted down. Speaker William Brockman Bankhead pounded his gavel. Massachusetts Representative Joseph Casey called for the vote. The Norton amendment lost by 56 to 192. Hallie had lost her first battle in the final round to save Federal Theatre. There remained the Senate.

Aided by her staff, she spent the next few days going through stacks of material—press releases, reviews, letters, and commenda-

tory articles, whatever could be used to combat the House allegations. Letters enclosing printed material went out to senators,
congressmen, the press—to everyone who might give aid and support. Many needed no prodding. Organized labor, Broadway professionals, and Hollywood stars rushed to the aid of Federal Theatre.
Telegrams urging presidential action poured into Hallie's Washington office from Eddie Cantor and dozens of other entertainers. Helen
Hayes, Lee Shubert, Burgess Meredith, Richard Rodgers, George
Abbott, Moss Hart, Clifford Odets, and Harold Clurman were but a
few of those who urged Congressman Cannon to read their endorse-
ments of the Theatre Project on the floor of Congress. Actors,
playwrights, and producers printed an appeal in the *New York
Times*: "If the theatre has ever brought you happiness and joy, join
with us now; write or wire your senator demanding the continuation
of Federal Theatre." On the West Coast, screen actors, directors, and
writers gathered in a mass rally. The number of those signing
petitions ran into the thousands.

Hallie called the response "magnificent." The battle to save
Federal Theatre came to have broad significance. In many people's
minds, it became a fight to get the public to recognize that *artists
counted,* that their talents were essential to the nation's well-being.
Shortly before the relief bill came before the House, President
Roosevelt wrote to Nelson Rockefeller about the widespread anti-
intellectualism among members of Congress. "I suppose," he commented, "these elected legislators are representing the view of their
constituents, for the simple reason that the average voter does not yet
appreciate the need of encouraging art, music, and literature. Unfortunately there are too many people who think that this type of
white-collar worker ought to be put to work digging ditches . . . We
need all the help we can get to educate the Congress." The Arts
Project employees, he added, had done an "amazingly constructive"
job. The President's words were borne out repeatedly. A couple of
weeks later, a congressman, in response to Senator Robert Wagner's
plea for the Arts Projects, exclaimed, "Culture! What the Hell—Let
'em have a pick and shovel."

Two days after the House voted to abolish Federal Theatre, the
New York Times reported that the administration might finally and
belatedly join the fight to urge the Senate to reverse the House

decision. Senator Claude Pepper gathered together a group of well-known stage people for a preliminary hearing before the Senate Appropriations Committee. When Hallie entered the senatorial chamber on June 20, the first person she saw was Tallulah Bankhead seated on top of a table in a manner Hallie later described as "probably rare in senatorial offices." Tallulah had arrived with her father, William, who was the Speaker of the House and a Federal Theatre supporter. Her Uncle John, a senator from Alabama but *not* a Federal Theatre supporter, was also present. She was giving one of her most theatrical performances, trying to persuade her uncle with pleas and kisses that actors had a right to earn a living. When her uncle remained unmoved, insisting that these "city fellers in Congress never vote to do anything for the farmers," she turned to the senators. "Actors are people, aren't they?" she demanded. In a voice breaking with emotion, she begged them not to deprive WPA employees of the chance "to hold up their heads with dignity and self-respect." Blanche Yurka added: "I do not think anybody questions that the Federal Theatre needs improvement. But after all, you do not chloroform a child who happens to have the measles. You help that child, you try to build up his strength."

When Hallie took the floor, she made a point of refuting the charges that had been made in the House. The project, she said, had been accused of competing with the commercial theatre: in fact, it had brought in audiences unable to afford commercial entertainment. It had also been accused of being overstaffed with persons not on relief; that charge too was incorrect: 95 percent of those in the project came from relief rolls. As for the objection of extravagance, Hallie admitted that the rehearsal time for *Sing for Your Supper* had been too long but pointed out that the revue had had to be recast almost entirely after government cuts were instituted. Several employees had returned to the private sector while rehearsals were going on and thus deprived the cast of talent even while aiding one of the purposes for which Federal Theatre had been set up, namely, returning theatrical workers to the commercial stage.

Herman Shumlin, speaking for the League of New York Theatres, and Frank Gillmore of Actors' Equity agreed with Hallie that the Federal Theatre did not compete with the commercial theatre. On the contrary: "the more plays on Broadway, the better." A New

York stagehand explained what the project meant to his profession. A social worker spoke of the great good that had been done by performances in hospitals, insane asylums, orphanages, and crippled children's clinics. Finally, Colonel Harrington, speaking for the administration, reiterated the project's accomplishments. Thus ended that particular session. The Senate subcommittee had still to present its own version of the relief bill to the Senate.

Hallie felt the hearing had been fair, that the majority of senators had been thoughtful rather than hostile. She came to feel that Federal Theatre's "double identity" as a relief organization and artistic enterprise was "at the root of many of our problems." As she later wrote:

> If an actor took pride in his work and turned in an excellent performance, he was accused of being a "careerist." On the other hand, if he gave all that was in him but if it was no longer of the best because of age or sickness, he might as easily be accused of being "incompetent" or "amateur." Because we were a relief enterprise, people found it difficult to believe that the good acting was turned in by actors actually in need of relief. Because we were also a theatre enterprise, they were impatient with the strange variety of talent which we took from the relief rolls.

The number of Federal Theatre supporters was meantime growing rapidly. In Hollywood, the Motion Picture Guild arranged for two coast-to-coast radio broadcasts. Movie stars, including Claudette Colbert, Melvyn Douglas, Ralph Bellamy, Joan Blondell, Henry Fonda, James Cagney, Dick Powell, and Al Jolson, spoke on behalf of the Theatre Project. Lionel Barrymore, who characterized himself as an old actor and an old citizen, said that eliminating the arts program was like "taking one of the stripes out of the American flag." Raymond Massey, who offered to debate Representative Woodrum, and Tyrone Power flew to Washington to support an amendment proposed by Senators Wagner, Downey, and Pepper which would have set aside one percent of the entire relief appropriation for the Arts Projects. On the East Coast, the Federation of Arts Union sponsored a broadcast from New York, sent lobbyists to Capitol Hill, and organized mass rallies in the Shuberts' Majestic

Theatre. Orson Welles debated three senators over the radio. Eleanor Roosevelt lobbied for Federal Theatre in her daily column, as did at least eight other journalists, including Walter Winchell, who told the nation that "you cannot budget the value of art" and that Federal Theatre productions were "important events in the history of the American theatre, and therefore in the history of the American people."

All of this encouraged Hallie to believe that Federal Theatre now had a "better than fighting chance in the Senate and a fairly good chance in the House."

During the Senate debates that followed, only one senator indulged in the smear tactics that had characterized the Dies and Woodrum Committee hearings. Getting the facts to the senators, as Hallie later said, had had the desired effect. The attacks of Senators Robert Reynolds of North Carolina and Rush Holt of West Virginia did not go unanswered.

After Reynolds rose to defend America from the danger of "Red" propaganda, Democratic senator Pat McCarran of Nevada used Roosevelt's often quoted remark that "the only thing we have to fear is fear itself" to point out how certain people used the "bugbear of communism" to enhance their own prestige. Senator Pepper then made the point that a new provision in the relief bill would require a formal oath of allegiance from all Arts Project employees, so that no one who advocated the overthrow of the government could earn compensation. Senator James M. Mead of New York, who presented a complete breakdown of the various unions on the New York project, made the point that the number of Communists among Workers' Alliance members was negligible. Reynolds wanted to know whether the Senate would accept an amendment to the bill providing that anyone who had ever been affiliated with the Workers' Alliance be barred from participating in the Theatre. "No," said Senator Alva B. Adams, chairman of the Senate Committee on Appropriations, "because while there may be Communists in the Workers' Alliance, I would not be willing to join in condemnation of everyone who belongs to that association."

In 1936, James Davis, a Republican senator from Pennsylvania, had stated that extreme radicals controlled the New York unit of the Federal Theatre. But now that Congress was "on the eve of saving

these theatrical projects from the extremists," he urged his colleagues
to "clean house . . . but not throw these men of the stage out on the
street." This defense from a former Federal Theatre critic urged
Reynolds on to his most virulent attack. He proceeded to reiterate
the testimony of a witness who had claimed that a supervisor
belonging to the Workers' Alliance had urged her to date a Negro.
"The cardinal keystone of Communism," he said "—free love and
racial equality—is being spread at the expense of the God-fearing,
home-loving American taxpayer who must pay the bills for all this
dangerous business." He insisted that the project's "unsavory collection of communistic, un-American doctrines" was being "spewed
from the gutters of the Kremlin"; indeed the project was not only
pro-Communist but also unprofitable. There was probably in America, he said, "no lady of higher character" than Mrs. Flanagan, but
what was needed was "someone with old-fashioned common horse
sense, rather than some college professor." "Tripe" was being
"served across the footlights." Federal Theatre did plays with such
titles as *Love 'em and Leave 'em, Up in Mabel's Room,* and *A New
Kind of Love.*

When Hallie read this testimony, she wondered about Reynolds's sincerity. It did not seem possible that Reynolds and his
associates really believed that Molière's *School for Wives* and
Sheridan's *School for Scandal,* which had also been attacked, were
dangerous and indecent. She thought of *Julius Caesar*—how those
who had attacked Cinna had said, "Not a conspirator? Then, tear
him for his verses," whether you've read them or not. Were Federal
Theatre's opponents afraid, she wondered, because the project was
educating people "to know more about government and politics and
the vital issues of housing, power, agriculture, and labor?" She could
understand why certain people would not want a government theatre
"to make the people in our democracy think," but Senator Reynolds's remarks about Negroes made her wonder if congressmen were
afraid of Federal Theatre because it gave Negro actors a chance. She
felt a special gratitude to Senator Henry F. Ashurst of Arizona, who
at a high moment in the hearings, declared: "The stage is art, and art
is truth, and in the final sum of worldly things, only art endures. The
sculptures outlast the dynasty . . . The coin outlasts Tiberius."

At the end of its debate, the Senate discussed whether one percent, or three-fourths of one percent, of the relief appropriation should go to the Arts Projects. It settled on the smaller amount. The Wagner-Downey-Pepper amendment restoring Federal Theatre to the relief bill was passed by a vote of 54 to 9. The "fair hearing" in the Senate, Hallie said later, was "all over so quickly we hardly knew we had won." But the news of the triumph, which flashed across the country and brought in hundreds of congratulatory telegrams, was premature.

The next day, the bill passed by the Senate was referred to a joint conference of the House and Senate Appropriations Committees. Relief appropriations were to end at midnight on the following day, and the conference was forced to make compromises. The main compromise settled on was Federal Theatre. Congressman Woodrum was quoted in the press as saying that he was going to put the government out of show business if it was the last thing he did. He prevailed. A senator later wrote Hallie: "The Theatre Project was the last concession made by the Senate conferees, and that concession was made only as the last resort in order to secure an agreement." No funds, the final bill stated, would be available for the Theatre after June 30, 1939.

President Roosevelt signed the bill, even though he felt it was unfair to "a special group of professional people":

> It is discrimination of the worst type. I have not objected to the provisions that a portion of the costs of projects for artists, musicians and writers should be paid for by local governments and sponsored by them, and the same provision could well have been applied to theatre projects. The House conferees declined to yield to the Senate and we have as a result an entering wedge of legislation against a specific class in the community.

The other three Arts Projects were permitted to continue under local sponsorship, but Federal Theatre had ended.

The President wrote to Hallie that she was "pioneering in a new field so far as this country was concerned. Not only did you accomplish the primary purpose of affording work for those who follow a particular calling—in itself no easy task—but you encouraged dramatic writing and production and at the same time made high-class entertainment available to large numbers of our people who otherwise might not have had such advantages." He offered his congratulations.

Editorials across the country also praised Federal Theatre. But the most touching wake for the Theatre took place on the stages where the last performances were given. For the final showing of *Pinocchio,* Yasha Frank provided a new ending. Pinocchio, who had concluded every other performance by turning into a real boy, this time died and was laid away in a pine coffin while the cast chanted, "So let the bells proclaim our grief—that his small life was all too brief." Stagehands knocked down the sets while the audience looked on. "Thus passed Pinocchio," an actor declared. "Born December 23, 1938, died June 30, 1939. Killed by an Act of Congress." Actors and crew walked out of the theatre with a placard reading WANTED: REPRESENTATIVE CLIFTON A. WOODRUM FOR THE MURDER OF PINOC- CHIO. At Duffy Square the demonstration ended. Those present sang the national anthem, then walked off into the night.

"It was over at last," Hallie wrote in *Arena.* She felt that Federal Theatre might have lived longer "if it had been less alive. But I do not believe anyone who worked on it regrets that it stood from first to last against reaction, against prejudice, against racial, religious, and political intolerance." In the coming months she was to be haunted by the thought of the thousands of people who had been thrown out of work. Their "loyalty and devotion" moved her to tears when, a few days later, they sent money to her secretary with instructions to "buy something with diamonds for Hallie." A committee went to Cartier's and purchased a platinum wristwatch set with diamonds, one for each state. "Someone, Winchell, I think," said Hallie, "wrote a column about the watch entitled *Actors Are Funny.*"

Malcolm Cowley's account of the New Deal theatre project, written for *The New Republic* in 1941, gives as good an assessment of Federal Theatre's achievements as any.

> In the first place, it provided steady work for eight thousand penniless theatrical people. That was its primary purpose, under the law setting up the WPA, and was quite enough to justify the money spent on the project. But in the second place, it also brought stage shows, at a low price or none at all, to people who were starved for entertainment and in many cases had never seen a living actor. It gave regional

pageants, comedies specially written to be played in the barracks of CCC camps, tent shows, marionette plays for children and Living Newspapers for the broad public; and much of what it did was tied up with the daily lives of people watching the performance. The Federal Theatre was creating an entirely new audience, just as free libraries had created a new audience for books; that explains why the commercial theatre tried hard to defend it later, when it was being attacked in Congress. And in the third place, it produced an astonishing number of good plays, old and new, highbrow and popular, everything from Marlowe and Shakespeare to surrealism and "The Swing Mikado." It was for a time the center of almost everything that was fresh and experimental on the American stage. More than that, it came closer than anything else we have had—perhaps closer than anything we shall get in the future—to being an American national theatre.

He asked himself why it had been stopped, and concluded that it conflicted with prejudices that are deeply ingrained in American society. "Americans tend to think that wealth is a divine reward for thrift and self-denial . . . and to see poverty and unemployment as God's punishment meted out to the lazy and shiftless." Under Roosevelt's leadership, they came to feel that the destitute should be fed, perhaps even clothed and housed, but they rebelled at the idea of entertaining the destitute at public expense. This was "not in keeping with the principles expounded by the Founding Fathers and Horatio Alger." Cowley thought Federal Theatre had also aroused class hatreds and, among some members of Congress, a "violent philistinism, a hatred not only for actors and playwrights but for every human activity faintly tinged with intelligence." But he put the chief blame for the eclipse of Federal Theatre on himself and other liberals. "We liked the idea of the Federal Theatre, we went to see some of the plays when they were sufficiently recommended by Brooks Atkinson . . . and at the very end, when it was too late, we perhaps signed protests against its suppression. That has been the career of too many progressive people, signing indignant protests when it was too late. Afterward we were properly regretful and perhaps wrote editorials ridiculing Mr. Starnes of Alabama. But during the four preceding years, when we might have helped to build up a sentiment for Federal Theatre so strong that Congress would not have dared to abolish it; when we might have proved to Mr. Roosevelt that his always good intentions were receiving wide popular approval, we had done, well not exactly nothing, but not really enough to matter."

> And, in a sense, this failure is typical of the whole decade that has just ended. In 1933, progressive opinion in America received a chance that it was never given before—a President in sympathy with its aims and a business community so frightened that for once it was willing to accept liberal measures. Brave things were done in the following years, but not enough of them; and some of the bravest attempts were permitted to fail through lack of intelligent support. The progressives had their chance and most of them lost it—sometimes because they failed to see it, sometimes because they saw but failed to grasp it, and sometimes because they were so busy quarreling among themselves that after grasping it they let it slip from their hands. The story would have been different if more of us had been as imaginative and hard-working and self-forgetful as Hallie Flanagan.

Hallie, who worried all her life that she was not being self-forgetful enough, particularly when she compared herself with her selfless mother, may have found consolation in Cowley's words. If so, she wasted no time in self-congratulation. By the time Cowley's article appeared, she had satisfied her ambition explaining Federal Theatre to the public and gone back to considering what contributions a college theatre might make in influencing the future of the country.

Aftermath
1940–1969

Return to Vassar

I N her later years Hallie was to recall the seven months after Federal Theatre ended as a "thoroughly happy time." With the help of a grant from the Rockefeller Foundation to write *Arena*, her book about the Theatre Project, she was able to hire a secretary and a small staff of researchers. Vassar gave her space to work in. "President Mac-Cracken arranged with President Roosevelt to have all Federal Theatre records sent to Vassar . . . I divided my time between my household, the Experimental Theatre and the writing of *Arena*."

Esther Porter Lane remembered the hectic days before the Roosevelt administration granted Hallie the permission she needed to transport the WPA records to Poughkeepsie. "When I was in New York, we'd fill the trunk of my car with papers. It was a snitchy kind of job, but Hallie needed them." She was impatient to get started. Getting clearance took time and was "so complicated that we just snitched, no other word for it, filled the trunk of the car and drove to Poughkeepsie."

Many of the people who had worked with Hallie on Federal Theatre, particularly those who felt angry at Hopkins for backing off when Hallie needed him, thought she would write a scathing attack on the WPA bureaucracy. "She was a fighter," said Irwin Rubinstein. He hoped she would denounce those who had let her down. So did

Emmet Lavery, who blamed Hopkins for not having lifted a finger "to stop the slaughter," and said so in an article he wrote for *Commonweal* in August 1939. Both men were to be disappointed. In Rubinstein's words, Hallie's comments on Washington were "sugar-coated. The book was no attack at all." But Rubinstein and Lavery failed to understand something basic about Hallie. She was as much a politician as Hopkins, Roosevelt, and the men who worked under them. She spent her whole life making concessions to get her own way. She knew the necessity of doing so and never blamed Hopkins for harboring ambitions that clashed with hers. In Hallie's view, Hopkins had fought for what he wanted and believed in until he saw that what he wanted was no longer possible. He had not wantonly abandoned her nor changed his ideals, as Lavery thought; but, rather, to further those ideals had adjusted his actions to the changing political climate.

Lavery never forgot the day Hopkins walked into the room where he and Hallie were working on *Arena*. "Hopkins said, Hello, Hallie, how's the book? Are you going to kick the hell out of me?" Lavery could not recall what else was said. "But Hallie and Harry went off to talk, and Mary McFarland went off to prepare tea for Harry at Garfield Place. Mary said, Isn't it wonderful? Two old friends getting together after the wars are over?—Maybe, I told her, but I think it would have been more wonderful if they had gotten together a bit earlier."

Hallie now had more time to be with her family. On weekends she and Dad took my brother, sister, and me on tours of Dutchess County. As part of its American Guide Series, the Federal Writers' Project had produced a number of local guidebooks. The one on Dutchess County, which my parents carried with them on our outings, led us up and down the Hudson, into small, sparsely populated towns and across broad stretches of farmland. We visited Hyde Park and the nearby Vanderbilt Mansion. In Red Hook we investigated a blacksmith shop. In Rhinebeck we lunched at the Beekman Arms Hotel, which, the guidebook informed us, was the oldest operating hotel in America. We looked at eighteenth-century houses in Fishkill, at nineteenth-century houses in Millbrook, and at dozens of Dutch doors. We drove past Bannerman's Island, with its imitation medieval castle, and learned from Hallie, who read aloud while Dad did the driving, that the island had once been inhabited by a fisherman whose wife had imagined herself the Queen of England. We saw sites where Revolutionary soldiers had built forts and fought battles. In Poughkeepsie, we visited a Coca-Cola plant, a printing press, and the Smith Brothers' cough drop factory. Hallie and Phil enjoyed discussing Dutchess County lore as much as they had enjoyed talking about Roosevelt's New Deal. This time was a second honeymoon for both of them. They set aside an hour each evening to read to us, then read to one another or went to the college to hear a lecture or concert. If Hallie had a theory about child-rearing it was that children grow like flowers: give them the proper setting and a little watering now and then and they will flourish. Quarrels among her children took her by surprise. On one memorable occasion while she was running Federal Theatre, we staged a pitched battle in the lobby of a large New York theatre minutes after photographers arrived to take pictures. While we punched one another in our fierce competition to see who could collect the biggest pile of programs, Hallie made valiant efforts to divert the photographers' attention. A month or so later she hired a different photographer to take pictures of Dad playing ball with Jack and her reading aloud to Helen and me in the garden. This time she made sure to set the scene and rehearse us thoroughly before the photographer arrived.

She was not always so successful in channeling the direction of her children's energies. Two months after Federal Theatre ended, Fred eloped. He was in his senior year at Brown University. Since students were forbidden to marry, Fred decided to keep his marriage a secret. His wife, Elizabeth Beckwith, a bright, attractive Pembroke College graduate who had visited the family with Fred on a number of occasions the previous year, had made a good impression on Philip. Betty, he pointed out, had a calm, self-assured manner. She was unlike the flighty girls Fred had previously dated, and she would be good for him. Hallie gave the matter little thought. Believing that Fred would finish college and find work before marrying, she also thought he would consult her before making any major decision. She was totally unprepared for what followed.

Fred had planned to announce his marriage in June, at the time of his graduation. But events intervened. One autumn weekend, while he and Betty were visiting her mother in Yonkers, they were discovered in bed together. The secret came out, and a day or two later, the young couple made a trip to Poughkeepsie to relay the news to Hallie and Philip. In Betty's recollection, Philip was pleased, "but Hallie was furious. It took all of Phil's patience to calm her down." Hallie imagined the worst: Brown might not allow Fred to graduate; Betty might become pregnant before Fred found work. And, in fact, the administrators at Brown did make a fuss. Hallie had to go to Providence to persuade university officials that her son, though he had broken a rule, had done the necessary work and should get a degree. At the same time she and Phil planned a June party to celebrate the marriage. It was the last big event they arranged together.

Hallie later wrote:

> One night in February, 1940, Phil and I started the evening as usual—our candlelit dinner, the children joining us for dessert and some reading aloud. Then we drove to the theatre where I was rehearsing a play and Phil was reading inscriptions in his office upstairs. After rehearsal we drove a car load of people home and then went on to 12 Garfield. We stood in the snow and looked at the garden and planned spring planting. I said something about what a wonderful spring it would be—at home and together—and Phil said, "Let Rome in Tiber melt, and the wide range of the vast empire fall—here is my place."
>
> We went in the back way and Phil said, "That's not quite right. Let's read the play. I'll bring it up. Go up and get your bath and pop into bed. I'll bring up something to drink and *Antony and Cleopatra*."
>
> I went up and while I was in the bath I heard a peculiar sound—a rapid, insistent tapping. I thought it was the furnace . . . I put on a robe and got into bed and called, "Come on up, darling. And what is that noise?" There was no answer and the noise in the dark house was terrifying. I ran downstairs and into the kitchen. On the table was a tray containing a bottle of wine, two glasses, crackers and cheese, and *Antony and Cleopatra*. Phil was lying on the floor, his feet making the terrible sound. He was in convul-

sions, from which, although we got him to the hospital, he never recovered . . . The doctor said coronary thrombosis. By three o'clock in the morning I was back home, knowing that in the morning I should have to tell the children that Phil was dead.

During the weeks that followed, Hallie received hundreds of letters from students, colleagues, and friends. One student wrote: "I remember thinking to myself after class on Monday, This is the happiest class I have ever been in, all because of Mr. Davis. He teaches you grammar and you think it's poetry. He makes you work five hours some nights but you'd work six if he asked you to." Another wrote: "I opened the letter with the awful news in it, in the little restaurant where I always have breakfast, and quite unashamedly sat at the counter and cried my eyes out. I think everyone who knew Phil loved him."

In replying to her closest friends, Hallie occasionally voiced a thought that haunted her; she had wasted four years living apart from Philip when she might have been with him. The idea was too painful to dwell on. "Phil never thought those years were wasted," she wrote E. C. Mabie. "He never let me stop until the final fight had been made." She came to feel that "his suffering over the end of the project, especially over the attack on me, had a connection with his death." Later, when she wrote *Notes on My Life*, her autobiography, she recalled Phil's reaction to the Dies Committee hearings. "He sat up in the gallery hearing me called Red, subversive and communistic and it made him sick. At one point—I found this out later—he almost fainted and had to be helped out."

Phil's close friends thought he had been pushing himself. "We were all worried about his health," Gordon Post recalled. "He used to drive to New York after a day of teaching to see a rehearsal with Hallie, then return the same night." Another friend remembered the Sunday before Phil's death. "There was a meeting of the Open Forum. Phil was exhausted and lying on the couch. Hallie said, Why do you go? He said, I have to."

After Phil's funeral Hallie met with his mother, brother Pen, and eldest sister Jean, to discuss the family's future. Pen, who worked for the State Department (later he was ambassador to Hungary and after that to Costa Rica), and Jean, who taught economics and sociology at Wells College, were concerned about Phil's children and Hallie's finances. Neither Pen nor Jean had children. Pen offered to adopt Jack, Jean offered to adopt all three children. Under New York State law, if one parent dies, the other automatically becomes guardian, but in the case of a surviving stepparent, the court is entitled to appoint a guardian without consulting the family. Jean remembered her family being "scared: any stranger, any lawyer or bank might be appointed." She had known cases of orphans going to unsuitable foster parents.

Hallie immediately settled all worries by saying that she wanted to be guardian. Her lawyer, Bill Walsh, told me he had several talks with her about this time. Hallie "dug in her heels at the idea of anyone else adopting you. She felt your Uncle Pen was a little conservative and rigid in his views. His philosophy differed about as far as it could from your father's. She didn't want you to grow up as conservatives, and also she wanted to keep you together. As I remember it, the final decision rested with your maternal grandmother, Mrs. Dwelle. She had the strongest claim." Nannie Dwelle, as we all called her, had taken the main responsibility for raising us after Mother died. It was Nannie who hired a nurse to care for my sister after Mother's death and Nannie who paid the nurse who looked after us after Dad married Hallie. She took us to Buffalo to live with her when Dad went on vacations and during the year he took a sabbatical in Greece and married Hallie. "In the beginning," Bill told me, "Mrs. Dwelle didn't see things Hallie's way, but eventually she came round and let Hallie be appointed guardian."

Money problems loomed large in the lengthy correspondence between Hallie and her in-laws. Hallie told the Davises that Philip had left unpaid bills. Pen, Jean, and Phil's mother sent checks to help, even though they considered Hallie extravagant. "My mother," Jean said, "remembered Hallie buying several elegant sets of towels at a time when she already had a full linen closet." Pen wrote Hallie, "I am afraid you are going to find that the household financing will require careful budgeting," but he offered to help "whenever and however I can." Phil's mother sent Hallie loving, supportive letters almost daily. But Hallie never felt entirely at ease with Phil's family.

The Davises, though well off, were frugal. Their interests, tastes, and way of life were different from Hallie's, and they were as strong-minded as Hallie herself. Philip's sister Marjorie, who of all his siblings was closest in age to Philip, remembered a summer when Hallie visited the Davises' summer home on Lake George shortly after her marriage. "Did you know," she asked me, "that Hallie got together with those who had married into the family and that they named themselves the Outlaws?" I hadn't known, but I could imagine it. I could also imagine Hallie initiating the movement. Hallie visited Lake George when she was working on *One-Third of a Nation* at Vassar. After receiving the accolades of opening night, she suddenly found herself surrounded by people more interested in swimming, hiking up mountains, and taking daylong boat trips on the lake than in talking about theatre or President Roosevelt. If anyone took center stage at the Lake George house, it was Philip's mother, who presided at mealtimes over a long table where the children spoke up as often as the adults. Philip's parents had bought the house before his father died; and it was a family house entirely. The large living room on the second floor was not a stage set designed for adult theatrical parties or a place set aside for adult living; it accommodated people of all ages. It was in this house that I first came to feel that children and adults might be thought of as equals.

Hallie, who wanted us to feel that we belonged to her, was well aware that she had competition. My brother, Jack, was Dad's mother's favorite grandchild. Helen always felt she was a Dwelle. In summer Dad's sister Marjorie "adopted" me. The years after Dad's death were made more difficult for Hallie because of this, but in another way, they were easier. We were not, after all, entirely dependent on Hallie.

As I see it now, one of the problems from Hallie's point of view was Nannie Dwelle. My mother had been her only child. Naturally Nannie wanted to keep Mother's memory alive. After Grandpa died, she moved to Poughkeepsie to be near us. Today Nannie would be considered old-fashioned: sewing, cooking, and caring for her family were her chief pleasures. She also voted the Republican ticket, which from Hallie's viewpoint was a strike against her. Grandpa had made a success of running a glass company in Buffalo, and Nannie had not had to worry about money for years. Hallie had worried about

money most of her life. Over time she had come to regard women
who did not work as somewhat frivolous, not quite her equals. But
the main cause of strain between Hallie and Nannie was their rivalry
for our affections.

Nannie saw us as her daughter's children. Your mother, she
would say to us, did this or that. She was beautiful (we could see that
from the pictures on the walls of Nannie's apartment); she was lively
and talented and had wanted many children. Before long I got the
idea, and I think my brother and sister did also, that Mother, if she
had lived, would have been the most exemplary mother of all time.
She would have stayed at home; not chosen to have a career. Hallie,
who liked to think she had managed a career, marriage, and
child-rearing with equal success, was naturally upset by any remarks
suggesting that we might have fared better had Mother lived.

After she moved to Poughkeepsie, Nannie began eating dinner
with us on Sundays. Those Sundays, which turned into nightmares
for everyone, began simply enough. Usually Nannie arrived a couple
of hours early so my sister and I could try on the clothes she was
making for us. After we sat down to dinner she often talked about
the trips she had taken abroad after her husband's death. Hallie, who
liked nothing better than traveling abroad but had never had the
money to do this without help from foundations, would sit and listen
and nod politely while Nannie described her most recent trip to see
the Egyptian pyramids. But after a while, Nannie would turn to us
and say something like, "Now the year your mother and I went
abroad . . ." She never got a chance to finish her sentence. At the
words *your mother,* Hallie would push back her chair from the table,
run upstairs, throw herself across the bed, and burst into tears.
Silence would reign at the table—a silence made more dreadful by
Nannie's realization that once more, without intending harm, she
had said the wrong thing.

Who was going to go after Hallie? Certainly not my sister. Not
my brother either. Jack always managed to look unruffled and
uninterested when the females in the family were at odds with one
another. It was going to have to be me. Presently I would rise from
the table, climb the stairs, and try to persuade Hallie to return,
though I have no recollection of what I said once I reached Hallie's
bedroom. I must have succeeded, for somehow we always managed

to get through those awful Sunday dinners without any further scenes. It might be thought that I enjoyed my peace-making missions, but this was not so. I was as embarrassed by Hallie's tears as everyone else. I do recall my grandmother once telling me, "We must all make an effort to be kind to Hallie and remember that her role is not easy." By the time she said this she had stopped talking about Mother on Sundays.

One night I heard Hallie telling Philip's mother, who was visiting, that Nannie Dwelle was making her life miserable. I forget the details, but Hallie was dramatizing her difficulties, as she often did in the years following Dad's death. The next day I told Hallie that I was sure Nannie did not mean to hurt her. I was perhaps twelve at the time. To my surprise, Hallie listened. She said she would think about what I had said. And she did; for a while, at least, there were no more scenes.

So Hallie began to think of me as her ally. Having a daughter, she told me, gave her a pleasure she had not known before. We had many discussions after that about her girlhood, a subject she knew would interest me. Hallie never told me she was "groping to get hold of life again," a thought she confided to a friend. Occasionally she mentioned Dad. Once or twice she told me how much she missed him. But nobody in the house realized the thoughts that haunted her at night. These she put in a letter to her friend Mary Crapo.

> I hear myself saying to the girls—Yes, Darlings, I think the pink hair ribbons with the blue sweaters are sweet. And to Jack—But you can't spell educate with two d's, Dear, because . . . because why? Because why anything? . . . And spring is starting again—and the book has to be finished— and the stone lions are still staring out to sea, seven centuries of staring out to sea on Delos . . .

If Hallie had told my brother and sister and me how she was feeling, it might have strengthened family ties. As it was, we grew apart. Hallie allied herself with me. Helen turned to Nannie for affection. Jack was invited to Washington for a year to live with Uncle Pen and became attached to Pen's wife, Louise; he returned reluctantly. Although there were times, especially at Christmas, when we got together with Fred and Betty and renewed family bonds, these occasions were rare. Hallie had not wanted it that way, but she was busy.

Lee Gantt wrote to her after Dad's death: "You have always shown yourself capable of mastering any difficulty and turning it to good account. I have no doubt that you will find the light again." Of course he was right. Hallie went back to writing *Arena* and to teaching her course in playwriting. She forgot her grief when she was working.

In 1938 Hallie's playwriting students wrote the first act of a Living Newspaper about the founding of Vassar College. Hallie then asked Esther Porter Lane, whom she had appointed to direct the Vassar Theatre in the last year of her absence, to produce the show. Esther, who had learned a good deal about staging shows from assisting Joe Losey on *Injunction Granted* and from running a Federal Theatre unit in Seattle, was pleased: she had been wanting to pursue a career in directing for some time. She rewrote the script and created a visual pageant. Slides of the Hudson River provided the background for the scenes students had written about Matthew Vassar's life. Her production was praised.

Then Hallie returned to the campus. Though still busy writing *Arena,* she began dropping into the theatre to watch rehearsals. *Vassar's Folly* was to be given a second showing for Vassar's seventy-fifth alumnae reunion that June. Theoretically, Esther was still in charge, but Hallie had her own ideas about how to improve the show. "It was a difficult situation," Esther recalled. "If you're doing a runthrough and Hallie suddenly turns up and says she would like to change scene seven and stop the show, what do you do?" Not wanting to argue, Esther gave in, but there were times when she felt so tense she was unable to eat. From Hallie's point of view, she and Esther were working together in a cooperative venture. Any theatrical enterprise, she liked to say, made use of everyone's talents. No one was to be billed as a star. Hallie used words so masterfully, that it was hard to argue with her. Esther stayed on at Vassar a year longer. Whatever bitterness she felt toward Hallie she eventually put aside. At the time she knew only that there was not room in a small college theatre for two directors with ambition, especially when one of them was Hallie.

During the summer after Dad's death, Hallie wrote a play about a middle-aged actress who gets the lead in a Broadway play but then loses it to a younger woman. *No Time for Tears,* based on a true story Hallie had heard from a friend, is slight. She wrote it quickly, probably from a need to keep herself occupied at a difficult time. Her protagonist ruefully remarks in a late scene that there is "no happy ending. Just a doubtful beginning." Her younger woman character, Isabel, is the same willful, self-centered but gifted woman Hallie had created in several earlier stories and plays. Hallie recognizes Isabel's talent while deploring the ambition which drives her to override others' feelings. If the characters learn anything, it is that people who have hurt others or been hurt by them must simply keep going as best they can.

Hallie finished *Arena* in mid-1940, and it came out in December. She must have been pleased when John Gassner in the *New York Times Book Review* called it "as exciting as a novel and twice as provocative." Miss Flanagan, he noted, "does not accept defeat. Although discouraged by her experience with politics, she turns briskly to the question of what lessons are now available to the next group to work for a government theatre." Whether briskly or not, Hallie by the time the review came out had also returned to the question of how to make a college theatre responsive to the larger community of which it is a part.

Her half-cinematic, half-staged version of Thornton Wilder's *Our Town,* which opened at Vassar in the fall, grew out of her fascination with movies. She sent her students to New York to see a series of film classics at the Museum of Modern Art. "We were impressed," she wrote later, "with the increasing virtuosity of the film in comparison to the static quality of stagecraft." In originating the Living Newspaper for Federal Theatre, Hallie had borrowed many cinematic techniques. Even before that, when producing *Romeo and Juliet* at Grinnell, she had tried to approximate the speed of film to convey the play's message.

Wilder and Sol Lesser, who had produced the movie version of *Our Town,* gave Hallie permission to adapt the text and shooting script. In her production, Hallie juxtaposed the two in a way that pointed up the different values of each. She started with the stage version, then moved to the screen to show images of the town, the horizon, the horse and milk wagon, and the exteriors and interiors of the houses where the main action takes place. Transition was made fluid by the Stage Manager Wilder had created, and for whom Hallie invented new lines. Moving back and forth between stage and screen, letting the movie tell the story at some points, the stage at others, Hallie ended by showing the last scene both ways. "So that's how it was," her Stage Manager announces. "Emily saw for a moment how things really are in *Our Town,* and how good it all was. Hardly any of us ever realizes that, even for a minute. The play says that she went back to her grave; the movie says that it was all a dream and that when she awakened there was her new baby and George, happy and anxious. But the main thing is that for just a minute she saw—and maybe we all saw—how fast it is going, and how we better take time right now to look at each other and to look around us."

One reason Hallie had chosen the play was because of what it said about families. One night when we were riding home in a cab after a late rehearsal, she told me that Dad had especially enjoyed the brief moments in life that many people take for granted. "Whether he was weeding the garden, or reading aloud, or mixing us drinks, or just driving to work, he refused to hurry. Our time together was brief but never wasted, perhaps because we both knew that love and pleasure cannot last forever."

When Esther Porter Lane left Vassar in 1941, Hallie offered the job of assistant director to Robert Schnitzer. Bob, as all of us in the family soon came to call him, had directed the controversial but successful run of *Julius Caesar* for Federal Theatre in Delaware. Later he had worked for Hallie in the Washington office. After Philip's death he made frequent trips to Poughkeepsie to offer Hallie whatever support and assistance he could. Hallie was touched by his kindness, and she was lonely. When Bob, a year and a half after Dad died, told her he had fallen in love and wanted to marry her, she did not immediately discourage him. During the year he taught at Vassar, and for several years afterwards, he was a frequent guest in our home. Unfortunately for Bob's hopes, he had little fondness for children. At family gatherings he was out of place. Hallie, who delighted in our games, inventions, and youthful high spirits, was as quick to realize this as we were. Many years later she told me that she never seriously considered marrying Bob, though she had had a love affair with him that lasted several years. It was an admission she would have preferred keeping secret, but by the time she told me she knew that I had already discovered the main facts of her life.

Hallie and Bob became intimate while working together on a production of *Murder in the Cathedral*. Hallie's new conception for Eliot's play grew out of her recognition, in the fall and winter of 1941, that the world was in crisis. "Youth, taught since childhood to work for peace, faced a world at war." Every play she and her students considered seemed slight. "We talked about doing an escape play of fantasy or laughter, but no one wanted to waste time on it. We considered a play about factory life by a member of the economics department, but since one intent of the play was to show the inhuman speed of factory life, it seemed inappropriate at a time when the successful outcome of the war might hinge on this very speed."

> One night during our search for a play we read *Murder in the Cathedral* . . . Here was a play which emphasized the common man and the part he must play in a great decision. Every word spoken by the women of Canterbury seemed to have an immediate urgency. The women desired peace and the ordinary way of life . . . They did not want anything to happen. Yet there was upon them, as upon all of us in the fall and winter of 1941, a sense of fate.

Hallie's 1941 production of Eliot's play emphasized two themes: the women of the chorus drawn into a "pattern of fate" against their will and the struggles of the Archbishop against inner temptations and outer forces over which he had little control. She did not want to repeat the Federal Theatre interpretation, the church calling for religious submission. "We did not believe that the comfort of the church was as accessible to the poor as the horizontal steps [of the earlier production] seemed to suggest . . . Our setting therefore suggested on one side a cathedral with broken arches, and on the other the perilous crags on which the poor live . . . The women of the chorus built up their characters, not only from the play but from a study of the lives of women who had known oppression." They pored over photographs by Dorothea Lange, and the drawings of Käthe Kollwitz.

Murder in the Cathedral was one of Hallie's biggest successes at Vassar. The poet Alan Porter, who was teaching at the college that year, was especially moved by the chorus. "This is something which our Vassar Experimental Theatre does superbly well—as far as my experience goes, unmatchably well." The chorus, Hallie was later to say, "is a symbol of our theatre: a group working together on something more important than any of us." The production opened on December 6, 1941. The next day all who had shared in creating it "realized with Becket that *The moment foreseen may be unexpected when it arrives."* On December 8 America entered World War II.

Hallie had meantime been offered the job of Dean at Smith College. She had been looking for a new challenge, wanting also to escape the attachment she felt to the home she and Philip had created together. Smith president Herbert Davis offered her the use of a large, beautiful house overlooking Paradise Pond in Northampton, a larger salary than she had been receiving, and the chance to create a theatre department. She accepted.

In a chapel talk before Vassar's 1941 graduating class, Hallie summed up the hopes and beliefs of a generation— *her* generation— when she told students that from the defeats, failures, and mistakes of the past they might learn "a sense of civilization beginning its struggle upward." The conquest of the earth, the sea, and the air, she said, was incomplete and still a challenge. Those lucky enough to have studied at Vassar could count themselves "kings of infinite space."

> At a time when we want to rely less and less upon pleasures to be bought, at a time when we shall be called upon for strict economy, when we wish to sacrifice to help our country and the suffering world, it is important that we have inner sources of joy; that we know how to make music as well as to listen to it; how to make plays as well as how to go to the movies; how to paint pictures as well as look at

them; how to move, speak, read, think, live in such a way
that we reflect some of the beauty about us.

Some of Hallie's students had told her they felt guilty enjoying the
arts when there was so much suffering in the world. Hallie disagreed.
The values taught by a liberal arts education, she said, were if
anything even more important in moments of crisis. "At a time when
our belief in our American way of life leaps to meet a challenge
greater than any yet thrown down to us, let us remember that the
final bulwark of any way of life, the thing that keeps it from
annihilation, lies in the number of people who believe through their
own experience that that way of life is worth living for."

Hallie received many tributes before she left Vassar. All of them
touched her, but none made her prouder than the letter written by
her students for an Alumnae House party. "Dear Hallie," they
wrote:

> We came to Vassar. We were starry-eyed. We thought that
> D.P. majors wore white sarongs on Sundays. People told us
> they wore blue nail polish. Other people said they never
> combed their hair. We knew we were great actresses. That
> was when we were freshmen.
>
> Then after our sophomore scuffles through the green-
> room, after we panted through our reading rehearsals, we
> began to learn something about the theatre. We found out
> that hammering a nail isn't glamorous but had something
> to do with the play going on—and even when all we had to
> show for it were a lot of splinters in our fingers, we were
> part of something that was pretty important . . . That made
> us work hard. It made us think. It made us take pride in
> what came out of the mad days of rehearsal.
>
> Before we got to be wise, we found out something
> more. We had a theatre that had something serious to say—
> that meant something in the world we live in. It was a
> special kind of theatre—the right kind, a theatre we were
> grateful to be part of.
>
> So it doesn't matter in the end that we weren't all great
> actresses. We were glad to learn that we were in a very

particular way, drama students at Vassar College, Poughkeepsie, Dutchess County, New York State, the United
States of America, the Western Hemisphere, the earth, the
universe, the mind of God. We thank you, Hallie, for all
you've taught us.

No one present missed the reference to the Western Hemisphere, the
earth, the universe, and the mind of God: it was a quotation from
Our Town.

18

Northampton: New Challenges

Hallie announced that we were moving to Northampton one evening in 1942 after calling the family together for a conference. Family conferences to discuss such subjects as how much allowance my brother, sister, and I should have had been established when Dad was alive. But this time it was not Dad but Bob Schnitzer who sat with Hallie on the living room couch. Jack, who had distressed Hallie by addressing her from time to time as Aunt Louise after his return from living for a year with Dad's brother's family, had by this time settled down and accepted his fate as one of us. He was pleased when Hallie announced the move. So was Helen, but I burst into tears at the thought of leaving my friends behind. Hallie had not expected this. She had planned the announcement, expecting to tell us that we were moving because she needed more money, hoping we'd ask her what Northampton was like. My tears spoiled her pleasure, infuriated Bob, and put an end to what Hallie may have hoped would become a new family enclave with Bob as its latest member.

Every now and then Hallie got the idea that Jack needed a father. In the summer of 1942 she asked Bob to take him on a walking tour of the Adirondacks. Jack's recollection was that "he didn't do this for me, he did it for Hallie." True, Bob had little fondness for children, though he would have slain dragons for Hallie. I always thought he regarded us as unfortunate orphans who had been saved by Hallie's generosity from a fate worse than death (adoption by Nannie Dwelle).

Hallie did not help matters. By confiding in Bob the difficulties she was having with Nannie, she nourished his wish to play the knight in shining armor. She needed an ally, and Bob fit the bill. One of Hallie's "lieutenants" on Federal Theatre, he kept this role ever after, sometimes with a vengeance. When Hallie many years later had to be cared for in a nursing home, he sent each of us a play about villainous children who abandon their mother to the care of others. For Bob, where Hallie was concerned, there were two kinds of people: villains and heroes.

Northampton, as Hallie had predicted, turned out to be a charming college town with wide streets and handsome buildings dating from colonial times. Shops, restaurants, and a nineteenth-century opera house called the Academy of Music were all within walking distance of Smith College. One could get in a car and quickly find oneself in the tranquil setting of the broad Connecticut River valley. Northampton's residents took pride in the town's cultural traditions. *Uncle Tom's Cabin* had been performed at the Academy in the author's presence. Sarah Bernhardt, Maude Adams, and Ellen Terry had appeared on its stage. Jenny Lind had sung next door at City Hall, and characterized the town, when she honeymooned there in 1852, as the Paradise of America. In 1870 Sophia Smith left her entire fortune to found a women's college—"not to render my sex any the less feminine but to develop as fully as may be the powers of womanhood." The house Hallie was offered had a view of skaters in winter and rowboats in summer. Town and college, Hallie felt, combined to form a community of exceptional charm. She never lost this feeling, even after she began to wish she had never left Vassar.

At first all prospects looked promising. The maintenance men at Smith helped Hallie put her house in order. They painted, papered, built bookcases, installed furniture, and voiced no objection when Hallie, disliking some detail, asked for changes. They transplanted trees, planted flowers, and mowed the broad, sloping lawn that overlooked the pond. They built a guest-room addition. Bob helped with the moving. Hallie wanted everything shipshape for the fall when her job would begin and her stepchildren would return from summering with grandparents. She hired a housekeeper and settled in. She was as yet unaware of the furor her appointment had caused on campus.

The new president, Herbert Davis, had made Hallie's job sound altogether attractive. "Do not be too much concerned with the title of dean," he wrote her during the months before she had made up her mind to accept his offer.

> I suggested that office for you because it is the highest we have to offer, and because if you were Dean there would be no one else there to obstruct you and limit your work.
>
> It would give you a free hand to organize the work of the theatre and all the creative arts round it. It would leave you free to do exactly whatever else you like best in teaching. You would be encouraged to do whatever writing you wished to do, and to undertake any teaching outside or any expert investigations you were keen about.

Davis, before coming to Smith, had taught English at the University of Toronto and later at Cornell. He had been reared in England and educated at Oxford. No doubt it was his scholarly attainments that had won him his new position. Smith's former president and board of trustees were proud of its academic traditions. No one apparently realized that Davis, although scholarly, cherished a vision of an artistic renaissance at Smith, or that he wished to attract practicing artists to the campus, or that he knew next to nothing about running an American college and was not interested in administration.

The first hint Hallie got that the deanship, contrary to Davis's assurances, would involve her in a great deal of administrative detail came from the woman who acted as dean during the president's first year. The dean's role, Mary McElwain wrote Hallie, "is designed to be, to some extent, a buffer for the President." He needs an aide "who will bother with the details of the academic machinery, which are so different from those he has been used to and which are, in themselves, distasteful to him." One of the women who was to act as a class dean under Hallie later echoed this opinion. "President

Davis," she wrote me, "was a fine scholar and gentleman but a very poor administrator. He was vacillating, often irresponsible, and basically unfamiliar with the organization of an American college."

Davis's first mistake was to appoint Hallie dean without consulting his faculty. After she had agreed to take the job, he wrote to her wondering how to announce the appointment. Hallie, with a premonition of a disaster she had yet to experience, replied by telegram to his request for her appearance: "Plan indicates high voltage dramatic imagination. Stop. Suggest rara avis emerge from conch shell or more appropriately from bomb shell." Hallie must have sensed that the announcement of her appointment would cause a violent explosion.

It did. Many faculty members were annoyed that they had had no say in the appointment. Hallie's predecessor, Marjorie Hope Nicolson, was a highly esteemed scholar, and a scholar was what a majority of Smith's faculty wanted. Some opposed Davis's idea of creating a theatre department at Smith. Theatre still had the stigma, one faculty member wrote me, of being nonacademic. Dramatics on campus before Hallie arrived had been extracurricular. "The disaffected faction opposed Hallie from the start: they looked for something to criticize in her speeches and her proposals. And she was dramatic: she didn't fit the stereotype of a dean. The undermining all went on behind the scenes. And President Davis, who should have stood behind his appointment and cleared the air, simply dismissed the rumblings as unworthy of consideration."

At first, none of this affected Hallie. She was hardly aware of it. Newspaper accounts of her arrival at Smith were complimentary. "She is very sweet," wrote the reporter for the Boston *Post,* "a rare, completely unflabbergasted type of female who is at home in any company; who is brimming with anecdotes and good humor . . . She looks and acts like a good companion . . . Smith College will be delighted to meet the Davis children, Joanne and Jack, fourteen-year-old twins, and Helen, twelve. The Dean's house ought to be merry and jolly for the youngsters and college students who drop in to visit."

Juliette Harvey, who accompanied Hallie to Smith from Vassar as general assistant, remembered the first at-home Hallie gave for the Smith faculty. Hallie served tea, of course: that was expected. But she also filled a pitcher of rum for the men. She had quickly made friends with the nonconventional faculty members—Otto Kraushaar, of the philosophy department, Daniel Aaron and Al Fisher of the English department, Oliver Larkin and George Cohen of the art department. She had also got to know the women she considered unconventional. "There was no conversation about recipes," Juliette recalled. "You children," she added, "put toothpicks in all the cigarettes. Hallie always put cigarettes out for a party. I started to light one for her and she laughed. That's the children, she said. They like to do that sort of thing."

I have no memory of sticking toothpicks in cigarettes at Hallie's party, but I do not doubt the truth of the story. My brother, sister, and I, all adolescents by this time, had always enjoyed poking fun at Hallie's parties—in earlier years by writing outrageous notes which we placed in the purses and coat pockets of her guests. (They left their wraps upstairs, where we had easy access.) Hallie indulged us in this as she had indulged many of her son's pranks. As a mother, she was both strict and indulgent, strict regarding our educations, indulgent in other matters. We responded by rebelling in ways we could get away with, perhaps because, as my brother put it later, "As a child I felt the adults were always hiding things. Hallie was more interested in her students than she was in us."

Hallie did make an effort, after we moved to Northampton, to include us in her life. Jack remembers that she placed him at the head of the table while he was still a teenager. "It had to do with carving. Hallie said Dad was a wonderful carver, and she thought I would be too. She wanted to put me in the role of the man of the house, but I felt I was acting a part." Hallie's intentions were good, but she did not realize how much Jack was missing his father nor how difficult it was for him to see himself in those years in an adult role. She understood Jack as little as she understood Frederic, whose greatest need then was to create a life that was as different from his mother's as possible. When Fred graduated from Brown University in 1940, Hallie wrote Henry Allen Moe asking if he would grant him an interview. "I realize," she wrote, "that you are concerned chiefly with grants to graduate students and he is not applying for a grant. However he does have, I think, rather an unusual background and combination of interests, and I wondered whether you employed young men in any research or writing capacity?" When Fred, instead of following Hallie's lead, chose to pursue a career in public relations, Hallie was disappointed. Fred had artistic talents and interests, and she did not like to think of them being used in advertising.

Many of Hallie's allies at Smith were younger than she was. Daniel Aaron, who was just beginning his teaching career in American Studies, remembered Smith as "a fairly starchy place in those days. I recall Margaret Locke, who was from Boston, saying about certain newcomers to the campus—My dear, they're much too eager . . . At that time, in the forties, people tended to be embarrassed by Hallie's kind of effusiveness. If you wanted to be popular, the trick was to be indirect, ironic, cutting. Hallie was outgoing and open." He enjoyed the many parties Hallie gave for students and faculty members whom she found congenial. "There was lots of talk. They were pleasant, informal affairs." That was one difficulty. Those who objected to Hallie complained about her lack of reserve. Hallie had become accustomed to easygoing relations with students at Vassar. But Smith, Juliette Harvey told me, was different. "There was a sharp line drawn between faculty and students. At Vassar we would invite members of the faculty to dinner. It was never a formal affair. We had the idea, let's sit down and pick these wonderful brains that are available to us. But at Smith there was Faculty Night: students would invite their professors to dinner, but the faculty would end up talking to the faculty."

Gradually, Hallie found herself wedged into an uncomfortable position between supporters and detractors. Those wanting to oppose her noticed, for example, that her legs did not reach the floor when she sat on the stage at college assemblies. Others minimized her training, pointing out that she had never got a Ph.D., forgetting or perhaps ignoring her training under George Pierce Baker and her extensive experience as a director and administrator. But in the dean's office, where Hallie spent much of her time, she felt that she was among friends. "I think I can say with confidence," one of her associates there told me, "that everyone who worked with Hallie and really knew her thought very highly of her . . . She stood by those of us who were class deans, she knew how to delegate authority, she coped vigorously and intelligently with the myriad problems raised by a college in war time . . . She was loyal to President Davis and covered up for him when he made mistakes."

John Duke, who taught music at Smith, later wrote to me: "No doubt, in giving her the appointment of dean of the college and head of the theatre department, the college had hopes that she would repeat her remarkable achievement as executor of Federal Theatre. However, I think it was too much to ask of such a dedicated artist that she should be able to cope with the academic infighting of a college faculty. As I see it, although it is true that at the present time the college milieu offers the artist a welcome respite from the competitive life of the outside world, it is also true that there is a fundamental cleavage between the artist and the academic world . . . I do think the dual nature of Hallie's appointment at Smith was a mistake . . . For myself I can only say that I remember Hallie with much admiration and affection and believe that she made many significant contributions to the artistic and intellectual life of the college."

In addition to Juliette Harvey, Hallie brought Bob Schnitzer to act as production director and Emmet Lavery to be playwright in residence, from Vassar. She had asked the Rockefeller Foundation for money to help start the new department, and this grant paid their salaries. Hallie wanted it understood that there should be no attempt to make the Smith theatre another Vassar Experimental Theatre, yet she must have been feeling nostalgic. Juliette remembered Hallie taking her aside one day to show her the pale gray and pink wall colors of the vestibule in her new house. "Do you think anyone will notice?" Hallie whispered. Gray and pink were the Vassar colors.

Before Hallie's arrival, Sam Eliot of the English department had taught one or two theatre courses and directed plays students put on in the auditorium in the Students Building in their free time. Naturally he expected to help Hallie create the new theatre department President Davis wanted. But Hallie had no intention of going along with anyone else's methods. If she was to start something new, she was going to do it her way. Davis agreed that the new department was to be entirely hers, though he hoped she would make use of Eliot's talents. This Hallie was not willing to do, as she considered his methods old-fashioned. The stage was set for a head-on collision.

It took Eliot some time to realize Hallie's intentions. When he finally saw that his help was not wanted, he reacted as anyone in his position would, with resentment. Those he worked with took up his cause, adding fuel to the opposition Hallie's appointment had already created. Eventually, however, he decided to make a conciliatory gesture and invite Hallie to a party in her honor. She accepted. But as the time for the party approached, she felt unable to face it. On the evening of the party, she was arranging books with my brother, sister and me in the downstairs lounge. None of us knew that Hallie was expected at a party. We were busy and in high spirits. From time to time, Hallie stopped what she was doing to read us a passage from one of her favorite books. This may have been the evening she went to the piano, plunked out a few notes, and began singing "Meet me in St. Louis, Louis, meet me at the fair."

When the phone rang, Hallie said, "Don't answer. Let's just go on doing what we're doing." The phone rang again a few minutes later, and once again, Hallie instructed us not to answer. The next morning she was filled with remorse. "I did an awful thing last night," she said. "I forgot Sam Eliot's party." Hallie never did resolve her feud with Eliot. She apologized and then tried to forget the whole affair. Her opponents' attacks had hurt her more than most people realized. Eliot had not spearheaded the opposition (he had simply reacted to Hallie's rejection), but because he had talked against her and Hallie knew it, he became a prime target.

Hallie wrote to a friend that contrary to the rosy picture President Davis had painted of the dean's job, it had turned out to be "a pretty stiff one, without much time to write, let alone undertake any teaching outside or any expert investigations I was keen about." She was almost as naive as Davis in thinking that the job *would* free her. The one prediction Davis made about Hallie that came true was that she would "constantly stir up the administration and everything else on campus."

Her first way of stirring things up was to create a campuswide Christmas celebration, a project she planned with Emmet Lavery. "Smith Celebrates Christmas, 1942" was conceived of as a modern version of a medieval religious pageant. Each department organized a "Station"—a display, panel discussion, recital, or dramatic presentation. For three days, members of the audience moved from place to place to participate in a heralding of Christmas and the liberal arts. The plant house exhibited flowers and plants of the Bible; the three language houses sang carols in German, French, and Spanish, and one of them presented a Nativity play; the speech department held a reading of Dickens's *A Christmas Carol* in the library, where exhibits of Dickens's Christmas books were on display; teachers of dance staged a recital; the music department presented concerts; the newly established theatre department produced a modern version of a morality play, and finally, on the last night of the celebration, a candlelight service was held in the students' quadrangle. Throughout the period, wassail was served from large bowls in the dormitories.

Hallie sent out over a hundred letters to friends, acquaintances, and people she knew in the theatre, announcing the event and inviting them to come to Smith for the big show. She referred to the event as a "dramatization of a liberal arts education." Ever the publicist, she even wrote to the Office of War Information, pointing out that the celebration embraced "the broad conception of theatre on which we are working. You will see that in the attempt to dramatize a liberal arts college, we have included demonstrations by the science departments, panel discussions by the social sciences and many other events not normally thought to be dramatic . . . If we can be of use to the government at this time, please let us know."

Audience response was not as favorable as Hallie had hoped. Though some participants thought the occasion, "joyous, unique, unforgettable," others concluded that the conception had been more impressive than the results. Hallie herself realized that she had not brought it off. She had not had the personnel to build audiences; she had not prepared the college to see the event as a coordinated effort; the final service in the quadrangle should have been more spectacular. But it was a first try at something she thought important. "If it had done no more than to prove that the various departments of a college can work together, it would have been enough."

She had other ideas for getting people to work together. In the fall of 1942 she arranged a meeting with theatre people from nearby colleges and universities to decide what they could do to help the war effort. Subsequent meetings resulted in a close tie between Smith and Amherst College, with Amherst supplying actors for Smith productions and vice versa. The more immediate outcome was *Factory Follies,* a music and dance revue written and designed to be played in nearby factories during lunch hours. With Nancy Davis, later Mrs. Ronald Reagan, in the lead, it played at the Fisk Rubber Plant, the

Westinghouse Electric Company, and the Springfield Armory. A year later, with revisions, it toured farther afield.

When Emmet Lavery and Bob Schnitzer left Smith after Hallie's first year—Emmet to write scripts for war movies in Hollywood, Bob to join the Overseas Red Cross Service in China—Hallie brought in other men to replace them. Halsted Welles, who had directed the Federal Theatre production of *Murder in the Cathedral,* was the first. Welles stayed several years, produced a number of highly acclaimed shows, and stirred up the campus in other ways. Many of his students fell in love with him. Hallie enjoyed watching these infatuations from the sidelines. Welles later characterized her as "the world's romantic," and, when he wrote a novel about two people who fall in love at Smith, he put Hallie into one of his chapters.

Welles's portrait points up Hallie's sentimental side. His two main characters go to see the dean to discuss their predicament: they are in love, but there are obstacles. The dean, liking both of them and wanting to be helpful, invites them into her office. They sit down but do not know how to begin.

> Every Friday, the Dean said cheerfully, trying to ease the silence, I die a little. I look out the window and watch those lovely young girls going off for weekends at Dartmouth or New Haven, and I groan with envy . . . The Dean fiddled with her frizzy hair. She fancied she had looked like Colette as a young woman. Then she turned to look out the window, leaned back, felt the languor of a Friday afternoon in spring. My God, I had a wild youth. And now I'm as sexless as every other old person around here. She sighed. She was little, but she could give such big sighs they blew papers off her desk.

Later in the conversation, after her guests have told their story, the dean tells them that it is the anniversary of her husband's death.

> Whenever the Dean became fond of a person, she told that person about Phil . . . He was a transcendent lover, the Dean confided . . . We knew transcendent love.

She gets up abruptly to keep from crying. The young heroine goes to her, puts an arm around her, and kisses her.

> She loved the Dean. She loved the Dean for knowing transcendent love, although she wasn't sure what transcendent love was.

How much of this scene Welles invented, how much he recalled, I do not know, but he caught a side of Hallie that she usually tried to submerge. My sister and I got a glimpse of it when we inspected Hallie's girlhood scrapbooks. On one page she had pasted a poem by Edgar Guest that sentimentalized the joys of home and children. When we laughed, Hallie was hurt. I have since wondered whether Hallie would have been hurt or amused by Welles's portrait. In general, she was a good sport about being satirized. One year her Smith students put on a skit. I forget the general drift, but at the climactic moment, the student impersonating Hallie appeared at a doorway wearing a gigantic hat. "Come in!" those on the other side call out. "I can't," says Hallie. "My hat is too big. Won't someone please call the War Department?"

Dynamo, Hallie's book about her work at Vassar that she wrote the summer before she left Poughkeepsie, came out in the spring of 1943. John Gassner's review was laudatory. "When the history of contemporary American culture is ultimately written, the name of Hallie Flanagan will recur often in its pages. One of the most forward-looking personalities of our time, this remarkable woman made history when she headed Federal Theatre . . . What is less well known is that Miss Flanagan also made history for more than a decade before coming into the limelight . . . Her orbit was small—a college for women in Poughkeepsie, but the light radiated to the furthest reaches of the land . . . Her students discovered theatrical uses that are now routine procedures in film technique . . . Indeed the whole range of documentary drama that has proved so valuable in film making for social reform, wartime morale and military training was explored by the Vassar Experimental Theatre . . . Undoubtedly these claims can be moderated by reflection that all Miss Flanagan's experiments had been tried before in Europe and were occasionally realized even on Broadway. The significance of her work lies in the fact that it was carried out in the influential field of education."

After we moved to Northampton, Hallie enrolled Jack as a day student at Deerfield Academy, Helen at a private school run by Smith College, and me at the Northampton School for Girls. She urged us to do well and sometimes helped with our work, but felt helpless and impatient when it came to coping with our adolescent rebellions. "I was a real trial to Hallie during my four years at Deerfield," my brother recalled. "I didn't do well academically and during my freshman year I played hookey a lot. Hallie worried about me and about my grades, but she didn't know how to cope." At the end of Jack's freshman year Hallie solved the problem by sending him to Deerfield as a boarder.

Helen, who more often than not kept her rebellious feelings hidden, was often shocked by Hallie's high-handedness. She recalled a weekend Hallie took the two of us to New York. We stayed at the apartment of one of Hallie's friends, but had it to ourselves as the friend was in Europe. Shortly after we arrived, Hallie was invited to an evening party at the Copacabana. Helen and I declined, since we had not brought suitable clothes. But Hallie wanted to take us. She looked into the closet of her fashionable friend and found two elegant dresses. "Well-made clothes," she assured us, "will fit anyone. Try them on." Helen didn't want to but did, and we both wondered what would happen if we spilled something on them. "In that case," said Hallie matter-of-factly, "we'll simply send them to the cleaners." Hallie, it seemed to me then, had answers for everything. Since I needed to believe that her answers were the right ones, I went along with almost all her suggestions. The upshot was, we went to the party, had a good time, and returned the dresses unharmed to the closet. Hallie's friend, of course, was never informed.

On my sixteenth birthday Hallie arranged a treasure hunt to celebrate the occasion. She prepared for it as if it were a major theatrical production. A friend of hers, William Walsh, who was a frequent guest in our house after Bob left for China, helped her with the plans. Together they created clues, rules, and prizes. Each clue contained lines of poetry or some literary allusion. I cannot remember how my friends felt about coming upon messages like "Some girls cling, and some take the lead. I cling to a wall like a delicate reed. I rise toward the sun and grow green in its light. If you keep up the search, you can find me all right"; but I was impressed. The message hit home, making me wonder whether I was developing into a leader or a clinging vine. Hallie, it was clear, had little respect for clinging vines, yet in many ways she had fostered that role in me as she had fostered it in Frederic, making us both feel that she would collapse without us. For all her independence, Hallie nurtured a protective feeling in those she was closest to. She could make you feel she needed you terribly, and do it in such a charming way that you forgot for the moment how strong and how determined to pursue her own course of action she was. I had just begun to have these thoughts when I accompanied Hallie to Iowa City in the summer of 1945. I still remember that time as one of the happiest of my girlhood.

E. C. Mabie, who headed the University of Iowa Theatre, and who had been a friend of Hallie's for years, invited her to give a course and direct a play for a summer session. She chose to do Muriel Rukeyser's *Middle of the Air,* about Lindbergh's solo flight across the Atlantic, and that, of course, became the focus of her summer. But aside from work, Hallie was unusually relaxed that season. She was not overwhelmed by her job, so she had time to look about and enjoy where she was.

We made dinners together. It was the first time since I had known Hallie that she did not have someone else running the house. We cooked chicken and a lot of corn and shared the cleaning up. In the early evening, looking out from the dining room over the rolling Iowa fields, or walking the half mile to the university theatre, we talked about Rukeyser's play, the friendliness of Midwesterners, or how landscape shaped character. When we passed strangers in the street, Hallie speculated about their lives. She had thoughts about everyone.

Two of the people we met almost as soon as we arrived were Vance and Virginia Morton. Vance was a teacher and director in the theatre department; Virginia had been reared in Texas. They had a son, Jim, who was one year younger than I. Jim, who years later became dean of the Cathedral of St. John the Divine in New York City, was a buoyant, energetic young man. Hallie took to him immediately. He became fond of me, and I of him, and Hallie thought that was wonderful. Vance, Virginia, Jim, Hallie and I made many trips into the countryside in the Mortons' car. We picnicked and dined together. Jim acted in Hallie's production of Rukeyser's play. I enrolled in an acting class with his father and fancied myself an actress after giving a reading of Alexandra in Lillian Hellman's *The Little Foxes.* Our trips into the Iowa countryside gave me a feeling for the largeness of the country I had not known before. It was a summer of innocence—my first and last. For Hallie it was a summer of pure pleasure. The only drawback was that as soon as Hallie saw that Jim and I liked one another, she began hearing wedding bells. She liked Jim, she liked the idea of acquiring him as a son-in-law. For years afterward they plotted our marriage like two directors planning the perfect romantic production. Jim has since become a producer himself. At the Cathedral of St. John the Divine, where he presides over cultural events as well as religious services, he often reminds me of Hallie in his fresh, vigorous approach to the social and economic problems of New York's Upper West Side. If Hallie were alive, she would approve. Their common roots in Iowa and their shared enthusiasms made them close companions and conspirators. If they did not succeed in writing a script for me, that is not to be wondered at. Like all of Hallie's students I at last realized that I had to find my own way.

Middle of the Air, played on a huge construction which revolved in the presence of the audience, was well received. One reviewer thought the play was "at times vague and puzzling" but that perhaps that didn't matter. "One thinks and wonders . . . It is a magnificent production." Lynne Anderson, who worked on the light crew, recalled that Hallie used "music, lighting, suspense—anything and everything—to achieve magic moments, unforgettably theatrical moments . . . For all her experience of Russian, European, and New York theatre, her work seemed totally non-derivative, totally spontaneous."

Hallie taught over thirty students that summer. Three of them (Lynne Anderson, Betty Lord, and Evelyn Clinton) followed her to Smith to become her graduate students. Her lead actor and lighting technician, Denton Snyder, became her full-time technical director at Smith two months later. Hallie returned to New England feeling rested and refreshed.

Living with Illness

HALLIE had taken a four-year leave of absence from Vassar, thinking she might want to return. Still undecided, she made a trip to Poughkeepsie in late 1944 to sound out the situation. No one encouraged her to return. Mary Virginia Heinlein, who had replaced Hallie as head of the theatre, was firmly entrenched and backed by Dean Thompson. President MacCracken, who was thinking of retiring, told Hallie that Dean Thompson had become a strong influence on campus and he did not feel able to put up a fight. Hallie talked to others about job possibilities. John Gassner, who taught theatre at Yale, said many people he knew in New York thought she would be the right person to head the Yale School of Drama. When Hallie did not discourage him, he took his suggestion to the president of the university, but nothing came of it. She had meanwhile invited Denton Snyder to Smith.

Snyder arrived on campus a few days after Japan surrendered to the Allied forces. "I had wanted to work with her," he said later, "from the first time I heard her speak. I should have known better, because there was nothing short of perfect she did not expect you to do." He had a twinkle in his eye when he said it. In fact he remembered his first two years with Hallie as "just great," largely because of her attitude toward teaching. "We had three people—Hal

Welles, Hallie, and myself . . . There was one class and everybody was in it. The productions were the basis for the course."

With the war over, Hallie's job as dean became somewhat less demanding. With Snyder on hand to take charge of technical details, she felt able to launch an ambitious show. She chose Marlowe's *Dr. Faustus,* in part because the art department was focusing its courses on the Renaissance, but even more, as she wrote in the program, "because it seemed an appropriate time to do a play about power, the desire for power and the misuse of power." Ross Finney of the music department composed a score, Randolph Johnston of the art department designed masks for the Seven Deadly Sins, Edith Burnett, in charge of dance, arranged the choreography, the physics department constructed two sound boxes, and Snyder designed a revolving stage, which was cranked by hand in the basement. Welles played Faustus, Snyder Mephostopilis. A reporter for *Stage Pictorial* noted: "What the theatre misses in size and equipment is more than made up by the talent, originality, and enthusiasm of the students." The *New York Times* reviewer was likewise impressed. Local critics liked the show, and audiences were delighted.

Naturally Hallie was pleased. But she was worried: she had begun to feel a twitch in the corner of one eye. When she consulted her doctor, he warned her to slow down, that the symptom could be the beginning of a nervous disorder. "At first," she wrote to a friend, "I refused to believe it. I was sure I could overcome it—that it would wear off like battle fatigue." She was only fifty-seven and looking forward to many more productive years. Realizing that her double role at Smith had exhausted her, she decided to give up the deanship, even though it was going to mean the loss of three thousand dollars a year and renewed financial worries. In late 1946 she became distressed by a second symptom, a tremor in one of her fingers. One of her graduate students remembered that she "developed a habit of pressing her hand against her waist to stop the trembling. But then she would get involved in what she was saying and let go, and the finger would start to shake." Hallie tried to ignore what was happening. A group of war veterans who had just arrived at Smith to study theatre absorbed her attention.

One of them, Ted Kazanoff, described how this came about.

"Some of my friends and I were wandering the streets of the theatre district in New York. This was just after the war. And there was a shingle hanging outside a little office in the old Hudson Theatre, saying Veterans Counseling Service. Bob Schnitzer was inside and we explained to him what we were after: we wanted to form a theatre group, something similar to the old Group Theatre. We wanted to work in an industrial town but first we wanted to try out our wings. Bob listened, then he said, I think I have just the thing for you. Hallie Flanagan is up at Smith and she might be willing to accept you in her master's program. We commented that this was a girls' school, and he said yes, but they will accept male veterans. He called Hallie on the phone right then and there and her response was immediate: come up. So we did, about six of us. We got off the train and marched to Hallie's house on Paradise Road. And there we stood, on her front steps, in a kind of army formation. Hallie was delighted to see us and we spoke with her for two or three hours. All of us were tremendously impressed by her forthrightness and by what she had to say. She said she would make up a program that would suit our needs. She told us we would have plenty of rope to try out what we wanted to do. There would be graduate shows we could do on our own. There would be shows in which we could participate along with the undergraduates." All of this worked out, though it caused a storm on campus.

Bob Baron, another veteran who went to Smith, though not as part of Ted Kazanoff's group, remembered how the "college attempted to throw us out. They notified us that Sophia Smith's will did not provide for the education of men and that therefore we were there illegally. The Veterans Administration went to bat for us. They finally found a reference in the will which could be interpreted in our favor." Baron thought Smith disapproved "because we were a ferment. Our hours were not traditional. We rehearsed often until ten at night." He remembered an incident. "After ten the dormitory doors were locked. One night we worked till after ten and I walked a student halfway back to her dormitory. There was a warden then, and I got a call from her office after I reached home wanting to know if I had the student with me. It turned out the student had decided to visit a friend instead of returning to her dormitory." Another student has mentioned hearing that one of the veterans "brought his mistress with him and installed her in Northampton. You can imagine how that went over in those days!"

Hallie, who believed that people's private lives were their own business, and that the real issue was what her students were learning, managed to handle the situation with tact. She continued to focus her energies on giving her students professional training. Ted Kazanoff, for one, felt he learned that from her. "When we went to Amherst with *Home of the Brave* and had to wait for a long time while some technical things were being taken care of, a few of us went to Hallie and said, My God, Hallie, how long do we have to wait before we rehearse? In her most charming but forceful way, she said: 'It's about time you people learn that if you don't take care of the technical needs of a show, then all the good acting will go for naught. It's my responsibility to take care of that end. I trust you as actors. You must trust me as directing producer.' I was thoroughly chastened."

Bob Baron, perhaps the male student who became closest to Hallie, learned something even more basic from her. "I'd just gone through the war," he said. "I had a degree in agriculture but I hated agriculture, I wanted to get into the theatre . . . But at Smith I was cowed by the other graduates. They had all gone to city colleges, they knew all about the Stanislavsky Method. I didn't understand it and felt out of place. So I went to Hallie and said, 'You made a mistake in accepting me, I can hardly spell Shakespeare, I must withdraw from the program.' Hallie then said to me something that has stayed with me all my life: 'We are a better department because you are here.' Nobody in my life had said such a thing. When I told her later I was grateful, she said she didn't want to hear that word, that my desire to accomplish something was her reward. That was a very fundamental thing to learn. She made me feel I counted."

Bob met the challenge. Looking around, he was shocked to discover that the Smith theatre department had no mechanized equipment and that its budget for shows was minimal. "I told Hallie we should charge for tickets, and she said, all right, you figure out how to do it." He did. He set up a subscription program that brought money into the theatre and received a fellowship to manage the program.

*   *   *

Despite the pleasure she felt in setting up a new program for veterans, Hallie was lonely and increasingly worried about her health. In the fall of 1946 Jack and I had left home to go to college. Helen remained behind, but she was in full-fledged adolescent rebellion. Hallie had hoped I would go to Smith, but Nannie Dwelle's money made it possible for me to choose from a number of colleges. I chose Vassar. If I had known how worried Hallie was about her health, I might have chosen differently. But Hallie did not press me: she was as careful about nurturing her stepchildren's freedom of choice as she had been about nurturing her students'.

After my first visit home from Vassar, and after Jack's from Brown University, Hallie drew up a will to which she attached a long letter. Frederic and his wife and two children, who had been with us for the Christmas holidays, had just left. So had Helen—for a holiday in Mexico with Nannie Dwelle. Jack had gone back to Brown, I had returned to Vassar. Our house on Paradise Road, and even the nearby campus, must have felt very large and empty to Hallie that evening. Small towns, when the lights are out, are desolate places. So are houses that have been filled with noise and laughter and are then suddenly emptied out. And Hallie, who was so often surrounded by people who loved her, felt particularly abandoned when left alone. "I can think of no better time than this, just after a marvelous Christmas in which we were all together," Hallie wrote in a letter that none of the family saw until after her death, "to sit down and plan what all of you should do in the event of my death." She made a list of her possessions, assigning each to one of her children. "You still seem very close to me," she wrote, "and all this planning will perhaps seem absurd years later when the objects described are broken up or moved or gone. But all the things I'm writing about are full of remembrance ... Objects have a wonderful way of bringing back beautiful times, and I have enjoyed imagining how each of you will use things which we have enjoyed together." Hallie was also remembering, as she looked about her study at souvenirs she had bought in Greece and Russia, at plays that had come out of Federal Theatre, at books she had received from friends in foreign countries, how "happy she had been in theatres all over the world."

Thinking too that when it's all over, what I really leave you,
I hope, is a sense of how wonderful life is, how courageous
and beautiful people can be, how high is the hunt for
justice, love, beauty.

The year just past had been a special one for Hallie despite the
start of her illness. Frederic, who had distressed Hallie by enlisting in
the Marine Corps, had returned from the war unharmed. He had
found a steady job in advertising and fathered two children. Hallie
had got over the shock of not being invited to his wedding and grown
fond of his wife, Betty. Fred and Betty had brought their two
children, Hallie Ann and Frederic, for frequent visits to Northampton, and Hallie had discovered the pleasures of being a grandmother.
Years later her granddaughter recalled that "Hallie was not maternal,
but she made up wonderful stories. I remember watching a violent
storm from one of her windows. She put two chairs together to make
me a bed and then invented a story with the storm as background."

When she was alone, Hallie turned to writing. In the summer of
1947 she began work on a Living Newspaper about the atomic age.
She called it $E = mc^2$. Scientists had recently called for a national
campaign to educate the public on atomic energy. "If told a few
facts," Albert Einstein said, "all men can understand that this bomb
and the danger of war is a very real thing. It directly concerns every
person in the civilized world. We cannot leave it to generals,
senators, and diplomats."

While running Federal Theatre, Hallie had been impressed by a
remark made to her by a man in the United States Treasury
Department, "It's my job to know how people's money is spent . . .
It's spent for war. Eighty-five cents out of every dollar of the
taxpayer's money goes for wars, past, present and future. So don't let
anybody fool you about these things. Five hundred dollars for ten
months for an artist's work? Why, it would cost more than that to
blow him to pieces in the trenches."

Sylvia Gassel, a graduate student, helped Hallie do the research
and wrote a couple of early scenes. But when Hallie rewrote them
and made it clear that she wanted a research assistant, not a
co-author, Gassel left in a huff. Hallie then turned to Day Tuttle, a

former director at the Washington Civic Theatre, whom she had just appointed an associate professor in the department. Tuttle recalled working with Hallie for hours each day during the fall of 1947. "She would read the dialogue to me. I would pace the floor and speak it back to her. Certain parts of it were entirely my own."

The script has a cast of over seventy-five characters. Of these, some (President Roosevelt, senators, secretaries of war, members of the Atomic Energy Commission, and others) speak lines that are historical, but the majority of characters (Atom, the Muse of History, the Stage Manager, newsboys, soldiers, businessmen, politicians, and civilians) are fictional, invented to point up the differing attitudes that people held in 1947 toward atomic energy. Atom, a central figure played by Sylvia Short, is introduced as an uncontrolled, Jekyll-and-Hyde character who is "too hot to handle." She shows her different sides throughout the play. She can be meek and mild when harnessed for peacetime purposes. She can be violent when used in wartime. She is volatile; she says it is up to the public to decide what to do about her. Early scenes portray the horror, relief, or indifference various people felt when they read that an atomic bomb had been dropped over Hiroshima. Following scenes go back in time. President Roosevelt orders work to proceed on the atomic bomb; Secretary of War Henry Stimson urges that the bomb be dropped on Japan, Mr. Bard, undersecretary of the navy, protests that Japan be given a preliminary warning because "the United States is a great humanitarian nation." Mr. Bard's advice is not heeded. Roosevelt dies and Truman orders the bombing of Hiroshima and Nagasaki. The audience sees this on film.

Act two focuses on the struggle for control of atomic energy. The audience sees newsreels covering the period when the United Nations proposed an international system of control and Russia insisted that any international agency should follow, not precede, the destruction of all atomic bombs. Senators on Capitol Hill—those who wanted the War Department given total control over atomic energy—imply that David Lilienthal, the head of the civilian-dominated Atomic Energy Commission, has Communist leanings. Other fictional characters—businessmen, politicians, people from the military—fight behind the scenes for the power to direct what happens. Several scenes dramatize the vision some people had at the time of a future

freed from drudgery through the peacetime use of atomic energy:
instantaneous laundry service, rapid trips to Mars, enormously
increased agricultural production. "The problem of the future," says
one of the characters, "will be to use a magnificent leisure—that is,
if we permit the race to continue." The audience is left with the
question: How can we stop a future war in which everyone will be
annihilated? ("Everybody wants peace," says Atom, "and everybody
is getting ready for war.") A last scene, in the spirit of *Catch-22* and
other postwar novels, depicts members of the military punching
buttons that precipitate the end of the world—one of them has
misinterpreted an earthquake for an atomic explosion. The Stage
Manager concludes:

> Ladies and gentlemen—the scene you just saw is not from
> the pen of a poet, a dramatist or a dreamer. It is by a
> physicist, Dr. Louis Ridenour. He is allowing us to use it
> because he wants as many people as possible to know that
> it could happen that way—that if we're not careful, it *will*
> happen that way . . .
>
> The shadow is still on the wall at Hiroshima—mute
> symbol of man's terrible power to destroy himself. The only
> way to obliterate that shadow is to throw across the sky a
> tremendous affirmation of man's will to save himself from
> destruction.—Whether we can do it and do it in time, rests
> not alone with the scientists, but with the psychologist, the
> economist, the philosopher, the artist—with you and with
> me. For it is still, in this moment of time, December 13,
> 1947—by some desperate miracle, *our world*.

The chief technical problem in producing $E = mc^2$ was the
staging of thirty-five scenes on a small stage. The "sheer topography"
of Hallie's direction, one assistant recalled, was "staggering." For
scene changes that had to be in split seconds, Denton constructed
two revolving platforms, which, as in *Dr. Faustus*, were operated by
students stationed in the basement. For actors, Hallie used students,
graduate students, and faculty members from Smith and Amherst.

Today, when the issues surrounding atomic energy have become
more complex than they were in 1947, and when television docu-
mentaries have proved more effective than the stage in presenting

current issues, $E = mc^2$ seems dated. Most of all, Hallie's one-dimensional characters seem unacceptable. There are the good guys and the bad guys: businessmen, politicians, and military personnel are on the whole the same shallow characters one meets in the muckraking novels of the twenties and thirties. This limits the play's appeal. But for Hallie, who was less concerned with creating masterpieces than in stirring audiences to confront the world around them, her production was a success; not merely at Smith but also in New York, where the play was produced a year and a half later by the American National Theatre and Academy.

The tremor in Hallie's hand grew worse during the next six months. Her doctor told her she was suffering from an early symptom of Parkinson's disease, a disease of the nervous system for which there is no known cure. She went to other doctors, who confirmed the diagnosis, but, not yet ready to accept what she heard and fearing that she might be on the verge of a nervous breakdown, Hallie spent two weeks in the summer of 1948 at the Austin Riggs Psychiatric Center in Stockbridge, Massachusetts. There her doctors helped her to face what was to come. She wrote then:

> When I came to Stockbridge I had hoped that some secret cause for my trouble would be found, some psychological or mental twist which could be untwisted . . . This seems not to be true. I must accept the fact of age, probably accelerated age, as a physical fact, must see its implications and prepare for them. This is hard because I feel so well in every other way. The sun is as amazing, the cobwebs on the wet grass as delicate, the morning glories on the summer house as blue. The letters from my children and my friends mean more, not less.

Her psychiatrist assigned her a task: every morning after break-fast, she was to write a chapter of her life. In the act of writing and reinventing her past, she regained courage. She recalled her childhood as close to idyllic, her education as inspiring, her marriages (despite the tragedies she endured) as fulfilling, her entire life as a challenge to do something worthwhile. But she decided that going to Smith had been a mistake.

My roots had gone down deep at Vassar. I loved the
college, the theatre, my friends . . . I was not the right
person for Smith and it was not the place for me. It is
literally true that only in our house and in the theatre have
I ever felt at home there . . . It is the only place where I have
felt loneliness and estrangement . . . Trying to be Dean and
at the same time to start a theatre, trying to master a
curriculum and a faculty, understand and help, trying to
help a president who was new to the college and the
country, setting up a summer session during the war years,
and working right through the summers . . . None of these
things would have mattered had I not felt, from the first,
undercurrents of distrust and misunderstanding . . . I do not
think this was personal dislike. It was part of the war years.
It was part of a doubt on the part of the faculty as to
President Davis, it was part of Smith's dislike of Vassar. It
was partially a justified feeling that I was a theatre person,
not an academic person.

With her doctors' help, Hallie struggled to confront the future.
"Death coming soon and without preliminary helplessness" did not
worry her, but the possibility that her disease might continue for a
long time while she grew "old, helpless and a burden" did. She
thought next about losing her home. The house on Paradise Road
belonged to the college; she would have to leave it if she gave up her
job. "How can I do it? Into that house I poured all my love for the
children . . . There is not an inch of that house and garden, not a
color, not a vista, that I did not plan. It seems like part of my body."
She had hoped her three stepchildren would be married there, "that
they would come back to bring their children," that in her retirement
there would be "long, peaceful times with friends, with children,
with books and flowers." She then tried to face giving up her work
in the theatre, wondering how she would manage without students
around her. "Yet, in another way, I feel it is time." Because of the
tremor, directing and teaching had become increasingly difficult. She
still had the energy to choose plays, read manuscripts, hold conferences with students. If Smith would allow her to stay on in semi-
retirement, all might still be possible. But this was a dream Hallie

scarcely dared hope would come true. She made up her mind to stay on at Smith as long as she could.

There was a last thing she was going to have to get used to: "the changed me. The tremor makes me shaky, stiff and slow, the exact opposite of myself. I must find a new rhythm of movement, speech and life."

Few of the thoughts Hallie wrote for herself and her doctors reached her friends or family. Even while putting them on paper, Hallie was writing her graduate student Bob Baron that her day consisted of breakfast on a tray "as I recline on a chaise longue with a soft rose silk quilt over my best negligee"; then a stroll through the orchard; then lunch with fascinating people; then a rest ("from what?") followed by an hour with her analyst ("He is nice. We laugh a lot"). Her dressing-table lights, she admitted, "make anyone look seductive—but to what end? I ask myself. Nobody answers. I turn lights off in a hurry. Not very fond of me as yet."

During her sabbatical from Smith in the spring of 1949, Hallie spent much of her time writing a play about Margaret Fuller, the nineteenth-century child prodigy from Massachusetts who under her father's tutelage knew Latin by the age of six and the works of Shakespeare, Cervantes, and Molière before she reached her teens. A friend of such men as Ralph Waldo Emerson, Horace Greeley, and Thomas Carlyle, a literary critic for *The Dial* and the New York *Tribune*, and later America's first woman correspondent in Europe, Margaret Fuller might have interested Hallie less had she remained content with her literary life. But Fuller came to feel that erudition without humanitarian concern—a life devoted to reason and intellect when not tempered by action and emotion—was hollow. Biographers have portrayed Margaret Fuller as impulsive, flamboyant, erudite, and sexually frustrated, a searcher for truth and for ways to put truth into action. It was this mixture of qualities that attracted Hallie. She came to see Fuller as a woman in some ways like herself.

There are many parallels between the two lives. Fuller, like Hallie, had been reared by her father to be a special person. In an early scene in the play, which is based on fact but partly invented, Margaret's father tells his daughter that she is all he has hoped for. "Life has somehow passed me by." He wants his daughter to take hold of her life and make something of it. "You have one of the minds of the century," he tells her. "Use it." Hallie, imagining their conversation dramatically, has Fuller say that she wants her freedom but that her father will be a part of her life forever, whatever she does. This was sheer invention on Hallie's part, more related to her own life than to Fuller's; indeed, Fuller later blamed her father's preoccupation with books for her ill health.

Hallie took the playwright's prerogative of shaping her heroine's life to fit her own conception. In a last scene she has her heroine say she has thought too much about herself, seen herself too often as "the center of the universe . . . We learn so slowly—and only, it seems to me, through love and pain. We learn more from a single hour with our lovers or our children than in all the books ever written. It would be simpler if we could put life up in little compartments—this for work, this for study, this for love . . . but instead all these things are mixed together. We must learn how to study while we are suffering, how to love while we are working."

During her last three years at Smith, Hallie taught playwriting, supervised productions directed by her associates, attended occasional classes, and conferred with students, but she did not direct. The friendships she developed with her graduate students and associates helped her to overcome intermittent feelings of loneliness and despair.

Doris Abramson, who had got her B.A. from the University of Massachusetts, recalled going to see Hallie about getting a graduate fellowship. "I wanted to work with her and had a portfolio of the work I had done in theatre," Doris recalled. "I put on a nice suit and spectator pumps and a hat to match, and rang Hallie's doorbell." Hallie surprised her. Doris had expected to meet a large, talkative woman, "but Hallie was small, and she was very good at listening. After a while I said, I'd like to work with you. Hallie said she'd like to work with me, but could I type? I couldn't but I said, Oh yes! There were six weeks before the fall season began. I went to business college and learned."

Doris became Hallie's production secretary in the fall of 1949. Hallie had another secretary, Norma Leas, who adored her and protected her from many administrative frustrations but who was sometimes shocked by Hallie's mail. Doris handled matters that Hallie wanted to keep from Norma. "One day," Doris recalled, "a play arrived from Pablo Picasso, *Desire Caught by the Tail*. Picasso wanted to know what Hallie thought of it." Hallie, though an admirer of Picasso's art, had to reply that she thought the play sounded like an old man trying to work himself up. "That was the gist of it. People in the play were pissing to put out the footlights, they were farting. Whatever they were doing, it hadn't very much to do with anything. Hallie told him what she thought."

Doris had meantime been writing a thesis about Ibsen. "I think it meant something special to Hallie. I can't remember which one of us initiated the theme of Ibsen's aging.—Have I sacrificed my family to my career? That was what Ibsen was asking in his last plays.— What do we sacrifice in order to create? Hallie would say, *Yes, I know* . . . I would go over to her house and we would sit and talk. I remember an occasion when she wasn't feeling well. She said, I'm going to lie down on my bed (she had twin beds in her bedroom); why don't you just lie down on the other bed?—Can you imagine? I've been teaching now for twenty-seven years, and I can't imagine anything like this with one of my students.—But it was all right. She knew it was all right, and I knew it was all right. The birches were budding just outside the window, it was very late in the afternoon. We lay there and talked about Ibsen."

Hallie's relations with other graduate students she was fond of were equally unconventional. When she realized that Bob Baron did not know what he wanted to do with his life, she suggested they write a play together. Bob did most of the writing; Hallie made suggestions and criticized. "Four characters came into view," Bob recalled, "a married couple and two others, a man and a woman. We put them in the Alps and called the play *Four in the Snow*." Hallie and Bob wrote an early scene, but could not decide what should happen next. For years afterward they kept up a correspondence about the plot, and Bob sent Hallie scenes he had written. "How mean of you," Hallie wrote Bob on one occasion, "to put glasses on Eve and to straighten out her hair which used to be red but which now, I'm sure, is mousey brown. A virgin of thirty wanting romance and pretending to be an artist is so unappetizing . . . And Michael? He seems to be in a highchair pounding with his spoon and yammering, I want

Mommy. No, sir, take back your idea." They discontinued the collaboration soon afterward. It had given them a good deal of fun, served its purpose, and, surprisingly perhaps, did not end their friendship.

Another graduate student who became a close friend during Hallie's last years at Smith was Lynne Anderson, who first met Hallie at the University of Iowa. Four years after the Iowa summer session Lynne turned up at Smith to pursue her study of theatre. During her two-year stay she rented a room in our house. (After my brother, sister, and I left home, Hallie took in roomers; she needed the money.) "Hallie was often in her study," Lynne recalled, "when I got home from rehearsals. If the door was open, it meant she'd like a short chat . . . I realize now that she was lonely. She often asked me to eat with her, and we always had Friday night suppers together, which I would bring from the local fish market." While Lynne fetched dinner Hallie set out place mats and candles. The setting, as always, mattered more to her than what she ate. It stimulated talk, and talk revived her spirits. Lynne recalled these occasions as special. "Then Hallie insisted on helping with the washing up—she washing, I drying." She described Hallie's dish-washing methods: something was always on her mind. As she talked, she would hold a plate under running water and run a dishrag lightly across it. "Her inattention to that particular task was extraordinary!" When she could do so without seeming impertinent, Lynne rewashed the dishes.

Hallie felt responsible for Lynne and the other students to whom she rented rooms. She tried to make sure that there would be food for their breakfasts but sometimes forgot. One of her night notes to Lynne read, "Terribly sorry but I fear you must eat bananas and crackers with your coffee tomorrow. I forgot to order bread and juice. Please forgive."

"Hallie had a characteristic gesture," Lynne added, "of raising her small right hand almost as if she was beginning a benediction. Such a gesture would accompany a request for the most impossible feat, usually a scenic or lighting effect. Those around her would attempt anything rather than disappoint her." Before Lynne left Smith, Hallie gave her a photograph to which she added a quotation from *Middle of the Air*: "Use yourself. Be. Fly." Lynne thought "that was what Hallie wanted for all young people."

Hallie's Vassar students remembered her for her magnetic leadership, her total devotion to what she was doing, her capacity for friendship. At Smith where Hallie was often less able to provide the individual attention she had given undergraduates earlier, she was remembered for other qualities—courage and endurance. Ruth Wolff, who was in Hallie's last playwriting class, elaborated. "The first time we met in her house I remember being surprised that she was so small and frail . . . She was trembling. Later I learned she had Parkinson's disease. She didn't tell us that then. What she did say was 'Don't let this bother you. It doesn't bother me.' I have never forgotten that statement. It put us all where she was, on a plane beyond human frailty."

By late 1950 Hallie was taking long rests between classes. She was meeting with her colleagues—Snyder, Tuttle, and a newcomer to the department, George Dowell—individually, and more and more leaning on their support. Tuttle thought many of Hallie's actions at this time were divisive. "She would take me aside, or she would take George or Denton aside. She would say the same thing to each one of us: You are the Rock of Gibraltar in the department. If it weren't for you, I don't know what I'd do." Looking back on this period, Snyder concluded that Hallie "needed moral support, and that was how she got it."

Sometimes she forgot to eat. George Dowell, who roomed in our house for a couple of years, remembers going to the china closet to get a dish or glass and discovering morsels of food Hallie had started to eat and then put away on the top shelf. There was usually someone in the house to cook Hallie's main meal. For years it was a housekeeper, later Hallie's cousin Julia Kuhl, who had come to Northampton to study at the School for the Deaf. But Hallie often missed breakfasts and lunches. She would eat a graham cracker and drink a glass of milk for lunch if she remembered. If people were around, she would drink orange juice and eat toast for breakfast. Her mind was on other matters—her work, her illness, her growing awareness that she would soon have to retire and leave the Northampton house. This was what she dreaded.

Her last big contribution to Smith was the show she produced for the seventy-fifth anniversary of the college in 1950. *Heritage,* which was written by students in Hallie's playwriting class, evolved from a seminar Hallie organized to give her students an overall view of American life from 1800 to 1875. Professors who were authorities on the art, literature, music, and religious movements of the period gave lectures. Students studied Sophia Smith's journals, the town records of her native Hatfield, and the reminiscences of old residents. They wrote scenes which Hallie and George Dowell edited. The show that resulted, using many techniques of the Living Newspaper, was directed by Dowell under Hallie's supervision. "I submerged my own point of view," Dowell said of his directing at Smith, "so Hallie's vision would come through. She was extremely sensitive, very delicate with actors in conveying her ideas . . . But her voice would get weak. She'd lose it sometimes. My assignment was difficult . . . I wanted the students to have the experience of working with her as a director."

That summer Hallie and I sailed on the Polish ship *Batory* for a theatre session at Dartington Hall in England, where Hallie had been invited to spend six weeks as artist in residence. Although her movements had been slowed by her illness, her mind was as quick and lively as ever. "We were wishing that you were with us," Hallie wrote to Bob Baron, "to interpret many things that are puzzling. Outwardly the *Batory* is much like any other ship—the usual deck tennis, dancing and shuffleboard. But underneath we feel tension. The U.S.S.R. publications are numerous and explicit in their praise of the rising standard of living in Russia. It seems that everyone is having a dandy time working on collective farms and building dams! Not only that, but Russia wants peace and the U.S. alone is inciting war. It is rather illuminating to have the ship's news slanted in the opposite direction from our own."

Dartington enchanted Hallie every bit as much as it had when she had gone there at Leonard Elmhirst's invitation in 1934. The five-hundred-year-old manor hall overlooking a courtyard, the gardens filled with gigantic purple thistles, yellow dahlias, heliotrope, and scarlet carnations, and, beyond, the rolling Devonshire countryside seemed to Hallie a perfect blending of past and present. She imagined how the gardens must have served as background for the "jousts and spectacles in a period more florid," then decided there was "no nostalgia for the past at Dartington and no attempt to live in the Hall as if it were 1380. We did not go to bed with candles, bait bears, or engage in jousting. Students wore tweeds, slacks, or shorts instead of medieval robes."

The Dartington art director, Peter Cox, had become convinced during a tour of American college and university theatres in 1947 that England could learn from what America was doing. Not quite sure that he liked Hallie after first meeting her in Northampton, he nevertheless decided that the theatre she was running was more exciting than educational theatres he found elsewhere. "There is this quite extraordinary feeling of creation going on," he wrote Dorothy and Leonard Elmhirst. "It's difficult to say why Hallie is exciting . . . She's just one of those people whom you could throw up a well-paid job to go and work for." The Elmhirsts asked Hallie to recommend a director and teacher of acting for the summer session. Hallie chose Arch Lauterer, who taught theatre at Mills College in Oakland, California, and Nadine Miles, who taught acting at Western Reserve University in Cleveland. They were joined by the Dartington staff, which included Rudolf von Laban, an internationally known choreographer, and Imogen Holst, a composer and a daughter of Gustav Holst.

Freed of the responsibility of teaching and administering, Hallie saved her strength for conferences with the forty-five young people who had come from all over England to take part in the summer session. Some came from the Nottingham People's Theatre, others from the Watergate Theatre, the Old Vic, and the Royal Academy of Dramatic Arts, in London, and from community theatres in Bristol, Lancashire, and Glasgow. A few came from further away—from Capetown, Rio de Janeiro, Bombay, and Uppsala. Most had already embarked on professional careers as producers, directors, actors, dancers, and writers. All talked with Hallie about their work and their experiences in wartime, making her realize how little she had understood the hardships the English and others had endured. It had been one thing to hear about the bombings on the radio, quite another to hear from people who had had their homes destroyed and their families uprooted.

During the hours reserved for recreation, Hallie and I would walk down the country lane leading from the high hill on which the manor hall stood toward the nearby village. We never got as far as the village, for Hallie's strength would give out and we stopped often, sometimes just to gaze at the cows grazing beyond the stone walls lining the lane. As we walked, we talked—about the country-side, the students, the war, the agricultural experiments Leonard Elmhirst was conducting, or about Peter Cox, who had fallen in love with my sister on his visit to Northampton. Nothing escaped Hallie's notice; everything she saw and heard aroused her curiosity and made her eager to share her observations. But she tired quickly and walked slowly, always holding on to my arm for support. Often, in the middle of a thought, she would suddenly say, "Let's turn back. I need to rest now. And you should be off swimming with your friends." I needed no persuasion. Having just finished college, I was eager to make my own explorations. Hallie knew that, and though she needed me in the years following her illness more than ever before, she never tried to persuade me to do anything different.

After the summer session, I stayed in England for several months. A year later I left Northampton to work at the Brattle Theatre in Cambridge, knowing that Hallie would have preferred it if I had remained at home. But she had taught me by her example to make something of my life, and she backed me in everything.

She remained at Smith two more years, running the department, suggesting plays, overseeing the work of her colleagues. During that time my brother, sister, and I persuaded Nannie Dwelle to let Hallie share the small house Nannie owned in Poughkeepsie across from the Vassar College campus. Hallie had friends in the community, so it was a good place for her to retire; and over the years she and Nannie Dwelle had (at least on the surface) become reconciled. But the move away from Northampton was difficult. Moving this time did not mean, as it had in the past, a new challenge, a new family to care for, a new work to be accomplished. It meant an ending.

I came home to help Hallie with the moving. So did Helen, but I was the only person present on the day the movers came to take everything away and put it in storage. Day Tuttle's wife, Lauralee, who had helped Hallie organize many theatre parties, turned up at the last minute to say good-bye. "The rugs were all rolled up," she recalled. "Packing cases were everywhere. There was a great feeling of The End. Hallie was lying on a cot and shaking. We talked a little, and then she said, 'My whole life has been a failure. Nothing that I cared about has turned out as I hoped it would.' " Lauralee thought about all the people she had known who had accomplished a great deal and led useful lives. She had imagined them feeling a final moment of satisfaction. "What Hallie said showed me, maybe for the first time, that the hopes we all have aren't really satisfied. The way Day and I had seen Hallie was not the way she saw herself . . . It was a very sad moment."

After the movers left, I settled Hallie in the 1938 Chevrolet my grandmother had given me and we began the three-hour trip to Poughkeepsie. Hallie at first said very little. She was as downhearted as I had ever seen her. It was a late afternoon in June and the light lingered long over the blue green Berkshire hills. Soon Hallie began to recall the trips we had taken each spring to buy scarlet geranium and blue ageratum for the garden. "We have had good times together," she said, "and we will have more. You will marry and have children and bring them to Poughkeepsie. Jack and Helen will marry and bring their children also. I still have my sight, I can still write. There is much I can do and much to live for." She patted my arm. I felt it was I who should be patting hers.

Hallie enjoyed her years of retirement in Nannie Dwelle's house more than she thought she would. After what Hallie described to a friend as a "year of loss and estrangement," of adjusting to her new surroundings and new way of life, Nannie died, leaving Hallie the use of the house for life. Hallie's cousin Julia, who had lived with her in Northampton during the two previous years, stayed on for five more. Friends came from all over to visit. People she had known stopped by for afternoon chats. She made frequent visits to Frederic and his wife, who were living in White Plains. She read, saw plays, went to concerts, and kept up a large correspondence. One of her greatest pleasures, great because it surprised her, was getting to know and love my husband. When Eric Bentley and I started living together in New York during Hallie's last year at Smith, Hallie was upset. First love affairs, she thought, should be saved for marriage. During one dreadful afternoon, after Eric and I had come for a visit, Hallie called him into her study to ask him what his "intentions" were. A few months later, when I told her that Eric and I planned to marry, she said he was not the sort of young man who would empty the garbage, that Englishmen never did. But after our marriage had taken place, Hallie read everything Eric wrote, and on our frequent visits, she made a point of getting to know him. They became fond of one another, and on the occasion of our first wedding anniversary, Hallie wrote him a poem:

> Our Eric should be sung in prose, not verse—
> His qualities are prose. Witness his terse
> Critique on all that's shallow, flat or stale.
> Witness his wit, on which he can impale
> Pretense, snap judgment, sentimental trash,
> The ill-digested fact, the statement rash.
> Witness his search relentless for the truth.
> (This is of course the secret of his youth.)
> He makes the proper study of mankind
> Within the generous framework of his mind.
> Such qualities are prose—
> Or so I think, because I am no poet,
> Only admirer—and proud to have him know it.

For Hallie, as for us, there were many happy moments in the fifties, despite the increasingly debilitating symptoms of her illness. When Eric and I went to Cape Cod in the summers, Hallie stayed in our New York apartment. During the one summer when we did not go away, we rented a suite for her in a nearby hotel. I remember the pleasure she and Julia took in preparing some simple dinners for us. Hallie was by this time saving all her energies for the moments she regarded as special—spending time with and writing to the people she loved.

The vigor of her mind remained unimpaired. When Frances Youtz wrote her in 1956, "Age brings wisdom," Hallie shot back, "Nonsense. I know less and less all the time. Your philosophy comes from your years in China. Let's go there." When Lynne Anderson wrote asking for advice about her teaching career, Hallie replied, "If you do not feel that teaching is creative and imaginative, then perhaps you should think of another vocation." In a second letter she commented, "I had such an unparalleled chance to see that theatre could be and might be a dynamic center of life that it seems unfair to ask anyone else to share the passion and the pain of such theatre, only to turn them loose in New York, Cleveland or any place else where the theatre is obviously no such thing."

Her letters to me were almost always cheerful. "You are a great pet," she wrote on one occasion, "and I am so glad we are on the same planet at the same time. It is still a good planet in spite of the coming elections—Adlai behaving stupidly and Eisenhower being made to play golf and smile all the time." After one of my letters, in which I had addressed her as Mums, she replied, "Of course I love to be called Mums, Tums, Mumsy or Tumsy, Nip and Tuck, Odd or Even . . . My name has always been bandied about. I once had a beau (whose letters you have no doubt read as you 'straightened out' my files) who called me Halliest, another who called me, most inappropriately as it turned out, My Happiness. And don't forget that I once had a gold mine named after me—the Hallie Mine; never struck pay dirt, however."

Hallie often wrote to me about Philip during her years of retirement. "Six marvelous years of making a home together, making a garden, making music, laughing together . . . I knew a little about sons and began then to know how incomplete my life had been without daughters." She was often troubled by the thought that she had put her career before her family. "I send you the review of *The Art of Loving* by Erich Fromm," she wrote me once. "I believe so deeply in his thesis though I have not attained it . . . One thing I know is that loving may start with being spontaneous, but it does not grow, or even stay the same unless you work at it . . . Now I'm going out to walk and reaffirm as I stumble along my love for my sons and daughters."

When she felt discouraged about seeing her children less often than she wished, she wrote to others, not to me. She told Bob Baron she was learning "that you cannot hold on to the past. You cannot hold on to light, or liberty, or love. You can only go forward, and in darkness not be afraid, and then possibly you may again find freedom, light, and even, incredibly as it may seem, love . . . If I have any insight, strength or love which my children need, it is theirs."

When young women wrote to Hallie seeking advice—Should they marry if they wanted careers? Should they have children?—Hallie sidestepped the issue. She herself, she said, had not chosen one alternative over the other; she had simply been faced with the need to make a living. But she did advise young married women to care for their husbands and be with their children.

When Helen and Jack, who had both married, took their children to visit, Hallie did her best to make these occasions memorable. "I fear I am a total loss as a grandmother," Hallie wrote to me after one of Jack's visits, "but I loved being wakened by Philip [Jack's eldest] opening my door and shouting, Hi Gramma! He and J.D. [Jack's second son] are too young for *Emil and the Detectives,* but I showed them all the books I could find on primitive art, on which they had very definite ideas. Of a fifth-century Aphrodite, Philip said, Too fat . . . J.D. spit on Picasso but I don't think it was an artistic judgment. After a week of the visit, Hazel [Hallie's housekeeper] and I are both wrecks—not the fault of our guests but of the septic tank which suddenly erupted, due to all sorts of foreign objects being dropped into the toilets by the enterprising young."

Hallie felt her uselessness as a grandmother most in relation to me. She imagined that I must be having a terribly difficult time as the mother of two small sons, and her letters were full of suggestions: to rest, to hire more help, to look after my health. She was reminded of her own years as the mother of two small boys. "How well I remember one dinner party Murray and I gave in St. Louis. Everything went wrong. My meat loaf flopped all over the kitchen floor and the baby chose that night to have the croup. And to finish the affair, one of my guests fell off the piano bench. I remember when I was scooping up the meat loaf thinking, *They expect me to do everything.*" On one occasion when I had a bad cold, she suggested that she and her later housekeeper might come to New York for several days, "put you to bed and do the work. Emma said she would love to get meals. I could do dishes and brush up the house. We could take the boys to market singing as we walked hymns, or more likely, To market, to market, to buy a fat pig." This was sheer fancy: Hallie by then needed constant care.

Frederic's visits, sometimes alone, sometimes with his son or daughter, always cheered Hallie, although she worried about his drinking and increasing ill health. Fred's troubled childhood (even if invisible to most people) had finally caught up with him. He began drinking to quiet his anxieties, but the drinking led to anger. Hallie never saw the anger (she had needed to believe Fred was carefree and cheerful, and he played this role to the end), but others did. In the sixties he developed a serious stomach disorder and underwent a series of operations. His marriage was failing. He did not tell Hallie, but she probably suspected. "I see my own failures as a mother so clearly and painfully now," she wrote me as early as 1956, "but one can't unravel life, and Fred is Fred." "The worst part of this disease," she told the Youtzes, "is that it makes me so dumb and helpless."

Fred committed suicide six months before Hallie died. None of us told her: it would have broken her heart.

Hallie was in an automobile accident in 1963 and had to be cared for afterward in a small nursing home overlooking the Hudson in Beacon, New York. She tried even then to turn visits from family and friends into joyful occasions. Day Tuttle recalled a late sixties visit. "Hallie had asked the nurse to bring two glasses of fruit punch and some slices of cake. There was a table between us. She used this to steady her arm. Then with a smile and in a voice I could hardly hear, but whose syllables were clearly articulated, she raised her glass and proposed a toast: To life—in lemonade."

Few of the people who visited Hallie in her last years realized that she was not just fighting a battle against failing health. She was haunted by memories of the Dies Committee hearings. In moments of self-doubt she would wonder if the voices she heard in the corridor outside her room were accusing her of being a Communist. A change of scenery, a drive in the country or a picnic by the Hudson, would momentarily revive her spirits. But the tormenting doubts returned. In her youth Hallie had quelled the attacks of her conscience by working. She found the attacks of HUAC and of the newspapers which printed them more difficult to overcome.

Hallie died on July 23, 1969. Two months later there was a memorial service for her at the Vivian Beaumont Theatre in Lincoln Center. Three hundred people attended. Eric Bentley led off by saying that we had not met so much to mourn a death as to celebrate a life—a life vibrant with purpose and with joy taken in that purpose. "On the one hand, she was a fighter for the big things. On the other, one who took endless pleasure in her work, one who was not only joyful in herself but the cause of joy in countless others. These two sides of Hallie are the two sides of the art she served, for when theatre is not dedicated to the big things, it is sick, and when it is not playful, it is dead. I would say that Hallie Flanagan was above all a patriot. Her dedication was to the people of this country, to improve the quality of their life, first by providing bread, second by providing work, and third by providing joy. And so Hallie is history, but I shall not call her a landmark since that suggests we have gone beyond her. Alas, we haven't. But her spirit is still with us, and I would say she is part not only of our present but of our future."

Muriel Rukeyser read a poem she had written about Hallie, Fritz Weaver read poems from Whitman. Brooks Atkinson, Howard Bay, Abe Feder, and Joseph Cotten were among the speakers. Just before the event got under way, Muriel Rukeyser hurried down the aisle and handed my twin sons, who were nine, two toy cars.

Afterwards, relatives and close friends of Hallie's gathered for lunch in my New York apartment. It was a clear autumn day and the view of the Hudson River and New Jersey coastline from the living room overlooking Riverside Park was more than usually spectacular. Hallie had enjoyed helping me select furniture and drapes for the thirty-foot-long room ten years earlier. As I prepared for the occasion by arranging flowers in vases, I remembered the pleasure we had shared. My sister, who helped me, was as concerned as I to create the sort of celebration Hallie would have liked.

It was. People who had not met for years exchanged memories of Hallie. Someone, I forget who, proposed a toast and spoke eloquently of Hallie's zest for life. All that was needed, I thought, was Clair Leonard going to the piano, Hallie calling out that she needed a chorus of singers or dancers, someone picking up the tune or improvising a role. If the event lacked drama, it at least provided a theatrical setting. Hallie would have called it a beginning.

ACKNOWLEDGMENTS

The number of people who helped me recreate the drama of Hallie's life is prodigious. Shirley Rich Krohn was the first person to urge me to write a biography. With her usual encouragement and enthusiasm she got me going. My first editor, Jacques Barzun, believed in the book from the start. Without his support I might not have proceeded. Audrey Naumann and Barbara Mendoza, who wrote graduate theses on Hallie, generously shared their findings, as did Jane Mathews, whose book, *The Federal Theatre,* is the best available record.

I am much indebted to Kay and Richard Hocking, who put me up during my brief stay in Cambridge, to Helen Chinoy, who guided me through a labyrinth of material when I visited Northampton, to Anne and Lee Warren, whose home was my refuge while I researched the records at the National Archives in Washington and at the Federal Theatre Research Center in northern Virginia. Howard Wicks entertained me royally in Des Moines, and Kenneth and Gladys Ferguson did the same when I visited Chicago. Margaret Kiesel was my guide during the week I spent in Grinnell, Lorraine Brown and her staff during the days I worked at George Mason University. All helped make my labors as much pleasure as work. Many people contributed letters, made copies of letters from their own collections, or sent other pertinent materials. Among them are Barbara Gratwick, Betty Flanagan, Frances Youtz, Mary Spurway, Esther Lane, Howard Wicks, Bob Baron, Mary Crapo Hyde, Florence Wislocki, Velda Tatter, Doris Abramson, Lynne Anderson, Winifred Beachler, Lillian Berkeley, Day Tuttle, Robert Schnitzer, May Sarton, Philena Lang, Barrie Stavis, Bernard Craven, Patsy Walsh, Dorothy Wallace, Eric Bentley, Evelyn Clinton, Kay Strelsky, Howard Backus, Kate Clugston, Jane Wylie, Julia Sloane, and Emmet Lavery. Librarians and others in charge of special collections were unfailingly helpful. I want particularly to thank Anne Kintner at the Burling Library in Grinnell, Stephen Schlesinger at the Guggenheim Foundation, Dorothy Swerdlove at the Performing Arts Center at Lincoln Center, Lisa Browar in charge of Special Collections at Vassar, Peter Cox at Dartington Hall in England, and Jane Knowles at the Radcliffe College Archives.

Hallie once said that a director's life was like a camel's: both must stop at oases to continue the trip through the desert. The same might be said of biographers, all of whom must refresh themselves from others' memories. For granting me interviews I am indebted to Kenneth Ferguson, Howard Wicks, Kay Hocking, Esther Porter Lane, Tony Buttitta, Bernard Craven, George Clifton, Henry Schubart, Mark Schubart, Barbara Gratwick, Claudia Stearns, Christine Lyman, Mary Crapo Hyde, Eleanor Phelps, Harriet Deknatel, Juliette Guthrie, Harriet Meyer, Mary McCarthy, Dorothy Wallace, Mary Villard, Anne Bassage, Jane Levin, Katharine White, Muriel White, Josephine Gleason, Ted Riley, Phelps Riley, Kay Strelsky, Patsy and Bill Walsh, Vernon and Ruth Venable, Gordon Post, Howard Bay, Robert Schnitzer, Philip Barber, Harold Bolton, Halsted Welles, Irwin Rubinstein, George Kondolf, Rosamond Gilder, Day and Lauralee Tuttle, Denton Snyder, Bob Baron, George Dowell, Suzanne Johnston, Doris Abramson,

Ted Kazanoff, Daniel Aaron, Ted Apstein, Jack Davis, Helen Norman, Hallie Wolfe, and Frederic Flanagan, Jr.

During the year that I spent collecting materials, the postman's arrival was the high point of many of my days. A great many people responded generously to my quest for information. Those not already mentioned include Renna Whitford, Elizabeth Clark, Helen MacEachron, Lyle Flanagan, Helen Hutchinson, Harold Swanson, Laurence Brierly, Don Wilson, Charles Meyers, Marie Edwards, Mary Tait, Homer Abegglen, Harriet Rust, Louise Carstens, Margaret Brooke, Lucy Bridgham, Pat Gallagher, Wilma Segrest, Marjorie Savage, John Talbott, Helen Rathje, Doris Halman, Dorothy Sherrill, Betty Brucker, Carolyn Brooks, Margaret Trask, Marjorie Meiss, Margaret LaFarge, Barbara Dowell, Barbara Clarke, Charlotte Kohler, Katrina Moore, Lillias Trowbridge, Kay Davies, Jane DeLay, Margaret Setton, Marion Bieth, Phyllis Maier, Catherine Little, Isabel Roberts, Dorothy Roudebush, Margaret Campbell, Nancy Goldsmith, Gwen Davenport, Alison Conner, Mary Taylor, Christine Helwig, Margaret Strauss, Sara Azrael, Doris Fortes, Blair Davies, Marie Haug, Catherine Fessenden, Nancy Ebsen, Ros Altemus, Molly Brylawski, Marjorie Laggia, Priscilla Robertson, Mildred Lynes, Sterling Dow, Barbara Swain, Toni Hamilton, Caroline Mercer, Thomas Hartmann, Jean Davis, Marjorie Weir, Lois Stevenson, Anne Swift, Virginia Farmer, Howard Miller, Joseph Losey, Arnold Sundgaard, Herbert Kline, Joan Shepardson, Eleanor Lincoln, Virginia Brautigam, John Duke, Marianne Heinemann, Helene Cantarella, Agnes Drake Bender, Ruth Wolff, Bobbie Leigh, Allen Wheelis, Bertha Sherman, Connie Canright, and Lawrence Morris.

I also want to thank the group of women writers with whom I met once a week during the early stages of writing this book. Jane Anderson, Pat Lowe, Janet Cicchetti, Flo Gould, Sally Kellin, Barbara Moment, Esther Van Slyke, and Nancy Desart offered encouragement at a time when I needed it most. My finished manuscript was given thoughtful readings by Eric Bentley, Jacques Barzun, Dorothy and Harry Davis, and by a California friend who prefers not to be mentioned because his political views differ so much from mine. I incorporated many of their ideas. My brother, Jack Davis, and my sister, Helen Norman, whose memories of Hallie were often at odds with my own, provided constant and useful reminders that no one person sees another in exactly the same way. I came to see that as an advantage. What a dull business the writing of a biography would be if people's memories matched! My good friend and peerless editor, Harry Ford, was the soul of patience and kindness at every step of the way.

NOTES

Hallie Flanagan's papers (journals, diaries, letters, scrapbooks, memos, drafts of speeches, copies of correspondence, unpublished stories and plays, an unpublished autobiography, and miscellaneous materials) are widely scattered. Many letters are privately owned; others are in special collections. To indicate the locations of the main sources used I have adopted the following abbreviations:

AC   Author's Collection includes interviews, many letters, all journals and diaries, copies or originals of unpublished stories and plays, the unpublished autobiography *Notes on My Life,* and much miscellaneous material.

GCL The Burling Library at Grinnell College has much material on Flanagan's undergraduate years and the years she taught at the college.

VCL The Archives at Vassar College have a large collection of Flanagan papers relating to the years she directed the Vassar Experimental Theatre.

LC   The Performing Arts Research Center at Lincoln Center, a branch of the New York Public Library, has the largest collection of Flanagan papers.

SCT The Smith College Theatre has material relating to the period Flanagan taught and directed at the college.

GMU The Institute on the Federal Theatre Project and New Deal Culture at George Mason University has taped interviews with former Federal Theatre employees. Manuscripts, production photographs, and posters are included in this large collection of Federal Theatre materials.

NA   The National Archives in Washington, D.C., has seventy-five boxes of Federal Theatre records. This collection is catalogued as Record Group No. 69: Records of the Work Projects Administration, Records of the Federal Theatre Project.

GF   The John Guggenheim Foundation in New York City has the collection of letters Flanagan wrote to Henry Allen Moe.

RCA The Radcliffe College Archives has programs and other materials relating to George Pierce Baker's 47 Workshop.

YUL The Yale University Library has the letters Flanagan wrote to George Pierce Baker, as well as copies of the letters Baker wrote to and about Flanagan.

DH   Flanagan's letters to Dorothy and Leonard Elmhirst are at Dartington Hall in Devon, England.

Books frequently cited are referred to by title only. They are:

Hallie Flanagan, *Shifting Scenes of the Modern European Theatre.* New York: Coward McCann, 1928.
Hallie Flanagan, *Arena.* New York: Duell, Sloan and Pearce, 1940.
Hallie Flanagan, *Dynamo.* New York: Duell, Sloan and Pearce, 1943.

Jane De Hart Mathews, *The Federal Theatre, 1935–1939; Plays, Relief, and Politics.* Princeton, New Jersey: Princeton University Press, 1967.
Hallie Flanagan's unpublished autobiography, *Notes on My Life,* is referred to as *Notes.*

Play reviews and local newspaper mentions for Federal Theatre productions, which are numerous, are not cited. References to these can be found in *Arena* or *The Federal Theatre.* The latter contains an extensive bibliography, which should be consulted by anyone wanting to know more about the Federal Theatre.

PART I

CHAPTER 1: GRINNELL

3 Ned Lehac. Letter to author from Ned Lehac, 1982.
4 Great-grandfather Alexander. Frances Ann Johnson, *The History of Monroe, N.H.* (New Hampshire: 1955).
  Many Fergusons. Records of Deeds for Madison County, Edwardsville, Ill.
  The early settlers. W. T. Norton, ed., *The Centennial History of Madison County, Illinois, and its People, 1812–1912.*
  Sometime in the 1880s. Interview with Kenneth Ferguson, 1980.
  The Dakotas were just then. Herbert Schell, *History of South Dakota* (Omaha, Nebraska: 1961).
5 Six weeks after Hallie's birth. "Madam Director," unpublished article by Dorothy Wallace. AC.
  Because the country. Letter to author from Bob Flood, history librarian, Omaha Public Library, 1980.
  Like many of Hallie's early stories. "The Truth," *The Unit* (October 1909). GCL.
  "She was especially fond." *Notes.*
6 Her father, Frederick Fischer. Telephone directories, Hayner Public Library, Alton, Illinois.
  But when Louisa was thirteen. Ferguson interview.
7 Louisa, as Hallie put it. *Notes.*
  When Hallie accompanied. Ferguson interview.
8 In his opinion. Ibid.
  There was a tree. *Notes.*
  But the Leffler Company. Ferguson interview.
  During the next year. *Notes.*
10 Fred worked. Ibid.
  With the return. "Obituary of F. M. Ferguson," December 1926. AC.
  In the Ferguson house. *Notes.*
11 Finally, the year. Office of Land Deed Records, Courthouse, Montezuma, Iowa.
  Fred soon knew. *Notes.*
12 Grinnell's Colonial Theatre. Interview with George Clifton, 1980.
  A short time. Ferguson interview.
  When Hallie took over. Letter to author from Renna Norris Whitford, 1980.
13 Hallie kept a diary. Journal, *St. Louis World's Fair.* AC.
  "Her timing was perfect." Ferguson interview.

14 "Life must have been." Whitford letter.
When she fell in love. *Notes.*

CHAPTER 2: MURRAY FLANAGAN

17 Renna Norris thought. Letter to author from Renna Norris Whitford, 1980.
His recollection was. Clifton interview.
Rachel Harris wrote. Letter to HF from Harris, 1940. AC.
18 "When we came to." *Notes.*
At later periods. Grinnell College Annuals, 1908–1911.
19 "She had more ability." Letter to author from Helen MacEachron, 1979.
Hallie was later to insist. *Notes.*
Murray came from. Letter to author from Lyle Flanagan, 1980.
In the words. Whitford letter.
During his first. Ferguson interview.
20 As Hallie recalled it. *Notes.*
One day he wrote. Letter to HF from John Ryan, 1909. AC.
Another instance. *Notes.*
"Two's Company." *The Unit* (March 1908). GCL.
21 As soon as. *Notes.*
He was even jealous. Ferguson interview.
22 His younger brother, Lyle. Flanagan letter, 1980.
During the period. *Notes.*
After Murray and Hallie. Ferguson interview.
On the occasion. Letter to HF from Murray Flanagan, 1913. AC.
23 And then suddenly. *Notes.*
She had us organize. Letter to author from Helen Hutchinson, 1980.
Their son, Jack. *Notes.*
At some point. *Free.* GCL.
24 Literary historian. Cowley, *Exile's Return* (New York, 1951).
In 1916 he wrote. Daniel Aaron, *Writers on the Left* (New York, 1977), p. 9.
It took us. *Notes.*
25 Kenneth thought Murray. Ferguson interview.
Two months after Hallie. *Notes.*
She wrote Deborah that. Letter to Deborah Wiley, 1917. AC.
26 At home. *Notes.*
"His letters." Letter to Deborah Wiley, 1917. AC.
27 Murray would have. *Notes.*
28 During Murray's rest periods. Ibid.
He sometimes tried. Whitford letter.
Much later Hallie wrote. *Notes.*
In a later play. *Free.* GCL.

CHAPTER 3: NEW DIRECTIONS

29 "I did not choose work." Comment to author, circa 1950.
Kenneth, in his last. Ferguson interview.
30 Hallie's own. Interview with Denton Snyder, 1981.
Kenneth's recollection. Ferguson interview.
The man in charge. Howard Backus scrapbook. GCL.
Bridge thought. *Notes.*

30 Baker was an innovator. Wisner Payne Kinne, *George Pierce Baker and the American Theatre* (Cambridge, Mass., 1954).
31 O'Neill was later. Ibid.
32 William Bridge's innovations. Barbara Mendoza, "Hallie Flanagan: Her Role in American Theatre," unpublished manuscript, New York University.
    Hallie's first venture. "The Garden of Wishes," unpublished script. AC.
33 Later, in a full-length play. *Free.* GCL.
    Jack had always. Letter to author from J. R. Gallagher, 1980.
    Jack told her. *Notes.*
34 On one occasion. Letter to author from John Talbott, 1980.
    Thirty years later. *Notes.*
    One day he blurted out. Ferguson interview.
    During the summer. Mendoza ms.
35 Hallie's prize-winning play. *The Curtain* (Boston: Samuel French, 1932).
36 He was barely able. Interview with Gladys Ferguson, 1980.
    "There was not a stick." Letter to Audrey Koran from Homer Abegglen, 1971.
    Ryan told you. Letter to author from Harriet Rust, 1980.
    Ryan then resigned. Abegglen letter.
37 One of the people. Comment from HF to author, circa 1950.
    Hallie was later to say. *Notes.*
    Tall, somewhat aristocratic. Letter to author from Dorothy Sherrill, 1980.
    During classes. Letter to author from Helen Rathje, 1980.
38 On a page. 47 Workshop Scrapbook. LC.
    Robinson was ten years. Letter to author from Philip Barber, 1980.
    What she did say. *Notes.*
    The plays Hallie saw. Flanagan papers. LC.
39 Hallie's heroine, Gloria. *Free.* GCL.
40 Later she was to say. Comment to author, circa 1950.
    Baker told her. Letter from Baker to Henry Allen Moe, 1925. YUL.
41 Before Hallie left. Ibid.
    Baker, in fact. Ibid.
    Those who worked. Rust letter.
42 Among Hallie's students. Interview with Howard Wicks, 1980.
    When Howard heard. Ibid.
43 One student. Letter to author from Charles Meyers, 1980.
    Grinnell's best actor. Interview with Bernard Craven, 1980.
    Hallie had no difficulty. *Notes.*
    Just before Christmas. Letter to Winifred Beachler, 1924.
    Hallie was an inspiring director. Letter to author from Winifred Beachler, 1980.
    The young woman in charge. Letter to Audrey Koran from Ruth Clure, 1971.
    Hallie's conception. Dramatic Club program for *Romeo and Juliet.* GCL.
44 "The love scenes." Letter from HF to Winifred Beachler, 1925.
    Spotlights were ordered. Margaret Kiesel, "Hallie Flanagan's First: Experimental Theatre at Grinnell," *The Grinnell Magazine,* November 1978. GCL.
    In the words. Meyers letter.
    Howard Wicks had constructed. Letter to author from Wicks, 1980.
    According to Winifred. Letter to author from Winifred Beachler, 1980.
45 A student spectator. Meyers letter.
    Frederick Keppel. *Notes.*
    She was offered. Letter to HF from Amy Reed, 1925. VCL.
46 From Pomona College. Letter to Winifred Beachler, 1925.
    Later, Hallie was to write. *Notes.*
    On the contrary. Letter to author from Mary Tait, 1980.

46 The "amount of work." Letter to Amy Reed from George Coffman, 1925. VCL.
   It was one. Rust letter.
   Hallie thought. Letter from HF to Velda Jordan, 1926. AC.
47 In return. Letter to author from Priscilla Robertson, 1982.
   She missed "the simple." *Notes*.
   "My God," European Journal, 1926
   When she went. Letter from Amy Reed to President MacCracken, 1926. VCL.
48 In fact. Wicks interview.
   As soon as she saw. *Dynamo*.
   Disregarding the deficiencies. Ibid.
   Thirty-six. Letter to author from Stephen Schlesinger, 1980.
   In applying. Application for a fellowship, 1925. GF.
49 Like his mother. Interview with Josephine Gleason, 1980.
   Hallie's first idea. Letter to Henry Allen Moe, 1926. GF.
   When Moe turned down. *Notes*.
   Just before. Letter to HF from Thomas Robinson, 1926. AC.
   Even before. European diary, 1926.

CHAPTER 4: EUROPEAN ADVENTURE

Except where otherwise indicated, all quotations are from the diary and journal Hallie wrote while traveling in Europe.

52 "Once there was belief." Ibid.
53 Every detail. Ibid.
   Hallie left England. Ibid.
54 During the long. Ibid.
   They still had. Letter to Baker, 1926. YUL.
55 "We are in great avenues." *Shifting Scenes*.
   I remember the evening. Ibid.
57 In the country. Ibid.
   In Uppsala. Ibid.
58 When I am thinking out. Ibid.
59 Stark Young. Young, *Immortal Shadows* (New York: Scribner's, 1948).
   Isadora Duncan. Duncan, *My Life* (New York, 1927).
   One of his critics. Lee Simonson, *The Stage Is Set* (New York, 1932).
60 No stage design. *Shifting Scenes*.
64 After the Revolution. Nikolai A. Gorchakov, *The Theatre in Soviet Russia* (New York, 1957).
66 Walking along. *Shifting Scenes*.
67 In Red Square. Ibid.
68 Stanislavsky told Hallie. Ibid.
69 "Insolent rhythms." Ibid.
   Harold Clurman. Clurman, *Theatre Arts Monthly*, November 1935.
70 "The man playing." *Shifting Scenes*.
71 Was Meyerhold. Ibid.
   When Stalin decided. Edward Braun, *The Theatre of Meyerhold* (London, 1979).
72 "Think of letting actors" Letter to Baker, 1926. YUL.
73 Russian friends. *Shifting Scenes*.

74 At the Leningrad School. Ibid.
78 "There is an appalling amount." Ibid.
79 "Max Reinhardt, unlike Meyerhold." Ibid.
80 Hallie nevertheless wrote. Letter to Moe, 1926. GF.
81 She was enchanted. *Shifting Scenes.*
    "Prague must be seen." Ibid.
83 The Kingdom of Marionettes. Ibid.
    To begin with. Ibid.
85 Travelers from the States. Ibid.
86 It was at this point. Letter to author from Harriet Meyer, 1980.
87 In the Goldoni Theatre. *Shifting Scenes.*
88 In Rome. Ibid.
89 "That is your." Ibid.
91 Hallie did not know. Interview with Mark Schubart, 1980.
92 In subsequent years. Interview with Henry Schubart, 1980.

CHAPTER 5: EXPERIMENTAL THEATRE AT VASSAR

93 Hallie returned. *Notes.*
    She spent the summer. Letters to Moe, 1927, 1928. GF.
    When she finished. Letter to HF from Gordon Craig, 1927. LC.
94 Velona told her. Letter to HF from Velona Pilcher, 1927. LC.
    Hallie entered. Interview with Kay Hocking, 1980.
95 Some had decided. Interview with Claudia Stearns, 1980.
    "She could command." Letter to author from Julie Sloane, 1980.
    Hallie's plan. *Dynamo.*
96 Hallie later described. Ibid.
97 As one student. Letter to author from Kay Davies, 1980.
    "I really don't think." Hocking interview.
    One of the first things. Wicks interview.
98 At one rehearsal. Hocking interview.
    The Marriage Proposal. Theatre Arts Monthly, June 1928; *Theatre Magazine,*
        May 1928.
99 Interest continued. *Dynamo.*
    "Our success and fame." Letter to author from Betty Brucker, 1980.
100 A few weeks later. *Dynamo.*
    The plot of *Blocks.* Unpublished script. VCL.
101 As Hallie's reputation grew. Stearns interview; Davies letter.
102 If a student's ideas. *Dynamo.*
103 Hallie's pioneer period. Davies letter.
    "Those who opposed Hallie." Stearns interview.
104 She had never imagined. Letter to author from Priscilla Robertson, 1982.
    Freddie, as he was called. Interview with Josephine Gleason.
    Phelps Riley. Interview with Riley, 1982.
105 Writing them. Letter from HF to Philip and Frances Youtz, 1963.
    Although Harold Clurman. *New York Times,* March 9, 1980.
    "It should not expect." *Dynamo.*
    "Feeling that." Howard Wicks, "A Quest for Perfection," unpublished memoir.
        AC.
106 The girl, who later became. Interview with Katherine White, 1982.
    Later in his life. Wicks interview.
107 Janet Hartmann was a loner. Davies letter.

107 Hallie encouraged Janet. Flanagan and Hartmann, *The Sky Will Be Lit Up,*
     unpublished script. VCL.
108 And then one afternoon. Hocking interview.
109 Kay was "breathlessly naive." Interview with Christine Ramsey, 1980.
     "The illusion." *Vassar Miscellany News,* April 1929. VCL.
     Hallie often made decisions. Wicks interview.
     One student thought. Davies letter.
     Janet Hartmann's brother. Letter to author from Thomas Hartmann, 1980.
110 "It might be possible." Letter to HF from Craig, 1928. LC.
111 "If I could have." Letter to Moe, February 1928. GF.
     Furthermore, Louisa. Interview with Gladys Ferguson, 1980.
     Hiram Motherwell. *The New York Times Book Review,* December 23, 1928.
112 As a student. Stearns interview.

CHAPTER 6: A CAMPUS ROMANCE

113 In the words. Letter to author from Charlotte Kohler, 1980.
     Hallie soon learned. Interview with Lauralee Tuttle, 1980.
     President MacCracken. Letter to author from Mary Crapo Hyde, 1981.
     MacCracken called Hallie. *Notes.*
114 *Masse Mensch.* Ernst Toller, *Man and the Masses* production script. VCL.
     The campus reviewer. *Vassar Miscellany News,* May 1930. VCL.
     Hallie sent Toller. Letter to HF from Toller, January 1930. VCL.
116 In Hallie's acting version. *Dynamo.*
117 Most of Hallie's productions. Davies letter.
     "Hallie was a task-master." Letter to author from Jane DeLay, 1980.
118 Even so. Letter from HF to Herbert Kline, January 1935. VCL.
     When Philip Davis heard. *Notes.*
     As Malcolm Cowley. Cowley, *The Dream of the Golden Mountains* (New
        York, 1964).
     On reaching Leningrad. Journal, 1930. AC.
     Her students, influenced by. Interview with Barbara Gratwick, 1980.
119 One production, *Oil.* Flanagan, "Blood and Oil," *Theatre Guild Magazine,*
        October 1930.
     After Moscow. Journal, 1930.
120 After he became. Interview with Philip Barber, 1980.
     When she returned. "In His Image," unpublished story. AC.
     Whittaker Chambers. Chambers, "Can You Make Out Their Voices," *New
        Masses,* March 1931.
121 Hallie and Margaret Ellen Clifford. Flanagan and Clifford, *Can You Hear Their
        Voices?* Published by the Vassar Experimental Theatre, 1931.
     The play, later considered. Malcolm Goldstein, *The Political Stage* (New York,
        1974).
     The *New York Times.* May 10, 1931.
     New Masses. June 1931.
     Hallie noted that. *Dynamo.*
122 They were not love letters. *Notes.*
     He had visited Hallie. Interview with Josephine Gleason, 1980.
     "Maps of the Moon." Unpublished story. AC.
123 Around this time. *The Ant and the Statue,* unpublished story. AC.
     Here was the "real thing." European Journal, 1927.
124 Envisioning a stage. *Dynamo.*

124 By June 1931. Letter from HF to Grace Macurdy, 1931. VCL.
　　To Gertrude Brown. *Dynamo.*
125 Philip was none. *Notes.*
　　In Philena Lang's recollection. Letter to author from Lang, 1982.
126 "It was a tremendously emotional experience." Interview with Patsy Walsh,
　　　1980.
　　A reporter from the *Herald Tribune.* November 29, 1931.
　　The novelist Mary McCarthy. Interview with McCarthy, 1982.
　　The reviewer for the *Herald Tribune.* December 12, 1931.
　　The Poughkeepsie *Sunday Courier.* December 13, 1931.
　　Mary McCarthy thought. McCarthy interview.
　　Gilbert Murray. Letter to HF from Murray, July 2, 1932. VCL.
127 "Here was this man." Walsh interview.
　　Whenever the love affair began. *Notes.*
128 Hallie disapproved. Letter to author from Jean Davis, 1980.
　　One of Philip's sisters. Letter to author from Marjorie Weir, 1980.
　　His eldest sister. Jean Davis letter.
129 *Miners on Strike* and *We Demand.* The first by A. Prentis; the second by
　　　Bernard Reines. Production scripts at VCL.
　　She liked to quote Walt Whitman. *The Seven Arts,* September 1917, p. 633.
130 Helen Lockwood. *Vassar Miscellany News,* May 11, 1932. VCL.
　　In an article. "A Theatre is Born," *Theatre Arts Monthly,* November 1931.
131 Nik. Interview with Kay Strelsky, 1980.
132 When he again. *Notes.*

CHAPTER 7: INDECISION

133 "I have never been." Letter from HF to Mrs. Dwelle, August 1932. AC.
　　As usual. "Pearls Found in a Bottle," *The Tanager* (March 1935). GCL.
134 When she asked him. *Notes.*
　　Hallie had sent. Letter from HF to Ethel Bebb, September 1933. VCL.
　　He often phoned her. Riley interview.
135 As a writer. Arthur Holmberg, *New York Times,* November 21, 1982.
　　Eliot replied. Letter to HF from Eliot, March 18, 1933. Copy at VCL.
136 Hallie had her own ideas. *Dynamo.*
137 "If you saw the play." Letter from HF to T. S. Eliot, May 17, 1933. Copy at
　　　VCL.
　　On the morning. Interview with Mary Hyde, 1980.
　　Eliot thought. *Vassar Miscellany News,* May 10, 1933.
　　"Mr. Davis rendered." May 6, 1933.
138 Hallie recalled. *Dynamo.*
　　It was helped along. Jean Davis letter.
　　Roaming about. *Dynamo.*
139 A few days after. Letter to HF from Bernard Reines, May 3, 1933. VCL.
　　When a young playwright. Letter to Mr. Belco, March 1933. VCL.
　　The new board. Correspondence between HF and Bernard Reines, November
　　　1933. VCL.
140 "I can't seem." Letter to Bernard Reines, May 1933. Copy at VCL.
　　"Lester Lang and I work": Letter to Grinnell College Registrar, March 1932.
　　　Copy at VCL.
　　In August. Letter from August Lenniger, August 1933. VCL.
　　September 1933. Interview with Mary Villard, 1980.

141 "Such an amount." Letter to Mary Crapo, September 1933.
"Muriel Rukeyser, Elizabeth Bishop." Villard interview.
142 She considered *Fear.* Letter from HF to President MacCracken, 1933. VCL.
When she first wrote Hallie. Letter from May Sarton, August 1933. VCL.
143 After meeting with Hallie. Letter from Sarton, undated. VCL.
"Our translation." Letter to Sarton, undated.
144 The play *Fear.* A. Afinogenov, *Fear,* translated by Dorothy Colman and Nikander Strelsky. Acting version by HF. VCL.
Lester Lang's set. *Dynamo.*
Hoping for. Letter to Moe, December 1932. GF.
145 This naturally. Correspondence between HF and President MacCracken, March 1930, May 1933. VCL.
146 "The last two years." Letter to Mary Crapo, undated.
In an effort. Dear Theatre letter, February 8, 1934. VCL.
147 In time. 1934 Journal. AC.
148 Hallie was charmed by. Flanagan, "Kurt Jooss at Dartington," *Theatre Arts Monthly,* May 1934.
149 She told Elmhirst. 1934 Journal.
"We have had." Letter to Esther Porter, undated. AC.
From Paris she wrote. Dear Theatre letter, March 13, 1934. VCL.
150 Craig's next communication. Undated letter. LC.
Ten days before. Letter to Leonard and Dorothy Elmhirst, April 21, 1934. DH.
151 It's a good thing. Craig letter, 1934. LC.
152 From Naples she wrote. March 26, 1934. AC.
It really started Friday. Dear Theatre letter, March 28, 1934. VCL.
153 It is best. 1934 Journal. AC.
Years later. Interview with Vernon Venable, 1980.
154 Here she witnessed. Dear Theatre letter, April 10, 1934. VCL.
"We are in a trance." 1934 Journal. AC.
157 "How it would amuse you." Dear Theatre letter, April 16, 1934. VCL.
But visiting. 1934 Journal. AC.
159 Twenty-five years. *Notes.*
160 "Perhaps," she added. Letter to students, April 30, 1934. VCL.
161 One, Nikias, came. "Chorus for the Delian Apollo," *Theatre Arts Monthly,* January 1935.
162 Every day is a cycle. 1934 Journal. AC.
164 Hallie's feeling. "Lorelei on Delos," unpublished story. AC.
165 *The Lost Aphrodite.* Unpublished play. AC.
166 Pat's speeches. Letter to Esther Porter, June 1934. AC.

CHAPTER 8: A NATION IN CRISIS

167 When President MacCracken. Letter to author from Philena Lang, 1980.
168 A couple of years. Radcliffe Alumnae Information Form. RCA.
169 "Really, it's some undertaking." Craig letter, undated. LC.
"Sometimes we turned up." Interview with Patsy and Bill Walsh, 1980.
Tina remembered a game. Interview with Christine Ramsey, 1980.
170 "I can still remember." Letter to author from Jane Wylie, 1980.
Later, on Delos. Jean Davis letter, 1980.
North Africa is full. *Dynamo.*
171 Plutarch is hard. Ibid.

174 She would have been amused. Letter to Dorothy Wallace from President
       MacCracken, August 16, 1938. AC.
175 Gordon Post. Letter to author from Post, 1969.
       Hallie was a great one. Interview with Anne Bassage, 1980.
176 William Randolph Hearst. February 24, 1935.
177 "Many on the Vassar faculty." Villard interview.
       To her former Grinnell student. March 19, 1935. Copy at VCL.
       American college students. *Dynamo.*
178 "Herb Mayer and I." Letter to author from Doris Fortes, 1981.
179 Schlesinger wrote Hallie. March 1935. VCL. A copy of Flanagan's reply is
       attached.
180 "You know I once wanted." Dear Theatre letter, March 7, 1934. VCL.
       Auden's *Dance of Death. Dynamo.*

PART II

CHAPTER 9: LAUNCHING THE PROJECT

185 "I am not willing." William E. Leuchtenburg, *Franklin D. Roosevelt and the
       New Deal* (New York, 1963).
       A year earlier. *Arena.*
186 Harry was later to recall. Introductory remarks before Flanagan's speech,
       Mayflower Hotel, May 1938. NA.
       He was also a practical joker. Charles Searles, *Minister of Relief* (Syracuse, New
       York, 1963).
       Few know that. Ibid.
       "Hell," he replied. Arthur Schlesinger, Jr. *The Coming of the New Deal*
       (Boston, 1958).
187 After telegraphing. *Arena.*
       Rice . . . told Hallie. Rice, *The Living Theatre* (New York, 1959).
       By the time. Letter to Philip Davis, May 17, 1935. AC.
188 In Washington. Letter to Philip Davis, May 19, 1935. AC.
       At the White House. *Arena.*
189 The Arts Projects. Flanagan, "Democracy and the Drama," quoted in *Free,
       Adult, Uncensored,* eds. John O'Connor and Lorraine Brown (Washington,
       D.C., 1978), 26.
190 "But I'm not going to do it." *Notes.*
       It would be "creating." Report to Jacob Baker, 1935. NA.
       "So excellent in nature." Letter from HF to Herbert Kline, 1935. LC.
191 Mabie's reply. July 1935. NA.
       "Can you spend money?" *Arena.*
193 When the newspapers announced. *The Federal Theatre.*
       And then from England. Alistair Cooke, broadcast quoted in *The Listener,*
       April 8, 1936.
       Mr. Bowser. Letter to Philip Davis, September 4, 1935. AC.
194 Esther Porter, who made. Interview with Esther Porter Lane, 1980.
       he "raised hell." Letter to Philip Davis, September 6, 1935. AC.
195 Hallie and Holger Cahill. Letter to Philip Davis, undated. AC.
       Barrett M. Clark. Letter to HF from Clark, August 1935. NA.
       Hallie was "comforted." Letter to Philip Davis, undated. AC.
       "Oh Darling." Letter to Philip Davis, September 4, 1935. AC.

195 "She was always asking." Interview with Vernon Venable, 1980.
"She depended on him." Interview with Patsy Walsh, 1980.
196 "marble court." Letter to Philip Davis, September 18, 1935. AC.
"Successful looking men." Letter to Philip Davis, September 11, 1935. AC.
197 According to Hallie's legal counsel. Interview with Irwin Rubinstein, 1980.
Barber was later to say. Interview with Barber, 1980.
198 "An absolutely new character." Letter to Philip Davis, October 21, 1935.
AC.
199 Martin Beck. Letter to Philip Davis, September 22, 1935. AC.
Lee Schubert, *Arena*.
As the *New York Times* put it. "Vassar's Hallie Flanagan," *New York Times*,
September 22, 1935.
Eva Le Gallienne remarked. *Arena*.
Katharine Cornell invited her. Letter to Philip Davis, October 1, 1935. AC.
She then "went." Letter to Philip Davis, September 4, 1935. AC.
200 The irony of meeting. "Address by Hallie Flanagan," October 8, 1935.
Roosevelt Archives, Hyde Park, N.Y.
When Hallie had tried. *Arena*.
201 Charles Coburn, who appeared. Letter to Philip Davis, October 8, 1935. AC.
Colonel Westbrook. Letter to Philip Davis, September 26, 1935. AC.
202 "We live." Flanagan address, Roosevelt Archives.
203 "The theatre may be art." Kate Clugston, unpublished autobiography.
Booth said . . . Hallie said. Letter to Philip Davis, undated. AC.
204 Sidney Howard. Letter from Howard, October 1935. NA.
"It was a struggle." *Arena*.
205 "Well, Hallie." Ibid.
Variety was informing. October 30, 1935; November 27, 1935.
"*You* try getting up." *Arena*.
"Do you enjoy working." Clugston autobiography.
When she got discouraged. Letter to Philip Davis, October 1, 1935. AC.
206 "Did you have a nice day." Letter to Philip Davis, October 6, 1935. AC.
207 "I certainly like." Letter to Philip Davis, October 20, 1935. AC.
Hallie found herself. Letter to Philip Davis, October 17, 1935. AC.
208 "Is that good army discipline." *Arena*.
"Do old plays here." Ibid.

CHAPTER 10: EARLY CRISES

210 Later, after she had been accused. *Arena*.
211 He "knew less." Ibid.
Watson's first loyalty. Interview with Wendell Phillips by members of the
Research Center at GMU, 1976. Phillips, who was a Communist Party
member, remembered Watson as a "power in the Party."
Ethiopia asked why. Text reprinted in *Educational Theatre Journal*, March
1968.
212 "This is war." William E. Leuchtenburg, *Franklin D. Roosevelt and the New
Deal* (New York, 1963).
"We are skating." *The Federal Theatre*.
"It all means." Letter to Philip Davis, January 16, 1936. LC.
"I have the gravest fears." Letter to Mrs. Roosevelt, January 1936. Hyde Park
Library.
213 "No issue." *Arena*.

213 "She told me." Interview with Esther Porter Lane by members of the Research
Center at GMU, 1976.
214 Rice had become. Clugston autobiography.
"When difficulties have arisen." *Arena.*
215 "The government's decision." *New York Times,* January 25, 1936.
Newspaper reaction. *The Federal Theatre.*
In a private conversation. Tony Buttitta and Barry Witham, *Uncle Sam Presents*
(Philadelphia, 1982).
216 "Hallie's name began to flare." Clugston autobiography.
Hallie had had dreams. Letter to Philip Davis, January 1936. AC.
Jacob Baker, "looking very grave." Letter to Philip Davis, January 8, 1936. LC.
"When I think." Letter to Philip Davis, February 18, 1936. AC.
217 She saw them. *Dynamo.*
218 Halsted Welles. Interview with Welles, 1985.
"But every time I turned up." Interview with Welles by members of the
Research Center at GMU, 1975.
"Many people," *Arena.*
Hallie wrote rather wistfully. Letter to Philip Davis, undated. AC.
219 *Triple-A Plowed Under.* Text published in *Federal Theatre Plays,* ed. Pierre de
Rohan (New York, 1938).
Hallie then invited. Letter from HF to Ira Knaster, July 1938. NA.
But as rehearsals. *Arena.*
220 Norman Lloyd. Interview with Lloyd by members of the Research Center at
GMU, 1976.
"We want an audience." Quoted in Willson Whitman's *Bread and Circuses*
(New York, 1937), p. 69.
221 She was also. Interview with Barber, 1980.
222 "Sometimes we'd all get." Interview with Harold Courlander by members of
the Research Center at GMU, 1977.
Hallie sent a telegram. January 15, 1936. AC.
Hopkins had told Hallie. *Arena.*
"Anyone who did not flirt." Rubinstein interview.
"This project." Interview with Gilder by members of the Research Center at
GMU, 1976.
223 An assistant in her office. Interview with Bud Fishel by members of the Research
Center at GMU, 1976.
She was exulting. Letters to Philip Davis, February 24 and 26, 1936. AC.
Farnsworth thought. Interview with Farnsworth by members of the Research
Center at GMU, 1977.
224 "I can scarcely give." Letter to Philip Davis, February 9, 1936. AC.
"I realize." "Report on Federal Theatre Projects," WPA document, unpub-
lished, March 13, 1936. LC.
The show, Hopkins replied. *The Federal Theatre.*
225 "Well, folks." Letter to Philip Davis, April 1936. AC.
he told her he owed. Letter to Philip Davis, undated. AC.
226 The idea of doing. John Houseman, *Run-through* (New York, 1972).
227 "Here we are." Letter to regional directors, February 12, 1936. NA.
228 Tony Buttitta. *Uncle Sam Presents.*
Pierre de Rohan. Interview with Andrew Slane by members of the Research
Center at GMU, 1979.
To illustrate an article. Letter to Philip Davis, April 25, 1936. LC.

228 "They had a terrible fight." Interview with Rosamond Gilder by members of
     Research Center at GMU, 1976.
     "Let's gang up." *Uncle Sam Presents.*
     "I'm not quarreling." Correspondence between Flanagan and Rohan,
     1936–1938. NA.
229 "We have not one thing." Report on New England trip, August 1936. NA.
230 Green was later to say. Interview with Paul Green by members of the Research
     Center at GMU, 1975.
231 Herbert Price. *Arena.*
232 Hallie told Hopkins. Letter to Philip Davis, May 28, 1936. AC.
     In one letter. Letter to Philip Davis, October 20, 1935. AC.
233 "I can't possibly tell you." Letter to Philip Davis, May 28, 1936.

CHAPTER 11: FEDERAL THEATRE AT MIDPOINT

234 According to Arthur Arent. *The Federal Theatre.*
     In style and tone. Arnold Goldman, "Life and Death of the Living Newspaper
     Unit," *Theatre Quarterly,* January-March 1973.
235 "I had a little piano." Lloyd interview.
     Irwin Rubinstein. Rubinstein interview.
     She asked Watson and Losey. *The Federal Theatre.*
237 "I broke." Goldman.
     "Terrified of." Letter to author from Joe Losey, 1984.
241 A week later. Letter to Philip Davis, September 30, 1936. AC.
242 "Lewis had frequent tantrums." Interview with Philip Barber by members of the
     Research Center at GMU, 1975.
     "At intervals." *Arena.*
244 "Any New York manager." Letter from HF to Kay Hocking, undated.
     In Hallie's opinion. *Arena*
246 "Picket lines with banners." Letter to Philip Davis, undated. AC.
     Somervell . . . was quoted." Clugston autobiography.
247 In late February. *The Federal Theatre.*
     Robert Schnitzer. Interview with Schnitzer, 1979.
248 Her play, she told. Letter to Isaacs from HF, January 18, 1935. VCL. Flanagan
     sent the script to Richard Madden, her agent. Present whereabouts
     unknown.
249 "facts which would fit in." Correspondence between HF and Watson, January
     1937. NA.
     Hallie wanted the production. Letter from HF to Walter Hart, February 17,
     1937. NA.
     "the most bungling and inept." Ibid.
250 "Far and away the best." James Agate, London *Times,* June 20, 1937.
     Norman Lloyd was. Text published in *Federal Theatre Plays,* ed. Pierre de
     Rohan (New York, 1938).
     "This is a great show." *Arena.*
251 "From offices." Ibid.
252 "Faustus, emerging," Ibid.
     "I suppose." Letter to Philip Davis, undated. AC.
     Houseman recalled. *Run-through.*
253 "We build a theatre." Letter to Philip Davis, undated. AC.

253 Irwin Rubinstein. Rubinstein interview.
     Robert Schnitzer. Schnitzer interview.
254 Philip Barber. Barber interview.
     When she discussed. Rubinstein interview.
     Shaw . . . his reply. Letter to HF from Shaw, May 22, 1937. GMU.

CHAPTER 12: RELEVANT THEATRE

257 "All of us." "Conversation between HF and Farnsworth," May 20, 1937. NA.
     Niles . . . asked her. "Conversation between HF and Niles," May 25, 1937.
        NA.
     in a speech. "Notes for speech," May 28, 1937. AC.
     "We hate to lose." "Conversation between HF and Farnsworth," May 19,
        1937. NA.
258 "It was up to." Fishel interview. GMU.
     William Leuchtenburg. *Franklin D. Roosevelt and the New Deal.*
260 Hallie, who had told. Letter to Philip Davis, November 8, 1936. AC.
     Blitzstein's inspiration. *Uncle Sam Presents.*
     As Houseman wrote, *Run-through.*
261 "Because of impending cuts." *Arena.*
262 Houseman, who later admitted. *Run-through.*
264 Like every Living Newspaper. Eugenie Birch, "Woman-Made America: The
        Case of Early Public Housing Policy," *Journal of the American Institute of
        Planners,* April 1978, pp. 130–142.
265 Though the Living Newspaper Unit. "Summer Theatre Results," Memorandum
        from Pierre de Rohan to HF, May 8, 1939. NA.
     "That didn't sit well." Slane interview.
266 She asked Howard Bay. Interview with Bay by members of the Research Center
        at GMU, 1976.
267 Act one. Text published in *Federal Theatre Plays.*
268 Eleanor Roosevelt. *Arena.*
     A neighbor of Hallie's. Interview with Emmet Lavery by members of the
        Research Center at GMU, 1976.
     But Philip Barber. Barber interview.
     Rhoda Rammelkamp. John O'Connor and Lorraine Brown, eds. *Free, Adult,
        Uncensored* (New Republic Books, Washington, D.C., 1978).
     Barber . . . felt triumphant. Barber interview.
269 Later Bay was to say. Interview with Howard Bay, 1980.
     The climax of act two. *Arena.*
270 Senator Josiah W. Bailey. *The Federal Theatre.*
     Senator Charles O. Andrews. Ibid.
271 "If senators and congressmen." *Arena.*
     "convicted the senators." Interview with Florence Kerr, 1967, by Kathryn
        Moliman. Association of American Colleges, Washington, D.C.
     "Living newspapers." *Arena.*
272 "We found what." Interview with Esther Porter Lane by members of the
        Research Center at GMU, 1976.

CHAPTER 13: MOUNTING OPPOSITION

275 "she read in *Variety.*" *The Federal Theatre.*
276 Hopkins had returned to Chicago. Interview with George Kondolf, 1984.

276 According to Philip Barber. Barber interview.
  Walter Hart. *The Federal Theatre.*
277 "We are being watched." Ibid.
  "Emmet Lavery." Interview with Francis Bosworth by members of the Research
    Center at GMU, 1978.
278 "Whether this means." Letter to Philip Davis, October 13, 1937. AC.
  "Dearest, I want very much." Letter to Philip Davis, October 25, 1937. AC.
279 Louisa Ferguson. Letter to Philip Davis, October 26, 1937. AC.
  But when she saw *Boy Meets Girl.* Letter to Philip Davis, October 28, 1937.
    AC.
280 "We wept." Letter to Philip Davis, October 26, 1937. AC.
  "I've had such a day." Letter to Philip Davis, October 31, 1937. AC.
281 After seeing her Negro Unit. Letter to Philip Davis, November 2, 1937. AC.
282 "He had only performed." Porter interview.
  "We should be building theatres." Letter to Philip Davis, November 7, 1939.
    AC.
  Later she wrote. *Arena.*
283 "It was a miracle." Letter to Philip Davis, November 9, 1937. AC.
  She had never been. Interview with Howard Miller by members of the Research
    Center at GMU, 1976.
  Two marionette shows. Letter to Philip Davis, November 9, 1937. AC.
  Mrs. O'Neill drove. Letter to Philip Davis, November 11, 1937. LC.
285 "Yasha Frank." Letter to Philip Davis, November 21, 1937. AC.
  It was "typical." Letter to Philip Davis, November 16, 1937. AC.
286 Miller later recalled. Miller interview. GMU.
  "I am so afraid." Letter to Philip Davis, November 21, 1937. AC.
  "No one can help." Letter to Philip Davis, November 23, 1937. AC.
287 Montgomery . . . Lawson. Letter to Philip Davis, November 21, 1937. AC.
  She was feeling homesick. Letter to Philip Davis, November 23, 1937. AC.
  "Ouray Building." Letter from HF to Esther Porter, December 9, 1937.
    AC.
  Writing Philip. Letter to Philip Davis, December 2, 1937. LC.
288 Hopkins . . . looked thin. Letter to Philip Davis, December 9, 1937. AC.
289 "Harry, I know you have been ill." *The Federal Theatre.*

CHAPTER 14: FURTHER CRISES

292 any theatre operating. *Arena.*
  "Despite local problems." "A Brief Delivered by Flanagan before the Committee
    on Patents," February 1938. AC.
293 "The melancholy fact." Atkinson, "Perpetuating the Federal Theatre," *New
    York Times,* February 20, 1938.
294 Later she was to admit. *Arena.*
  Hallie produced. Ibid.
  "I wish very much." Ibid.
295 Our chief enemies. "Murder in the Federal Theatre." NA.
  In his letter of resignation. Goodman letter, February 1, 1938. NA.
  But George Kondolf. Interview with Kondolf, 1984.
296 They met in secret. Ibid.
  Malcolm Cowley. Cowley, "The People's Theatre," *The New Republic,*
    January 13, 1941.
  "When I found that someone." Kondolf interview.

296 "Many times." Interview with Kondolf by members of the Research Center at
      GMU, 1976.
297 "The worst morale." *Arena.*
      "I would like to conclude." Letter to HF from Morgan, May 5, 1938. NA.
      Hallie replied that. Letter to Morgan from HF, May 1938. NA.
      "As I studied." *Arena.*
299 The production, Bolton recalled. Telephone interview with Bolton, 1984.
      A few days before. Letter from HF to Kondolf, April 1938. NA.
      In a widely publicized interview. *The Federal Theatre.*
      "No, Hallie, no." Remark made to author by HF, circa 1950.
300 "If the WPA can build schools." "Second session of the Regional Conference of
      the Eastern Region," March 3, 1938. NA.
301 Hallie proposed. "Report on Trip to South," March 18, 1938. NA.
      Koch wanted the building. Interview with Paul Green by members of the
      Research Center at GMU, 1975.
302 "This girl." "Comments made at Mayflower Hotel, Washington, D.C.," May
      19, 1938. NA.
303 The Relief Administrator. *The Federal Theatre.*
      "J. Parnell Thomas called the Federal Theatre." *The Federal Theatre.*
      Hallie replied. Letter from HF to Erford Gage, June 9, 1938. NA.
      Anne Fremantle. Letter from Fremantle to HF, August 1938. NA.

                        CHAPTER 15: HUAC

304 A month before the hearings. *The Federal Theatre.*
      Chairman Dies's extreme. Ibid.
305 "the fashion at that time." *Arena.*
      In July. *The Federal Theatre.*
      "If your presence." Ibid.
306 Huffman testified. Ibid.
307 "one of the weirdest." August Ogden, *The Dies Committee* (Washington,
      1945).
      What the newspapers. *The Federal Theatre.*
      "She was not a weeping person." Interview with Kay Strelsky, 1980.
308 Emmet Lavery. *The Federal Theatre.*
      Congressman Thomas told. Ibid.
      Paul Edwards discovered. Ibid.
      "Day after day." Ibid.
309 Over Station WQXR. Ibid.
      Hallie was quick. Letter from HF to Emanuel Celler, September 14, 1938. NA.
      New Jersey State Guidebook. Jerry Mangione, *The Dream and the Deal* (Avon
      Books, 1972).
      Ellen Woodward reacted. *The Federal Theatre.*
      Hallie later said. *Arena.*
310 a letter from Mrs. Roosevelt. *The Federal Theatre.*
      Roosevelt delivered. Ibid.
311 Woodward's remarks. Ibid.
312 After swearing her in. All quotes from testimony can be found in Eric Bentley's
      Thirty Years of Treason (New York, 1971).
323 As the hearing broke up. *Arena.*
324 Henry Alsberg's testimony. *The Dream and the Deal.*
325 Dies grew more. Ibid.

325 No one else gave. Ibid.
326 "They'll have to include." *Arena.*
    "six months." Ibid.
    "Hallie was greatly disturbed." Miller interview. GMU.
327 "I feel you might be." Letter to Dies from HF, December 19, 1938. NA.
    the "Committee proceeded." *Arena.*

CHAPTER 16: FINAL FIGHT

328 Yasha Frank. Lane interview. GMU.
    "I once told you." Letter from HF to David Stevens, September 19, 1938. NA.
329 Burns Mantle. Letter from HF to Mantle, December 16, 1938. NA.
330 "We are trying." Letter from HF to Mrs. Roosevelt, January 25, 1939. Hyde
    Park: Roosevelt papers.
    Senator Claude Pepper. Letter from HF to Pepper, January 13, 1939. NA.
331 "no loan of personnel." Memorandum from HF to Florence Kerr, February 9,
    1939. NA.
    The President of the University. "Notes on Chicago Trip," February 1939. NA.
    Arnold Sundgaard. Letter to author from Sundgaard, 1984.
    Toby Leach. *Arena.*
332 "I want it to be." Ibid.
    "in the worst tradition." "Report on Western Trip," February 1939. NA.
333 On the morning. Ibid.
    "We spent all Friday." Letter to Philip Davis, February 18, 1939. AC.
    "almost frail-looking." John Hobart, "No Boondoggling in the Federal
    Theatre," *San Francisco Chronicle,* February 19, 1939.
334 "She took a hell of a chance." Interview with Izenour by members of the
    Research Center at GMU, 1976.
    The Los Angeles Project. *Arena.*
    "If we go out." Letter from HF to Herbert Biberman, March 23, 1939. NA.
335 "until the last gun." Ibid.
    "One day I went." Kondolf interview. GMU.
336 "narrow thread." Letter from HF to Morris Ankrum, April 19, 1939. NA.
    By May. *The Federal Theatre.*
    "I have here." Ibid.
    "it cost money." *Arena.*
337 When Brooks Atkinson. *The Federal Theatre.*
    Representative Cannon. *Arena.*
338 "They can't do that." Ibid.
    "It's your baby." Interview with Irwin Rubinstein by members of the Research
    Center at GMU, 1977.
339 Hallie later commented. *Arena.*
    "Art seems like." *Uncle Sam Presents.*
    Representative Mary Norton. *Arena.*
340 "If the theatre." Ibid.
    President Roosevelt wrote. *The Federal Theatre.*
    A couple of weeks later. Ibid.
341 "probably rare." *Arena.*
342 If an actor. Ibid.
    Lionel Barrymore. Ibid.
343 In 1936, James Davis. *The Federal Theatre.*
344 "no lady of higher character." Ibid.

344 *Julius Caesar. Arena.*
345 A senator later wrote Hallie. Ibid.
    It is discrimination. Ibid.
    The President wrote to Hallie. Letter to HF from Roosevelt, July 19, 1939. NA.
346 "So let the bells." *Arena.*
    Federal Theatre might have lived. Ibid.
    Malcolm Cowley's account. Cowley, "The People's Theatre," *The New Republic,* January 13, 1941.

PART III

CHAPTER 17: RETURN TO VASSAR

351 "thoroughly happy time." *Notes.*
    "President MacCracken arranged." Ibid.
    Esther Porter Lane remembered. Lane interview. GMU.
    "She was a fighter." Rubinstein interview.
352 So did Emmet Lavery. Lavery, "Who Killed Federal Theatre?" *Commonweal,* August 4, 1939.
    Lavery never forgot. Lavery interview. GMU, 1976.
354 In Betty's recollection. Interview with Betty Flanagan, 1986.
    One night in February. *Notes.*
355 "I remember thinking." Letter to HF from Angela Lang, 1940. AC.
    Another wrote. Letter to HF from Rosemary Messner, 1940. AC.
    "Phil never thought." Letter from HF to E. C. Mabie, March 7, 1940. Mabie Papers, University of Iowa.
    "He sat up in the gallery." *Notes.*
    "We were all worried." Interview with Gordon Post, 1984.
    "There was a meeting." Interview with William and Patsy Walsh, 1980.
356 Jean remembered. Letter to author from Jean Davis, March 19, 1980.
    Hallie "dug in her heels." Walsh interview.
    "My mother." Jean Davis letter.
    "I am afraid." Letter to HF from Nathaniel Davis, March 1, 1940. AC.
357 Philip's sister Marjorie. Letter to author from Marjorie Weir, October 10, 1980.
359 Hallie never said. Letter from HF to Mary Crapo Hyde, April 21, 1940.
    I hear myself saying. Ibid.
360 Lee Gantt. Letter to HF, March 14, 1940. AC.
    "It was a difficult situation." Lane interview. GMU.
361 *No Time for Tears.* Unpublished play. AC.
    John Gassner. Gassner, *The New York Times Book Review,* December 22, 1940.
    "We were impressed." *Dynamo.*
363 "Youth, taught since childhood." Ibid.
    "We did not believe." Ibid.
364 In a chapel talk. Flanagan, "Education For Use," May 21, 1941. VCL.
365 the letter written by her students. Letter read by students at farewell party, May 4, 1942. LC.

CHAPTER 18: NORTHAMPTON: NEW CHALLENGES

369 "Do not be." Letter from Davis to HF, August 29, 1941. LC.
    "President Davis." Letter to author from Eleanor Lincoln, 1980.

370 "Plan indicates." Helen Chinoy, "Hallie Flanagan Davis: The Smith Years." SCT.

"The disaffected faction." Lincoln letter.

"She is very sweet." Boston *Post,* August 23, 1942.

371 "There was no conversation." Interview with Juliette Guthrie, 1980.

"As a child." Interview with Jack Davis, 1980.

"It had to do with carving." Ibid.

Hallie wrote Henry Allen Moe. Letter from HF to Moe, July 1940. GF.

372 Daniel Aaron. Interview with Aaron, 1980.

"There was a sharp line." Guthrie interview.

"I think I can say." Lincoln letter.

373 John Duke. Letter to author from Duke, December 1979.

Juliette Harvey remembered. Guthrie interview.

374 When the phone rang. Recollection contributed by Helen Norman, 1980.

"a pretty stiff one." Janet Clarke, "Hallie Flanagan: The Smith Years," 1975. SCT.

375 Hallie sent out. Chinoy, "Hallie Flanagan Davis: The Smith Years."

Though some participants thought. Letter to author from Marianne Heinemann, July 1980.

"If it had done no more." Chinoy, "Hallie Flanagan Davis: The Smith Years."

376 Hal's portrait. Halsted Welles, *Love and Terror,* unpublished novel.

377 John Gassner's review. Gassner, "Dynamo," *New York Times Book Review,* August 1943.

378 "I was a real trial." Jack Davis interview, 1980.

Helen . . . recalled. Interview with Helen Norman, 1980.

379 *Middle of the Air.* Program, reviews, and other material on production at LC.

380 Lynne Anderson . . . recalled. Letter to author from Anderson, October 1980.

CHAPTER 19: LIVING WITH ILLNESS

381 President MacCracken . . . told Hallie. Letter from HF to Mary Crapo Hyde, January 1945.

Denton arrived. Interview with Snyder, 1980.

382 Marlowe's *Dr. Faustus. Dr. Faustus* program, December 1945. SCT.

A reporter for *Stage Pictorial.* Reviews of production at LC.

"At first." Comment to Kay Hocking, summer 1948.

One of her graduate students. Interview with Ted Kazanoff, 1980.

383 "Some of my friends." Ibid.

Bob Baron. Interview with Baron, 1980.

Another student. Letter to author from Joan Shepardson, 1980.

384 "When we went to Amherst." Kazanoff interview.

"I'd just gone through." Baron interview.

385 Hallie drew up a will. Letter from HF to her children, January 1947.

386 Years later. Comment to author by Hallie Wolfe, 1987.

"If told a few facts." Einstein, *The New York Times Magazine,* undated, quoted in "The Newsletter of the Smith College Department of Theatre," 1948. LC.

"It's my job." *Arena.*

387 Day recalled working. Letter to author from Tuttle, December 19, 1979.

The script has a cast. HF assisted by Sylvia Gassel and Day Tuttle, $E = Mc^2$ (Boston, 1948).

389 Austin Riggs Psychiatric Center. *Notes.*

390 My roots. Ibid.
391 Hallie . . . Bob Baron. Letter from HF to Baron, undated. AC.
    In an early scene. Flanagan, *Margaret Fuller,* undated, unpublished manuscript.
       AC.
392 Doris Abramson. Interview with Abramson, 1980.
393 "Four characters." Baron interview.
    "How mean of you." Letter from HF to Baron, April 14, 1951. AC.
394 "Hallie was often." Letter to author from Lynne Anderson, October 25, 1980.
    "Terribly sorry." Note from HF to Anderson, undated.
    "Hallie had a characteristic gesture." Anderson letter.
395 Ruth Wolff. Letter to author from Wolff, May 6, 1980.
    Day thought many. Letter to author from Day Tuttle, December 13, 1979.
    Denton concluded. Snyder interview, 1980.
    George Dowell . . . remembers. Interview with Dowell, 1980.
396 "I submerged." Ibid.
    "We were wishing." Letter from HF to Baron, undated. AC.
    She imagined how the gardens. Hallie Flanagan Davis, "Notes on the Theatre
       Session at Dartington Hall." AC, LC.
397 "There is this quite." Letter from Peter Cox to Dorothy Elmhirst, January 25,
       1947. DH.
398 "The rugs." Interview with Lauralee Tuttle, 1980.
399 After what she described. Letter from HF to Lynne Anderson, November 25,
       1952.
400 Our Eric. HF, "For Eric Bentley, in remembrance of May 8, 1953." AC.
    When Frances Youtz. Letter from HF to Youtz, August 16, 1956. AC.
    When Lynne Anderson wrote. Letter from HF to Anderson, December 19,
       1955.
    In a second letter. Letter from HF to Anderson, November 25, 1952.
401 "You are a great pet." Letter from HF to author, April 1956.
    "Of course I love." Letter from HF to author, February 1956.
    "Six marvelous years." Letter from HF to author, April 1956.
    "I send you the review." Letter from HF to author, March 1956.
    She told Bob Baron. Letter from HF to Baron, January 19, 1953. AC.
402 But she did advise. Letter from HF to Lynne Anderson, January 17, 1954.
    "I fear I am a total loss." Letter from HF to author, undated.
    "How well I remember." Letter from HF to author, undated.
    On one occasion. Letter from HF to author, January 5, 1963.
403 "I see my own failures." Letter from HF to author, undated.
    "The worst part." Letter from HF to the Youtzes, undated. AC.
    Day Tuttle recalled. Interview with Day Tuttle.
    Eric Bentley. Bentley, "Introductory address at HF Memorial," Vivian Beau-
       mont Theatre, Lincoln Center, September 16, 1969. AC.

INDEX

A NOTE ON THE TYPE

The text of this book was set in Sabon, a type face designed by Jan Tschichold (1902–1974), the well-known German typographer. Because it was designed in Frankfurt, Sabon was named for the famous Frankfurt type founder Jacques Sabon, who died in 1850 while manager of the Egenolff foundry.

Based loosely on the original designs of Claude Garamond (c. 1480–1561), Sabon is unique in that it was explicitly designed for hot-metal composition on both the Monotype and Linotype machines as well as for film composition.

Composition by American–Stratford Graphic Services, Inc.
Printed and bound by Fairfield Graphics, Fairfield, Pennsylvania
Designed by Harry Ford